BARRON'S
STUDENTS' #1 CHOICE

D0379065

PASS KEY

TO THE

GMAT

GRADUATE MANAGEMENT ADMISSION TEST

BARRON'S
STUDENTS' #1 CHOICE

PASS KEY

TO THE

GMAT

GRADUATE MANAGEMENT ADMISSION TEST

Fourth Edition

Eugene D. Jaffe, M.B.A., Ph.D.
Formerly Visiting Professor of Marketing
and International Business
Baruch College, City University of New York

and

Stephen Hilbert, Ph.D.
Professor of Mathematics, Ithaca College

BARRON'S EDUCATIONAL SERIES, INC.

All inquiries should be addressed to:
Barron's Educational Series, Inc.
250 Wireless Boulevard
Hauppauge, New York 11788
http://www.barronseduc.com

International Standard Book No. 0-7641-2355-6
Library of Congress Catalog No. 2003060088

Library of Congress Cataloging-in-Publication Data

Jaffe, Eugene D.
    Barron's pass key to the GMAT (Computer-Adaptive Graduate
Management Admission Test) / Eugene D. Jaffe and Stephen
Hilbert.—4th ed.
        p.   cm.
    "Students' #1 choice."
    ISBN 0-7641-2355-6 (alk. paper)
    1. Graduate Management Admission Test—Study guides.
2. Management—Examinations, questions, etc.   3. Computer adaptive
testing.   I. Title: Pass key to the GMAT.   II. Hilbert, Stephen.
III. Barron's Educational Series, Inc.   IV. Title.

HF1118.J333   2004
650′.076—dc22   2003060088

PRINTED IN THE UNITED STATES OF AMERICA
9 8 7 6 5 4 3 2 1

CONTENTS

Preface ix

Acknowledgments x

At-a-Glance Checklist for the CAT GMAT xii

1/An Introduction to the CAT GMAT 1

The Purpose of the GMAT 1
Where to Apply 2
The Test Format 3
What Is a Computer-Adaptive Test (CAT)? 3
Importance of the GMAT 5
How to Prepare for the CAT GMAT 6
Test-Taking Strategies 8

2/Reading Comprehension Review 11

Description of the Test 11
Tips to Help You Cope 11
Types of Questions 12
Sample Passage with Questions, Answers,
  and Analysis 14
A Method of Approach 18
  Basic Reading Skills 18
  Applying Basic Reading Skills 19
  Finding the Topic Sentence 19
  Finding the General Theme 21
  Finding Logical Relationships 22
  Making Inferences 24
Practice Exercise with Answers and Analysis 25
Reading Comprehension Strategies 28

3/Sentence Correction Review · 29

Description of the Test · 29

Tips to Help You Cope · 29

Sample Question with Answer and Analysis · 30
Review of Errors Commonly Found in the
    Sentence Correction Section · 30
    Verb Errors · 30
    Pronoun Errors · 37
    Adjective and Adverb Errors · 39
    Errors in Usage · 44
A Tactic for Sentence Correction Questions · 48
Practice Exercise with Answers and Analysis · 49

Sentence Correction Strategies · 51

4/Critical Reasoning Review · 52

Description of the Test · 52

Tips to Help You Cope · 52

Types of Questions · 53
Identifying the Premise and Conclusion · 53
Deductive and Inductive Arguments · 55
Determining the Logical Sequence
    of an Argument · 56
Attacking the Assumptions of an Argument · 56
Fallacies · 57
    Guilt by Association · 57
    Faulty Analogy · 58
    Causal Fallacies · 59
    Fallacies of Relevance · 59
    Fallacies of Language (Ambiguity) · 60
Final Hints · 61

Critical Reasoning Strategies · 61

5/Problem Solving and Data Sufficiency Review   62

Problem Solving   62
     Description of the Test   62
     Tips to Help You Cope   62
     Methods of Approaching the Test   63
     Sample Problem Solving Questions
       with Answers and Analysis   64
     Problem Solving Strategies   67
Data Sufficiency   68
     Description of the Test   68
     Tips to Help You Cope   68
     Methods of Approaching the Test   69
     Sample Data Sufficiency Questions
       with Answers and Analysis   71
     Data Sufficiency Strategies   75
Quick Mathematics Review   75
   Arithmetic   76
   Algebra   92
   Geometry   108

6/Analytical Writing Assessment   122

7/Three Sample GMATs with Answers and Analysis   129

Sample Test 1   129
   Answers   178
   Analysis   180
   Evaluating Your Score   206
Sample Test 2   209
   Answers   256
   Analysis   258
   Evaluating Your Score   279
Sample Test 3   283
   Answers   333
   Analysis   334
   Evaluating Your Score   360

PREFACE

How ready are you for the computer-adaptive Graduate Management Admission Test (CAT GMAT)? How familiar are you with the sorts of questions the exam contains? Do you know what level of mathematical and grammatical ability is necessary to get a high score on the GMAT? Do you have the computer skills you'll need for success? This book will provide you with strategies, review, and practice for taking the actual test. Since the results of the GMAT are used by many graduate schools of business as a means for measuring the qualifications of their applicants, it is important that you do as well as you can on this exam. Your admission to graduate business school may well depend on it.

This book describes in detail the question types found on the CAT GMAT exam. It offers you invaluable advice on how to prepare for the exam, including a step-by-step program designed to help you discover and correct weak points.

If you have scored well on the sample tests in this book, you may take the actual exam with confidence. If this book has shown that you need further practice, then you may wish to begin working with Barron's How to Prepare for the Graduate Management Admission Test, complete with CD-ROM to simulate actual test-taking conditions. The most complete GMAT study guide available, it covers all areas on the test with explanations and numerous practice exercises. The book/CD-ROM package features a diagnostic test and five full-length model exams with answer analyses and self-scoring charts, as well as a computer-adaptive test that allows you to tackle progressively difficult questions as you develop your test-taking proficiency.

ACKNOWLEDGMENTS

The authors gratefully acknowledge the permission to reprint passages. The copyright holders and publishers are given on this and the following page.

Pages 129–130, Passage 1: *The Hebrew Impact on Western Civilization,* edited by Dagobert Runes. The Philosophical Library. Published by arrangement with Carol Publishing Group.

Pages 132–133, Passage 2: *Budgeting for National Objectives* by the Committee on Economic Development, © 1966.

Pages 135–136, Passage 3: *The American Guide,* edited by Henry G. Alsberg, © 1949.

Pages 158–165, Section V, 25 Questions (with Explained Answers): *Barron's How to Prepare for the New High School Equivalency Examination (GED)* by Murray Rockowitz et al., © 1979. Barron's Educational Series, Inc.

Pages 217–218, Passage 2: *The Social Bond* by Robert A. Nisbet, © 1970 by Alfred A. Knopf, Inc. Reprinted by permission.

Pages 228–236, Section IV, 9 Questions (with Explained Answers): *Barron's How to Prepare for the Test of Standard Written English* by Sharon Green and Mitchel Weiner, © 1982. Barron's Educational Series, Inc.

Pages 228–236, Section IV, 3 Questions (with Explained Answers): *Barron's How to Prepare for the College Entrance Examinations (SAT)* by Samuel C. Brownstein and Mitchel Weiner, © 1980. Barron's Educational Series, Inc.

Pages 283–284, Passage 1: *Improving Executive Development in the Federal Government,* © 1964 by the Committee for Economic Development.

Pages 286–287, Passage 2: G. R. Crone, *Background to Geography,* © 1964, Pitman Publishing Ltd., London.

AT-A-GLANCE
CHECKLIST FOR THE CAT GMAT

BASIC STRATEGIES

1. *Be prepared.* Make sure you practice taking a computer-adaptive test (CAT) ahead of time so you don't waste time during the actual GMAT.
2. *Budget your time.* Calculate the time you may spend on each question.
3. *Read questions carefully.* Make sure you answer the questions that are asked. Consider *all* choices. Remember you must pick the *best* choice, not just a good choice.
4. *Make sure you have clicked on the letter corresponding to your answer.* Once you've confirmed your answer, you cannot go back to that question.
5. *Make educated guesses.* You must answer every question in the CAT, so study the guessing tips in this book.
6. *Get plenty of rest before the exam.* The GMAT exam takes over four hours. Try to get as much rest as possible before the exam.

THE FINER POINTS

Reading Comprehension Questions test your ability to understand *main points* and *significant details* contained in material you have read, and your ability to draw inferences from this material. Tactics to use:

1. Identify the central theme of the passage.
2. Organize mentally how the passage is put together and determine how each part is related to the whole.
3. Determine the opinion or viewpoint that the writer wants the reader to follow or assume.

Sentence Correction Questions test your understanding of the basic rules of English grammar and usage. Tactics to use:

> 1. Read the sentence carefully, paying more attention to the <u>underlined</u> part.
> 2. Assume any part of the sentence that is *not* underlined is correct.
> 3. Verb and pronoun errors are the most common examples—check for these first.
> 4. Other common errors include misuse of adjectives and adverbs.

Critical Reasoning Questions test your ability to evaluate an assumption, inference, or argument. Each question has five possible answers. Your task is to evaluate each of the five possible choices and select the one that is the best alternative. Tactics to use:

> 1. Read the question and then read the passage.
> 2. Learn to spot the major critical reasoning question types.
> 3. Look for the conclusion first.
> 4. Find the premises.
> 5. Do not be opinionated.
> 6. Do not be intimidated by unfamiliar subjects.

Problem Solving Questions test your ability to work with numbers and require a basic knowledge of arithmetic, algebra, and geometry. Tactics to use:

> 1. Use educated guesses on questions you can't figure out in two or three minutes.
> 2. Budget your time so you can concentrate on each question in the test.
> 3. Try to answer questions by *estimating* or doing a rough calculation.
> 4. Make sure your answer is in the units asked for.
> 5. Remember that the more answers you can eliminate, the better your chance of guessing correctly when time is running out.

Data Sufficiency Questions test your reasoning ability. Like the Problem Solving questions, they require a basic knowledge of arithmetic, algebra, and geometry. Each Data Sufficiency question consists of a mathematical problem and two statements containing information relating to it. You must decide whether the problem can be solved by using information from: (A) the first statement alone, but not the second statement alone; (B) the second statement alone, but not the first statement alone; (C) both statements together, but neither alone; or (D) either of the statements alone. Choose (E) if the problem cannot be solved, even by using both statements together. Tactics to use:

1. Don't waste time figuring out the exact answer.
2. Use the strategies in Chapter 5 to make intelligent guesses, if you can't answer the questions.

1

AN INTRODUCTION TO THE CAT GMAT

The most productive approach to undertaking the actual study and review necessary for any examination is first to determine the answers to some basic questions: What? Where? When? and How? In this case, what is the purpose of the Graduate Management Admission Test (GMAT)? What does it measure? Where and when is the exam given? And most important, how can you prepare to demonstrate aptitude and ability to study business at the graduate level?

The following discussion centers on the purpose behind the Graduate Management Admission Test and answers basic questions about the general format and procedure used on the computer-adaptive GMAT.

THE PURPOSE OF THE GMAT

The purpose of the GMAT is to measure your ability to think systematically and to employ the verbal and mathematical skills that you have acquired throughout your years of schooling. The types of questions that are used to test these abilities are discussed in the next chapter. It should be noted that the test does not aim to measure your knowledge of specific business or academic subjects. No specific business experience is necessary, nor will any specific academic subject area be covered. You are assumed to have knowledge of basic algebra (but not calculus), geometry, and arithmetic, and of the basic conventions of standard written English.

In effect, the GMAT provides business school admission officers with an objective measure of academic abilities to supplement subjective criteria used in the selection process, such as interviews, grades, and references. Suppose you are an average student in a college with high grading standards. Your overall grade average may be lower than that of a student from a college with lower grading standards. The GMAT allows you and the other student to be tested under similar conditions using the same grading standard. In this way, a more accurate picture of your all-around ability can be established.

WHERE TO APPLY

Information about the GMAT can be found in the "GMAT Bulletin of Information" for candidates published by ETS. You can obtain a copy by writing:

> Graduate Management Admission Test
> Educational Testing Service
> P.O. Box 6103
> Princeton, New Jersey 08541-6103
> http://www.mba.com

Unlike the pencil and paper GMAT exam, which was scheduled on fixed dates four times a year, the computer-adaptive test may be taken three weeks per month, six days a week, ten hours a day at 400 testing centers in the United States and Canada and major cities throughout the world. The test-taker will be seated in a testing alcove with only a few others present at the same time. One may register for a test a few days before a preferred time. To schedule a test, simply call the ETS toll-free number 1-800-GMAT-NOW or on-line at *http://www.mba.com*. Payment may be made by credit card, check, or money order. It is wise to schedule your exam early to ensure that the schools to which you are applying receive your scores in time.

THE TEST FORMAT

The CAT GMAT contains questions of the following types: Analytical Writing, Reading Comprehension, Problem Solving, Data Sufficiency, Critical Reasoning, and Sentence Correction. In the past, exams have included Analysis of Situations questions, but these questions have now been replaced by questions on Critical Reasoning.

WHAT IS A COMPUTER-ADAPTIVE TEST (CAT)?

In a computer-adaptive test, each question is shown on a personal computer screen one at a time. On the test, questions are of high, medium, and low difficulty. The first question on a test is of medium difficulty; the relative difficulty of the next question depends on your answer to the first question. If you answered correctly, the next question will be of greater difficulty. If your answer was incorrect, the next question will be less difficult, and so on. However, the choice of subsequent questions is not only based on whether the preceding answer was correct or incorrect, but also on the difficulty level of the preceding question, whether previous questions have covered a variety of question types, and specific test content. This procedure is repeated for each of your answers. In this way, the CAT adjusts questions to your ability.

The computer-adaptive GMAT will have three parts: a writing section which consists of writing two essays, a quantitative test, and a verbal test.

You will have 30 minutes to write each essay.

The quantitative test will be composed of Problem Solving and Data Sufficiency type questions. There will be 37 questions and you will have 75 minutes to finish this section.

The verbal test will be composed of Reading Comprehension, Critical Reasoning, and Sentence Correction type questions. There will be 41 questions and you will have 75 minutes to finish this section.

There is an optional five-minute break between each section of the exam.

You can download free test tutorials from *www.mba.com*. These will help you to review the basic skills of taking a computer-adaptive test, such as entering answers and accessing HELP. You should review these procedures before you arrive at the test center, because any time that you use to review HELP screens will mean less time for you to work on the test questions.

It is possible that your tests may contain some experimental questions. These questions may or may not be labeled experimental. You should do your best on any question that is not labeled experimental. Experimental questions are **not** counted in your scores.

In the CAT version of the GMAT once you enter and confirm your answer you **cannot** change the answer. You can't go back and work on previous questions if you finish a section early. Furthermore, you must answer each question before you can see the next question. (You will not be able to skip any questions.)

YOU'VE ANSWERED THE FIRST QUESTION: WHAT'S NEXT?

Suppose that you answered that first question correctly and then get a more difficult one that you also answer correctly and then an even harder one that you answer incorrectly. Will you get a lower score than say a candidate that answers the first question incorrectly and then gets an easier one that is answered correctly? No, because difficult questions are worth more points than easier ones. So, in the end, the mixture of questions that each candidate gets should be balanced to reflect his or her ability and performance. There is little possibility that a candidate will have a higher score because he or she answered more easy questions correctly.

These rules apply to both the quantitative (problem solving and data sufficiency) and qualitative (reading comprehension, sentence correction, and critical reasoning) multiple-choice type questions. The Analytical Writing Assessment (AWA), described in Chapter 6, will be written using the computer, but it will not be adaptive. Test-takers will write essays in response to two questions as was the case in the paper and pencil test. The overall quality of your thinking and writing will be evaluated by faculty members from a number of academic disciplines, including management. It will also be rated by an automated essay scoring system, developed by ETS, called an e-rater™. After extensive testing, the e-rater™ system was found to have a 92% agreement with human readers, which is about the same rate at which two human readers agree.

Another fact about the CAT is that questions cannot be skipped. You must answer the present question in order to proceed to the next one. This means that if you do not know the answer, you must guess (tips for guessing are given on page 9.) Answering a question means entering your choice by clicking the mouse next to the alternative you have chosen and then clicking on the "confirm" icon. Once you have confirmed your answer, you cannot go back to check.

IMPORTANCE OF THE GMAT

Your score on the GMAT is only one of the several factors examined by admissions officers. Your undergraduate record, for example, is at least as important as your GMAT score. Thus, a low score does not mean that no school will accept you, nor does a high GMAT score guarantee acceptance at the school of your choice. However, since your score is one important factor, you should try to do as well as you can on the exam. Using this book should help you to maximize your score.

Most college catalogs do not state what the minimum GMAT requirement is, but the annual reports of most MBA programs do note the average GMAT score of the last incoming student body. This is probably a good indication of the necessary ballpark figure for admission. However, obtaining a score somewhat below that figure does not mean that acceptance is not possible. First of all, it is an average figure. Some scored below, but were accepted. The GMAT is only one of a number of criteria for admission.

Before applying to a college or university, determine what criteria are considered for admission and how these criteria are ranked by order of importance. Directors of MBA programs, admissions officers, college catalogs, and annual reports should provide this information.

HOW TO PREPARE FOR THE CAT GMAT

You should now be aware of the purpose of the GMAT and have a general idea of the format of the test. With this basic information, you are in a position to begin your study and review. The rest of this guide represents a study plan that will enable you to prepare for the GMAT. If used properly, it will help you diagnose your weak areas and take steps to remedy them.

Begin your preparation by becoming as familiar as possible with the various types of questions that appear on the exam. The analysis of typical GMAT questions in the next chapter is designed for this purpose. Test-taking tactics provide hints on how to approach the different types of questions. When you feel you understand this material completely, take the Diagnostic Test that follows and evaluate your results on the self-scoring table provided at the end of the test. (An explanation of how to use these tables follows.) A low score in any area indicates that you should spend more time reviewing that particular material. Study the review section for that area until you feel you have mastered it and then take one of the sample GMATs at the back of the book. Continue this pattern of study until you are completely satisfied with your performance. For best results, try to simulate exam conditions as closely as possible when taking sample tests: no unscheduled breaks or interruptions, strict adherence to time limits, and no use of outside aids.

THE SELF-SCORING TABLES

The Self-Scoring Tables for each sample test in this guide can be used as a means of evaluating your weaknesses in particular subject areas and should help you plan your study program most effectively.

After completing a sample test, turn to the Answers section that immediately follows each test. First, determine the number of *correct* answers you had for each section. Next, subtract *one-fourth* the number of *wrong* answers for each part from the number of correct answers. For example, suppose that in Section I you answered 15 out of 25 questions correctly. Subtract ¼ of 10 (2.5) from 15 to obtain a final score of 12.5. Now turn to the section Evaluating Your Score, which follows the Answers Explained section of each test. Record your scores in the appropriate score boxes in the Self-Scoring Table as shown below.

SELF-SCORING TABLE		
Section	Score	Rating
1	12.5	POOR
2		
3		
4		
5		
6		
7		

Use the rating scale to find your rating for each section. A typical rating scale follows.

SELF-SCORING SCALE—RATING				
Section	Poor	Fair	Good	Excellent
1	0–12+	13–17+	18–21+	22–25
2	0–9+	10–13+	14–17+	18–20
3	0–12+	13–17+	18–21+	22–25
4	0–9+	10–13+	14–17+	18–20
5	0–9+	10–13+	14–17+	18–20
6	0–12+	13–17+	18–21+	22–25
7	0–12+	13–17+	18–21+	22–25

In the rating scale, numbers such as 12+ mean numbers larger than 12 but less than 13. For example, if your raw score on Section 6 of the exam was 21.5, then this translates to GOOD on the Self-scoring Table.

A rating of FAIR or POOR in any area indicates that you need to spend more time reviewing that material.

Next, be familiar with the CAT system. Make sure you know how everything works (e.g., scrolling) before you start the exam. Pace is very important. Losing time because of unfamiliarity with the CAT is avoidable with practice using this manual and other tools.

TEST-TAKING STRATEGIES

1. **The first five or so questions count more than later questions.** Budget a little more time for these questions. You have about 1¾ minutes for each verbal question and 2 minutes for each quantitative question. So, be prepared to spend more time with the initial questions.

2. **Answer as many questions as possible.** While there is no minimum number to answer in order to get a score, your score will be lower if fewer questions are answered.

3. **If you are not sure, guess.** Unlike the former GMAT version, there is no penalty for a wrong answer, so if you are running out of time, guess. Also, since you have to give an answer in order to proceed to the next question, guessing may be necessary. For some tips see the Guessing section that follows.

4. **Pace yourself and be aware of remaining time.** Be aware of the number of questions and remaining time. How much time is left in a test section can be determined by pressing the time icon and a clock will appear on the upper left-hand side of the screen.

5. **Confirm your answer only when you are confident that it is correct.** Remember, you cannot return to a previous ques-

tion and you must confirm your answer in order to move on to the next question.

6. **Be careful about section exit and test quit commands.** Once you confirm a section exit command you cannot go back. Confirming the test quit command automatically ends the session with no chance of continuing.

GUESSING

Two elements should be considered in addressing the area of guessing. First, consider the way your score is determined by the Educational Testing Service, the administrators of the GMAT. If you do not answer a question, you cannot proceed to the next one. So, if you are stuck it helps to guess. Or, if you are near the end of a test section and time is running out, you have two options. You can guess the answers to questions that you are unsure of the correct answer, or you can quit the section when time runs out. As we pointed out before, it is best to spend more time with the first five questions and less time with the remaining ones. So, guessing becomes an important strategy when time is critical. The probability of selecting the correct answer by random guessing is 1 out of 5, or 0.20, which is rather low. However, suppose that you have had time to read the question and have been able to eliminate two answer alternatives, but are still unsure of the correct answer. Now, a random guess of the correct answer among the remaining alternatives has a probability of 0.33. Obviously, if you are able to eliminate three alternatives, you then have a 50-50 chance of guessing the correct answer. Assuming that time has run out, guessing in this situation is a very low risk.

MANEUVERING THE GMAT CAT PC SCREEN

While you will have the opportunity to try out the so-called "Testing Tools" of the CAT before taking the test, you will have an advantage if you are already familiar with them beforehand.

These testing tools consist of a number of icons or commands by which you navigate the test.

Test Quit. If you click this, you terminate the test. Only do this if you have completed the entire test.

Section Exit. Clicking this button terminates a test section and enables you to go on to the next test section.

Time. Clicking this icon will show you how much time (shown in hours, minutes, and seconds) remains on the test.

? Help. Clicking this button will activate the help function. The help function contains directions for the question you are working on, directions for the section you are working on, general directions, how to scroll, and information about the testing tools.

Next and **Answer Confirm.** Both of these buttons work in sequence. When you are sure of your answer, click the *Next* button to move on to the next question. You will then see that the Answer Confirm button will become dark. Clicking it will save your answer and bring the next question to the screen.

You should also practice the word processing tools needed for the Analytical Writing Assessment (AWA).

Page up—moves the cursor up one page.
Page down—moves the cursor down one page.
Backspace—removes the text to the left of the cursor.
Delete—removes text to the right of the cursor.
Home—moves the cursor to the beginning of a line.
End—moves the cursor to the end of a line.
Arrows—move the cursor up, down, left, and right.
Enter—move the cursor to the beginning of the next line.

There are also *Cut, Paste,* and *Undo* functions.

2

READING COMPREHENSION REVIEW

DESCRIPTION OF THE TEST

The Reading Comprehension section tests your ability to analyze written information and includes passages from the humanities, the social sciences, and the physical and biological sciences.

The typical Reading Comprehension section consists of a passage with a total of approximately 11 questions. You will be allowed to scroll through the passages when answering the questions. However, many of the questions may be based on what is *implied* in the passages, rather than on what is explicitly stated. Your ability to draw inferences from the material is critical to successfully completing this section. You are to select the best answer from five alternatives.

TIPS TO HELP YOU COPE

1. Read the passage, noting important points, names, and so on on your scratch paper.
2. Determine the central thought. Is there a topic sentence that expresses the main idea succinctly? What title would you give the passage?
3. Notice the specific details or statements that the writer gives to support the main idea.
4. Note the special techniques used by the author. These may include reasoning from experimental data (inductive method) or from principles accepted in advance (deductive method) and the use of examples, anecdotes, analogies, and comparisons.

5. Determine the author's purpose. Is he or she seeking to inform, to persuade, to satirize, to evoke pity, to amuse, to arouse to action?

6. Look at the questions, noting the type of information called for.

7. Pay attention to the wording of each question. A question that begins "The main idea of the passage is…" calls for a different kind of reasoning from a question that begins "Which of the following is mentioned…?" Watch out for questions that specify "All of the following EXCEPT…" or "Which of the following is NOT…" since these phrases mean you should look for the *false* or *inapplicable* answer rather than the *true* one.

8. All reading comprehension questions on the GMAT can be answered on the basis of information provided in the passage. Therefore, don't bring in your own prior knowledge or your personal opinions when answering the questions; they may be inapplicable, inaccurate, or misleading.

9. Read all five answer choices carefully before selecting an answer. Sometimes two or more choices will have elements of truth; however, only one answer will be the best. Don't overlook the best answer by hastily choosing the first choice that seems reasonable.

TYPES OF QUESTIONS

Reading comprehension questions usually fall into several general categories. In most questions, you will be asked about one of the following:

Main Idea. In this type of question you may be asked about the main idea or theme of the passage, about a possible title, or about the author's primary objective. Usually the main idea refers to the passage as a whole, not to some segment or part of the passage. The main idea is typically (but not always) found in the first paragraph. It will be a statement that gives the overall theme of the passage. In many cases, it will be in the form of an argument, including a premise and conclusion.

Supporting Ideas. In this type of question, you may be asked about the idea expressed in one part of the passage, rather than about the passage as a whole. Questions of this type test your ability to distinguish between the main idea and those themes that support it, some of which may be implicit or implied rather than explicitly stated.

Drawing Inferences. Questions of this sort ask about ideas that are not explicitly stated in a passage. These questions refer to meanings implied by the author based on information given in the passage. Typical questions are:

1. The author feels (believes) that...
2. In reference to (event) it may be inferred that...

Specific Details. In this type of question you may be asked about specific facts or details the author has stated explicitly in the passage. This sort of question may take the following forms:

1. Which of the following statements is mentioned by the author?
2. All of the following are given as reasons for (   ) EXCEPT:
3. The author argues that...

Applying Information from the Passage to Other Situations. These questions ask you to make an analogy between a situation described in the passage and a similar situation or event listed in the question. Unlike other types of questions, these describe situations *not* given in the passage, but rather those that are analogous to those in the passage. In order to answer a question of this kind, you must be able to draw a parallel between the situation in the question and its counterpart in the passage.

Tone or Attitude of the Passage. These questions concentrate on the author's style, attitude, or mood. In order to determine this attitude, look for key words, such as adjectives that reveal if the author is "pessimistic," "critical," "supportive," or "objective" about an event, idea, or situation in the passage.

The Logical Structure of the Passage. These types of questions test your understanding of the overall meaning, logic, or organization of a passage. You may be asked how several ideas in a passage are interrelated or how a passage is constructed, classifies, compares, or describes events or situations. You may be asked about the strengths or weaknesses the author is making, to identify assumptions, or to evaluate counterarguments.

Determining the Meaning of Words from the Context. When a question asks for the meaning of a word, it can usually be deduced from the context of the passage. Remember, you are not required to know the meaning of technical or foreign words.

SAMPLE PASSAGE WITH QUESTIONS, ANSWERS, AND ANALYSIS

The following passage will give you an idea of the format of the Reading Comprehension section. Read the passage through and then answer the questions, making sure to leave yourself enough time to complete them all.

TIME: 10 minutes

Political theories have, in fact, very little more to do with musical creation than electronics theories have. Both merely determine methods of distribution. The exploitation of these methods is subject to political regulation and is quite rigidly
(5) regulated in many countries. The revolutionary parties, both in Russia and elsewhere, have tried to turn composers on to supposedly revolutionary subject-matter. The net result for either art or revolution has not been very important. Neither has official fascist music accomplished much either for music or for
(10) Italy or Germany.

Political party-influence on music is just censorship anyway. Performances can be forbidden and composers disciplined for what they write, but the creative stimulus comes from elsewhere. Nothing really "inspires" an author but money or food or
(15) love.

That persons or parties subventioning musical uses should wish to retain veto power over the works used is not at all surprising. That our political masters (or our representatives) should exercise a certain negative authority, a censorship, over (20) the exploitation of works whose content they consider dangerous to public welfare is also in no way novel or surprising. But that such political executives should think to turn the musical profession into a college of political theorists or a bunch of hired propagandists is naïve of them. Our musical civilization is older (25) than any political party. We can deal on terms of intellectual equality with acoustical engineers, with architects, with poets, painters, and historians, even with the Roman clergy if necessary. We cannot be expected to take very seriously the inspirational dictates of persons or of groups who think they can (30) pay us to get emotional about ideas. They can pay us to get emotional all right. Anybody can. Nothing is so emotion-producing as money. But emotions are factual; they are not generated by ideas. On the contrary, ideas are generated by emotions; and emotions, in turn, are visceral states produced (35) directly by facts like money and food and sexual intercourse. To have any inspirational quality there must be present facts or immediate anticipations, not pie-in-the-sky.

Now pie-in-the-sky has its virtues as a political ideal, I presume. Certainly most men want to work for an eventual (40) common good. I simply want to make it quite clear that ideals about the common good (not to speak of mere political necessity) are not very stimulating subject-matter for music. They don't produce visceral movements the way facts do. It is notorious that musical descriptions of hell, which is something (45) we can all imagine, are more varied and vigorous than the placid banalities that even the best composers have used to describe heaven; and that all composers do better on really present matters than on either: matters like love and hatred and hunting and war and dancing around and around.

(50)   The moral of all this is that the vetoing of objective subject

matter is as far as political stimulation or censorship can go in advance. Style is personal and emotional, not political at all. And form or design, which is impersonal, is not subject to any political differences of opinion.

1. The author is making a statement defending

    I. intellectual freedom
    II. the apolitical stance of most musicians
    III. emotional honesty

    (A) I only
    (B) II only
    (C) I and II only
    (D) I and III only
    (E) I, II, and III

2. The tone of the author in the passage is

    (A) exacting
    (B) pessimistic
    (C) critical
    (D) optimistic
    (E) fatalistic

3. The author's reaction to political influence on music is one of

    (A) surprise
    (B) disbelief
    (C) resignation
    (D) deference
    (E) rancor

4. According to the author, political attempts to control the subject matter of music

    (A) will be resisted by artists wherever they are made
    (B) may succeed in censoring but not in inspiring musical works
    (C) will succeed only if the eventual goal is the common good
    (D) are less effective than the indirect use of social and economic pressure
    (E) have profoundly influenced the course of modern musical history

5. The author refers to "musical descriptions of hell" (line 44) to make the point that

 (A) musical inspiration depends on the degree to which the composer's imagination is stimulated by his subject
 (B) composers are better at evoking negative emotions and ideas than positive ones
 (C) music is basically unsuited to a role in support of political tyranny
 (D) religious doctrines have inspired numerous musical compositions
 (E) political ideals are a basic motivating force for most contemporary composers

6. The author implies that political doctrines usually fail to generate artistic creativity because they are too

 (A) naïve
 (B) abstract
 (C) rigidly controlled
 (D) concrete
 (E) ambiguous

Answers:

1. **(D)**   2. **(C)**   3. **(C)**   4. **(B)**   5. **(A)**   6. **(B)**

Analysis:

 1. **(D)** The author is arguing that musicians will not conform to any control over their creativity. Thus, they want to be intellectually free and emotionally honest. It does not mean that they could not be active in politics (apolitical).
 2. **(C)** The author is critical of attempts to censor the arts, especially music.
 3. **(C)** The author does not find censorship surprising (lines 18–21), nor does he take it seriously (line 28). He is resigned to attempts at censorship, although he does not believe it can inspire creativity.

4. **(B)** See paragraph 2.
5. **(A)** See lines 43–49.
6. **(B)** See paragraph 4, in which the author states that "ideals" do not inspire music as "facts" do; and also see lines 14–15 and 35–37.

A METHOD OF APPROACH

BASIC READING SKILLS

A primary skill necessary for good reading comprehension is the understanding of the meanings of individual words. Knowledge of a wide and diversified vocabulary enables you to detect subtle differences in sentence meaning that may hold the key to the meaning of an entire paragraph or passage. For this reason, it is important that you familiarize yourself with as many words as possible.

A second reading skill to be developed is the ability to discover the central theme of a passage. By making yourself aware of what the entire passage is about, you are in a position to relate what you read to this central theme, logically picking out the main points and significant details as you go along. Although the manner in which the central theme is stated may vary from passage to passage, it can usually be found in the title (if one is presented), in the "topic sentence" of a paragraph in shorter passages, or, in longer passages, by reading several paragraphs.

A third essential skill is the capacity to organize mentally how the passage is put together and determine how each part is related to the whole. This is the skill you will have to use to the greatest degree on the GMAT, where you must pick out significant and insignificant factors, remember main details, and relate information you have read to the central theme.

In general, a mastery of these three basic skills will provide you with a solid basis for better reading comprehension wherein you will be able to read carefully to draw a conclusion from the material, decide the meanings of words and ideas presented and how they in turn affect the meaning of the passage, and recognize opinions and views that are expressed.

APPLYING BASIC READING SKILLS

The only way to become adept at the three basic reading skills outlined above is to practice using the techniques involved as much as possible. Studying the meanings of new words you encounter in all your reading material will soon help you establish a working knowledge of many words. In the same manner, making an effort to locate topic sentences, general themes, and specific details in material you read will enable you to improve your skills in these areas. The following drills will help. After you have read through them and answered the questions satisfactorily, you can try the longer practice exercise at the end.

FINDING THE TOPIC SENTENCE

The term "topic sentence" is used to describe the sentence that gives the key to an entire paragraph. Usually the topic sentence is found in the beginning of a paragraph. However, there is no absolute rule. A writer may build the paragraph to a conclusion, putting the key sentence at the end. Here is an example in which the topic sentence is located at the beginning:

EXAMPLE 1:
The world faces a serious problem of overpopulation. Right now many people starve from lack of adequate food. Efforts are being made to increase the rate of food production, but the number of people to be fed increases at a faster rate.

The idea is stated directly in the opening sentence. You know that the passage will be about "a serious problem of overpopulation." Like a heading or caption, the topic sentence sets the stage or gets your mind ready for what follows in that paragraph.

Before you try to locate the topic sentence in a paragraph you must remember that this technique depends upon reading and judgment. Read the whole passage first. Then try to decide which sentence comes closest to expressing the main point of the paragraph. Do not worry about the position of the topic sentence in the paragraph; look for the most important statement. Find the idea to which all the other sentences relate.

Try to identify the topic sentence in this passage:

EXAMPLE 2:
During the later years of the American Revolution, the Articles of Confederation government was formed. This government suffered severely from a lack of power. Each state distrusted the others and gave little authority to the central or federal government. The Articles of Confederation produced a government that could not raise money from taxes, prevent Indian raids, or force the British out of the United States.

What is the topic sentence? Certainly the paragraph is about the Articles of Confederation. However, is the key idea in the first sentence or in the second sentence? In this instance, the *second* sentence does a better job of giving you the key to this paragraph—the lack of centralized power that characterized the Articles of Confederation. The sentences that complete the paragraph relate more to the idea of "lack of power" than to the time when the government was formed. Don't assume that the topic sentence is always the first sentence of a paragraph. Try this:

EXAMPLE 3:
There is a strong relation between limited education and low income. Statistics show that unemployment rates are highest among those adults who attended school the fewest years. Most jobs in a modern industrial society require technical or advanced training. The best pay goes with the jobs that demand thinking and decisions based on knowledge. A few people manage to overcome their limited education by personality or a "lucky break." However, studies of lifetime earnings show that the average high school graduate earns more than the average high school dropout, who in turn earns more than the average adult who has not finished eighth grade.

Here, the first sentence contains the main idea of the whole paragraph. One more example should be helpful:

EXAMPLE 4:

They had fewer men available as soldiers. Less than one-third of the railroads and only a small proportion of the nation's industrial production was theirs. For most of the war their coastline was blockaded by Northern ships. It is a tribute to Southern leadership and the courage of the people that they were not defeated for four years.

In this case you will note that the passage builds up to its main point. The topic sentence is the last one. Practice picking out the topic sentences in other material you read until it becomes an easy task.

FINDING THE GENERAL THEME

A more advanced skill is the ability to read several paragraphs and relate them to one general theme or main idea. The procedure involves careful reading of the entire passage and deciding which idea is the central or main one. You can tell you have the right idea when it is most frequent or most important, or when every sentence relates to it. As you read the next passage, note the underlined parts.

EXAMPLE:

True democracy means direct rule by the people. A good example can be found in a modern town meeting in many small New England towns. All citizens aged twenty-one or over may vote. They not only vote for officials, but they also get together to vote on local laws (or ordinances). The small size of the town and the limited number of voters make this possible.

In the cities, voters cast ballots for officials who get together to make the laws. Because the voters do not make the laws directly, this system is called indirect democracy or representative government. There is no problem of distance to travel, but it is difficult to run a meeting with hundreds of thousands of citizens.

Representation of voters and a direct voice in making laws are more of a problem in state or national governments. The numbers

of citizens and the distances to travel make representative government the most practical way to make laws.

Think about the passage in general and the underlined parts in
particular. Several examples discuss voting for officials and making laws. In the first paragraph both of these are done by the voters. The second paragraph describes representative government
in which voters elect officials who make laws. The last paragraph
emphasizes the problem of size and numbers and says that representative government is more practical. In the following question, put all these ideas together.

The main theme of this passage is that
(A) the United States is not democratic
(B) citizens cannot vote for lawmakers
(C) representative government does not make laws
(D) every citizen makes laws directly
(E) increasing populations lead to less direct democracy

The answer is choice (E). Choices (B), (C), and (D) can be
eliminated because they are not true of the passage. Choice (A)
may have made you hesitate a little. The passage makes com-
ments about *less direct* democracy, but it never says that representative government is *not democratic.*

In summary, in order to find the general theme:
1. Read at your normal speed.
2. Locate the topic sentence in each paragraph.
3. Note ideas that are frequent or emphasized.
4. Find the idea to which most of the passage is related.

FINDING LOGICAL RELATIONSHIPS

In order to fully understand the meaning of a passage, you must
first look for the general theme and then relate the ideas and opinions found in the passage to this general theme. In this way, you
can determine not only what is important but also how the ideas
interrelate to form the whole. From this understanding, you will be
better able to answer questions that refer to the passage.

As you read the following passages, look for general theme and supporting facts, words, or phrases that signal emphasis or shift in thought, and the relation of one idea to another.

EXAMPLE:

The candidate who wants to be elected pays close attention to statements and actions that will make the voters see him favorably. In ancient Rome candidates wore pure white togas (the Latin word *candidatus* means "clothed in white") to indicate that they were pure, clean, and above any "dirty work." However, it is interesting to note that such a toga was not worn after election.

In more modern history, candidates have allied themselves with political parties. Once a voter knows and favors the views of a certain political party, he may vote for anyone with that party's label. Nevertheless, divisions of opinion develop, so that today there is a wide range of candidate views in any major party.

The best conclusion to be drawn from the first paragraph is that after an election
(A) all candidates are dishonest
(B) candidates are less concerned with symbols of integrity
(C) candidates do not change their ideas
(D) officials are always honest
(E) policies always change

You noted the ideas about a candidate in Rome. You saw the word "however" signal a shift in ideas or thinking. Now the third step rests with your judgment. You cannot jump to a conclusion; you must see which conclusion is reasonable or fair. Choices (A), (D), and (E) should make you wary. They say "all" or "always" which means without exception. The last sentence is not that strong or positive. Choices (B) and (C) must be considered. There is nothing in the paragraph that supports the fact that candidates do not change their ideas. This forces you into choice (B) as the only statement logically related to what the paragraph said.

MAKING INFERENCES

An inference is not stated. It is assumed by the reader from something said by the writer. An inference is the likely or probable conclusion rather than the direct, logical one. It usually involves an opinion or viewpoint that the writer wants the reader to follow or assume. In another kind of inference, the reader figures out the author's opinion even though it is not stated. The clues are generally found in the manner in which facts are presented and in the choice of words and phrases. Opinion is revealed by the one-sided nature of a passage in which no opposing facts are given. It is shown further by "loaded" words that reveal the author's feelings.

It is well worth noting that opinionated writing is often more interesting than straight factual accounts. Some writers are very colorful, forceful, or amusing in presenting their views. You should understand that there is nothing wrong with reading opinions. You should read varied opinions, but know that they are opinions. Then make up your own mind.

Not every writer will insert an opinion obviously. However, you can get clues from how often the same idea is said (frequency), whether arguments are balanced on both sides (fairness), and the choice of wording (emotional or loaded words). Look for the clues in this next passage.

EXAMPLE:
Slowly but surely the great passenger trains of the United States have been fading from the rails. Short-run commuter trains still rattle in and out of the cities. Between major cities you can still find a train, but the schedules are becoming less frequent. The Twentieth Century Limited, The Broadway Limited, and other luxury trains that sang along the rails at 60 to 80 miles an hour are no longer running. Passengers on other long runs complain of poor service, old equipment, and costs in time and money. The long distance traveller today accepts the noise of jets, the congestion at airports, and the traffic between airport and city. A more elegant and graceful way is becoming only a memory.

1. With respect to the reduction of long-run passenger trains, this writer expresses

    (A) regret
    (B) pleasure
    (C) grief
    (D) elation
    (E) anger

Before you choose the answer, you must deduce what the writer's feeling is. He does not actually state his feeling, but clues are available so that you may infer what it is. Choices (B) and (D) are impossible, because he gives no word that shows he is pleased by the change. Choice (C) is too strong, as is choice (E). Choice (A) is the most reasonable inference to make. He is sorry to see the change. He is expressing regret.

2. The author seems to feel that air travel is

    (A) costly   (D) elegant
    (B) slow   (E) uncomfortable
    (C) streamlined

Here we must be careful because he says very little about air travel. However, his one sentence about it presents three negative or annoying points. The choice now becomes fairly clear. Answer (E) is correct.

PRACTICE EXERCISE
WITH ANSWERS AND ANALYSIS

Time: 9 minutes

Directions: This part contains a reading passage. You are to read it carefully. When answering the questions, you *will* be able to refer to the passages. The questions are based on what is *stated* or *implied* in the passage. You have nine minutes to complete this part.

Above all, colonialism was hated for its explicit assumption that the civilizations of colonized peoples were inferior. Using

slogans like *The White Man's Burden* and *La Mission Civilica-trice,* Europeans asserted their moral obligation to impose their
(5) way of life on those endowed with inferior cultures. This orientation was particularly blatant among the French. In the colonies, business was conducted in French. Schools used that language and employed curricula designed for children in France. One scholar suggests that Muslim children probably
(10) learned no more about the Maghreb than they did about Australia. In the Metropole, intellectuals discoursed on the weakness of Arabo-Islamic culture. A noted historian accused Islam of being hostile to science. An academician wrote that Arabic—the holy language of religion, art, and the Muslim sciences—is
(15) "more of an encumbrance than an aid to the mind. It is absolutely devoid of precision." There was of course an element of truth in the criticisms. After all, Arab reformists had been engaging in self-criticism for decades. Also, at least some Frenchmen honestly believed they were helping the colonized. A Resident
(20) General in Tunisia, for example, told an assemblage of Muslims with sincerity, "We shall distribute to you all that we have of learning; we shall make you a party to everything that makes for the strength of our intelligence." But none of this could change or justify the cultural racism in colonial ideologies. To the
(25) French, North Africans were only partly civilized and could be saved only by becoming Frenchmen. The reaction of the colonized was of course to defend their identity and to label colonial policy, in the words of Algerian writer Malek Hadad, "cultural asphyxia." Throughout North Africa, nationalists made the
(30) defense of Arabo-Islamic civilization a major objective, a value in whose name they demanded independence. Yet the crisis of identity, provoked by colonial experiences, has not been readily assured and lingers into the post-colonial period. A French scholar describes the devastating impact of colonialism by
(35) likening it to "the role played for us (in Europe) by the doctrine of original sin." Frantz Fanon, especially in his *Studies in a Dying Colonialism,* well expresses the North African perspective.

Factors producing militant and romantic cultural nationalism are anchored in time. Memories of colonialism are already
(40) beginning to fade and, when the Maghreb has had a few decades
in which to grow, dislocations associated with social change
can also be expected to be fewer. Whether this means that the
cultural nationalism characteristic of the Maghreb today will
disappear in the future cannot be known. But a preoccupation
(45) with identity and culture and an affirmation of Arabism and
Islam have characterized the Maghreb since independence and
these still remain today important elements in North African life.

A second great preoccupation in independent North Africa is
the promotion of a modernist social revolution. The countries
(50) of the Maghreb do not pursue development in the same way and
there have been variations in policies within each country. But
all three spend heavily on development. In Tunisia, for example,
the government devotes 20–25% of its annual budget to
education, and literacy has climbed from 15% in 1956 to about
(55) 50% today. A problem, however, is that such advances are not
always compatible with objectives flowing from North African
nationalism. In Morocco, for instance, when the government
decided to give children an "Arab" education, it was forced to
limit enrollments because, among other things, most Moroc-
(60) cans had been educated in French and the country consequently
had few teachers qualified to teach in Arabic. Two years later,
with literacy rates declining, this part of the Arabization program
was postponed. The director of Arabization declared, "We are
not fanatics; we want to enter the modern world."

1. Which of the following titles best describes the content of
   the passage?

   (A) *Education in the Levant*
   (B) *Nationalism in North Africa*
   (C) *Civilization in the Middle East*
   (D) *Muslim Science*
   (E) *Culture and Language*

2. Which of the following is *not* used by the author in the presentation of his arguments?

   (A) Colonialism demoralized the local inhabitants.
   (B) Colonialism produced an identity crisis.
   (C) Cultural nationalism will soon disappear.
   (D) Decolonization does not always run smoothly.
   (E) Colonialists assumed that local cultures were inferior.

3. The author's attitude toward colonialism is best described as one of

   (A) sympathy   (D) hostility
   (B) bewilderment   (E) ambivalence
   (C) support

ANSWERS AND ANALYSIS

1. **(B)** Clearly, the main subject of the passage is nationalism. This is given in the statement on line 1, "Above all, colonialism was hated…" and in lines 29–31 and 38–39.

2. **(C)** Choice (E) is given in lines 1–2, (D) in lines 55–57, (B) in lines 31–33, and (A) is implied throughout; while the opposite of (C) is found in lines 42–44.

3. **(D)** See, for instance, the reference to "cultural racism" in lines 23–24, as well as the general tone of paragraph 1.

READING COMPREHENSION STRATEGIES

1. Use only the information in the passage.
2. Read the questions first, then the passage.
3. Note key words and ideas on your scratch paper.
4. Read *all* the answer alternatives.
5. Learn to identify the major question types.

3

SENTENCE CORRECTION REVIEW

DESCRIPTION OF THE TEST

The Sentence Correction part of the exam tests your understanding of the basic rules of English grammar and usage. To succeed in this section, you need a command of sentence structure including tense and mood, subject and verb agreement, proper case, parallel structure, and other basics. No attempt is made to test for punctuation, spelling, or capitalization.

You will be given a sentence in which all or part of the sentence is underlined. You will then be asked to choose the best phrasing of the underlined part from five alternatives. (A) will always be the original phrasing.

TIPS TO HELP YOU COPE

1. Read the sentence, concentrating on the underlined part.
2. Check for pronoun errors. (Look for errors in words like *he, him, her, we, us, them, who, whom, whoever, whomever, you, it, which,* or *that.*)
3. If there are no pronoun errors, check the verbs.
4. If you find no errors in either verbs or pronouns, look at adjectives and adverbs.
5. Other possible errors include the use of incorrect idioms and faulty parallelism.
6. If the sentence is correct, select (A) as your answer.

SAMPLE QUESTION WITH ANSWER AND ANALYSIS

Since the advent of cable television, at the beginning of <u>this decade, the video industry took</u> a giant stride forward in this country.

(A) this decade, the video industry took
(B) this decade, the video industry had taken
(C) this decade, the video industry has taken
(D) this decade saw the video industry taking
(E) the decade that let the video industry take

Answer:
   (C)

Analysis:
   The phrase "Since the advent..." demands a verb in the present perfect form; thus, "*has taken,*" not "*took,*" is correct. Choice (E) changes the meaning of the original sentence.

REVIEW OF ERRORS COMMONLY FOUND IN THE SENTENCE CORRECTION SECTION

Since you need only *recognize* errors in grammar and usage for this part of the exam, this section of the book will review those errors most commonly presented in the GMAT and teach you *what to look for.* We will not review the basic rules of grammar, such as the formation and use of the different tenses and the passive voice, the subjective and objective cases of pronouns, the position of adjectives and adverbs, and the like. We assume that a candidate for the GMAT is familiar with basic grammar, and we will concentrate on error recognition based on that knowledge.

VERB ERRORS

1. ERRORS IN VERB TENSE

Check if the correct verb *tense* has been used in the sentence.

INCORRECT: When I came home, the children still didn't finish dinner.

CORRECT: When I came home, the children still <u>hadn't finished</u> dinner.

In REPORTED SPEECH, check that the rule of *sequence of tenses* has been observed.

INCORRECT: She promised she will come.

CORRECT: She promised she <u>would</u> come.

2. ERRORS IN TENSE FORMATION

Check if the tense has been formed correctly. *Know* the past participle of irregular verbs!

INCORRECT: He throwed it out the window.

CORRECT: He <u>threw</u> it out the window.

3. ERRORS IN SUBJECT-VERB AGREEMENT

Check if the subject of the verb is singular or plural. Does the verb agree in number?

Multiple subjects will be connected by the word AND:

Ted, John, <u>and</u> I <u>are</u> going.

If a singular subject is separated by a comma from an accompanying phrase, *it remains singular.*

<u>The bride</u>, together with the groom and her parents, <u>is receiving</u> at the door.

INCORRECT: There is many reasons why I can't help you.

CORRECT: There <u>are many reasons</u> why I can't help you.

4. ERRORS IN CONDITIONAL SENTENCES

In conditional sentences, the word *if* will NEVER be followed by the words *will* or *would.*

Here are the correct conditional forms:

FUTURE: If I <u>have</u> time, I <u>will do</u> it tomorrow.

PRESENT: If I <u>had</u> time, I <u>would do</u> it now.

PAST: If I <u>had had</u> time, I <u>would have done</u> it yesterday.

Sentences using the words *when, as soon as, the moment,* etc., are formed like future conditionals:

> I will tell him <u>if</u> I <u>see</u> him.
> I will tell him <u>when</u> I <u>see</u> him.

The verb *to be* will ALWAYS appear as *were* in the present conditional:

> If I <u>were</u> you, I wouldn't do that.
> She wouldn't say so if she <u>weren't</u> sure.

NOTE: Not all sentences containing *if* are conditionals. When *if* appears in the meaning of *whether,* it may take the future:

> I don't know <u>if</u> he <u>will be</u> there. (I don't know <u>whether</u> he will be there.)

INCORRECT: If I would have known, I wouldn't have gone.
CORRECT: If I <u>had known</u>, I wouldn't have gone.

5. ERRORS IN EXPRESSIONS OF DESIRE

Unfulfilled desires are expressed by the form "_____ had hoped that _____ would (or *could,* or *might*) do _____ ."

> I <u>had hoped</u> that I <u>would pass</u> the exam.
> Expressions with *wish* are formed as follows:

PRESENT: I wish I <u>knew</u> him.
FUTURE: I wish you <u>could</u> (<u>would</u>) <u>come</u>.
PAST: I wish he <u>had come</u> (or <u>could have come</u>, <u>would have come</u>, <u>might have come</u>).

NOTE: As in conditionals, the verb *to be* will ALWAYS appear as *were* in the present: I wish she <u>were</u> here.

INCORRECT: I wish I heard that story about him before I met him.
CORRECT: I wish I <u>had heard</u> (or <u>could have heard</u> or <u>would have heard</u>) that story about him before I met him.

6. ERRORS IN VERBS FOLLOWED BY VERB WORDS

The following list consists of words and expressions that are followed by a VERB WORD (the infinitive without the *to*):

ask	prefer	requirement
demand	recommend	suggest
desire	recommendation	suggestion
insist	require	urge

It is essential/imperative/important/necessary that…

INCORRECT: She ignored the doctor's recommendation that she stops smoking.

CORRECT: She ignored the doctor's recommendation that she stop smoking.

7. ERRORS IN NEGATIVE IMPERATIVES

Note the two forms for negative imperatives:

   a. Please don't do that.

   b. Would you please not do that.

INCORRECT: Would you please don't smoke here.

CORRECT: Please don't smoke here.

OR

Would you please not smoke here.

8. ERRORS IN AFFIRMATIVE AND NEGATIVE AGREEMENT OF VERBS

Note the two correct forms for *affirmative* agreement:

   a. I am an American and so is she.

   b. I am an American and she is too.

   a. Mary likes Bach and so does John.

   b. Mary likes Bach and John does too.

   a. My father will be there and so will my mother.

   b. My father will be there and my mother will too.

INCORRECT: I have seen the film and she also has.
CORRECT: <u>I have seen</u> the film and <u>so has she</u>.

OR

<u>I have seen</u> the film and <u>she has too</u>.

Note the two correct forms for *negative* agreement:

    a. I'm not American and <u>he isn't either</u>.
    b. I'm not American and <u>neither is he</u>.

    a. Mary doesn't like Bach and <u>John doesn't either</u>.
    b. Mary doesn't like Bach and <u>neither does John</u>.

    a. My father won't be there and <u>my mother won't either</u>.
    b. My father won't be there and <u>neither will my mother</u>.

INCORRECT: I haven't seen the film and she hasn't neither.
CORRECT: I haven't seen the film and <u>she hasn't either</u>.

OR

I haven't seen the film and <u>neither has she</u>.

9. ERRORS OF INFINITIVES OR GERUNDS IN THE COMPLEMENT OF VERBS

Some verbs may be followed by either an infinitive or a gerund:

    I love <u>swimming</u> at night.
    I love <u>to swim</u> at night.

Other verbs, however, may require either one *or* the other for idiomatic reasons. Following is a list of the more commonly used verbs in this category:

Verbs requiring an INFINITIVE:

agree	fail	intend	promise
decide	hope	learn	refuse
expect	want	plan	

Verbs requiring a GERUND:

admit	deny	quit
appreciate	enjoy	regret
avoid	finish	risk
consider	practice	stop

Phrases requiring a GERUND:

approve of	do not mind	keep on
be better off	forget about	look forward to
can't help	insist on	think about
count on	get through	think of

INCORRECT: I intend learning French next semester.
CORRECT: I intend <u>to learn</u> French next semester.

10. ERRORS IN VERBS REQUIRING *HOW* IN THE COMPLEMENT

The verbs KNOW, TEACH, LEARN, and SHOW require the word *HOW* before an infinitive in the complement.

INCORRECT: She knows to drive.
CORRECT: She knows <u>how</u> to drive.

11. ERRORS IN TAG ENDINGS

Check for *three* things in tag endings:

a. Does the ending use the *same person* as the sentence verb?
b. Does the ending use the *same tense* as the sentence verb?
c. If the sentence verb is positive, is the ending negative; if the sentence verb is negative, is the ending positive?

<u>It's</u> nice here, <u>isn't it</u>?
<u>It isn't</u> nice here, <u>is it</u>?

<u>She speaks</u> French, <u>doesn't she</u>?
<u>She doesn't speak</u> French, <u>does she</u>?

<u>They'll be</u> here tomorrow, <u>won't they</u>?
<u>They won't be</u> here tomorrow, <u>will they</u>?

EXCEPTIONS:

<u>I'm</u> right, <u>aren't I</u>?
<u>We ought</u> to go, <u>shouldn't we</u>?
<u>Let's</u> see, <u>shall we</u>?

NOTE: If there is a contraction in the sentence verb, make sure you know what the contraction stands for:

INCORRECT: She's been there before, isn't she?
CORRECT: <u>She's been</u> there before, <u>hasn't she</u>?

12. ERRORS IN IDIOMATIC VERB EXPRESSIONS

Following are a few commonly used idiomatic verb expressions. Notice whether they are followed by a verb word, a participle, an infinitive, or a gerund. Memorize a sample of each to check yourself when choosing an answer:

a. *must have (done)*—meaning "it is a logical conclusion"

They're late. They <u>must have missed</u> the bus.
There's no answer. They <u>must have gone</u> out.

b. *had better (do)*—meaning "it is advisable"

It's getting cold. You <u>had better take</u> your coat.
He still has a fever. He <u>had better not go</u> out yet.

c. *used to (do)*—meaning "was in the habit of doing in the past"

I <u>used to smoke</u> a pack of cigarettes a day, but I stopped.
When I worked on a farm, I <u>used to get up</u> at 4:30 in the morning.

d. *to be used to*—meaning "to be accustomed to"

to get used to
to become used to }—meaning "to become accustomed to"

The noise doesn't bother me; I'm <u>used to studying</u> with the radio on.
In America you'll <u>get used to hearing</u> only English all day long.

e. *make* someone *do*—meaning "force someone to do"
   have someone *do*—meaning "cause someone to do"
   let someone *do*—meaning "allow someone to do"

My mother <u>made me take</u> my little sister with me to the movies.

The teacher <u>had us write</u> an essay instead of taking an exam.
The usher didn't <u>let us come</u> in until the intermission.

  f. *would rather*—meaning "would prefer"

I <u>would rather speak</u> to her myself.
I <u>would rather not speak</u> to her myself.

But if the preference is for someone *other than the subject* to do the action, use the PAST:

I <u>would rather</u> you <u>spoke</u> to her.
I <u>would rather</u> you <u>didn't speak</u> to her.

PRONOUN ERRORS

1. ERRORS IN PRONOUN SUBJECT/OBJECT

Check if a pronoun is the SUBJECT or the OBJECT of a verb or preposition.

INCORRECT: All of us—Fred, Jane, Alice, and me—were late.
CORRECT: <u>All of us</u>—Fred, Jane, Alice, and I—<u>were</u> late.

2. ERRORS WITH WHO AND WHOM

When in doubt about the correctness of WHO/WHOM, try substituting the subject/object of a simpler pronoun to clarify the meaning:

I don't know <u>who/whom</u> Sarah meant.

Try substituting *he/him;* then rearrange the clause in its proper order:

<u>he/him</u> Sarah meant/Sarah meant <u>him</u>.

Now it is clear that the pronoun is the *object* of the verb *meant*, so *whom* is called for.

CORRECT: I don't know <u>whom</u> Sarah meant.

ANOTHER EXAMPLE:
There was a discussion as to <u>who/whom</u> was better suited.

Try substituting *she/her.*

<u>she</u> was better suited/<u>her</u> was better suited.

Here the pronoun is the *subject* of the verb *was suited:*

CORRECT: There was a discussion as to <u>who</u> was better suited.

3. ERRORS OF PRONOUN SUBJECT-VERB AGREEMENT

Check if the pronoun and its verb agree in number. Remember that the following are *singular:*

anyone	either	neither	what
anything	everyone	no one	whatever
each	everything	nothing	whoever

These are *plural:*

both	many	several	others
few			

INCORRECT: John is absent, but a few of the class is here.
CORRECT: John is absent, but <u>a few</u> of the class <u>are</u> here.

INCORRECT: Everyone on the project have to come to the meeting.
CORRECT: <u>Everyone</u> on the project <u>has</u> to come to the meeting.

NOTE: In the forms *either ... or* and *neither ... nor*, the word directly preceding the verb will determine whether the verb should be singular or plural:

Either his parents or <u>he is</u> bringing it.
Either he or <u>his parents are</u> bringing it.

Neither his parents nor <u>he was</u> there.
Neither he nor <u>his parents were</u> there.

4. ERRORS OF POSSESSIVE PRONOUN AGREEMENT

Check if possessive pronouns agree in *person* and *number.*

INCORRECT: If anyone calls, take their name.
CORRECT: If <u>anyone</u> calls, take <u>his</u> name.

5. ERRORS IN PRONOUNS AFTER THE VERB TO BE

TO BE is an intransitive verb and will always be followed by a subject pronoun.

INCORRECT: It must have been her at the door.
CORRECT: It must have <u>been she</u> at the door.

6. ERRORS IN POSITION OF RELATIVE PRONOUNS

A relative pronoun refers to the word preceding it. If the meaning is unclear, the pronoun is in the wrong position.

INCORRECT: He could park right in front of the door, which was very convenient.

Since it was not the door which was convenient, the "which" is illogical in this position. In order to correct the sentence, it is necessary to rewrite it completely:

CORRECT: His being allowed to park right in front of the door was very convenient.

7. ERRORS IN PARALLELISM OF IMPERSONAL PRONOUNS

In forms using impersonal pronouns, use *either* "one ... one's/his or her" *or* "you ... your."

INCORRECT: One should take your duties seriously.
CORRECT: <u>One</u> should take <u>one's/his or her</u> duties seriously.

OR

<u>You</u> should take <u>your</u> duties seriously.

ADJECTIVE AND ADVERB ERRORS

1. ERRORS IN THE USE OF ADJECTIVES AND ADVERBS

Check if a word modifier is an ADJECTIVE or an ADVERB. Make sure the correct form has been used.

An ADJECTIVE describes a <u>noun</u> and answers the question *What kind?*

She is a <u>good</u> cook. (What kind of cook?)

An ADVERB describes either a <u>verb</u> or an <u>adjective</u> and answers the question *How?*

She cooks <u>well</u>. (She cooks how?)

This exercise is <u>relatively</u> <u>easy</u>. (How easy?)

Most adverbs are formed by adding -*ly* to the adjective.

EXCEPTIONS:

Adjective	*Adverb*
early	early
fast	fast
good	well
hard	hard *(hardly means almost not)*
late	late *(lately means recently)*

INCORRECT: I sure wish I were rich!

CORRECT: I <u>surely</u> wish I were rich!

2. ERRORS OF ADJECTIVES WITH VERBS OF SENSE

The following verbs of sense are intransitive and are described by ADJECTIVES:

be	look	smell	taste
feel	seem	sound	

INCORRECT: She looked very well.

CORRECT: She looked very <u>good</u>.

NOTE: "He is well" is also correct in the meaning of "He is healthy" or in describing a person's well-being.

INCORRECT: The food tastes deliciously.

CORRECT: The food tastes <u>delicious</u>.

NOTE: When the above verbs are used as transitive verbs, modify with an adverb, as usual: She tasted the soup <u>quickly</u>.

3. ERRORS IN COMPARATIVES

a. Similar comparison

ADJECTIVE: She is <u>as</u> <u>pretty</u> <u>as</u> her sister.

ADVERB: He works <u>as</u> <u>hard</u> <u>as</u> his father.

b. Comparative (of two things)

ADJECTIVE: She is <u>prettier</u> <u>than</u> her sister.

She is <u>more beautiful</u> <u>than</u> her sister.

She is <u>less</u> <u>successful</u> <u>than</u> her sister.

ADVERB: He works <u>harder</u> <u>than</u> his father.

He reads <u>more</u> <u>quickly</u> <u>than</u> I.

He drives <u>less</u> <u>carelessly</u> <u>than</u> he used to.

NOTE 1: A pronoun following *than* in a comparison will be the *subject pronoun:*

You are prettier than <u>she</u> (is).

You drive better than <u>he</u> (does).

NOTE 2: In using comparisons, <u>adjectives</u> of one syllable, or of two syllables ending in *-y,* add *-er:* smart, smarter; pretty, prettier. Other words of more than one syllable use *more:* interesting, more interesting. <u>Adverbs</u> of one syllable add *-er,* longer adverbs use *more:* fast, faster; quickly, more quickly.

NOTE 3: The word *different* is followed by *from:*

You are <u>different</u> <u>from</u> me.

c. Superlative (comparison of more than two things)

ADJECTIVE: She is <u>the</u> <u>prettiest</u> girl <u>in</u> her class.

He is <u>the</u> <u>most</u> <u>successful</u> <u>of</u> his brothers.

This one is <u>the</u> <u>least</u> <u>interesting</u> <u>of</u> the three.

ADVERB: He plays <u>the</u> <u>best</u> <u>of</u> all.

He speaks <u>the</u> <u>most</u> <u>interestingly</u>.

He spoke to them <u>the</u> <u>least</u> <u>patronizingly</u>.

EXCEPTIONAL FORMS:

good	better	best
bad	worse	worst
much/many	more	most
little	less	least

INCORRECT: This exercise is harder then the last one.
CORRECT: This exercise is harder <u>than</u> the last one.

4. ERRORS IN PARALLEL COMPARISONS

In parallel comparisons, check if the correct form has been used.

INCORRECT: The more you practice, you will get better.
CORRECT: <u>The more</u> you practice, <u>the better</u> you will get.

5. ERRORS OF ILLOGICAL COMPARATIVES

Check comparisons to make sure they *make sense*.

INCORRECT: Alaska is bigger than any state in the United States.
CORRECT: Alaska is bigger than any <u>other</u> state in the United States. (If Alaska were bigger than *any state,* it would be bigger than itself!)

6. ERRORS OF IDENTICAL COMPARISONS

Something can be *the same as* OR *like* something else. Do not mix up the two forms.

INCORRECT: Your dress is the same like mine.
CORRECT: Your dress is <u>like</u> mine.

OR

Your dress is <u>the same as</u> mine.

7. ERRORS IN IDIOMS USING COMPARATIVE STRUCTURES

Some idiomatic terms are formed like comparatives, although they are not true comparisons:

as high as   as much as   as few as
as little as   as many as

INCORRECT: You may have to spend so much as two hours waiting.
CORRECT: You may have to spend <u>as much as</u> two hours waiting.

8. ERRORS IN NOUN-ADJECTIVES

When a NOUN is used as an ADJECTIVE, treat it as an adjective. Do not pluralize or add *s*.

INCORRECT: You're talking like a two-years-old child!
CORRECT: You're talking like a <u>two-year-old</u> child!

9. ERRORS IN ORDINAL AND CARDINAL NUMBERS

Ordinal numbers (first, second, third, etc.) are preceded by *the*. Cardinal numbers (one, two, three, etc.) are not.

We missed <u>the first</u> act.
We missed Act <u>One</u>.

NOTE: Ordinarily, either form is correct. There are two exceptions:

a. In *dates* use only *ordinal* numbers:
   May <u>first</u> (*not* May one)
   the <u>first</u> of May

b. In terms dealing with *travel,* use only *cardinal* numbers, as "Gate Three" may not actually be the third gate. It is <u>Gate Number Three</u>.

INCORRECT: We leave from the second pier.
CORRECT: We leave from Pier <u>Two</u>.

10. ERRORS IN MODIFYING COUNTABLE AND NONCOUNTABLE NOUNS

If a noun can be preceded by a number, it is a countable noun and will be modified by these words:

a few   many, more   some
few, fewer   number of

If it cannot be preceded by a number, it is noncountable and will be modified by these words:

amount of   little, less   some
a little   much, more

INCORRECT: I was surprised by the large amount of people who came.
CORRECT: I was surprised by the large <u>number of people</u> who came.

ERRORS IN USAGE

1. ERRORS IN CONNECTORS

There are several ways of connecting ideas. Do not mix the different forms:

and	also	not only…but also
too	as well as	both…and

INCORRECT: She speaks not only Spanish but French as well.
CORRECT: She speaks Spanish <u>and</u> French.
             She speaks Spanish. She <u>also</u> speaks French.
             She speaks Spanish <u>and</u> French <u>too</u>.
             She speaks <u>not only</u> Spanish <u>but also</u> French.
             She speaks <u>both</u> Spanish <u>and</u> French.
             She speaks Spanish <u>as well as</u> French.

2. ERRORS IN QUESTION WORD CONNECTORS

When a question word such as *when* or *what* is used as a connector, the clause that follows is *not* a question. Do not use the interrogative form.

INCORRECT: Do you know when does the movie start?
CORRECT: Do you know <u>when</u> the movie <u>starts</u>?

3. ERRORS IN PURPOSE CONNECTORS

The word *so* by itself means *therefore*.

It was too hot to study, <u>so</u> we went to the beach.

So that means *in order to* or *in order that*.

INCORRECT: We took a cab so we would be on time.
CORRECT: We took a cab <u>so that</u> we would be on time.

4. ERRORS WITH BECAUSE

It is incorrect to say: *The reason is because…* Use: *The reason is that…*

INCORRECT: The reason he was rejected was because he was too young.

CORRECT: The reason he was rejected was <u>that</u> he was too young.

OR

He was rejected <u>because of</u> his young age.

OR

He was rejected <u>because</u> he was too young.

5. ERRORS OF DANGLING MODIFIERS

An introductory verbal modifier should be directly followed by the noun or pronoun that it modifies. Such a modifier will start with a gerund or participial phrase and be followed by a comma. Look for the modified noun or pronoun *immediately* after the comma.

INCORRECT: Seeing that the hour was late, it was decided to postpone the committee vote.

CORRECT: <u>Seeing</u> that the hour was late, <u>the committee</u> decided to postpone the vote.

6. ERRORS IN PARALLEL CONSTRUCTION

In sentences containing a series of two or more items, check to see if the same form has been used for all the items in the series. Do *not* mix infinitives with gerunds, adjectives with participial phrases, or verbs with nouns.

INCORRECT: The film was interesting, exciting, and it was made well.

CORRECT: The film was <u>interesting</u>, <u>exciting</u>, and <u>well made</u>.

7. ERRORS OF UNNECESSARY MODIFIERS

In general, the more simply an idea is stated, the better it is. An adverb or adjective can often eliminate extraneous words.

INCORRECT: He drove in a careful way.

CORRECT: He drove carefully.

Beware of words with the same meaning in the same sentence.

INCORRECT: The new innovations were startling.

CORRECT: The innovations were startling.

Beware of general wordiness.

INCORRECT: That depends on the state of the general condition of the situation.

CORRECT: That depends on the situation.

8. ERRORS OF COMMONLY CONFUSED WORDS

Following are some of the more commonly misused words in English:

a. **to lie**	lied	lied	lying	to tell an untruth
to lie	lay	lain	lying	to recline
to lay	laid	laid	laying	to put down (*Idiomatic* usage: LAY THE TABLE, put dishes, etc., on the table; CHICKENS LAY EGGS; LAY A BET, make a bet)
b. **to rise**	rose	risen	rising	to go up; to get up
to arise	arose	arisen	arising	to wake up; to get up (*Idiomatic* usage: A PROBLEM HAS ARISEN, a problem has come up)
to raise	raised	raised	raising	to lift; bring up (*Idiomatic* usage: TO RAISE CHILDREN, to bring up children; TO RAISE VEGETABLES, to grow vegetables; TO RAISE MONEY, to collect funds for a cause)
c. **to set**	set	set	setting	to put down (*Idiomatic* usage: SET A DATE, arrange a date; SET THE TABLE, put dishes, etc., on the table; THE SUN SET, the sun went down

for the night; TO SET THE CLOCK, to adjust the timing mechanism of a clock)

to sit	sat	sat	sitting	to be in or get into a sitting position
d. **to let**	let	let	letting	to allow; to rent
to leave	left	left	leaving	to go away

e. **formerly**—previously
   formally—in a formal way

f. **to affect**—to influence (verb)
   effect—result (noun)

INCORRECT: He was laying in bed all day yesterday.
CORRECT: He was <u>lying</u> in bed all day yesterday.

INCORRECT: The price of gas has raised three times last year.
CORRECT: The price of gas <u>rose</u> three times last year.

OR

The price of gas <u>was raised</u> three times last year.

INCORRECT: He raised slowly from his chair.
CORRECT: He <u>arose</u> slowly from his chair.

9. ERRORS OF MISUSED WORDS AND PREPOSITIONAL IDIOMS

a. **in spite of; despite**

The two expressions are synonymous; use *either* one *or* the other.

INCORRECT: They came despite of the rain.
CORRECT: They came <u>in spite of</u> the rain.

OR

They came <u>despite</u> the rain.

b. **scarcely; barely; hardly**

All three words mean *almost not at all;* do NOT use a negative with them.

INCORRECT:	I hardly never see him.
CORRECT:	I <u>hardly ever</u> see him.

INCORRECT:	He has scarcely no money.
CORRECT:	He has <u>scarcely any</u> money.

    c. Note and memorize the prepositions in these common idioms:

approve/disapprove <u>of</u>	agree/disagree <u>with</u>
be ashamed <u>of</u>	compare <u>with</u> (point out
capable/incapable <u>of</u>	similarities between things of a
be conscious <u>of</u>	different order)
be afraid <u>of</u>	compare <u>to</u> (point out differences
independent <u>of</u>	between things of the same
in the habit <u>of</u>	order)
be interested <u>in</u>	be equal <u>to</u>
except <u>for</u>	next <u>to</u>
dependent <u>on</u>	related <u>to</u>
be bored <u>with</u>	similar <u>to</u>

A TACTIC FOR SENTENCE CORRECTION QUESTIONS

The first step in the Sentence Correction part of the exam is to read the sentence carefully in order to spot an error of grammar or usage. Once you have found an error, eliminate choice (A) and ALL OTHER ALTERNATIVES CONTAINING THAT ERROR. Concentrate on the remaining alternatives to choose your answer. Do not select an alternative that has changed the *meaning* of the original sentence.

EXAMPLE 1:

If I knew him better, <u>I would have insisted that he change</u> the hour of the lecture.

    (A) I would have insisted that he change
    (B) I would have insisted that he changed
    (C) I would insist that he change
    (D) I would insist for him to change
    (E) I would have insisted him to change

Since we must assume the unmarked part of the sentence to be correct, this is a PRESENT CONDITIONAL sentence; therefore, the second verb in the sentence should read *I would insist*. Glancing through the alternatives, you can eliminate (A), (B), and (E). You are left with (C) and (D). Remember that the word *insist* takes a *verb word* after it. (C) is the only correct answer.

If you do not find any grammatical error in the underlined part, read the alternatives to see if one of them uses a clearer or more concise style to express the same thing. Do not choose an alternative that changes the meaning of the original sentence.

EXAMPLE 2:
<u>The couple, who had been married recently, booked their honeymoon passage through an agent who lived near them.</u>

- (A) The couple, who had been married recently, booked their honeymoon passage through an agent who lived near them.
- (B) The couple, who had been recently married, booked their honeymoon passage through an agent who lived not far from them.
- (C) The newlyweds booked their honeymoon passage through a local agent.
- (D) The newlyweds booked their passage through an agent that lived not far from them.
- (E) The couple lived not far from the agent who through him they booked their passage.

Although (A), the original, has no real errors, (C) expresses the same thing more concisely, without distorting the original meaning of the sentence.

Remember: If you find no errors, and if you find that none of the alternatives improve the original, choose (A).

PRACTICE EXERCISE WITH ANSWERS AND ANALYSIS

Directions: This exercise consists of a number of sentences, in each of which some part or the whole is underlined. Each sentence is followed by five alternative versions of the underlined portion. Select the alternative you consider both most correct and most effective according to the requirements of standard written English. Answer (A) is the same as the original version; if you think the original version is best, select answer (A).

In considering the answer choices, be attentive to matters of grammar, diction, and syntax, as well as clarity, precision, and fluency. Do not select an answer that alters the meaning of the original sentence.

1. A good doctor inquires not only about patients' physical health, <u>but about their mental health too</u>.

    (A) but about their mental health too
    (B) but their mental health also
    (C) but also inquires about their mental health
    (D) but also about their mental health
    (E) but too about their mental health

2. <u>Knowing that the area was prone to earthquakes</u>, all the buildings were reinforced with additional steel and concrete.

    (A) Knowing that the area was prone to earthquakes,
    (B) Having known that the area was prone to earthquakes,
    (C) Since the area was known to be prone to earthquakes,
    (D) Since they knew that the area was prone to earthquakes,
    (E) Being prone to earthquakes,

3. John would never have taken the job <u>if he had known</u> what great demands it would make on his time.

    (A) if he had known
    (B) if he knew
    (C) if he had been knowing
    (D) if he knows
    (E) if he was knowing

ANSWERS AND ANALYSIS

1. **(D)** The connective *not only* MUST be accompanied by *but also*. Eliminate (A), (B), and (E). (C) repeats *inquires* unnecessarily. (D) is correct.

2. **(C)** *All the buildings* couldn't have known that the area was prone to earthquakes. Since the unmarked part of the sentence must be assumed to be correct, eliminate all alternatives beginning with a dangling modifier: (A), (B), and (E). In (D) the word *they* is unclear. Where there is no definite subject, the passive is preferable. (C) is correct.

3. **(A)** This is a past conditional sentence. (A) is correct.

SENTENCE CORRECTION STRATEGIES

1. Remember that any error in the sentence must be in the underlined part.

2. If you determine that there is an error in the underlined part of the sentence, immediately eliminate answer choice (A).

3. Do not choose as an answer any alternative that changes the meaning of the original sentence.

4. Determine if the parts of the sentence are linked logically.

5. Look at the changes made in the answer alternatives.

6. Be aware of the common grammar and usage errors tested on the GMAT.

4

CRITICAL REASONING REVIEW

DESCRIPTION OF THE TEST

The Critical Reasoning section of the GMAT is designed to test your ability to evaluate an assumption, inference, or argument. Each question consists of a short statement followed by a question or assumption about the statement. Each question or assumption has five possible answers. Your task is to evaluate each of the five possible choices and select the one that is the best alternative.

TIPS TO HELP YOU COPE

1. *Before reading the passage, read the questions pertaining to it.* By reading the questions first, *carefully,* you familiarize yourself with the type of argument being presented and the factors you will have to consider in choosing your answer.

2. *Look for the conclusion first.* Critical reasoning questions are preceded by an argument or statement that has a conclusion or claim. While it may seem logical that a conclusion appears at the end of a passage, it might be given at the beginning or in the middle.

3. *Find the premises.* Premises are facts or evidence. Determine whether the conclusion follows logically from the premises or whether it is merely alleged. A conclusion may not follow, even though premises may be true. You must determine the legitimacy of assumptions and final conclusions.

TYPES OF QUESTIONS

Inference or Assumption. These questions test your ability to evaluate an assumption, inference, or argument. You will be given a statement, position, argument, or fact and will be asked to identify a conclusion or claim and the premise on which it is based.

Flaws. In this type of question you are asked to choose the best alternative answer that either represents a flaw in the statement position, or, if true, would weaken the argument or conclusion.

Statements of Fact. With this type of question, you will be asked to find the answer that best agrees with, summarizes, or completes the statement.

IDENTIFYING THE PREMISE AND CONCLUSION

In evaluating an argument and its strength and validity, the first step is to identify the components—the premises and conclusion. There are several things to keep in mind when doing this.

Cue Words. Very often you will be helped in identifying the parts of an argument by the presence of cue words. Words such as "if," "given that," "since," "because," "for," "suppose," and "in view of" signal the presentation of evidence and reasons in support of a fact or claim. These cues identify premises. Conclusions, on the other hand, may often be preceded by words such as "thus," "hence," "so," and "therefore." Without cue words, identifying and analyzing an argument becomes more difficult.

Position of Conclusion. Conclusions do not have to be at the end of an argument. Conclusions and premises may be reversed while the same meaning is conveyed. For example:

> "David was talking during the lesson, so he didn't understand the teacher's instructions."

> "David did not understand the teacher's instructions because he was talking during the lesson."

In both statements, the conclusion is "David did not understand the teacher's instructions."

Connecting Events to Draw Conclusions. Arguments frequently contain a number of premises and possibly more than one conclusion. Therefore, it is necessary to classify and connect things and events in order to analyze the arguments. To aid this analysis, think of events in terms of time sequence or causal relationships. For example:

> "Sarah overslept, which caused her to be late leaving for school; therefore, she ran all the way, causing her to be out of breath."

Determining What the Writer Is Trying to Prove. At first glance the analysis of some arguments looks difficult because of the absence of cue words. In these cases, ask yourself, "What is the writer trying to prove?" Once you have identified the main point of the argument, define it. Ask "How great a claim (or 'How limited a claim') is the author making?" "What precisely is the author talking about?" "What was the author's purpose in making the claim?"

To answer the first of these questions, look again for signal words—for instance "all," "none," "never," "always," "some," and "sometimes." There is a big difference, for example, between "all cars are red" and "some cars are red." The first statement is false. The second is most definitely true. Similarly, note the difference between "I have never seen him before" and "I have not seen him today."

Often the use of different verbs and adverbs can change the meaning of similar claims. "The ground was wet, so it must have been raining." We can limit the claim by changing "must" to "probably." "The ground was wet. So it probably has been raining." The first statement stands more chance of being proven false. Anything else that can be shown to have made the ground wet limits the chance that it must have been the rain that caused the wetness. However, it could still have been raining, and there is always the probability, no matter how small, that it may have been.

Descriptive words, both nouns and adjectives, in a passage are also used to limit or expand claims made by another. Take the example:

"Prisoners in San Quentin rioted today because they were angry about their conditions."

The author's choice of the word "Prisoners" indicates merely that more than one prisoner rioted. Maybe all or maybe only some prisoners rioted. Note also that the author claims to know the reason for the riot—namely, that the prisoners were angry about their conditions and for no other reason. However, you cannot assume that just because an author states a reason for a claim, he or she is correct in that assumption. And if an author makes a claim about the cause of some event, he or she may either endorse or condemn it. Endorsement of a claim without any supporting evidence is not a substitute for proof.

The use of assumptions is vital in evaluating an argument, but the strength of an argument depends on the legitimacy of its assumptions.

DEDUCTIVE AND INDUCTIVE ARGUMENTS

An argument may be deductive or inductive, depending on how the conclusion follows or is inferred from the premises.

An argument may be defined as deductive if it is *impossible* for the conclusion to be false if all the premises are true. In other words, in a deductive argument, the premises necessitate the conclusion. An example of a deductive argument is:

(1) All men are mortal.
(2) Brian is a man.
(3) Therefore, Brian is a mortal.

If both premises are true, then the conclusion follows automatically.

An argument is inductive if it is *improbable* that the conclusion is false if all premises are true. The premises do not necessitate but do make probable the conclusion. The conclusion may be false even if all the premises are true.

Determining if the conclusion in an argument has been arrived at through deductive reasoning or through inductive reasoning can often be discerned from the wording of the statement or sentence.

Words such as "usually," "sometimes," and "generally" are usually signals of induction.

An example of an inductive argument is:

(1) Freshmen usually find economics I difficult.

(2) Jones is a freshman.

(3) Therefore, Jones finds economics I difficult.

In the above statement, both premises are true. If the premises are true, does the conclusion automatically follow? No, because not all freshmen find economics I difficult, and Jones may be one of the minority of freshmen who do not.

The distinction between deduction and induction should not be taken as a distinction between a good or superior way of arguing or reasoning and an inferior way. An inductive argument is not necessarily a bad argument. The two methods of argument serve different and complementary purposes. The distinction is in the manner by which a conclusion follows its premise(s).

DETERMINING THE LOGICAL SEQUENCE OF AN ARGUMENT

Having discussed types of arguments, we will now demonstrate in more detail how an argument can be identified and analyzed. You must be able to determine what the writer is trying to establish.

In order to identify an argument:

1. Find the conclusion first. This may be done by locating the cue that introduces the conclusion.
2. Find the premise(s). Again, locate the cue words (if present) that signal premises.
3. Determine if the premise(s) are true.
4. Determine the logical form of the argument.

ATTACKING THE ASSUMPTIONS OF AN ARGUMENT

In the GMAT, one often has to attack or find a fact that weakens an argument. The most effective way of doing this is to defeat the assumptions. Consider the following argument:

(1) Cooking classes take place on Tuesdays.
(2) Today is Tuesday.
(3) Therefore, cooking classes take place today.

We may be able to defeat this argument by analyzing the first premise. If we assume that cooking classes usually take place on a Tuesday, then there is a probability that if today is Tuesday it will be one of those Tuesdays when cooking classes are held, but this is obviously not certain. Premise (1) does not state that cooking classes take place every Tuesday; classes could be held every other Tuesday or every third Tuesday. Therefore, the third sentence, the conclusion of the argument, *may* be false.

Often, the attack on the argument will not be so obvious because the assumptions on which the argument is built are hidden or concealed. Someone who is making a totally honest and correct argument will not explicitly acknowledge all of the assumptions he or she makes. These hidden assumptions may be open to attack. Bear this in mind, particularly if you are presented with an argument that seems logical and correct but which reaches a factually impossible or absurd result. This could indicate the existence of hidden assumptions that make the argument invalid.

FALLACIES

As mentioned earlier, the thought process that links the premise of an argument to its conclusion is called an inference. Errors may occur in any part of the argumentation process. These errors in reasoning are called *fallacies,* or *flaws*.

A fallacy is a form of reasoning that is illogical or violates the rules of argumentation. A fallacy is, in other words, an argument that seems to be sound but is not. The following common types of fallacies are those that appear most often on the GMAT.

GUILT BY ASSOCIATION

One type of fallacy is guilt by association. Suppose that one proves that educator John Doe is a dues-paying member of the

Association for Fairy Teeth (A.F.T.), a fact not denied by Doe. Suppose that three members of the association have been found to be subversives. An argument may be:

(1) John Doe is a member of the A.F.T.
(2) X, Y, and Z are members of the A.F.T. and subversives.
(3) Therefore, John Doe is a subversive.

This argument involves an invalid induction from premise (2) to a (missing) premise: all members of the A.F.T. are subversives. This has not been proven in the argument. It is left for the reader to draw his or her own—in this case, fallacious—conclusion, namely, that John Doe is a subversive.

FAULTY ANALOGY

Another type of fallacy is that of faulty analogy. A faulty analogy assumes that things that are similar in one respect must be similar in other respects. In general, analogies may be a useful form of communication. They enable a speaker to convey concepts in terms already familiar to the audience. A statement such as "our civilization is flowering" may be helpful in making a point, but the generalization is faulty. May we conclude that civilizations are in need of fertilizer?

Suppose that an economist argues that a "tariff on textiles will help our textile industry; a tariff on steel will help the steel industry; a tariff on every imported product will benefit the economy."

The above analogy may be stated as:

(1) Tariffs on textiles benefit the textile industry.
(2) Tariffs on steel benefit the steel industry.
(3) Therefore, a tariff on every imported product benefits the economy.

The analogy here assumes that, because two industries benefit from tariffs, all others will also benefit. However, no proof for this argument is given.

CAUSAL FALLACIES

Some of the common causal fallacies are treating an insignificant relationship as a causal factor and assuming that a sequential relationship implies a causal relationship. That two events occur in sequence is not evidence of a causal relationship. For example, Herbert Hoover was elected President of the United States in 1928, an act followed by a recession in 1929. Did Hoover's policies cause the recession or were there other intervening factors? (There were.)

FALLACIES OF RELEVANCE

Fallacies of relevance involve arguments wherein one or more of the premises are irrelevant to the conclusion. For example:

Ad Hominem (Personal attacks). One type of fallacy of relevance is the *ad hominem* fallacy. In this type of fallacy, the person is attacked, not his or her argument. Attacking an opponent may well be easier than rebutting the merit of the argument. The role of the demagogue is to assassinate the character of his or her opponent, thereby casting doubt on his/her argument.

For example, an economics professor exclaims to her class: "Even a freshman knows that good economists don't necessarily have to be good mathematicians." Or "Congressman Goodboy has argued eloquently in favor of increasing public spending in his district. Isn't he the same congressman who was accused of wasting taxpayers' money on new autobuses whose air conditioning systems didn't work?"

The fallacy in these examples is that arguments are not treated on their merit. The arguments follow the form:

(1) Z asserts B.
(2) Z would benefit if we accept B.
(3) Z's assertion of B is insufficient to accept B as true.

This sort of argument attempts to show that B is not a reliable source because of some self-interest.

FALLACIES OF LANGUAGE (AMBIGUITY)

Ambiguity occurs when there are two or more meanings for a word, phrase, statement, or expression, especially when the meanings are easily confused. Another problem occurs when it is not clear in what context the meaning is being used. Words and expressions such as "democracy," "teamwork," "the American way," and "payoff" have different meanings to different people and may be used in different contexts. For example, is the United States government a democracy in the same sense as the Indian government? Does teamwork mean the same thing to Japanese and American workers? The only way to avoid ambiguity is to carefully define the meaning of words in context.

Let us look at some cases where ambiguity is used with intent to deceive or confuse.

Equivocation (Double meaning). The fallacy of equivocation occurs when words or phrases that have more than one meaning are used. An arguer using this fallacy relies on the fact that the audience fails to realize that some word or expression occurring more than once is used in different ways. The ambiguity may occur in both premises or in a premise and the conclusion. In the following, for example, the structure of the argument is valid but an equivocation occurs.

> (1) Happiness is the end of life (X is Y).
> (2) The end of life is death (Y is Z).
> (3) So happiness is death (X is Z).

The fallacy is that the expression "end of life" has a different meaning in each premise. What has been asserted with one sense of the expression is then wrongly regarded as having been proved with respect to the other expression. An equivocation has been committed on the expression.

Amphiboly (Double talk). This fallacy results whenever there is ambiguity in sentence structure. For example:

> "Can you spell backwards?"

"I have filled out the claim form for my damaged car which I enclose."

FINAL HINTS

Sherlock Holmes once said, "When you have ruled out the possible solutions, only the impossible remain." Can this statement be a true guide to critical reasoning problems? When taking the test, be sure to relate the possible answers to the actual statements, without drawing on prior conceptions or possibly misconceptions. Each of us perceives a thing in his or her own way, but critical reasoning problems can only have one solution.

1. Never rule out the blatantly obvious; it may just be the only solution possible.

2. Never rule out the blatantly ridiculous; it could also be the only reasonable conclusion to be drawn from a specific set of criteria.

3. Always treat each conclusion in isolation, since only one answer can be correct.

CRITICAL REASONING STRATEGIES

1. First, read the question, and then read the passage.

2. Learn to spot major critical reasoning question types.

3. Look for the conclusion first.

4. Find the premises.

5. Do not be opinionated.

6. Do not be overwhelmed by unfamiliar subjects.

5

PROBLEM SOLVING AND DATA SUFFICIENCY REVIEW

PROBLEM SOLVING

DESCRIPTION OF THE TEST

The Quantitative section of the GMAT is designed to test your ability to work with numbers. There are a variety of questions in this section dealing with the basic principles of arithmetic, algebra, and geometry. These questions may take the form of word problems or require straight calculation. In addition, questions involving the interpretation of tables and graphs may be included.

The typical Problem Solving and Data Sufficiency section on the CAT GMAT consists of 37 questions that must be answered within a time limit of 75 minutes. These questions range from very easy to quite challenging and are not always arranged in order of difficulty. Make sure you budget your time so that you can try each question.

TIPS TO HELP YOU COPE

1. If a problem involves geometry, and a diagram is not provided, draw a picture.
2. Before you start to work a problem, check the answers to see how accurate the answer must be. For example, if all the answers are given in tenths, don't use five decimal places in your computations.
3. Don't waste time on unnecessary calculations. If you can answer the question by estimating or doing a rough

calculation, the time you save can be used to work on other questions. Keep this in mind especially when doing problems that involve tables or graphs.

4. Make sure your answer is in the units asked for. Change all measurements to the same units before you do any calculations.

5. Reread the question to make sure you answered the question that was asked as opposed to the question you THOUGHT would be asked.

6. If possible check your answer. For example, if you solve an equation, check that the number you obtained actually solves the equation. Always ask yourself if an answer makes sense.

7. You will not be allowed to use a calculator on the exam. Practice doing arithmetic without a calculator a week before the test.

8. Remember that you must answer all questions on the CAT GMAT. If you are unsure of the correct answer, eliminate one or more answers and make an educated guess. Be sure to budget your time so you can answer each question.

9. You cannot return to a question once you have confirmed your answer, so be satisfied that you have chosen the best answer before you move on.

10. Use the scratch paper for your calculations.

METHODS OF APPROACHING THE TEST

1. **Practice arithmetic.** Most problem solving sections contain one or two basic computational questions, such as multiplying two decimals or finding the largest number in a collection of fractions. *You cannot use a calculator on the GMAT,* so practice your arithmetic before you take the exam. You already know how to do basic computation; you just need to practice to improve your speed and accuracy.

2. **Try to think quantitatively.** If you want to improve your quantitative skills, you should exercise them frequently. When you go grocery shopping, try to figure out whether the giant size is cheaper per ounce than the economy size. When you look at the news, try to make comparisons when figures are given. If you get used to thinking quantitatively, the problem solving sections will be much easier and you will feel more confident about the entire exam.

SAMPLE PROBLEM SOLVING QUESTIONS WITH ANSWERS AND ANALYSIS
Time: 12 minutes

Solve the sample questions below, allowing yourself 12 minutes to complete all of them. As you work, try to make use of the above strategy. Any figure that appears with a problem is drawn as accurately as possible to provide information that may help in answering the question. All numbers used are real numbers.

1. A train travels from Albany to Syracuse, a distance of 120 miles, at the average rate of 50 miles per hour. The train then travels back to Albany from Syracuse. The total traveling time of the train is 5 hours and 24 minutes. What was the average rate of speed of the train on the return trip to Albany?

   (A) 60 mph   (D) 40 mph
   (B) 50 mph   (E) 35 mph
   (C) 48 mph

2. A parking lot charges a flat rate of X dollars for any amount of time up to two hours, and $\frac{1}{6}X$ for each hour or fraction of an hour after the first two hours. How much does it cost to park for 5 hours and 15 minutes?

   (A) $3X$ (D) $1\frac{1}{2}X$
   (B) $2X$ (E) $1\frac{1}{6}X$
   (C) $1\frac{2}{3}X$

Use the following table for questions 3–5.

NUMBER OF STUDENTS BY MAJOR IN STATE UNIVERSITY		
	1950	1970
Division of Business	990	2,504
Division of Sciences	350	790
Division of Humanities	1,210	4,056
Division of Engineering	820	1,600
Division of Agriculture	630	1,050
TOTAL	4,000	10,000

3. From 1950 to 1970, the change in the percentage of university students enrolled in Engineering was

(A) roughly no change
(B) an increase of more than 4%
(C) an increase of more than 1% but less than 4%
(D) a decrease of more than 4%
(E) a decrease of more than 1% but less than 4%

4. The number of students enrolled in Business in 1970 divided by the number of Business students in 1950 is

(A) almost 3
(B) about 2.5
(C) roughly 2
(D) about 1
(E) about 40%

5. By 1970 how many of the divisions had an enrollment greater than 200% of the enrollment of that division in 1950?

(A) 0   (D) 3
(B) 1   (E) 4
(C) 2

ANSWERS AND ANALYSIS

1. **(D)** The train took 120/50 = 2⅖ hours to travel from Albany to Syracuse. Since the total traveling time of the train was 5⅖ hours, it must have taken the train 3 hours for the trip from Syracuse to Albany. Since the distance traveled is 120 miles, the average rate of speed on the return trip to Albany was (⅓) (120) mph = 40 mph.

2. **(C)** It costs X for the first 2 hours. If you park 5 hours and 15 minutes there are 3 hours and 15 minutes left after the first 2 hours. Since this time is charged at the rate of $X/6$ for each hour or fraction thereof, it costs $4(X/6)$ for the last 3 hours and 15 minutes. Thus the total $X + ⅔X = 1⅔X$.

3. **(D)** Since 820/4,000 = .205, the percentage of university students enrolled in Engineering in 1950 was 20.5%; since 1,600/10,000 = .16, the percentage in 1970 was 16%. Thus the percentage of university students enrolled in Engineering was 4.5% less in 1970 than it was in 1950.

4. **(B)** In 1950 there were 990 Business students and in 1970 there were 2,504. Since (2.5) (1,000) = 2,500, the correct answer is thus (B), about 2.5. Note that this is an easy way to save yourself time. Instead of dividing 990 into 2,504 to find the exact answer, simply use numbers close to the original numbers to get an estimate. In many cases this gives enough information to answer the question and saves valuable time.

5. **(D)** If a division in 1970 has more than 200% of the number of students it had in 1950, that means that the number of students more than doubled between 1950 and 1970. Therefore simply double each entry in the 1950 column and if this is less than the corresponding entry in the 1970 column, that division has more than 200% of the number of students it had in 1950. Since (2)(990) = 1980, which is less than 2,504, the number of Business students more

than doubled. Since $(2)(1,210) = 2,420$, which is less than 4,056, Humanities more than doubled, and because $(2)(350) = 700$, which is less than 790, Sciences more than doubled. Engineering did not double in size because $(2)(820) = 1640$, which is larger than 1,600. Also since $(2)(630) = 1,260$, which is larger than 1,050, the number of Agricultural students in 1970 was less than 200% of the number of Agricultural students in 1950. Therefore three of the divisions (Business, Humanities, and Sciences) more than doubled between 1950 and 1970.

PROBLEM SOLVING STRATEGIES

1. Don't waste time.

2. Don't perform unnecessary calculations.

3. Answer the question that is asked.

4. Use intelligent guessing to improve your score.

5. Do calculations on your scratch paper.

6. Remember that you cannot go back to a question once you've confirmed the answer.

7. Check your work if you can.

8. If a problem involves units, keep track of the units. Make sure your answer has the correct units.

9. Use numerical values to check answers that involve formulas.

DATA SUFFICIENCY

DESCRIPTION OF THE TEST

These questions, included in the Quantitative section of the GMAT, are designed to test your reasoning ability. Like the Problem Solving questions, they require a basic knowledge of the principles of arithmetic, algebra, and geometry. Each Data Sufficiency question consists of a mathematical problem and two statements containing information relating to it. You must decide whether the problem can be solved by using information from: (A) the first statement alone, but not the second statement alone; (B) the second statement alone, but not the first statement alone; (C) both statements together, but neither alone; or (D) either of the statements alone. Choose (E) if the problem cannot be solved, even by using both statements together. A typical section will consist of 25 questions to be worked in 30 minutes. As in the Problem Solving questions, time is of the utmost importance. Approaching Data Sufficiency problems properly will help you use this time wisely.

TIPS TO HELP YOU COPE

1. *Don't waste time figuring out the exact answer.* Always keep in mind that you are never asked to supply an answer for the problem; you need only determine if there is sufficient data available to find the answer. Once you know whether or not it is possible to find the answer with the given information, you are through. If you spend too much time doing unnecessary work on one question, you may not be able to finish the entire section.
2. *Don't make extra assumptions.* In particular, don't make inferences based on the diagram supplied with some problems. You can't really tell if an angle is 90 degrees or 89 degrees by looking at a picture.
3. *Use the strategies described below to improve your score on these questions.*

METHODS OF APPROACHING THE TEST

Practice working data sufficiency questions. Most people have not had much experience with these types of questions. The more examples you work out the better you will perform on this section of the test. By the time you have finished the sample exams, you should feel confident about your ability to answer Data Sufficiency questions.

Eliminate choices with three questions. A systematic analysis can improve your score on Data Sufficiency sections. By answering three questions, you will always arrive at the correct choice. In addition, if you can answer any one of the three questions, you can eliminate at least one of the possible choices so that you can make an intelligent guess.

The three questions are:
  I Is the first statement alone sufficient to solve the problem?
  II Is the second statement alone sufficient to solve the problem?
  III Are both statements together sufficient to solve the problem?

As a general rule try to answer the questions in the order I, II, III, since in many cases you will not have to answer all three to get the correct choice.

Here is how to use the three questions:

If the answer to I is YES, then the only possible choices are (A) or (D). Now, if the answer to II is YES, the choice must be (D), and if the answer to II is NO, the choice must be (A).

If the answer to I is NO then the only possible choices are (B), (C), or (E). Now, if the answer to II is YES, then the choice must be (B), and if the answer to II is NO, the only possible choices are (C) or (E).

So, finally, if the answer to III is YES, the choice is (C), and if the answer to III is NO, the choice is (E).

A good way to see this is to use a decision tree.

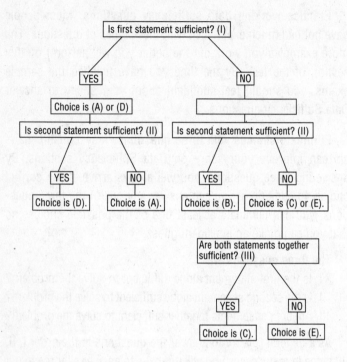

To use the tree simply start at the top and by answering YES or NO move down the tree until you arrive at the correct choice. For example, if the answer to I is YES and the answer to II is NO, then the correct choice is (A). (Notice that in this case you don't need to answer III to find the correct choice.)

The decision tree can also help you make intelligent guesses. If you can only answer one of the three questions, then you can eliminate the choices that follow from the wrong answer to the question.

Example 1.   You know the answer to I is YES. You can eliminate choices (B), (C), and (E).

Example 2.   You know the answer to II is NO. You can eliminate choices (D) and (B) since they follow from YES for II.

Example 3. You know the answer to III is YES. You can eliminate choice (E) since it follows from NO for III.

Example 4. You know the answer to I is NO and the answer to III is YES. You can eliminate (E) since it follows from NO to III. You also can eliminate (A) and (D) since they follow from YES to I.

Because you must answer every question, these guessing strategies can help you answer any data sufficiency question.

SAMPLE DATA SUFFICIENCY QUESTIONS WITH ANSWERS AND ANALYSIS

Time: 8 minutes

Directions: Each of the following problems has a question and two statements which are labeled (1) and (2). Use the data given in (1) and (2) together with other available information (such as the number of hours in a day, the definition of *clockwise,* mathematical facts, etc.) to decide whether the statements are *sufficient* to answer the question. Then choose

- (A) if you can get the answer from (1) alone but not from (2) alone;
- (B) if you can get the answer from (2) alone but not from (1) alone;
- (C) if you can get the answer from (1) and (2) together, although neither statement by itself suffices;
- (D) if statement (1) alone suffices and statement (2) alone suffices;
- (E) if you cannot get the answer from statements (1) and (2) together, but need even more data.

All numbers used are real numbers. A figure given for a problem is intended to provide information consistent with that in the question, but not necessarily consistent with the additional information contained in the statements.

1. A rectangular field is 40 yards long. Find the area of the field.

   (1) A fence around the entire boundary of the field is 140 yards long.
   (2) The field is more than 20 yards wide.

2. Is X a number greater than zero?

   (1) $X^2 - 1 = 0$
   (2) $X^3 + 1 = 0$

3. An industrial plant produces bottles. In 2001 the number of bottles produced by the plant was twice the number produced in 2000. How many bottles were produced altogether in the years 2000, 2001, and 2002?

   (1) In 2002 the number of bottles produced was 3 times the number produced in 2000.
   (2) In 2003 the number of bottles produced was one half the total produced in the years 2000, 2001, and 2002.

4. A man 6 feet tall is standing near a light on the top of a pole. What is the length of the shadow cast by the man?

   (1) The pole is 18 feet high.
   (2) The man is 12 feet from the pole.

5. Find the length of RS if z is 90° and $PS = 6$.

   (1) $PR = 6$
   (2) $x = 45°$

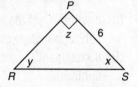

6. Working at a constant rate and by himself, it takes worker U 3 hours to fill up a ditch with sand. How long would it take for worker V to fill up the same ditch working by himself?

   (1) Working together but at the same time U and V can fill in the ditch in 1 hour 52½ minutes.
   (2) In any length of time worker V fills in only 60% as much as worker U does in the same time.

7. Did John go to the beach yesterday?

   (1) If John goes to the beach, he will be sunburned the next day.

   (2) John is sunburned today.

ANSWERS AND ANALYSIS

Answers:

1. **(A)**   4. **(C)**   7. **(E)**
2. **(B)**   5. **(D)**
3. **(E)**   6. **(D)**

Analysis:

1. **(A)** The area of a rectangle is the length multiplied by the width. Since you know the length is 40 yards, you must find out the width in order to solve the problem. Since statement (2) simply says the width is greater than 20 yards you cannot find out the exact width using (2). So (2) alone is not sufficient. Statement (1) says the length of a fence around the entire boundary of the field is 140 yards. The length of this fence is the perimeter of the rectangle, the sum of twice the length and twice the width. If we replace the length by 40 in $P = 2L + 2W$ we have $140 = 2(40) + 2W$ and solving for W yields $2W = 60$, or $W = 30$ yards. Hence the area is $(40)(30) = 1200$ square yards. Thus (1) alone is sufficient but (2) alone is not.

2. **(B)** Statement (1) means $X^2 = 1$, but there are two possible solutions to this equation, $X = 1$, $X = -1$. Thus using (1) alone you cannot deduce whether X is positive or negative. Statement (2) means $X^3 = -1$, but there is only one possible (real) solution to this, $X = -1$. Thus X is not greater than zero, which answers the question. And (2) alone is sufficient.

3. **(E)** T, the total produced in the three years, is the sum of $P_0 + P_1 + P_2$, where P_0 is the number produced in 2000, P_1 the number produced in 2001, and P_2 the number produced in 2002. You are given that $P_1 = 2P_0$. Thus $T = P_0 + P_1 + P_2 =$

$P_0 + 2P_0 + P_2 = 3P_0 + P_2$. So we must find out P_0 and P_2 to answer the question. Statement (1) says $P_2 = 3P_0$; thus, by using (1), if we can find the value of P_0, we can find T. But (1) gives us no further information about P_0. Statement (2) says $\frac{1}{2}T$ equals the number produced in 2003, but it does not say what this number is. Since there are no relations given between production in 2003 and production in the individual years 2000, 2001, or 2002, you cannot use (2) to find out what P_0 is. Thus (1) and (2) together are not sufficient.

4. **(C)** Sometimes it may help to draw a picture. By proportions or by similar triangles the height of the pole, h, is to 6 feet as the length of shadow, s, + the distance to the pole, x, is to s. So $h/6 = (s + x)/s$. Thus $hs = 6s + 6x$ by cross-multiplication. Solving for s gives $hs - 6s = 6x$, or $s(h-6) = 6x$ or finally we have $s = 6x/(h-6)$. Statement (1) says $h = 18$; thus $s = 6x/12 = x/2$, but using (1) alone we cannot deduce the value of x. Thus (1) alone is not sufficient. Statement (2) says x equals 12; thus using (1) and (2) together we deduce $s = 6$, but using (2) alone all we can deduce is that $s = 72/(h-6)$, which cannot be solved for s unless we know h. Thus using (1) and (2) together we can deduce the answer, but (1) alone is not sufficient, nor is (2) alone.

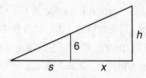

5. **(D)** Since z is a right angle, $(RS)^2 = (PS)^2 + (PR)^2$, so $(RS)^2 = (6)^2 + (PR)^2$, and RS will be the positive square root of $36 + (PR)^2$. Thus if you can find the length of PR the problem is solved. Statement (1) says $PR = 6$, thus $(RS)^2 = 36 + 36$, so $RS = 6\sqrt{2}$. Thus (1) alone is sufficient. Statement (2) says $x = 45°$ but, since the sum of the angles in a triangle is $180°$ and z is $90°$, then $y = 45°$. So x and y are equal angles and that means the sides opposite x and opposite y must

be equal, or $PS = PR$. Thus $PR = 6$ and $RS = 6$, so (2) alone is also sufficient.

6. **(D)** (1) says U and V together can fill in the ditch in $1\frac{7}{8}$ hours. Since U can fill in the ditch in 3 hours, in 1 hour he can fill in one–third of the ditch. Hence, in $1\frac{7}{8}$ hours U would fill in $(\frac{1}{3})$ $(\frac{15}{8}) = \frac{5}{8}$ of the ditch. So V fills in $\frac{3}{8}$ of the ditch in $1\frac{7}{8}$ hours. Thus V would take $(\frac{8}{3})(\frac{15}{8}) = 5$ hours to fill in the ditch working by himself. Therefore statement (1) alone is sufficient. According to statement (2), since U fills the ditch in 3 hours, V will fill $\frac{3}{5}$ of the ditch in 3 hours. Thus V will take 5 hours to fill in the ditch working by himself.

7. **(E)** Obviously, neither statement alone is sufficient. John *could* have gotten sunburned at the beach, but he might have gotten sunburned somewhere else. Therefore (1) and (2) together are not sufficient. This problem tests your grasp of an elementary rule of logic rather than your mathematical knowledge.

DATA SUFFICIENCY STRATEGIES

1. Make sure you understand the directions.
2. Don't waste time figuring out the exact answer.
3. Draw a picture whenever possible.
4. Don't make extra assumptions.
5. Use a system to work through the questions.

QUICK MATHEMATICS REVIEW

The Problem Solving and Data Sufficiency areas of the GMAT require a working knowledge of mathematical principles. The following is a brief review of topics that many people need to brush up on. If you want a more comprehensive review of mathematics, we recommend the review that appears in *Barron's How to Prepare for the GMAT*.

ARITHMETIC

FRACTIONS

A *fraction* is a number which represents a ratio or division of two whole numbers (integers). A fraction is written in the form $\frac{a}{b}$. The number on the top, *a,* is called the numerator; the number on the bottom, *b,* is called the denominator. The denominator tells how many equal parts there are (for example, parts of a pie); the numerator tells how many of these equal parts are taken.

For example, $\frac{5}{8}$ is a fraction whose numerator is 5 and whose denominator is 8; it represents taking 5 of 8 equal parts, or dividing 8 into 5.

> *A fraction cannot have 0 as a denominator since division by 0 is not defined.*

A fraction with 1 as the denominator is the same as the whole number which is its numerator. For example, $\frac{12}{1}$ is 12, $\frac{0}{1}$ is 0.

If the numerator and denominator of a fraction are identical, the fraction represents 1. For example, $\frac{3}{3} = \frac{9}{9} = \frac{13}{13} = 1$. Any whole number, *k,* is represented by a fraction with a numerator equal to *k* times the denominator. For example, $\frac{18}{6} = 3$, and $\frac{30}{5} = 6$.

Mixed Numbers

A *mixed number* consists of a whole number and a fraction. For example, $7\frac{1}{4}$ is a mixed number; it means $7 + \frac{1}{4}$ and $\frac{1}{4}$ is called the fractional part of the mixed number $7\frac{1}{4}$. Any mixed number

can be changed into a fraction:

   (A) Multiply the whole number by the denominator of the fractional part.
   (B) Add the numerator of the fraction to the result of step A.
   (C) Use the result of step B as the numerator and use the denominator of the fractional part of the mixed number as the denominator. This fraction is equal to the mixed number.

EXAMPLE:

29/4

Write $7\frac{1}{4}$ as a fraction.

   (A) $4 \cdot 7 = 28$ (B) $28 + 1 = 29$ (C) so $7\frac{1}{4} = \frac{29}{4}$.

In calculations with mixed numbers, change the mixed numbers into fractions.

Multiplying Fractions

To multiply two fractions, multiply their numerators and divide this result by the product of their denominators.

In word problems, *of* usually indicates multiplication.

EXAMPLE:

John saves $\frac{1}{3}$ of $240. How much does he save?

$\frac{1}{3} \cdot \frac{240}{1} = \frac{240}{3} = \$80$, the amount John saves.

Dividing Fractions

One fraction is a *reciprocal* of another if their product is 1. So $\frac{1}{2}$ and 2 are reciprocals. To find the reciprocal of a fraction, simply interchange the numerator and denominator (turn the fraction upside down). This is called *inverting* the fraction. So when you invert $\frac{15}{17}$ you get $\frac{17}{15}$. When a fraction is inverted the inverted fraction and the original fraction are reciprocals. Thus $\frac{15}{17} \cdot \frac{17}{15} = \frac{255}{255} = \frac{1}{1} = 1.$

To divide one fraction (the dividend) by another fraction (the divisor), invert the divisor and multiply.

EXAMPLE:

$$\frac{5}{6} \div \frac{3}{4} = \frac{5}{6} \cdot \frac{4}{3} = \frac{20}{18}$$

Dividing and Multiplying by the Same Number

Since multiplication or division by 1 does not change the value of a number, you can multiply or divide any fraction by 1 and the fraction will remain the same. Remember that $\frac{a}{a} = 1$ for any nonzero number a. Therefore, if you multiply or divide any fraction by $\frac{a}{a}$, the result is the same as if you multiplied the numerator and denominator by a or divided the numerator and denominator by a.

If you multiply the numerator and denominator of a fraction by the same nonzero number, the fraction remains the same.

If you divide the numerator and denominator of any fraction by the same nonzero number, the fraction remains the same.

Consider the fraction $\frac{3}{4}$. If we multiply 3 by 10 and 4 by 10, then $\frac{30}{40}$ must equal $\frac{3}{4}$.

Equivalent Fractions

Two fractions are equivalent or equal if they represent the same ratio or number. In the last section, you saw that if you multiply or divide the numerator and denominator of a fraction by the same nonzero number the result is equivalent to the original fraction. For example,

$\frac{7}{8} = \frac{70}{80}$ since $70 = 10 \times 7$ and $80 = 10 \times 8$.

In the test there will only be five choices, so your answer to a problem may not be the same as any of the given choices. You may have to express a fraction as an equivalent fraction.

To find a fraction with a known denominator equal to a given fraction:

- (A) divide the denominator of the given fraction into the known denominator;
- (B) multiply the result of (A) by the numerator of the given fraction; this is the numerator of the required equivalent fraction.

EXAMPLE:

Find a fraction with a denominator of 30 which is equal to $\frac{2}{5}$:

- (A) 5 into 30 is 6;

- (B) $6 \cdot 2 = 12$ so $\frac{12}{30} = \frac{2}{5}$.

Reducing a Fraction to Lowest Terms

A fraction has been reduced to lowest terms when the numerator and denominator have no common factors. For example, $\frac{3}{4}$ is reduced to lowest terms, but $\frac{3}{6}$ is not because 3 is a common factor of 3 and 6.

To reduce a fraction to lowest terms, cancel all the common factors of the numerator and denominator. (Cancelling common factors will not change the value of the fraction.)

For example, $\dfrac{100}{100} = \dfrac{10 \cdot 10}{10 \cdot 15} = \dfrac{10}{15} = \dfrac{5 \cdot 2}{5 \cdot 3} = \dfrac{2}{3}$. Since 2 and 3 have no

common factors, $\dfrac{2}{3}$ is $\dfrac{100}{150}$ reduced to lowest terms. A fraction is

equivalent to the fraction reduced to lowest terms.

Adding Fractions

If the fractions have the same denominator, then the denominator is called a *common denominator*. Add the numerators, and use this sum as the new numerator with the common denominator as the denominator of the sum.

If the fractions don't have the same denominator, you must first find a common denominator. Multiply all the denominators together; the result is a common denominator.

EXAMPLE:

To add $\dfrac{1}{2} + \dfrac{2}{3} + \dfrac{7}{4}$, $2 \cdot 3 \cdot 4 = 24$ is a common denominator.

There are many common denominators; the smallest one is called the *least common denominator*. For the previous example, 12 is the least common denominator.

Once you have found a common denominator, express each fraction as an equivalent fraction with the common denominator, and add as you did for the case when the fractions had the same denominator.

EXAMPLE:

$\dfrac{1}{2} + \dfrac{2}{3} + \dfrac{7}{4} = ?$

(A) 24 is a common denominator.

(B) $\dfrac{1}{2} = \dfrac{12}{24}, \dfrac{2}{3} = \dfrac{16}{24}, \dfrac{7}{4} = \dfrac{42}{24}$.

(C) $\dfrac{1}{2} + \dfrac{2}{3} + \dfrac{7}{4} = \dfrac{12}{24} + \dfrac{16}{24} + \dfrac{42}{24} = \dfrac{12+16+42}{24} = \dfrac{70}{24} = \dfrac{35}{12}$.

Subtracting Fractions

When the fractions have the same denominator, subtract the numerators and place the result over the denominator.

When the fractions have different denominators:

(A) Find a common denominator.
(B) Express the fractions as equivalent fractions with the same denominator.
(C) Subtract.

Complex Fractions

A fraction whose numerator and denominator are themselves fractions is called a *complex fraction*. For example, $\dfrac{\frac{2}{3}}{\frac{4}{5}}$ is a complex fraction. A complex fraction can always be simplified by dividing the fraction.

EXAMPLE:

$$\frac{2}{3} \div \frac{4}{5} = \frac{2}{3} \cdot \frac{5}{4} = \frac{1}{3} \cdot \frac{5}{2} = \frac{5}{6}$$

Converting a Fraction into a Decimal

To convert a fraction into a decimal, divide the denominator into the numerator. For example, $\dfrac{3}{4} = \dfrac{3.00}{4} = .75$. Some fractions give an infinite decimal when you divide the denominator into the numerator, for example, $\dfrac{1}{3} = .333\ldots$ where the three dots mean you keep on getting 3 with each step of division. $.333\ldots$ is an *infinite decimal*. If a fraction has an infinite decimal, use the fraction in any computation.

EXAMPLE:

What is $\dfrac{2}{9}$ of \$3,690.90?

Since the decimal for $\frac{2}{9}$ is .2222..., use the fraction

$$\frac{2}{9} \cdot \frac{2}{9} \times \$3,690.90 = 2 \times \$410.10 = \$820.20.$$

PERCENTAGE

Percentage is another method of expressing fractions or parts of an object. Percentages are expressed in terms of hundredths, so 100% means 100 hundredths or 1, and 50% would be 50 hundredths or $\frac{1}{2}$.

A decimal is converted to a percentage by multiplying the decimal by 100. Since multiplying a decimal by 100 is accomplished by moving the decimal point two places to the right, *you convert a decimal into a percentage by moving the decimal point two places to the right.* For example, .134 = 13.4%.

If you wish to convert a percentage into a decimal, you divide the percentage by 100. There is a shortcut for this also. To divide by 100 you move the decimal point two places to the left.

Therefore, *to convert a percentage into a decimal, move the decimal point two places to the left.* For example, 24% = .24.

A fraction is converted into a percentage by changing the fraction to a decimal and then changing the decimal to a percentage. A percentage is changed into a fraction by first converting the percentage into a decimal and then changing the decimal to a fraction.

> *When you compute with percentages, it is usually easier to change the percentages to decimals or fractions.*

EXAMPLE 1:
A company has 6,435 bars of soap. If the company sells 20% of its bars of soap, how many bars of soap did it sell?
Change 20% into .2. Thus, the company sold (.2)(6,435) = 1287.0 = 1,287 bars of soap. An alternative method would be to convert 20% to $\frac{1}{5}$. Then $\frac{1}{5} \times 6,435 = 1,287$.

EXAMPLE 2:

If the population of Dryden was 10,000 in 1960 and the population of Dryden increased by 15% between 1960 and 1970, what was the population of Dryden in 1970?

The population increased by 15% between 1960 and 1970, so the increase was (.15)(10,000), which is 1,500. The population in 1970 was 10,000 + 1,500 = 11,500.

A quicker method: The population increased 15%, so the population in 1970 is 115% of the population in 1960. Therefore, the population in 1970 is 115% of 10,000, which is (1.15)(10,000) = 11,500.

INTEREST AND DISCOUNT

Two of the most common uses of percentages are in interest and discount problems.

The rate of interest is usually given as a percentage. The basic formula for interest problems is:

$$\text{INTEREST} = \text{AMOUNT} \times \text{TIME} \times \text{RATE}$$

You can assume the rate of interest is the annual rate of interest unless the problem states otherwise; so you should express the time in years.

EXAMPLE 1:

What annual rate of interest was paid if $5,000 earned $300 in interest in 2 years?

Since the interest was earned in 2 years, $150 is the interest earned in one year. $\frac{150}{5,000} = .03 = 3\%$, so the annual rate of interest was 3%.

This type of interest is called *simple interest.*

There is another method of computing interest called *compound interest.* In computing compound interest, the interest is periodically added to the amount (or principal) which is earning interest.

EXAMPLE 2:

What will $1,000 be worth after three years if it earns interest at the rate of 5% compounded annually?

Compounded annually means that the interest earned during one year is added to the amount (or principal) at the end of each year. The interest on $1,000 at 5% for one year is $(1,000)(.05) = $50. So you must compute the interest on $1,050 (not $1,000) for the second year. The interest is $(1,050)(.05) = 52.50. Therefore, during the third year interest will be computed for $1,102.50. During the third year the interest is $(1,102.50)(.05) = $55.125 = $55.13. Therefore, after 3 years the original $1,000 will be worth $1,157.63.

If you calculated simple interest on $1,000 at 5% for three years, the answer would be $(1,000)(.05)(3) = $150. Therefore, using simple interest, $1,000 is worth $1,150 after 3 years. Notice that this is not the same as the money was worth using compound interest.

You can assume that interest means simple interest unless a problem states otherwise.

The basic formula for discount problems is:

$$\text{DISCOUNT} = \text{COST} \times \text{RATE OF DISCOUNT}$$

EXAMPLE 1:

What is the discount if a car which cost $3,000 is discounted 7%?

The discount is $3,000 × .07 = $210 since 7% = .07.

If we know the cost of an item and its discounted price, we can find the rate of discount by using the formula

$$\text{rate of discount} = \frac{\text{cost} - \text{price}}{\text{cost}}.$$

After an item has been discounted once, it may be discounted again. This procedure is called *successive* discounting.

EXAMPLE 2:

A bicycle originally cost $100 and was discounted 10%. After three months it was sold after being discounted 15%. How much was the bicycle sold for?

After the 10% discount the bicycle was selling for $100 (.90) = $90. An item which costs $90 and is discounted 15% will sell for $90 (.85) = $76.50, so the bicycle was sold for $76.50.

Notice that if you added the two discounts of 10% and 15% and treated the successive discounts as a single discount of 25%, your answer would be that the bicycle sold for $75, which is incorrect. Successive discounts are not identical to a single discount of the sum of the discounts. The previous example shows that successive discounts of 10% and 15% are not identical to a single discount of 25%.

SIGNED NUMBERS

A number preceded by either a plus or a minus sign is called a *signed number*. For example, +5, –6, –4.2, and +¾ are all signed numbers. If no sign is given with a number, a plus sign is assumed; thus, 5 is interpreted as +5.

Signed numbers can often be used to distinguish different concepts. For example, a profit of $10 can be denoted by +$10 and a loss of $10 by –$10. A temperature of 20 degees below zero can be denoted –20°.

Absolute Value

The absolute value of a signed number is the distance of the number from 0. The absolute value of any nonzero number is *positive*. For example, the absolute value of 2 is 2; the absolute value of –2 is 2. The absolute value of a number a is denoted by $|a|$, so $|-2| = 2$. The absolute value of any number can be found by dropping its sign, $|-12| = 12$, $|4| = 4$. *Thus $|-a| = |a|$ for any number a.* The only number whose absolute value is zero is zero.

Adding Signed Numbers

Case I. Adding numbers with the *same sign:*
   (A) The sign of the sum is the same as the sign of the numbers being added.
   (B) Add the absolute values.
   (C) Put the sign from step (A) in front of the number you obtained in step (B).

EXAMPLE 1:
What is $-2 + (-3.1) + (-.02)$?

    (A) The sign of the sum will be $-$.
    (B) $|-2| = 2$, $|-3.1| = 3.1$, $|-.02| = .02$, and $2 + 3.1 + .02 = 5.12$.
    (C) The answer is -5.12.

Case II. Adding two numbers with *different signs:*

    (A) The sign of the sum is the sign of the number which is largest in absolute value.
    (B) Subtract the absolute value of the number with the smaller absolute value from the absolute value of the number with the larger absolute value.
    (C) The answer is the number you obtained in step (B) preceded by the sign from part (A).

EXAMPLE 2:
How much is $-5.1 + 3$?

    (A) The absolute value of -5.1 is 5.1 and the absolute value of 3 is 3, so the sign of the sum will be $-$.
    (B) 5.1 is larger than 3, and $5.1 - 3 = 2.1$.
    (C) The sum is -2.1.

Case III. Adding *more than two* numbers with *different* signs:

    (A) Add all the positive numbers; the result is positive (this is Case I).
    (B) Add all the negative numbers, the result is negative (this is Case I).
    (C) Add the result of step (A) to the result of step (B), by using Case II.

EXAMPLE 3:
Find the value of $5 + 52 + (-3) + 7 + (-5.1)$.

    (A) $5 + 52 + 7 = 64$.
    (B) $-3 + (-5.1) = -8.1$.
    (C) $64 + (-8.1) = 55.9$, so the answer is 55.9.

Subtracting Signed Numbers

When subtracting signed numbers:

(A) Change the sign of the number you are subtracting (the subtrahend).

(B) <u>Add</u> the result of step (A) to the number being subtracted from (the minuend) using the rules of the preceding section.

EXAMPLE 1:

Subtract 4.1 from 6.5.

(A) 4.1 becomes –4.1.

(B) $6.5 + (–4.1) = 2.4$.

EXAMPLE 2:

What is $7.8 – (–10.1)$?

(A) –10.1 becomes 10.1.

(B) $7.8 + 10.1 = 17.9$.

So we subtract a negative number by adding a positive number with the same absolute value, and we subtract a positive number by adding a negative number of the same absolute value.

Multiplying Signed Numbers

Case I. Multiplying two numbers:

(A) Multiply the absolute values of the numbers.

(B) If both numbers have the same sign, the result of step (A) is the answer—i.e., the product is positive. If the numbers have different signs, then the answer is the result of step (A) with a minus sign.

EXAMPLE 1:

$(4)(–3) = ?$

(A) $4 \times 3 = 12$

(B) The signs are different, so the answer is –12. You can

remember the sign of the product in the following way:

$$(-)(-) = +$$
$$(+)(+) = +$$
$$(-)(+) = -$$
$$(+)(-) = -$$

Case II. Multiplying more than two numbers:

    (A) Multiply the first two factors using Case I.

    (B) Multiply the result of (A) by the third factor.

    (C) Multiply the result of (B) by the fourth factor.

    (D) Continue until you have used each factor.

EXAMPLE 2:

$(-5)(4)(2)\left(-\frac{1}{2}\right)\left(\frac{3}{4}\right) = ?$

    (A) $(-5)(4) = -20$

    (B) $(-20)(2) = -40$

    (C) $(-40)\left(-\frac{1}{2}\right) = 20$

    (D) $(20)\left(\frac{3}{4}\right) = 15$, so the answer is 15.

> The sign of the product is + if there are no negative factors or an even number of negative factors. The sign of the product is − if there is an odd number of negative factors.

Dividing Signed Numbers

Divide the absolute values of the numbers; the sign of the quotient is determined by the same rules as you used to determine the sign of a product. Thus,

$$+ \div + = +$$
$$- \div - = +$$
$$+ \div - = -$$
$$- \div + = -$$

EXAMPLE:

Divide 53.2 by –4.

53.2 divided by 4 is 13.3. Since one of the numbers is positive and the other negative, the answer is –13.3.

AVERAGES AND MEDIANS

Mean

The *average* or *arithmetic mean* of a collection of N numbers is the result of dividing the sum of all the numbers in the collection by N.

EXAMPLE:

The scores of 9 students on a test were 72, 78, 81, 64, 85, 92, 95, 60, and 55. What was the average score of the students?

Since there are 9 students, the average is the total of all the scores divided by 9.

So the average is $\frac{1}{9}$ of $(72+78+81+64+85+92+95+60+55)$,

which is $\frac{1}{9}$ of 682 or $75\frac{7}{9}$.

Median

The number that is in the middle, if the numbers in a collection of numbers are arranged in chronological order, is called the *median*. In the example above, the median score was 78. Notice that the median was different from the average.

In general, the median and the average of a collection of numbers are different.

If the number of objects in the collection is even, the median is the average of the two numbers in the middle of the array. For example, the median of 64, 66, 72, 75, 76, and 77 is the average of 72 and 75, which is 73.5.

POWERS, EXPONENTS, AND ROOTS

If b is any number and n is a whole number greater than 0, b^n means the product of n factors, each of which is equal to b. Thus,

$b^n = b \times b \times b \times \dots \times b$, where there are n copies of b.

If $n = 1$, there is only one copy of b, so $b^1 = b$. Here are some examples:

$$2^5 = 2 \times 2 \times 2 \times 2 \times 2 = 32, \quad (-4)^3 = (-4) \times (-4) \times (-4) = -64,$$

$$\frac{3^2}{4} = \frac{3 \times 3}{4} = \frac{9}{4},$$

$$1^n = 1 \text{ for any } n, \quad 0^n = 0 \text{ for any } n.$$

b^n is read as "b raised to the nth power." b^2 is read "b squared." b^2 is always greater than 0 (positive) if b is not zero, since the product of two negative numbers is positive. b^3 is read "b cubed." b^3 can be negative or positive.

If you raise a fraction, $\frac{p}{q}$, to a power, then $\left(\dfrac{p}{q}\right)^n = \dfrac{p^n}{q^n}$. For example,

$$\left(\frac{5}{4}\right)^3 = \frac{5^3}{4^3} = \frac{125}{64}$$

Exponents

In the expression b^n, b is called the *base* and n is called the *exponent*. In the expression 2^5, 2 is the base and 5 is the exponent. The exponent tells how many factors there are.

The two basic formulas for problems involving exponents are:
  (A) $b^n \times b^m = b^{n+m}$
  (B) $a^n \times b^n = (a \cdot b)^n$
(A) and (B) are called *laws of exponents.*

EXAMPLE:
What is 6^3?

Since $6 = 3 \times 2$, $6^3 = 3^3 \times 2^3 = 27 \times 8 = 216$.

or

$$6^3 = 6 \times 6 \times 6 = 216$$

Roots

If you raise a number d to the nth power and the result is b, then d is called the nth root of b, which is usually written $\sqrt[n]{b} = d$. Since $2^5 = 32$, then $\sqrt[5]{32} = 2$. The second root is called the square root and is written $\sqrt{\ }$; the third root is called the cube root. For example, $\sqrt{225} = 15$; $\sqrt{81} = 9$; $\sqrt[3]{64} = 4$.

There are two possibilities for the square root of a positive number; the positive one is called the square root. Thus we say $\sqrt{9} = 3$ although $(-3) \times (-3) = 9$.

Since the square of any nonzero number is positive, *the square root of a negative number is not defined as a real number.* Thus $\sqrt{-2}$ is not a real number. There are cube roots of negative numbers. $\sqrt[3]{-8} = -2$, because $(-2) \times (-2) \times (-2) = -8$.

You can also write roots as exponents; for example,

$$\sqrt[n]{b} = b^{\frac{1}{n}}; \text{ so } \sqrt{b} = b^{\frac{1}{2}}, \sqrt[3]{b} \quad b^{\frac{1}{3}}.$$

Since you can write roots as exponents, formula (B) above is especially useful.

$a^{\frac{1}{n}} \times b^{\frac{1}{n}} = (a \cdot b)^{\frac{1}{n}}$ or $\sqrt[n]{a \times b} = \sqrt[n]{a} \times \sqrt[n]{b}$. This formula is the basic formula for simplifying square roots, cube roots, and so on. *On the test you must state your answer in a form that matches one of the choices given.*

EXAMPLE:

$\sqrt{54} = ?$

Since $54 = 9 \times 6$, $\sqrt{54} = \sqrt{9 \times 6} = \sqrt{9} \times \sqrt{6}$. Since $\sqrt{9} = 3$, $\sqrt{54} = 3\sqrt{6}$.

You cannot simplify by adding square roots unless you are taking square roots of the same number. For example, $\sqrt{3} + 2\sqrt{3} - 4\sqrt{3} = -\sqrt{3}$, but $\sqrt{3} + \sqrt{2}$ is not equal to $\sqrt{5}$.

ALGEBRA

ALGEBRAIC EXPRESSIONS

Often it is necessary to deal with quantities which have a numerical value which is unknown. For example, we may know that Tom's salary is twice as much as Joe's salary. If we let the value of Tom's salary be called T and the value of Joe's salary be J, then T and J are numbers which are unknown. However, we do know that the value of T must be twice the value of J, or $T = 2J$.

T and $2J$ are examples of algebraic expressions. An algebraic expression may involve letters in addition to numbers and symbols; however, *in an algebraic expression a letter always stands for a number*. Therefore, you can multiply, divide, add, subtract and perform other mathematical operations on a letter. Thus, x^2 would mean x times x. Some examples of algebraic expressions are: $2x + y$, $y^3 + 9y$, $z^3 - 5ab$, $c + d + 4$, $5x + 2y(6x - 4y + z)$. When letters or numbers are written together without any sign or symbol between them, multiplication is assumed. Thus $6xy$ means 6 times x times y. $6xy$ is called a term; terms are separated by + or − signs. The expression $5z + 2 + 4x^2$ has three terms, $5z$, 2, and $4x^2$. Terms are often called monomials (mono = one). If an expression has more than one term, it is called a *polynomial* (poly = many). The letters in an algebraic expression are called *variables* or *unknowns*. When a variable is multiplied by a number, the number is called the *coefficient* of the variable. So in the expression $5x^2 + 2yz$, the coefficient of x^2 is 5, and the coefficient of yz is 2.

Simplifying Algebraic Expressions

Since there are only five choices of an answer given for the test questions, you must be able to recognize algebraic expressions that are equal. It will also save time when you are working problems if you can change a complicated expression into a simpler one.

Case I. Simplifying expressions that don't contain parentheses:

(A) Perform any multiplications or divisions before performing additions or subtractions. Thus, the expression $6x + y \div x$ means add $6x$ to the quotient of y divided by x. Another way of writing the expression would be $6x + \dfrac{y}{x}$. This is not the same as $\dfrac{6x + y}{x}$.

(B) The order in which you multiply numbers and letters in a term does not matter. So $6xy$ is the same as $6yx$.

(C) The order in which you add terms does not matter; for instance, $6x + 2y - x = 6x - x + 2y$.

(D) If there are roots or powers in any terms, you may be able to simplify the term by using the laws of exponents. For example, $5xy \cdot 3x^2y = 15x^3y^2$.

(E) Combine like terms. *Like terms* (or similar terms) are terms which have exactly the same letters raised to the same powers. So $x, -2x, \frac{1}{3}x$ are like terms. For example, $6x - 2x + x + y$ is equal to $5x + y$. In combining like terms, you simply add or subtract the coefficients of the like terms, and the result is the coefficient of that term in the simplified expression. In the example given, the coefficients of x were $+6, -2$, and $+1$; since $6 - 2 + 1 = 5$, the coefficient of x in the simplified expression is 5.

(F) Algebraic expressions which involve divisions or factors can be simplified by using the techniques for handling fractions and the laws of exponents. Remember, dividing by b^n is the same as multiplying by b^{-n}.

EXAMPLE 1:
$3x^2 - 4\sqrt{x} + \sqrt{4x} + xy + 7x^2 = ?$
(D) $\sqrt{4x} = \sqrt{4}\sqrt{x} = 2\sqrt{x}$.
(E) $3x^2 + 7x^2 = 10x^2, -4\sqrt{x} + 2\sqrt{x} = -2\sqrt{x}$.

The original expression equals $3x^2 + 7x^2 - 4\sqrt{x} + 2\sqrt{x} + xy$. Therefore, the simplified expression is $10x^2 - 2\sqrt{x} + xy$.

Case II. Simplifying expressions that have parentheses:

The first rule is to perform the operations inside parentheses first. So $(6x + y) \div x$ means divide the sum of $6x$ and y by x. Notice that $(6x + y) \div x$ is different from $6x + y \div x$.

The main rule for getting rid of parentheses is the distributive law, which is expressed as $a(b + c) = ab + ac$. In other words, if any monomial is followed by an expression contained in parentheses, then *each* term of the expression is multiplied by the monomial. Once we have gotten rid of the parentheses, we proceed as we did in Case 1.

> If an expression has more than one set of parentheses, get rid of the *inner parentheses first* and then *work out* through the rest of the parentheses.

EXAMPLE 2:
$2x - (x + 6(x - 3y) + 4y) = ?$

To remove the inner parentheses we multiply $6(x - 3y)$, getting $6x - 18y$. Now we have $2x - (x + 6x - 18y + 4y)$, which equals $2x - (7x - 14y)$. Distribute the minus sign (multiply by -1), getting $2x - 7x - (-14y) = -5x + 14y$. Sometimes brackets are used instead of parentheses.

Adding and Subtracting Algebraic Expressions
Since algebraic expressions are numbers, they can be added and subtracted.

> *The only algebraic terms which can be combined are like terms.*

EXAMPLE:

$(3x + 4y - xy^2) + (3x + 2x(x - y)) = ?$

The expression $= (3x + 4y - xy^2) + (3x + 2x^2 - 2xy)$, removing the inner parentheses;

$\qquad = 6x + 4y + 2x^2 - xy^2 - 2xy$, combining like terms.

Multiplying Algebraic Expressions

When you multiply two expressions, you multiply *each term of the first by each term of the second*.

EXAMPLE 1:

$(2h - 4)(h + 2h^2 + h^3) = ?$

$\quad = 2h(h + 2h^2 + h^3) - 4(h + 2h^2 + h^3)$

$\quad = 2h^2 + 4h^3 + 2h^4 - 4h - 8h^2 - 4h^3$

$\quad = -4h - 6h^2 + 2h^4$, which is the product.

If you need to multiply more than two expressions, multiply the first two expressions, then multiply the result by the third expression, and so on until you have used each factor. Since algebraic expressions can be multiplied, they can be squared, cubed, or raised to other powers.

EXAMPLE 2:

$(x - 2y)^3 = (x - 2y)(x - 2y)(x - 2y).$

Since $(x - 2y)(x - 2y) = x^2 - 2yx - 2yx + 4y^2$

$\qquad\qquad\qquad\qquad\quad = x^2 - 4xy + 4y^2$

$\qquad (x - 2y)^3 = (x^2 - 4xy + 4y^2)(x - 2y)$

$\qquad\qquad\qquad = x(x^2 - 4xy + 4y^2) - 2y(x^2 - 4xy + 4y^2)$

$\qquad\qquad\qquad = x^3 - 4x^2y + 4xy^2 - 2x^2y + 8xy^2 - 8y^3$

$\qquad\qquad\qquad = x^3 - 6x^2y + 12xy^2 - 8y^3.$

The order in which you multiply algebraic expressions does not matter. Thus $(2a + b)(x^2 + 2x) = (x^2 + 2x)(2a + b)$.

Factoring Algebraic Expressions

If an algebraic expression is the product of other algebraic expressions, then the expressions are called factors of the original expression. For instance, we claim that $(2h - 4)$ and $(h + 2h^2 + h^3)$ are factors of $-4h - 6h^2 + 2h^4$. We can always check to see if we have the correct factors by multiplying; so by example 1 above we see that our claim is correct. We need to be able to factor algebraic expressions in order to solve quadratic equations. It also can be helpful in dividing algebraic expressions.

First remove any monomial factor which appears in every term of the expression. Some examples:

$$3x + 3y = 3(x + y)\text{: 3 is a monomial factor.}$$
$$15a^2b + 10ab = 5ab(3a + 2)\text{: } 5ab \text{ is a monomial factor.}$$
$$\frac{1}{2}hy - 3h^3 + 4hy = h\left(\frac{1}{2}y - 3h^2 + 4y\right).$$

$$= h\left(\frac{9}{2}y - 3h^2\right)\text{: } h \text{ is a monomial factor.}$$

You may also need to factor expressions which contain squares or higher powers into factors which only contain linear terms. (Linear terms are terms in which variables are raised only to the first power.) The first rule to remember is that since $(a + b)(a - b) = a^2 + ba - ba - b^2 = a^2 - b^2$, the difference of two squares can always be factored.

EXAMPLE 1:
Factor $(9m^2 - 16)$.

$9m^2 = (3m)^2$ and $16 = 4^2$, so the factors are $(3m - 4)(3m + 4)$. Since $(3m - 4)(3m + 4) = 9m^2 - 16$, these factors are correct.

You also may need to factor expressions which contain squared terms and linear terms, such as $x^2 + 4x + 3$. The factors will be of the form $(x + a)$ and $(x + b)$. Since $(x + a)(x + b) = x^2 + (a + b)x + ab$, you must look for a pair of numbers a and b such that $a \cdot b$ is the numerical term in the expression and $a + b$ is the coefficient of the linear term (the term with exponent 1).

EXAMPLE 2:
Factor $y^2 + y - 6$.

Since -6 is negative, the two numbers a and b must be of opposite sign. Possible pairs of factors for -6 are -6 and $+1$, 6 and -1, 3 and -2, and -3 and 2. Since $-2 + 3 = 1$, the factors are $(y + 3)$ and $(y - 2)$. So $(y + 3)(y - 2) = y^2 + y - 6$.

There are some expressions which cannot be factored, for example, $x^2 + 4x + 6$. In general, if you can't factor something by using the methods given above, don't waste a lot of time on the question. Sometimes you may be able to check the answers given to find out what the correct factors are.

Dividing Algebraic Expressions

The main things to remember in division are:

(1) When you divide a sum, you can get the same result by dividing each term and adding quotients. For example,

$$\frac{9x + 4xy + y^2}{x} = \frac{9x}{x} + \frac{4xy}{x} + \frac{y^2}{x} = 9 + 4y + \frac{y^2}{x}.$$

(2) You can cancel common factors, so the results on factoring will be helpful. For example,

$$\frac{x^2 - 2x}{x - 2} = \frac{x(x - 2)}{x - 2} = x.$$

EQUATIONS

An *equation* is a statement that says two algebraic expressions are equal. $x + 2 = 3$, $4 + 2 = 6$, $3x^2 + 2x - 6 = 0$, $x^2 + y^2 = z^2$, $\dfrac{y}{x} = 2 + z$, and $A = LW$ are all examples of equations. We will refer to the algebraic expressions on each side of the equal sign as the left side or the right side of the equation. Thus, in the equation $2x + 4 = 6y + x$, $2x + 4$ is the left side and $6y + x$ is the right side.

If we assign specific numbers to each variable or unknown in an algebraic expression, then the algebraic expression will be equal to a number. This is called *evaluating* the expression. For example, if you evaluate $2x + 4y^2 + 3$ for $x = -1$ and $y = 2$, the expression is equal to $2(-1) + 4 \cdot 2^2 + 3 = -2 + 4 \cdot 4 + 3 = 17$.

If we evaluate each side of an equation and the number obtained is the same for each side of the equation, then the specific values assigned to the unknowns are called a *solution of the equation*. Another way of saying this is that the choices for the unknowns satisfy the equation.

EXAMPLE:

Consider the equation $x^2 + y^2 = 5x$.

If $x = 1$ and $y = 2$, then the left side is $1^2 + 2^2$, which equals $1 + 4 = 5$. The right side is $5 \cdot 1 = 5$; since both sides are equal to 5, $x = 1$ and $y = 2$ is a solution.

If $x = 1$ and $y = 1$, then the left side is $1^2 + 1^2 = 2$ and the right side is $5 \cdot 1 = 5$. Therefore, since $2 \neq 5$, $x = 1$ and $y = 1$ is not a solution.

There are some equations that *do not have any solutions that are real numbers*. Since the square of any real number is positive or zero, the equation $x^2 = -4$ does not have any solutions that are real numbers.

Equivalence

One equation is *equivalent* to another equation if they have exactly the same solutions. The basic idea in solving equations is to transform a given equation into an equivalent equation whose solutions are obvious.

The two main tools for solving equations are:
- (A) If you add or subtract the same algebraic expression to or from *each side* of an equation, the resulting equation is equivalent to the original equation.
- (B) If you multiply or divide both sides of an equation by the same *nonzero* algebraic expression, the resulting equation is equivalent to the original equation.

Solving Linear Equations with One Unknown

The most common type of equation is the linear equation with only one unknown. $6z = 4z - 3$, $3 + a = 2a - 4$, $3b + 2b = b - 4b$ are all examples of linear equations with only one unknown.

Using (A) and (B), you can solve a linear equation with one unknown in the following way:

(1) Group all the terms which involve the unknown on one side of the equation and all the terms which are purely numerical on the other side of the equation. This is called *isolating the unknown*.

(2) Combine the terms on each side.

(3) Divide each side by the coefficient of the unknown.

EXAMPLE 1:

Solve $3x + 15 = 3 - 4x$ for x.

(1) Add $4x$ to each side and subtract 15 from each side;
$3x + 15 - 15 + 4x = 3 - 15 - 4x + 4x$.

(2) $7x = -12$.

(3) Divide each side by 7 so $x = \dfrac{-12}{7}$ is the solution.

CHECK: $3\left(\dfrac{-12}{7}\right) + 15 = \dfrac{-36}{7} + 15 = \dfrac{69}{7}$ and $3 - 4\left(\dfrac{-12}{7}\right) = 3 + \dfrac{48}{7}$

$= \dfrac{69}{7}$.

If you do the same thing to each side of an equation, the result is still an equation but it may not be equivalent to the original equation. Be especially careful if you square each side of an equation. For example, $x = -4$ is an equation; square both sides and you get $x^2 = 16$ which has both $x = 4$ and $x = -4$ as solutions. *Always check your answer in the original equation.*

If the equation you want to solve involves square roots, get rid of the square roots by squaring each side of the equation. Remember to check your answer since squaring each side does not always give an equivalent equation.

EXAMPLE 2:

Solve $\sqrt{4x + 34} = 5$.

Square both sides: $\left(\sqrt{4x + 3}\right)^2 = 4x + 3$ and $5^2 = 25$, so the new equation is $4x + 3 = 25$. Subtract 3 from each side to get $4x = 22$ and now divide each side by 4. The solution is $x = \frac{22}{4} = 5.5$. Since 4 (5.5) + 3 = 25 and $\sqrt{25} = 5$, $x = 5.5$ is a solution to the equation $\sqrt{4x + 3} = 5$.

If an equation involves fractions, multiply through by a common denominator and then solve. Check your answer to make sure you did not multiply or divide by zero.

Solving Two Equations with Two Unknowns

You may be asked to solve two equations with two unknowns. Use one equation to solve for one unknown in terms of the other; now change the second equation into an equation with only one unknown which can be solved by the methods of the preceding section.

EXAMPLE:

Solve for x and y: $\begin{cases} \dfrac{x}{y} = 3 \\ 2x + 4y = 20. \end{cases}$

The first equation gives $x = 3y$. Using $x = 3y$, the second equation is $2(3y) + 4y = 6y + 4y$ or $10y = 20$, so $y = \frac{20}{10} = 2$. Since $x = 3y$, $x = 6$.

CHECK: $\frac{6}{2} = 3$, and $2 \cdot 6 + 4 \cdot 2 = 20$, so $x = 6$ and $y = 2$ is a solution.

Solving Quadratic Equations

If the terms of an equation contain squares of the unknown as well as linear terms, the equation is called *quadratic*. Some examples of quadratic equations are $x^2 + 4x = 3$, $2z^2 - 1 = 3z^2 - 2z$, and $a + 6 = a^2 + 6$.

To solve a quadratic equation:

(A) Group all the terms on one side of the equation so that the other side is *zero*.

(B) Combine the terms on the nonzero side.

(C) Factor the expression into linear expressions.

(D) Set the linear factors equal to zero and solve.

The method depends on the fact that if a product of expressions is zero, then at least one of the expressions must be zero.

EXAMPLE:

Solve $x^2 + 4x = -3$.

(A) $x^2 + 4x + 3 = 0$

(C) $x^2 + 4x + 3 = (x + 3)(x + 1) = 0$

(D) So $x + 3 = 0$ or $x + 1 = 0$. Therefore, the solutions are $x = -3$ and $x = -1$.

CHECK: $(-3)^2 + 4(-3) = 9 - 12 = -3$

$(-1)^2 + 4(-1) = 1 - 4 = -3$, so $x = -3$ and $x = -1$ are solutions.

A quadratic equation will usually have 2 different solutions, but it is possible for a quadratic to have only one solution or even no real solution.

WORD PROBLEMS

The general method for solving word problems is to translate them into algebraic problems. The quantities you are seeking are the unknowns, which are usually represented by letters. The information you are given in the problem is then turned into equations. Words such as "is," "was," "are," and "were" mean equals, and words like "of" and "as much as" mean multiplication.

EXAMPLE 1:

A coat was sold for $75. The coat was sold for 150% of the cost of the coat. How much did the coat cost?

You want to find the cost of the coat. Let $\$C$ be the cost of the coat. You know that the coat was sold for $75 and that $75 was 150% of the cost. So $75 = 150\%$ of $\$C$ or $75 = 1.5C$. Solving for C you get

$C = \dfrac{75}{1.5} = 50$, so the coat cost \$50.

CHECK: $(1.5)\$50 = \$75$.

EXAMPLE 2:

Tom's salary is 125% of Joe's salary; Mary's salary is 80% of Joe's salary. The total of all three salaries is \$61,000. What is Mary's salary?

Let $M =$ Mary's salary, $J =$ Joe's salary, and $T =$ Tom's salary. The first sentence says $T = 125\%$ of J or $T = \dfrac{5}{4} J$, and $M = 80\%$ of J

or $M = \dfrac{4}{5} J$. The second sentence says that $T + M + J = \$61,000$. Using

the information from the first sentence, $T + M + J = \dfrac{5}{4} J + \dfrac{4}{5} J + J =$

$\dfrac{25}{20} J + \dfrac{16}{20} J + J = \dfrac{61}{20} J$. So $\dfrac{61}{20} J = 61,000$; solving for J you have

$J = \dfrac{20}{61} \times 61,000 = 20,000$. Therefore, $T = \dfrac{5}{4} \times \$20,000 = \$25,000$

and $M = \dfrac{4}{5} \times \$20,000 = \$16,000$.

CHECK: $\$25,000 + \$16,000 + \$20,000 = \$61,000$.
So Mary's salary is \$16,000.

EXAMPLE 3:

Steve weighs 25 pounds more than Jim. The combined weight of Jim and Steve is 325 pounds. How much does Jim weigh?

Let $S =$ Steve's weight in pounds and $J =$ Jim's weight in pounds. The first sentence says $S = J + 25$, and the second sentence becomes $S + J = 325$. Since $S = J + 25$, $S + J = 325$ becomes $(J + 25) + J = 2J + 25 = 325$. So $2J = 300$ and $J = 150$. Therefore, Jim weighs 150 pounds.

CHECK: If Jim weighs 150 pounds, then Steve weighs 175 pounds and $150 + 175 = 325$.

EXAMPLE 4:

A carpenter is designing a closet. The floor will be in the shape of a rectangle whose length is 2 feet more than its width. How long should the closet be if the carpenter wants the area of the floor to be 15 square feet?

The area of a rectangle is length times width, usually written $A = LW$, where A is the area, L is the length, and W is the width. We know $A = 15$ and $L = 2 + W$. Therefore, $LW = (2 + W)W = W^2 + 2W$; this must equal 15. So we need to solve $W^2 + 2W = 15$ or $W^2 + 2W - 15 = 0$. Since $W^2 + 2W - 15$ factors into $(W + 5)(W - 3)$, the only possible solutions are $W = -5$ and $W = 3$. Since W represents a width, -5 cannot be the answer; therefore the width is 3 feet. The length is the width plus two feet, so the length is 5 feet. Since $5 \times 3 = 15$, the answer checks.

Distance Problems

A common type of word problem is a distance or velocity problem. The basic formula is

DISTANCE TRAVELED = RATE × TIME

The formula is abbreviated $d = rt$.

EXAMPLE:

A train travels at an average speed of 50 miles per hour for $2\frac{1}{2}$ hours and then travels at a speed of 70 miles per hour for $1\frac{1}{2}$ hours. How far did the train travel in the entire 4 hours?

The train traveled for $2\frac{1}{2}$ hours at an average speed of 50 miles per hour, so it traveled $50 \times \frac{5}{2} = 125$ miles in the first $2\frac{1}{2}$ hours.

Traveling at a speed of 70 miles per hour for $1\frac{1}{2}$ hours, the distance traveled will be equal to $r \times t$ where $r = 70$ m.p.h. and $t = 1\frac{1}{2}$, so the distance is $70 \times \frac{3}{2} = 105$ miles. Therefore, the total distance traveled is $125 + 105 = 230$ miles.

Work Problems

In this type of problem you can always assume all workers in the same category work at the same rate. The main idea is: If it takes k workers 1 hour to do a job, then *each worker does $\frac{1}{k}$ of the job in an hour* or she works at the rate of $\frac{1}{k}$ of the job per hour. If it takes m workers h hours to finish a job then each worker does $\frac{1}{m}$ of the job in h hours so she does $\frac{1}{h}$ of $\frac{1}{m}$ in an hour. Therefore, each worker *works at the rate of $\frac{1}{hm}$ of the job per hour.*

EXAMPLE:
If 5 men take an hour to dig a ditch, how long should it take 12 men to dig a ditch of the same type?

Since 5 workers took an hour, each worker does $\frac{1}{5}$ of the job in an hour. So 12 workers will work at the rate of $\frac{12}{5}$ of the job per hour.

Thus if T is the time it takes for 12 workers to do the job, $\frac{12}{5} \times T = 1$ job and $T = \frac{5}{12} \times 1$, so $T = \frac{5}{12}$ hour or 25 minutes.

INEQUALITIES

A number is positive if it is greater than 0, so 1, $\frac{1}{1,000}$, and 53.4 are all positive numbers. Positive numbers are signed numbers whose sign is +. If you think of numbers as points on a number line, positive numbers correspond to points to the right of 0.

A number is negative if it is less than 0. $-\frac{4}{5}$, −50, and −.0001 are all negative numbers. Negative numbers are signed numbers whose sign is −. Negative numbers correspond to points to the left of 0 on a number line.

0 is the only number which is neither positive nor negative.

$a > b$ means the number a is greater than the number b; that is, $a = b + x$ where x is a positive number. If we look at a number line, $a > b$ means a is to the right of b. $a > b$ can also be read as b is less than a, which is also written $b < a$. For example, $-5 > -7.5$ because $-5 = -7.5 + 2.5$ and 2.5 is positive.

The notation $a'' \ b$ means a is less than or equal to b, or b is greater than or equal to a. For example, $5 \geq 4$; also $4 \geq 4$. $a \neq b$ means a is not equal to b.

If you need to know whether one fraction is greater than another fraction, put the fractions over a common denominator and compare the numerators.

EXAMPLE:

Which is larger, $\frac{13}{16}$ or $\frac{31}{40}$?

A common denominator is 80. $\frac{13}{16} = \frac{65}{80}$, and $\frac{31}{40} = \frac{62}{80}$; since

$65 > 62$, $\frac{65}{80} > \frac{62}{80}$, so $\frac{13}{16} > \frac{31}{40}$.

Inequalities have certain properties which are similar to equations. We can talk about the left side and the right side of an inequality, and we can use algebraic expressions for the sides of an inequality. For example, $6x < 5x + 4$. A value for an unknown *satisfies an inequality* if when you evaluate each side of the inequality the numbers satisfy the inequality. So if $x = 2$, then $6x = 12$ and $5x + 4 = 14$, and since $12 < 14$, $x = 2$ satisfies $6x < 5x + 4$. Two inequalities are equivalent if the same collection of numbers satisfies both inequalities.

The following basic principles are used in work with inequalities:

(A) Adding the same expression to *each* side of an inequality gives an equivalent inequality (written $a < b \leftrightarrow a + c < b + c$ where $\leftrightarrow$ means equivalent).

(B) Subtracting the same expression from *each* side of an inequality gives an equivalent inequality ($a < b \leftrightarrow a - c < b - c$).

(C) Multiplying or dividing *each* side of an inequality by the same *positive* expression gives an equivalent inequality ($a < b \leftrightarrow ca < cb$ for $c > 0$).

(D) Multiplying or dividing each side of an inequality by the same *negative* expression *reverses* the inequality ($a < b \leftrightarrow ca > cb$ for $c < 0$).

(E) If both sides of an inequality have the same sign, inverting both sides of the inequality *reverses* the inequality.

$$0 < a < b \leftrightarrow 0 < \frac{1}{b} < \frac{1}{a}$$

$$a < b < 0 \leftrightarrow \frac{1}{b} < \frac{1}{a} < 0$$

(F) If two inequalities are of the same type (both greater or both less), adding the respective sides gives the same type of inequality.

$(a < b$ and $c < d$, then $a + c < b + d)$

Note that the inequalities are *not* equivalent.

(G) If $a < b$ and $b < c$, then $a < c$.

EXAMPLE 1:

Find the values of x for which $5x - 4 < 7x + 2$.

Using principle (B) subtract $5x + 2$ from each side, so $(5x - 4 < 7x + 2) \leftrightarrow -6 < 2x$. Now use principle (C) and divide each side by 2, so $-6 < 2x \leftrightarrow -3 < x$.

So any x greater than -3 satisfies the inequality. It is a good idea to make a spot check. -1 is > -3; let $x = -1$, then $5x - 4 = -9$ and $7x + 2 = -5$. Since $-9 < -5$, the answer is correct for at least the particular value $x = -1$.

EXAMPLE 2:

Find the values of a which satisfy $a^2 + 1 > 2a + 4$.

Subtract $2a$ from each side, so
$(a^2 + 1 > 2a + 4) \leftrightarrow a^2 - 2a + 1 > 4$.
$a^2 - 2a + 1 = (a - 1)^2$, so
$a^2 - 2a + 1 > 4 \leftrightarrow (a - 1)^2 > 2^2$.

We need to be careful when we take the square roots of inequalities. If $q^2 > 4$ and if $q > 0$, then $q > 2$; but if $q < 0$, then $q < -2$. We must look at two cases in example 2. First, if $(a - 1) \geq 0$, then

$(a - 1)^2 > 2^2 \leftrightarrow a - 1 > 2$ or $a > 3$.
If $(a - 1) < 0$ then $(a - 1)^2 > 2^2 \leftrightarrow a - 1 < -2 \leftrightarrow a < -1$.
So the inequality is satisfied if $a > 3$ or if $a < -1$.

CHECK: $(-2)^2 + 1 = 5 > 2(-2) + 4 = 0$, and $5^2 + 1 = 26 > 14 = 2 \cdot 5 + 4$.

Some inequalities are not satisfied by *any* real number. For example, since $x^2 \geq 0$ for all x, there is no real number x such that $x^2 < -9$.

You may be given an inequality and asked whether other inequalities follow from the original inequality. You should be able to answer such questions by using principles (A) through (G).

If there is any property of inequalities you can't remember, try out some specific numbers. If $x < y$, then what is the relation between $-x$ and $-y$? Since $4 < 5$ but $-5 < -4$, the relation is probably $-x > -y$, which is true by (D).

Probably the most common mistake is forgetting to reverse the inequalities if you multiply or divide by a negative number.

GEOMETRY

ANGLES

If two straight lines meet at a point they form an *angle*. The point is called the *vertex* of the angle and the lines are called the *sides* or *rays* of the angle. The sign for angle is $\angle$.

If two lines intersect at a point, they form 4 angles. The angles opposite each other are called *vertical* angles. $\angle 1$ and $\angle 3$ are vertical angles. $\angle 2$ and $\angle 4$ are vertical angles.

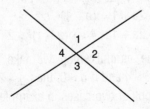

Vertical angles are equal.

A straight angle is an angle whose sides lie on a straight line. *A straight angle equals 180°.*

If the sum of two adjacent angles is a straight angle, then the angles are *supplementary* and each angle is the supplement of the other.

If an angle of $x°$ and an angle of $y°$ are supplements, then $x + y = 180$.

If two supplementary angles are equal, they are both *right angles*. A right angle is half of a straight angle. A right angle = 90°.

If the sum of two adjacent angles is a right angle, then the angles are *complementary* and each angle is the complement of the other.

If an angle of $x°$ and an angle of $y°$ are complementary, then $x + y = 90$.

LINES

A line is understood to be a straight line. A line is assumed to extend indefinitely in both directions. *There is one and only one line between two distinct points.*

Parallel Lines

Two lines in the same plane are *parallel* if they do not intersect no matter how far they are extended.

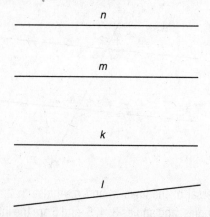

m and n are parallel, but k and l are not parallel since if k and l are extended they will intersect. Parallel lines are denoted by the symbol ||; so $m \parallel n$ means m is parallel to n.

If two lines are parallel to a third line, then they are parallel to each other.

If a third line intersects two given lines, it is called a *transversal*. A transversal and the two given lines form eight angles. The four inside angles are called *interior* angles. The four outside angles are called *exterior* angles. If two angles are on opposite sides of the transversal they are called *alternate* angles.

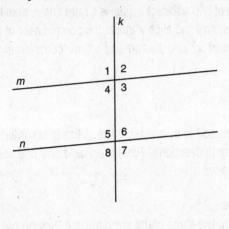

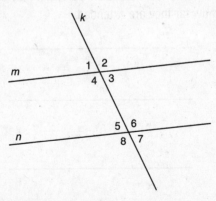

k is a transversal of the lines *m* and *n*. Angles 1, 2, 7, and 8 are the exterior angles, and angles 3, 4, 5, and 6 are the interior angles. ∠4 and ∠6 are an example of a pair of alternate angles. ∠1 and ∠5, ∠2 and ∠6, ∠3 and ∠7, and ∠4 and ∠8 are pairs of *corresponding* angles.

If two parallel lines are intersected by a transversal, then:
  (1) Alternate interior angles are equal.
  (2) Corresponding angles are equal.
  (3) Interior angles on the same side of the transversal
      are supplementary.

If we use the fact that vertical angles are equal, we can replace "interior" by "exterior" in (1) and (3).

Perpendicular Lines

When two lines intersect and all four of the angles formed are equal, the lines are said to be *perpendicular*. If two lines are perpendicular, they are the sides of right angles whose vertex is the point of intersection.

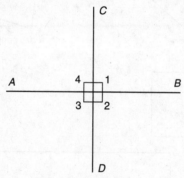

AB is perpendicular to *CD*, and angles 1, 2, 3, and 4 are all right angles. ⊥ is the symbol for perpendicular; so *AB* ⊥ *CD*.

If *any one* of the angles formed when two lines intersect is a right angle, then the lines are perpendicular.

POLYGONS

A *polygon* is a closed figure in a plane which is composed of line segments which meet only at their endpoints. The line segments are called *sides* of the polygon, and a point where two sides meet is called a *vertex* (plural *vertices*) of the polygon.

Polygons are classified by the number of angles or sides they have. A polygon with three angles is called a *triangle:* a four-sided polygon is a *quadrilateral;* a polygon with five angles is a *pentagon;* a polygon with six angles is a *hexagon;* an eight-sided polygon is an *octagon.* The number of angles is always equal to the number of sides in a polygon, so a six-sided polygon is a hexagon. The term *n*-gon refers to a polygon with *n* sides.

If the corresponding sides and the corresponding angles of two polygons are equal, the polygons are *congruent.* Congruent polygons have the same size and the same shape.

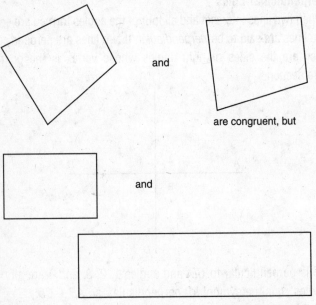

The sum of all the angles of an *n*-gon is $(n-2)180°$. So the sum of the angles in a hexagon is $(6-2)180° = 720°$.

TRIANGLES

A *triangle* is a 3-sided polygon. If two sides of a triangle are equal, it is called *isosceles.* If all three sides are equal, it is an *equilateral* triangle. The symbol for a triangle is △; so △*ABC* means a triangle whose vertices are *A*, *B*, and *C*.

The sum of the angles in a triangle is 180°.

The sum of the lengths of any two sides of a triangle must be longer than the remaining side.

If two angles in a triangle are equal, then the lengths of the sides opposite the equal angles are equal. If two sides of a triangle are equal, then the angles opposite the two equal sides are equal. In an equilateral triangle all the angles are equal and each angle = 60°. If each of the angles in a triangle is 60°, then the triangle is equilateral.

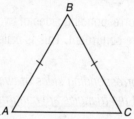

If $AB = BC$, then $\angle BAC = \angle BCA$.

In a right triangle, the side opposite the right angle is called the *hypotenuse,* and the remaining two sides are called legs.

The *Pythagorean Theorem* states that *the square of the length of the hypotenuse is equal to the sum of the squares of the lengths of the legs.*

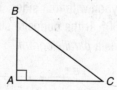

$(BC)^2 = (AB)^2 + (AC)^2$

If $AB = 4$ and $AC = 3$, then $(BC)^2 = 4^2 + 3^2 = 25$, so $BC = 5$. If $BC = 13$ and $AC = 5$, then $13^2 = 169 = (AB)^2 + 5^2$. So $(AB)^2 = 169 - 25 = 144$ and $AB = 12$.

If the lengths of the three sides of a triangle are a, b, and c and $a^2 + b^2 = c^2$, then the triangle is a right triangle where c is the length of the hypotenuse.

Congruence

Two triangles are congruent if two pairs of corresponding sides and the corresponding *included* angles are equal. This is called *Side-Angle-Side* and is denoted by S.A.S.

Two triangles are congruent if two pairs of corresponding angles and the corresponding *included* sides are equal. This is called *Angle-Side-Angle* or A.S.A.

If all three pairs of corresponding sides of two triangles are equal, then the triangles are congruent. This is called *Side-Side-Side* or S.S.S.

In general, if two corresponding sides of two triangles are equal, we cannot infer that the triangles are congruent.

The symbol $\cong$ means congruent.

Similarity

Two triangles are similar if all three pairs of corresponding angles are equal. Since the sum of the angles in a triangle is 180°, it follows that if two corresponding angles are equal, the third angles must be equal. The symbol $\sim$ means similar.

QUADRILATERALS

A *quadrilateral* is a polygon with four sides. The sum of the angles in a quadrilateral is 360°. If the opposite sides of a quadrilateral are parallel, the figure is a *parallelogram*.

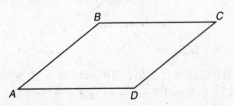

ABCD is a parallelogram.

In a parallelogram:

   (1) Opposite sides are equal.

   (2) Opposite angles are equal.

   (3) All diagonals divide the parallelogram into two congruent triangles.

   (4) The diagonals bisect each other. (A line *bisects* a line segment if it intersects the segment at the midpoint of the segment.)

If *any* of the statements (1), (2), (3), and (4) are true for a quadrilateral, then the quadrilateral is a parallelogram.

If all the angles of a parallelogram are right angles, the figure is a *rectangle*.

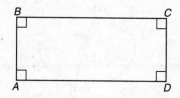

ABCD is a rectangle.

Since the sum of the angles in a quadrilateral is 360°, if *all* the angles of a quadrilateral are equal, then the figure is a rectangle. The diagonals of a rectangle are equal. The length of a diagonal can be found by using the Pythagorean theorem.

If all the sides of a rectangle are equal, the figure is a *square*.

A quadrilateral with two parallel sides and two sides that are not parallel is called a *trapezoid*. The parallel sides are called bases, and the nonparallel sides are called legs.

If *BC* || *AD*, then *ABCD* is a trapezoid; *BC* and *AD* are the bases.

CIRCLES

A *circle* is a figure in a plane consisting of all the points which are the same distance from a fixed point called the *center* of the circle. A line segment from any point on the circle to the center of the circle is called a *radius* (plural: *radii*) of the circle. All radii of the same circle have the same length.

A line segment whose endpoints are on a circle is called a *chord*. A chord which passes through the center of the circle is a *diameter*. *The length of a diameter is twice the length of a radius.* A diameter divides a circle into two congruent halves which are called *semi-circles*.

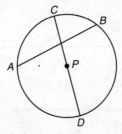

P is the center of the circle.
AB is a chord, *CD* is a diameter, and *PC* and *PD* are radii.

A diameter which is perpendicular to a chord bisects the chord.

If a line intersects a circle at one and only one point, the line is said to be a *tangent* to the circle. The point common to a circle and a tangent to the circle is called the *point of tangency*. The radius from the center to the point of tangency is perpendicular to the tangent.

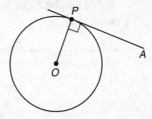

AP is tangent to the circle with center *O*. *P* is the point of tangency and *OP* ⊥ *PA*.

An angle whose vertex is a point on a circle and whose sides are chords of the circle is called an *inscribed angle*. An angle whose vertex is the center of a circle and whose sides are radii of the circle is called a *central angle*.

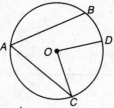

∠*BAC* is an inscribed angle.

∠*DOC* is a central angle.

An *arc* is a part of a circle.

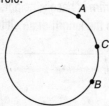

ACB is an arc. Arc *ACB* is written $\overset{\frown}{ACB}$.

An arc can be measured in degrees. The entire circle is 360°, thus an arc of 120° would be $\frac{1}{3}$ of a circle.

A central angle is equal in measure to the arc it intercepts.

An inscribed angle is equal in measure to $\frac{1}{2}$ the arc it intercepts.

AREA AND PERIMETER

Area

The *area of a square* equals s^2, where s is the length of a side of the square. Thus, $A = s^2$.

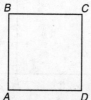

If $AD = 5$ inches, the area of square *ABCD* is 25 square inches.

The *area of a rectangle* equals length times width; if *L* is the length of one side and *W* is the length of a perpendicular side, then the area is $A = LW$.

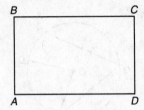

If $AB = 5$ feet and $AD = 8$ feet, then the area of rectangle *ABCD* is 40 square feet.

The *area of a parallelogram* is base × height; $A = bh$, where *b* is the length of a side and *h* is the length of an altitude to the base.

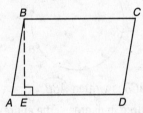

If $AD = 6$ yards and $BE = 4$ yards, then the area of the parallelogram *ABCD* is 6 · 4 or 24 square yards.

The *area of a trapezoid* is the (average of the bases) × height. $A = [(b_1 + b_2)/2]h$, where b_1 and b_2 are the lengths of the parallel sides and *h* is the length of an altitude to one of the bases.

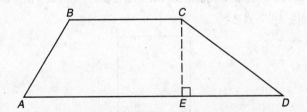

If $BC = 3$ miles, $AD = 7$ miles, and $CE = 2$ miles, then the area of trapezoid $ABCD$ is $[(3 + 7)/2] \cdot 2 = 10$ square miles.

The *area of a triangle* is $\frac{1}{2}$ (base × height); $A = \frac{1}{2} bh$, where b is the length of a side and h is the length of the altitude to that side.

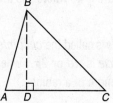

If $AC = 5$ miles and $BD = 4$ miles, then the area of the triangle is $\frac{1}{2}$ × 5 × 4 = 10 square miles.

If we want to find the *area of a polygon* which is not of a type already mentioned, we break the polygon up into smaller figures such as triangles or rectangles, find the area of each piece, and add these to get the area of the given polygon.

The *area of a circle* is πr^2, where r is the length of a radius. Since $d = 2r$ where d is the length of a diameter, $A = \pi \left(\dfrac{d}{2}\right)^2 = \pi \dfrac{d^2}{4}$. π is a number which is approximately $\dfrac{22}{7}$ or 3.14; however, there is *no fraction which is exactly equal to π. π is called an irrational number.*

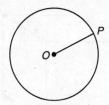

If $OP = 2$ inches, then the area of the circle with center O is $\pi 2^2$ or 4π square inches.

$d = 2(2)$

$d = 4$

$3.14(2)^2$

$3.14(4)$

Perimeter

The *perimeter of a polygon* is the sum of the lengths of the sides.

The *perimeter of a rectangle* is $2(L + W)$, where L is the length and W is the width.

The *perimeter of a square* is $4s$ where s is the length of a side of the square.

The *perimeter of a circle* is called the *circumference* of the circle. The *circumference of a circle* is πd or $2\pi r$, where d is the length of a diameter and r is the length of a radius.

VOLUME AND SURFACE AREA

Volume

The *volume of a rectangular prism or box* is length times width times height.

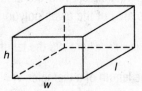

If each of the faces of a rectangular prism is a congruent square, then the solid is a *cube*. The *volume of a cube* is the length of a side (or edge) cubed.

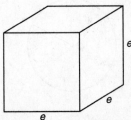

If the side of a cube is 4 feet long, then the volume of the cube is 4^3 or 64 cubic feet.

This solid is a circular cylinder. The top and the bottom are congruent circles. Most tin cans are circular cylinders. The *volume of a circular cylinder* is the product of the area of the circular base and the height.

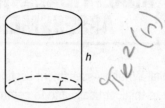

A *sphere* is the set of points in space equidistant from a fixed point called the center. The length of a segment from any point on the sphere to the center is called the radius of the sphere. *The volume of a sphere* of radius r is $\frac{4}{3}\pi r^3$.

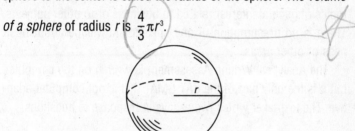

The volume of a sphere with radius 3 feet is $\frac{4}{3}\pi 3^3 = 36\pi$ cubic feet.

Surface Area

The *surface area of a rectangular prism* is $2LW + 2LH + 2WH$, where L is the length, W is the width, and H is the height.

The *surface area of a cube* is $6e^2$, where e is the length of an edge.

The *area of the circular part of a cylinder* is called the lateral area. The *lateral area of a cylinder* is $2\pi rh$, since if we unroll the circular part we get a rectangle whose dimensions are the circumference of the circle and the height of the cylinder. The total surface area is the lateral surface area plus the areas of the circles on top and bottom, so the total surface area is $2\pi rh + 2\pi r^2$.

6
ANALYTICAL WRITING ASSESSMENT

The Analytical Writing Assessment section is designed to assess your ability to think critically and to communicate complex ideas. The writing task consists of two sections that require you to examine the composition of an issue, take a position on the basis of the details of the issue, and present a critique of the conclusion derived from a specific way of thinking. The issues are taken from topics of general interest related to business or to other subjects. There is no presumption of any specific knowledge about business or other areas.

The Analytical Writing Assessment is written on the computer, but it is the only part of the CAT GMAT that is not computer adaptive. The test taker writes two essays in response to questions.

ANALYTICAL WRITING ASSESSMENT TASKS

There are two types of Analytical Writing Assessment tasks: *Analysis of an Issue* and *Analysis of an Argument.* Following is an example of each:

EXAMPLE:

Analysis of an Issue

Some analysts complain that consumers do not receive enough information to make rational purchase decisions. When the consumer is unable to make rational decisions, the economy suffers. Behavioral scientists contend that emotional and psychological factors play an important role in the satisfaction of consumer wants and that the measurable quantitative information being proposed by others is not as relevant for consumer decision-making as purported to be.

Which do you find more convincing: the complaint of the analysts or the contention of the behavioral scientists? State your position using relevant reasons and examples from your own experience, observation, or reading.

TIPS TO HELP YOU COPE

1. **Identify the issue or argument.** In the example, the claim or conclusion is that the economy suffers when consumers cannot make rational decisions. Consumers cannot make rational decisions whenever information is lacking. The counterview is that consumer decision-making is based more on emotion than on rational reasoning. If that is the case, then information is not so important.

2. **Outline your ideas.** You are asked to take sides. If you believe that consumers make decisions mainly on a rational basis, you will have to support your view by giving examples based on experience or on the facts that you have acquired from study or reading. You must state why you support this view and not the other. Do you have any facts on the issue? If so, list them along with examples. If you do not have any facts, you will need to deal with the issue inferentially—by reasoning inductively. Here, experience and observation will be important to buttress your claims.

   Another possibility in this case is that consumer decision-making depends on the sort of product. When it comes to purchasing a house or making a similar capital investment, the decision is mainly rational, and so it depends on a good deal of information. Most consumer purchases, however, are not of this kind; for example, clothing, food, leisure activities—whose motivation is largely emotional. Thus, for most purchases, a lot of information is not necessary, and so the economy does not suffer as is claimed.

EXAMPLE:

Analysis of an Argument

The computerized water-irrigation system to be installed by farmers will prevent crops from drying out. The soil moisture is measured by sensors in the ground that send signals back to the irrigation control system. On the basis of this information, the system automatically regulates the amount and time of irrigation.

Discuss how logically persuasive you find this argument. In presenting your point of view, analyze the sort of reasoning used and its supporting evidence. In addition, state what further evidence, if any, would make the argument more sound and convincing or would make you better able to evaluate its conclusion.

TIPS TO HELP YOU COPE

1. **Identify the parts of the argument.**
2. **State how convincing (or unconvincing) you find the argument.** The persuasiveness of an argument depends on its logic; that is, on whether the conclusion follows from the evidence presented. You are also asked to discuss what would make the argument more sound and persuasive or would help to evaluate its conclusion. To make an argument more sound, it is necessary to provide more evidence that will buttress the conclusion.

   In the example, the conclusion is found in the first sentence: the irrigation system wil prevent crops from drying out. What evidence is given that the irrigation system will indead perform its task? Overall, the argument is sound and convincing, assuming that proper irrigation is all that is needed to keep crops from drying out. What then could strengthen the conclusion? Evidence that systems similar to the one described are already in place and working. This last point is important because we have no evidence about the reliability of the system. Moreover, there may be a question of cost-effectiveness. Will farmers be willing to adopt such a system? If evidence of these factors could be provided, the conclusion would be strengthened.

Answer Sheet—Sample Test 1

Section I Reading Comprehension	Section II Problem Solving	Section III Critical Reasoning	Section IV Data Sufficiency
1. Ⓐ Ⓑ Ⓒ Ⓓ Ⓔ	1. Ⓐ Ⓑ Ⓒ Ⓓ Ⓔ	1. Ⓐ Ⓑ Ⓒ Ⓓ Ⓔ	1. Ⓐ Ⓑ Ⓒ Ⓓ Ⓔ
2. Ⓐ Ⓑ Ⓒ Ⓓ Ⓔ	2. Ⓐ Ⓑ Ⓒ Ⓓ Ⓔ	2. Ⓐ Ⓑ Ⓒ Ⓓ Ⓔ	2. Ⓐ Ⓑ Ⓒ Ⓓ Ⓔ
3. Ⓐ Ⓑ Ⓒ Ⓓ Ⓔ	3. Ⓐ Ⓑ Ⓒ Ⓓ Ⓔ	3. Ⓐ Ⓑ Ⓒ Ⓓ Ⓔ	3. Ⓐ Ⓑ Ⓒ Ⓓ Ⓔ
4. Ⓐ Ⓑ Ⓒ Ⓓ Ⓔ	4. Ⓐ Ⓑ Ⓒ Ⓓ Ⓔ	4. Ⓐ Ⓑ Ⓒ Ⓓ Ⓔ	4. Ⓐ Ⓑ Ⓒ Ⓓ Ⓔ
5. Ⓐ Ⓑ Ⓒ Ⓓ Ⓔ	5. Ⓐ Ⓑ Ⓒ Ⓓ Ⓔ	5. Ⓐ Ⓑ Ⓒ Ⓓ Ⓔ	5. Ⓐ Ⓑ Ⓒ Ⓓ Ⓔ
6. Ⓐ Ⓑ Ⓒ Ⓓ Ⓔ	6. Ⓐ Ⓑ Ⓒ Ⓓ Ⓔ	6. Ⓐ Ⓑ Ⓒ Ⓓ Ⓔ	6. Ⓐ Ⓑ Ⓒ Ⓓ Ⓔ
7. Ⓐ Ⓑ Ⓒ Ⓓ Ⓔ	7. Ⓐ Ⓑ Ⓒ Ⓓ Ⓔ	7. Ⓐ Ⓑ Ⓒ Ⓓ Ⓔ	7. Ⓐ Ⓑ Ⓒ Ⓓ Ⓔ
8. Ⓐ Ⓑ Ⓒ Ⓓ Ⓔ	8. Ⓐ Ⓑ Ⓒ Ⓓ Ⓔ	8. Ⓐ Ⓑ Ⓒ Ⓓ Ⓔ	8. Ⓐ Ⓑ Ⓒ Ⓓ Ⓔ
9. Ⓐ Ⓑ Ⓒ Ⓓ Ⓔ	9. Ⓐ Ⓑ Ⓒ Ⓓ Ⓔ	9. Ⓐ Ⓑ Ⓒ Ⓓ Ⓔ	9. Ⓐ Ⓑ Ⓒ Ⓓ Ⓔ
10. Ⓐ Ⓑ Ⓒ Ⓓ Ⓔ	10. Ⓐ Ⓑ Ⓒ Ⓓ Ⓔ	10. Ⓐ Ⓑ Ⓒ Ⓓ Ⓔ	10. Ⓐ Ⓑ Ⓒ Ⓓ Ⓔ
11. Ⓐ Ⓑ Ⓒ Ⓓ Ⓔ	11. Ⓐ Ⓑ Ⓒ Ⓓ Ⓔ	11. Ⓐ Ⓑ Ⓒ Ⓓ Ⓔ	11. Ⓐ Ⓑ Ⓒ Ⓓ Ⓔ
12. Ⓐ Ⓑ Ⓒ Ⓓ Ⓔ	12. Ⓐ Ⓑ Ⓒ Ⓓ Ⓔ	12. Ⓐ Ⓑ Ⓒ Ⓓ Ⓔ	12. Ⓐ Ⓑ Ⓒ Ⓓ Ⓔ
13. Ⓐ Ⓑ Ⓒ Ⓓ Ⓔ	13. Ⓐ Ⓑ Ⓒ Ⓓ Ⓔ	13. Ⓐ Ⓑ Ⓒ Ⓓ Ⓔ	13. Ⓐ Ⓑ Ⓒ Ⓓ Ⓔ
14. Ⓐ Ⓑ Ⓒ Ⓓ Ⓔ	14. Ⓐ Ⓑ Ⓒ Ⓓ Ⓔ	14. Ⓐ Ⓑ Ⓒ Ⓓ Ⓔ	14. Ⓐ Ⓑ Ⓒ Ⓓ Ⓔ
15. Ⓐ Ⓑ Ⓒ Ⓓ Ⓔ	15. Ⓐ Ⓑ Ⓒ Ⓓ Ⓔ	15. Ⓐ Ⓑ Ⓒ Ⓓ Ⓔ	15. Ⓐ Ⓑ Ⓒ Ⓓ Ⓔ
16. Ⓐ Ⓑ Ⓒ Ⓓ Ⓔ	16. Ⓐ Ⓑ Ⓒ Ⓓ Ⓔ	16. Ⓐ Ⓑ Ⓒ Ⓓ Ⓔ	16. Ⓐ Ⓑ Ⓒ Ⓓ Ⓔ
17. Ⓐ Ⓑ Ⓒ Ⓓ Ⓔ	17. Ⓐ Ⓑ Ⓒ Ⓓ Ⓔ	17. Ⓐ Ⓑ Ⓒ Ⓓ Ⓔ	17. Ⓐ Ⓑ Ⓒ Ⓓ Ⓔ
18. Ⓐ Ⓑ Ⓒ Ⓓ Ⓔ	18. Ⓐ Ⓑ Ⓒ Ⓓ Ⓔ	18. Ⓐ Ⓑ Ⓒ Ⓓ Ⓔ	18. Ⓐ Ⓑ Ⓒ Ⓓ Ⓔ
19. Ⓐ Ⓑ Ⓒ Ⓓ Ⓔ	19. Ⓐ Ⓑ Ⓒ Ⓓ Ⓔ	19. Ⓐ Ⓑ Ⓒ Ⓓ Ⓔ	19. Ⓐ Ⓑ Ⓒ Ⓓ Ⓔ
20. Ⓐ Ⓑ Ⓒ Ⓓ Ⓔ	20. Ⓐ Ⓑ Ⓒ Ⓓ Ⓔ	20. Ⓐ Ⓑ Ⓒ Ⓓ Ⓔ	20. Ⓐ Ⓑ Ⓒ Ⓓ Ⓔ
21. Ⓐ Ⓑ Ⓒ Ⓓ Ⓔ			21. Ⓐ Ⓑ Ⓒ Ⓓ Ⓔ
22. Ⓐ Ⓑ Ⓒ Ⓓ Ⓔ			22. Ⓐ Ⓑ Ⓒ Ⓓ Ⓔ
23. Ⓐ Ⓑ Ⓒ Ⓓ Ⓔ			23. Ⓐ Ⓑ Ⓒ Ⓓ Ⓔ
24. Ⓐ Ⓑ Ⓒ Ⓓ Ⓔ			24. Ⓐ Ⓑ Ⓒ Ⓓ Ⓔ
25. Ⓐ Ⓑ Ⓒ Ⓓ Ⓔ			25. Ⓐ Ⓑ Ⓒ Ⓓ Ⓔ

Section V Sentence Correction	Section VI Problem Solving	Section VII Critical Reasoning
1. Ⓐ Ⓑ Ⓒ Ⓓ Ⓔ	1. Ⓐ Ⓑ Ⓒ Ⓓ Ⓔ	1. Ⓐ Ⓑ Ⓒ Ⓓ Ⓔ
2. Ⓐ Ⓑ Ⓒ Ⓓ Ⓔ	2. Ⓐ Ⓑ Ⓒ Ⓓ Ⓔ	2. Ⓐ Ⓑ Ⓒ Ⓓ Ⓔ
3. Ⓐ Ⓑ Ⓒ Ⓓ Ⓔ	3. Ⓐ Ⓑ Ⓒ Ⓓ Ⓔ	3. Ⓐ Ⓑ Ⓒ Ⓓ Ⓔ
4. Ⓐ Ⓑ Ⓒ Ⓓ Ⓔ	4. Ⓐ Ⓑ Ⓒ Ⓓ Ⓔ	4. Ⓐ Ⓑ Ⓒ Ⓓ Ⓔ
5. Ⓐ Ⓑ Ⓒ Ⓓ Ⓔ	5. Ⓐ Ⓑ Ⓒ Ⓓ Ⓔ	5. Ⓐ Ⓑ Ⓒ Ⓓ Ⓔ
6. Ⓐ Ⓑ Ⓒ Ⓓ Ⓔ	6. Ⓐ Ⓑ Ⓒ Ⓓ Ⓔ	6. Ⓐ Ⓑ Ⓒ Ⓓ Ⓔ
7. Ⓐ Ⓑ Ⓒ Ⓓ Ⓔ	7. Ⓐ Ⓑ Ⓒ Ⓓ Ⓔ	7. Ⓐ Ⓑ Ⓒ Ⓓ Ⓔ
8. Ⓐ Ⓑ Ⓒ Ⓓ Ⓔ	8. Ⓐ Ⓑ Ⓒ Ⓓ Ⓔ	8. Ⓐ Ⓑ Ⓒ Ⓓ Ⓔ
9. Ⓐ Ⓑ Ⓒ Ⓓ Ⓔ	9. Ⓐ Ⓑ Ⓒ Ⓓ Ⓔ	9. Ⓐ Ⓑ Ⓒ Ⓓ Ⓔ
10. Ⓐ Ⓑ Ⓒ Ⓓ Ⓔ	10. Ⓐ Ⓑ Ⓒ Ⓓ Ⓔ	10. Ⓐ Ⓑ Ⓒ Ⓓ Ⓔ
11. Ⓐ Ⓑ Ⓒ Ⓓ Ⓔ	11. Ⓐ Ⓑ Ⓒ Ⓓ Ⓔ	11. Ⓐ Ⓑ Ⓒ Ⓓ Ⓔ
12. Ⓐ Ⓑ Ⓒ Ⓓ Ⓔ	12. Ⓐ Ⓑ Ⓒ Ⓓ Ⓔ	12. Ⓐ Ⓑ Ⓒ Ⓓ Ⓔ
13. Ⓐ Ⓑ Ⓒ Ⓓ Ⓔ	13. Ⓐ Ⓑ Ⓒ Ⓓ Ⓔ	13. Ⓐ Ⓑ Ⓒ Ⓓ Ⓔ
14. Ⓐ Ⓑ Ⓒ Ⓓ Ⓔ	14. Ⓐ Ⓑ Ⓒ Ⓓ Ⓔ	14. Ⓐ Ⓑ Ⓒ Ⓓ Ⓔ
15. Ⓐ Ⓑ Ⓒ Ⓓ Ⓔ	15. Ⓐ Ⓑ Ⓒ Ⓓ Ⓔ	15. Ⓐ Ⓑ Ⓒ Ⓓ Ⓔ
16. Ⓐ Ⓑ Ⓒ Ⓓ Ⓔ	16. Ⓐ Ⓑ Ⓒ Ⓓ Ⓔ	16. Ⓐ Ⓑ Ⓒ Ⓓ Ⓔ
17. Ⓐ Ⓑ Ⓒ Ⓓ Ⓔ	17. Ⓐ Ⓑ Ⓒ Ⓓ Ⓔ	17. Ⓐ Ⓑ Ⓒ Ⓓ Ⓔ
18. Ⓐ Ⓑ Ⓒ Ⓓ Ⓔ	18. Ⓐ Ⓑ Ⓒ Ⓓ Ⓔ	18. Ⓐ Ⓑ Ⓒ Ⓓ Ⓔ
19. Ⓐ Ⓑ Ⓒ Ⓓ Ⓔ	19. Ⓐ Ⓑ Ⓒ Ⓓ Ⓔ	19. Ⓐ Ⓑ Ⓒ Ⓓ Ⓔ
20. Ⓐ Ⓑ Ⓒ Ⓓ Ⓔ	20. Ⓐ Ⓑ Ⓒ Ⓓ Ⓔ	20. Ⓐ Ⓑ Ⓒ Ⓓ Ⓔ
21. Ⓐ Ⓑ Ⓒ Ⓓ Ⓔ		
22. Ⓐ Ⓑ Ⓒ Ⓓ Ⓔ		
23. Ⓐ Ⓑ Ⓒ Ⓓ Ⓔ		
24. Ⓐ Ⓑ Ⓒ Ⓓ Ⓔ		
25. Ⓐ Ⓑ Ⓒ Ⓓ Ⓔ		

7

THREE SAMPLE GMATS WITH ANSWERS AND ANALYSIS

This chapter contains three full-length GMAT exams. They have the same formats and degrees of difficulty as typical GMAT exams. A detailed analysis of the answers is included after each exam.

SAMPLE TEST 1

SECTION I   READING COMPREHENSION   Time: 30 minutes

Directions: This part contains three reading passages. You are to read each one carefully. When answering the questions, you *will* be allowed to refer to the passages. The questions are based on what is *stated* or *implied* in each passage.

This pasage was written before the fall of the Soviet Union.

Passage 1:

With Friedrich Engels, Karl Marx in 1848 published the *Communist Manifesto*, calling upon the masses to rise and throw off their economic chains. His maturer theories of society were later elaborated in his large and abstruse work *Das Kapital*. Starting as a non-violent
(5) revolutionist, he ended life as a major social theorist more or less sympathetic with violent revolution, if such became necessary in order to change the social system which he believed to be frankly predatory upon the masses.

On the theoretical side, Marx set up the doctrine of surplus value
(10) as the chief element in capitalistic exploitation. According to this theory, the ruling classes no longer employed military force primarily as a means to plundering the people. Instead, they used their control over employment and working conditions under the bourgeois capitalistic system for this purpose, paying only a bare subsistence wage
(15) to the worker while they appropriated all surplus values in the

productive process. He further taught that the strategic disadvantage of the worker in industry prevented him from obtaining a fairer share of the earnings by bargaining methods and drove him to revolutionary procedures as a means to establishing his economic and social rights.

(20) This revolution might be peacefully consummated by parliamentary procedures if the people prepared themselves for political action by mastering the materialistic interpretation of history and by organizing politically for the final event. It was his belief that the aggressions of the capitalist class would eventually destroy the middle class and take

(25) over all their sources of income by a process of capitalistic absorption of industry—a process which has failed to occur in most countries.

With minor exceptions, Marx's social philosophy is now generally accepted by left-wing labor movements in many countries, but rejected by centrist labor groups, especially those in the United States.

(30) In Russia and other Eastern European countries, however, Socialist leaders adopted the methods of violent revolution because of the opposition of the ruling classes. Yet, many now hold that the present Communist regime in Russia and her satellite countries is no longer a proletarian movement based on Marxist social and political theory,

(35) but a camouflaged imperialistic effort to dominate the world in the interest of a new ruling class.

It is important, however, that those who wish to approach Marx as a teacher should not be "buffaloed" by his philosophic approach. They are very likely to in these days, because those most interested in

(40) propagating the ideas of Marx, the Russian Bolsheviks, have swallowed down his Hegelian philosophy along with his science of revolutionary engineering, and they look upon us irreverent peoples, who presume to mediate social and even revolutionary problems without making our obeisance to the mysteries of Dialectic Materialism, as a

(45) species of unredeemed and well-nigh unredeemable barbarians. They are right in scorning our ignorance of the scientific ideas of Karl Marx and our indifference to them. They are wrong in scorning our distaste for having practical programs presented in the form of systems of philosophy. In that we simply represent a more progressive intellec-

(50) tual culture than that in which Marx received his education—a culture farther emerged from the dominance of religious attitudes.

1. According to the passage, the chief element in Marx's analysis of capitalist exploitation was the doctrine of

   (A) just wages.
   (B) the price system.
   (C) surplus value.
   (D) predatory production.
   (E) subsistence work.

2. *Das Kapital* differs from the *Communist Manifesto* in that it

   (A) was written with the help of Friedrich Engels.
   (B) retreated from Marx's earlier revolutionary stance.
   (C) expressed a more fully developed form of Marxist theory.
   (D) denounced the predatory nature of the capitalist system.
   (E) expressed sympathy for the plight of the middle class.

3. According to the passage, Marx ended his life

   I. a believer in nonviolent revolution.
   II. accepting violent revolution.
   III. a major social theorist.

   (A) I only
   (B) III only
   (C) I and III only
   (D) II and III only
   (E) Neither I, II, nor III

4. The author suggests that the then-present Communist regime in Russia may best be categorized as a(n)

   (A) proletarian movement.
   (B) social government.
   (C) imperialistic state.
   (D) revolutionary government.
   (E) social democracy.

5. Marx's social philosophy is now generally accepted by

   (A) centrist labor groups.
   (B) most labor unions.
   (C) left-wing labor unions.
   (D) only those in Communist countries.
   (E) only those in Russia.

6. It can be concluded that the author of the passage is

   (A) sympathetic to Marx's ideas.
   (B) unsympathetic to Marx's ideas.
   (C) uncritical of Marx's interpretation of history.
   (D) a believer in Hegelian philosophy.
   (E) a Leninist-Marxist.

7. Which of the following classes did Marx believe should control the economy?

(A) the working class   (D) the lower class
(B) the upper class   (E) the capitalist class
(C) the middle class

8. According to Marx, a social and economic revolution could take place through

   I. parliamentary procedures.
  II. political action.
 III. violent revolution.

(A) I only   (D) II or III only
(B) III only   (E) I, II, or III
(C) I or II only

Passage 2:

In 1789 Alexander Hamilton, as the first Secretary of the Treasury, affirmed and successfully established a position of strong executive leadership in matters of public finance. His proposals on revenues, banking, and the assumption of prior debts of both national and state
(5) governments were based on his philosophy that federal fiscal policies should be designed to encourage economic growth. However, Hamilton's successors, and the Presidents under whom they served, did not follow his concept of executive responsibility for "plans of finance."

(10) Partly through default, Congress took charge of all phases of fiscal policy. At the outset, each chamber was so small that coherent initiative was possible. (The first House had some 60 members—about the number of its present Appropriations Committee.) Spending estimates, considered in Committee of the Whole in 1789, were later
(15) referred to the Committee on Ways and Means. In 1865, expenditures were assigned to a new Appropriations Committee while revenues remained with the Ways and Means Committee.

By the turn of the century there was a clear need for reform in financial management. At all levels of government, officials spent money on
(20) activities "as authorized by law" and in line with "appropriations" made by legislative bodies—usually after committee consideration.

Several factors played a part in the eventual breakthrough. In the first decade of the twentieth century, an "executive budget" came into successful use by some cities and states. President Taft's Commission
(25) on Efficiency and Economy prepared an illustrative federal budget which—while rejected by Congress—commanded broad public support. The more advanced methods developed by European governments came to American attention. World War I precipitated accounting chaos, with an aftermath of scandal. The need for new and better
(30) methods was established beyond dispute.

The Budget and Accounting Act of 1921 placed direct responsibility for preparation and execution of the federal budget upon the President, making a unified federal budget possible for the first time. The Act set up two new organizational units, the General Accounting Office (GAO)
(35) and the Bureau of the Budget. GAO is headed by the Comptroller General, appointed by the President *with* Senate approval for a 15-year term, and is regarded as primarily a congressional rather than an executive resource. The Bureau, under a Director appointed by the President *without* Senate confirmation and serving at his pleasure, has
(40) from its inception been the President's chief reliance in budgetary and related matters.

9. Alexander Hamilton's philosophy was that federal fiscal policies should

   (A) be expansionary.
   (B) encourage economic growth.
   (C) be determined by Congress.
   (D) encourage a balanced budget.
   (E) be determined by the President.

10. Hamilton's successors

   I.   followed his economic philosophy of "plans of finance."
   II. followed his social philosophy.
   III. did not follow his philosophy of strong executive leadership.

   (A) I only
   (B) III only
   (C) I and II only
   (D) II and III only
   (E) I, II, and III

11. In the history of U.S. fiscal management, spending estimates were *first* considered by the

    (A) Committee of the Whole.
    (B) Appropriations Committee.
    (C) Ways and Means Committee.
    (D) Commission on Efficiency and Economy.
    (E) General Accounting Office.

12. At the end of the 19th century, there was a need for

    (A) more restrained executive leadership.
    (B) a new finance commission.
    (C) more Congressional interest in finance.
    (D) overall reform of financial management.
    (E) creation of a new Appropriations Committee.

13. The "executive budget" was first used

    (A) by Alexander Hamilton.
    (B) in the 19th century.
    (C) in the first decade of the 20th century.
    (D) by President Eisenhower.
    (E) by President Truman.

14. President Taft's federal budget was

    (A) based on procedures used by some European governments.
    (B) enthusiastically accepted by Congress.
    (C) a partial cause of accounting chaos during World War I.
    (D) rejected by Congress.
    (E) vilified by the public.

15. In 1921, the responsibility for preparation and execution of the federal budget fell upon the

    (A) President.   (D) House of Representatives.
    (B) Congress.   (E) Senate.
    (C) Bureau of the Budget.

16. All of the following are true about the Bureau of the Budget except

  (A) its Director is appointed by the President.
  (B) it assists the President in budgetary matters.
  (C) its Director need not be approved by the Senate.
  (D) it was established in 1921.
  (E) its Director serves for a 15-year term.

Passage 3:

The basic physical similarity of the Native Americans from Alaska to Patagonia is explained by the fact that they all came originally from Asia by way of the Bering Strait and the Aleutian Islands into Alaska and then southward. They came in different waves, the earliest around
(5) 25,000 years ago, the latest probably not long before America was discovered by Europeans. Because these people all came from Asia and were therefore drawn from the same pool of Asiatic people, they tended to look somewhat alike. But since the various waves of migration crossed into Alaska at widely separated times, there were differ-
(10) ences among them in their physical characteristics.

Despite their limited technical equipment, some of the New Mexico Indians were very successful big game hunters. Twenty-five thousand years ago they were hunting the woolly mammoth, the giant bison, the ground sloth and the camel, all characteristic animals of the closing
(15) phases of the last ice age.

After their arrival from Asia in various waves across the Bering Strait, the early peoples in the Americas slowly spread southward into the vast empty spaces of the two continents. A group of people moving slowly down the Mackenzie River valley east of the Rockies into the
(20) general region of Southern Alberta, then eastward across the northern prairies reaching the wooded country around the upper Mississippi and the Western Great Lakes, then in a southeastward movement following the Mississippi valley until some final settlement was reached in the Gulf states, would encounter a wide variety of physical
(25) environments. At various stages of such wanderings they would have to evolve methods of coping with the cold, barren, tundra country of northern Canada; the prairies, cold, treeless, but well stocked with large game; then later the completely different flora and fauna of the Minnesota-Wisconsin-Illinois area, thickly forested and well watered

(30) and providing an abundance of small game and wild vegetable foods; then the semi-tropical character of the lower Mississippi country as they neared the Gulf of Mexico. Since such a migration would be spread over many centuries, the modification of whatever basic culture they had on their arrival from Asia would be very slow. Yet the *(35)* end result would be completely different from their original culture. It would also be different from the final culture of a closely allied group who became separated from them early in their wanderings and whose movements led them into different types of country. In its final form, the culture of this second group would have little in common with that *(40)* of the first, except perhaps a continuing resemblance in language and in general physical type.

17. According to the passage, Native Americans who migrated to what is now the United States originated in

(A) Asia.   (D) Alaska.
(B) Africa.   (E) Patagonia.
(C) South America.

18. Physical differences among Native Americans who migrated to Alaska can be accounted for by the fact that they came

(A) from different places.
(B) from different tribes.
(C) at different times.
(D) from different races.
(E) to different places.

19. It is estimated that Native Americans first came to what is now the United States about

(A) 5,000 years ago.   (D) 25,000 years ago.
(B) 10,000 years ago.   (E) 50,000 years ago.
(C) 15,000 years ago.

20. The author is most interested in discussing the Native Americans'

(A) cultural background.

(B) eating habits.

(C) technical abilities.

(D) migration patterns.

(E) physical characteristics.

21. According to the passage, the southernmost area reached by the earliest settlers was the

(A) northern prairies.

(B) upper Mississippi.

(C) Great Lakes.

(D) Mackenzie River valley.

(E) Gulf states.

22. Particularly noted for their hunting prowess were the Native Americans who settled in

(A) Mississippi.

(B) Southern Alberta.

(C) the Mackenzie River valley.

(D) New Mexico.

(E) the American prairies.

23. What characteristics of Native American culture remained fairly stable despite the Native American migrations?

I. Language

II. Physical type

III. Technical abilities

(A) I only

(B) III only

(C) I and II only

(D) II and III only

(E) I, II, and III

24. Which animals were hunted by the Native Americans during the last ice age?

I. Bison

II. Woolly mammoth

III. Camel

(A) I only

(B) III only

(C) I and II only

(D) II and III only

(E) I, II, and III

25. The passage most likely was written by a(n)

(A) economist.   (D) social scientist.
(B) historian.   (E) anthropologist.
(C) educator.

If there is still time remaining, you may review the questions in this section only. In the actual CAT GMAT, you cannot return to a question after you have confirmed your answer.

SECTION II   PROBLEM SOLVING   Time: 30 minutes

Directions: Solve each of the following problems; then indicate the correct answer on the answer sheet. [On the actual test you will be permitted to use any space available on the examination paper for scratch work.]

NOTE: A figure that appears with a problem is drawn as accurately as possible so as to provide information that may help in answering the question. Numbers in this test are real numbers.

1. A college has raised 75% of the amount it needs for a new building by receiving an average donation of $60 from the people already solicited. The people already solicited represent 60% of the people the college will ask for donations. If the college is to raise exactly the amount needed for the new building, how much must the remaining people donate per person?

   (A) $25   (D) $50
   (B) $30   (E) $60
   (C) $40

2. If $2x + y = 10$ and $x = 3$, what is $x - y$?

   (A) −4   (D) 1
   (B) −1   (E) 7
   (C) 0

3. If a worker can pack $\frac{1}{6}$ of a carton of canned food in 15 minutes and there are 40 workers in a factory, how many cartons should be packed in the factory in $1\frac{2}{3}$ hours?

   (A) 33   (D) $44\frac{4}{9}$
   (B) $40\frac{2}{9}$ (E) $45\frac{2}{3}$
   (C) $43\frac{4}{9}$

4. Which of the following inequalities is the solution to the inequality $7x - 5 < 2x + 18$?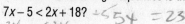

   (A) $x < \dfrac{13}{5}$ (D) $x > \dfrac{23}{5}$

   (B) $x > \dfrac{23}{9}$ (E) $x < \dfrac{23}{5}$

   (C) $x < \dfrac{23}{9}$

5. A truck driver must complete a 180-mile trip in 4 hours. If he averages 50 miles an hour for the first three hours of his trip, how fast must he travel in the final hour?

   (A) 30 mph   (D) 45 mph
   (B) 35 mph   (E) 50 mph
   (C) 40 mph

6. If a triangle has base B and the altitude of the triangle is twice the base, then the area of the triangle is

   (A) $\frac{1}{2}AB$ (D) B^2
   (B) AB (E) $2B^2$
   (C) $\frac{1}{2}B^2$

7. If the product of two numbers is 10 and the sum of the two numbers is 7, then the larger of the two numbers is

   (A) −2   (D) 4¼
   (B) 2   (E) 5
   (C) 3

8. Oranges cost $x a bag for the first 100 bags a store buys from a wholesaler. All bags bought in addition to the first 100 get a discount of 10%. How much does it cost to buy 150 bags of oranges from the wholesaler?

   (A) $100   (D) $150x
   (B) $140x   (E) $100x + $50
   (C) $145x

9. If the lengths of the two sides of a right triangle adjacent to the right angle are 8 and 15 respectively, then the length of the side opposite the right angle is

(A) $\sqrt{258}$ (D) 17
(B) 15.8   (E) 17.9
(C) 16

10. It costs x¢ each to print the first 600 copies of a newspaper. It costs $\left(x - \dfrac{y}{10}\right)$¢ for every copy after the first 600. How much does it cost to print 1,500 copies of the newspaper?

(A) 1500x¢   (D) $(150x - 9y)$
(B) 150y¢   (E) $15x$
(C) $(1,500x - 90y)$¢

11. Which of the following sets of values for w, x, y, and z respectively are possible if $ABCD$ is a parallelogram?

   I.   50, 130, 50, 130
   II. 60, 110, 70, 120
   III. 60, 150, 50, 150

(A) I only
(B) II only
(C) I and II only
(D) I and III only
(E) I, II, and III

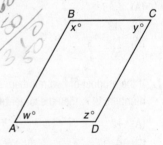

12. John weighs twice as much as Marcia. Marcia's weight is 60% of Bob's weight. Dave weighs 50% of Lee's weight. Lee weighs 190% of John's weight. Which of these 5 persons weighs the least?

(A) Bob   (D) Lee
(B) Dave   (E) Marcia
(C) John

13. The sum of 5 consecutive integers is 35. How many of the five consecutive integers are prime numbers?

(A) 0   (D) 3
(B) 1   (E) 4
(C) 2

14. Circle 1 has the same radius as circle 2. *A* is the center of circle 1, and *B* is the center of circle 2. Circle 1 and circle 2 meet only at *C*. *ACB* is a straight line segment of length 10. What is the length of *DB* if *DA* is perpendicular to *AC*?

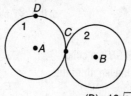

(A) 10

(B) $5\sqrt{5}$

(C) 11

(D) $10\sqrt{2}$

(E) 15

15. The assessed value of a house is $72,000. The assessed value is 60% of the market value of the house. If taxes are $3 for every $1,000 of the market value of the house, how much are the taxes on the house?

(A) $216

(B) $360

(C) $1,386

(D) $2,160

(E) $3,600

16. If the operation $*$ is defined by $*a = a^2 - 2$, then $*(*5)$ is

(A) 23

(B) 527

(C) 529

(D) 621

(E) 623

17. If $\frac{y}{x} = \frac{1}{3}$ and $x + 2y = 10$, then x is

(A) 2   (B) 3   (C) 4   (D) 5   (E) 6

18. What is the area of the parallelogram *ABCD*? $A = (1, -1)$, $B = (2, 2)$, $C = (5, 2)$, and $D = (4, -1)$.

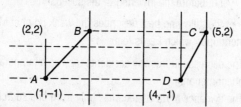

(A) 3   (B) 4   (C) $4\frac{1}{2}$ (D) 9   (E) 10

19. The area of a rectangular field is 1,000 square yards. If the length of the field is y yards, then how many yards is the perimeter of the field?

   (A) $y + 1,000/y$ (D) $2y + 1,000/y$
   (B) $2y + 1,000$ (E) $2y + 2,000/y$
   (C) $1,000$

20. The figure *ABCDEFGH* is a cube. $AB = 10$. What is the length of the line segment *AF*?

   (A) 10   (D) 20
   (B) $10\sqrt{2}$ (E) $10\sqrt{5}$
   (C) $10\sqrt{3}$

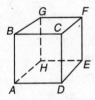

If there is still time remaining, you may review the questions in this section only. In the actual CAT GMAT, you cannot return to a question after you have confirmed your answer.

SECTION III   CRITICAL REASONING   Time: 30 minutes

Directions: For each question, choose the best answer among the listed alternatives.

1. Myra: The number of freeway accidents this year in the state of North Carolina, where the speed limit on freeways was low-ered to fifty miles an hour two years ago, is clear evidence that speed restrictions, rigorously enforced, make drivers more aware of the dangers of going too fast.

   Lewis: Wrong. A close look at the records shows that the number of freeway accidents has been falling ever since the forma-tion of a new special traffic division, which happened two years before the lowering of the speed limit.

   Which of the following best describes the weak point in Myra's statement upon which Lewis focuses?

   (A) The decrease in freeway accidents may be a temporary phenomenon.
   (B) The evidence Myra cites comes only from one source— the state of North Carolina.
   (C) Myra's claim leaves open the possibility that the cause she cites came after the effect she attributes to it.

(D)   No exact statistics for freeway accidents are given by Myra.

(E)   No mention is made of deaths caused on roads other than freeways.

2. Imagine you are a prisoner. Two prison guards, Jake and Jim, defend two doors. One door leads to death, the other to your life and freedom.

Each of the guards either always tells the truth or always lies. Both may be truth-tellers, both may be liars, or one may be a liar and the other a truth-teller.

You are allowed to choose from the following questions to discover which door leads to your release.

1. Is your comrade the same as you?
2. Are you guarding the door to life and liberty?
3. Is your comrade lying?
4. Are you telling the truth?

Which of the following combinations of questions will lead to your certain freedom?

(A)   3 to Jake, 4 to Jim, 2 to Jake.
(B)   3 to Jim, 2 to Jake, 1 to Jim.
(C)   2 to Jim, 2 to Jake, 3 to Jake.
(D)   4 to Jim, 1 to Jim, 2 to Jake.
(E)   1 to Jim, 1 to Jake, 2 to Jim.

3. The Pistons have more points than the Nuggets. The Bullets have less points than the Lakers. The Nuggets and the Suns have the same number of points. The Suns have more points than the Bullets.

If the above is true, which of the following must also be true?

(A)   The Nuggets have fewer points than the Bullets.
(B)   The Pistons have more points than the Bullets.
(C)   The Nuggets have fewer points than the Lakers.
(D)   The Lakers have more points than the Pistons.
(E)   The Lakers have more points than the Suns.

4. A train leaves New Jersey for New York every minute, all trains traveling on the same line. At the same time, and leaving at the

same one-minute intervals, trains make the journey in the opposite direction (New York to New Jersey) traveling all the time on rails parallel to the New York–bound trains. All the trains complete the 60-mile journey in exactly one hour. No other trains use these tracks.

Given the above facts, which of the following conclusions cannot be made?

(A) A train leaving New Jersey at 3 P.M. will pass the train which left New York at 3:15 P.M. after the latter has completed one quarter of its journey.

(B) The 3:30 P.M. out of New York will reach its destination before the train due to arrive in New York at 6 P.M. has left its home station.

(C) The train that leaves New York at 4 P.M. will pass 60 trains during its journey.

(D) The average speed of the train that leaves New York at 5 P.M. is 60 miles per hour.

(E) None of the above.

5. The states of New York, Ohio, Pennsylvania, and California provide extensive free higher education to their residents. These states are representative of different geographic areas of the United States. There is little reason why most states cannot provide the same service to their residents.

Which of the following, if true, would weaken the above argument?

(A) Free education is not guaranteed by the constitution.

(B) New York, Ohio, Pennsylvania, and California have more qualified high school graduates than other states.

(C) Most other states do not have the tax base that New York, Ohio, Pennsylvania, and California have.

(D) Other states do not have as many high school graduates.

(E) Quality education cannot be free; it must be paid for.

6. Professor Archibald had the task of giving grades (ranging from A–D in descending value) to his 100 students, based upon the marks they received in three examinations in which the passing mark was 50%. He is instructed to follow the following criteria:

I. All students who scored between 90 and 100% in any two examinations could receive an A grade.

II. Students that came in the top decile overall were to be awarded an A.

III. Notwithstanding I and II, if any student failed a paper, the highest he or she could get was a B.

IV. The top 20 students in the whole year, when the overall exam percentages were averaged, could receive an A.

Given the above criteria, which of the following, in the absence of further information, would definitely not be permissible?

(A) A. Brown, who got 95% in Chemistry and 92% in Biology, received a B grade.

(B) B. White, who was first in Physics and got 96% in History, received a B grade.

(C) C. Green failed English but, because he ranked ninth overall out of the 100 students, he was awarded an A grade.

(D) D. Black was given an A after he came in twentieth out of the 100 students and failed to get above 90% in any of the three examinations.

(E) E. Gray failed his Math paper, but came in top in his other two tests and was awarded a B.

7. A company, Marson Ltd., included in its annual financial statements the following note on its policy of accounting for fixed assets and depreciation:

Fixed Assets

Fixed assets are stated in the consolidated balance sheet at cost less accumulated depreciation and amortization. Depreciation is provided on all fixed assets, except land, to write off their cost in equal annual installments over the estimated economic useful lives of the assets. The cost of leasehold improvements is amortized over the term of the remaining number of years of the lease in equal annual installments.

Which of the following statements is relevant to, but not consistent with, the above accounting policy?

(A) The economic useful life of land and buildings is assumed to be 50 years, and Marson Ltd., therefore, employs a depreciation rate of 2% per annum.

(B) Marson Ltd. included in their plant inventory equipment that cost $100,000, even though this equipment is more than 10 years old and the depreciation rate on plant and machinery has been 15% for many years.

(C) Marson Ltd. spent $30,000 on improving a building, which is leased. The period of the lease was seven years, but the lease must be renewed in two years' time. Marson Ltd. provided for amortization at 50% for this year.

(D) Inventories and negotiable securities are not included in fixed assets.

(E) Amortization of other assets, e.g., goodwill, is provided separately in the financial statements.

8. "The last five Wimbledon men's singles champions have all changed to Gallenger's new tennis rackets—the only racket that uses genuine X-lon strengthened frames. In that case, isn't now the time to add power to your tennis strokes and to trade in your old racket for a Gallenger?"

Which of the following claims is not made and cannot be inferred from the above ad?

(A) Frames strengthened by X-lon are used only in Gallenger's new rackets.

(B) X-lon strengthened frames make tennis rackets stronger and allow the player to make more powerful strokes.

(C) Former Wimbledon champions know a great deal about tennis and their equipment.

(D) Gallenger tennis rackets helped the last five Wimbledon singles champions achieve their status.

(E) You will improve your tennis play with a Gallenger.

9. The fact that more and more married women are working has placed stress on marriages. The census published data showing the divorce rate for married women earning over $75,000 annually is twice the national average and four times the national average for women in the $150,000 bracket.

Which of the following, if true, would weaken the statement?

(A) Fifteen percent of married women earn over $75,000 per year.

(B) Married couples are more stressed because of their careers.

(C) When both spouses work, married couples have less time to spend together.

(D) Sixty percent of married women earn over $75,000 per year.

(E) The average divorce rate for unemployed women is 40 percent.

10. Prompted by a proposal to convert a shipyard into a complex of condominiums with a full-service marina and boat repair center and by concern about the proposal from local residents, baymen, and environmentalists, the town is considering a one-year building moratorium for the waterfront area.

Which of the following, if true, would most seriously weaken opposition to the complex?

(A) Condominiums would sell for $350,000 each.

(B) There is a large demand for boat repair services.

(C) A growing population results in the closure of shellfish.

(D) There are already 1,200 moorings on the waterfront.

(E) The shipyard may be sold for another commercial use.

11. The local education authorities in England have recently issued a "prescribed" list of books that are approved for reading in schools by children aged between 5 and 11.

A furor has arisen among many parents because an author by the name of Enid Blyton, very popular with children, has been omitted from the said list. When asked to comment on the omission, the head of the committee that was responsible for preparing the list of books said that the books of Ms. Blyton have been omitted because "we thought they are of an inferior quality and do not sufficiently stimulate the children's intellectual ability and not because they contain characters that are stereotypes or may show racial prejudice."

Which one of the following statements can be inferred from the above paragraph?

(A) Children are very angry that they will not be reading Enid Blyton in school once this decision is implemented.

(B) The parents' view is that Mrs. Blyton's books have been left off the list because some of her characters were racist.

(C) If the parents had been consulted, Enid Blyton's books would have been prescribed.

(D) The head of the deciding committee implied that Mrs. Blyton was not the only author whose books were banned.

(E) Mrs. Blyton was popular with children and parents
     because she included stereotype characters in her books.

12. A recent statement published by a prominent accounting body in the
    United States introducing new disclosure requirements in cash flow
    statements in corporate annual financial statements includes a
    paragraph stating *inter alia* the following:

    The provisions of this statement shall be effective for annual
    financial statements for fiscal years ending after July 15, 1988.
    Earlier application is encouraged. This statement need not be
    applied in financial statements for interim periods in the initial year
    of application, but cash flow information for those interim periods
    shall be restated if reported with annual financial statements for that
    fiscal year. Restatement of comparative (previous) annual financial
    statements for earlier years is encouraged but not required.

    The date is December 31, 1988. According to the above provision,
    in which one or more of the following cases, if any, is it required to
    adopt the new disclosure requirements?

    I.   Interim financial statements for seven months ended July 30,
         1988, accompanying the actual financial statements for the
         year ended December 31, 1987.
    II. Interim financial statements for the six months ended
         December 31, 1988, for a company who has a usual fiscal
         year-end of June 30.
    III. The first annual financial statements of a company for the three
         months ended December 31, 1988.

    (A) I but not II and III.
    (B) II and III but not I.
    (C) I and III but not II.
    (D) III only.
    (E) None of them.

13. Pioneers of the motor-car industry realized that if they were going to
    meet the growing demand for their product, they had to adapt the
    labor force used in the productive process. Instead of many men
    working to complete all the stages of one car at a time, they
    assigned defined tasks to each man which they would repeat on
    every car.

Which of the following can be concluded from the passage?

(A) Early motor-car manufacturers intended to increase productivity by applying the principle of division of labor.

(B) The car workers became disgruntled because they were assigned monotonous, repetitive tasks on the assembly line.

(C) Economies of scale enabled early motor companies to expand.

(D) A bad worker would perform the same task badly on each car, leading to many more rejects.

(E) The new production process enabled certain car workers to become specialists in the part of the process to which they were assigned.

14. In 1989, Japanese economic growth is expected to increase 50 times more than that of the United States.

Japanese economic policy ensures that faster growth is caused by greater investment in modern industrial plants. The initial investment leads to lower production costs, increased competitiveness, higher living standards, and low inflation.

The United States, on the other hand, is more concerned with curbing inflation and is pursuing a policy of slow growth, thus preventing investment in the modernization of American industry.

Which of the following conclusions can be drawn from the above?

(A) Slow growth prevents inflation.

(B) Slow-growth policies reduce inflation, but also decrease the efficiency and competitiveness of industry.

(C) Investment in industry causes inflation.

(D) Inflation can be reduced by increasing productivity.

(E) The U.S. must cure inflation before it can modernize and streamline its industry.

15. A pill that can induce abortions in pregnant women has become available in France. The drug, RU486, has proved more than 95% effective in tests conducted by a scientific team in Paris. The drug is an antihormone which disrupts pregnancy by blocking the implantation of a fertilized egg in the wall of the uterus. In France, the pill will be available to women who are 49 days late in their

menstrual cycle. The company that manufactures the pill, Roussel Uclaf, states, however, that the pill is not a "morning after" pill for use as a contraceptive.

Which of the following statements can be correctly deduced from the text above?

(A) The drug RU486 is a new type of contraceptive.

(B) The drug RU486 blocks egg production.

(C) The drug RU486 can be used to terminate pregnancy.

(D) The drug RU486 will replace conventional abortion techniques.

(E) The drug RU486 will only be available in France.

16. Jane and Bella are both successful women who are also members of a minority group. Jane believes in positive discrimination. She believes that if positions of power and honor are offered principally to minority groups, then these groups will begin to play a more significant role in society today.

Bella, on the other hand, feels that she has succeeded in her chosen field of work on her own merits. She thinks that positive discrimination will lower standards and decrease competition between similarly qualified personnel who will expect to achieve positions because of their minority status rather than their suitability for the particular position.

Which of the following best sums up Jane's argument?

(A) Positive discrimination will encourage more people to apply for jobs previously unavailable to them.

(B) Positive discrimination will give extra opportunities to minority groups.

(C) Quality and professionalism will improve because of the greater number of positions held by members of minority groups.

(D) Positive discrimination will ensure that each position is filled by the most suitably qualified candidate.

(E) Positive discrimination will eradicate prejudice from the work arena.

17. Many countries are facing a potential crisis in 20 to 30 years' time. The ratio of pensioners to workers will be changing drastically with

a declining birth rate, with more lengthy education of the young, and with a reduced working life. In general, the number of people paying into pension schemes is decreasing all the time. Meanwhile, with increased health care and living standards, more people are living long enough to draw their pension funds.

A controversial solution to this problem has been proposed in Germany—changing the age of retirement, for both men and women, from the current qualifying age of 63 for men and 60 for women.

A radical, but socially acceptable, solution to this problem must be found. If this is not done, it is predicted that by the year 2050, one person in three will be 65 or over and the projected work force will be unable to support pensions.

Assuming the following were all socially acceptable, which one would not improve the situation in the future?

(A) Lower the retirement age.
(B) Decrease the school-leaving age.
(C) Impose larger contributions on employees and employers.
(D) Cut pensions in half.
(E) Only give state pensions to retired persons whose income is below a certain level.

18. Before the arrival of Joe, a new partner, sales output in Bill's company, Midas In Reverse Ltd., had been rising by 10% per year on average. Innovations by Joe included computerization of technical processes and reductions in the work force, but annual sales output has only risen by 5% per year. It appears that Joe's innovations have caused the reduction in the annual growth rate.

Which of the following, if true, would most seriously weaken the conclusion above?

(A) The investment in new machinery entails a provision for depreciation of the cost of the fixed assets, which causes a reduction in profit.
(B) Midas In Reverse Ltd. does not base increases in the selling price of its products with costs.
(C) Joe's innovations were intended as long-term investment and not made for short-term profit growth.

    (D) General demand for the product manufactured by the company has declined.

    (E) Workers laid off by Midas In Reverse Ltd. have been hired by a competitor, who is taking an increasing share of the market.

19. Complete the following paragraph with the most suitable sentence. In order to boost sales of toys at times other than the peak sale time—Christmas—manufacturers use many techniques. Character toys from movies or TV series are promoted, and all sets are "collectible" by their young purchasers. Collections, however, never appear to be complete, because as soon as all the characters are acquired, the child then requires the "car," the "home," the "mobile home," and even the "airplane" to ensure a happy environment for the toys. Ultimately, the elusive final piece of the series is attained just as the manufacturer and promoter release the next series of "collectibles."

The prime aim of the manufacturer and promoter is to ensure that

    (A) all children should be happy and no child can be happy without a complete series of toys.

    (B) as soon as one set is complete or almost complete, then the next one arrives on the scene.

    (C) children should be encouraged to complete their collections of toys.

    (D) Christmas must be the peak selling period for toys.

    (E) sales are bolstered throughout the year.

20. John Wyndham Lewis, the famous sociologist, postulated that if murder is a worse crime than blackmail and blackmail is a worse crime than theft, how much more so is murder a worse crime than theft.

Which is a correct analysis of the above argument?

    (A) A case operating in one situation will also be operative in another situation, if both situations are characterized in identical terms.

    (B) A case that operates under certain conditions will surely be operative in other situations in which the same conditions are present in a more acute form.

(C) A case that clearly expresses the purpose it was meant to serve will also apply in other situations in which the identical purpose may be served.

(D) A case that begins with a generalization as to its intended application, then continues until the specification of particular cases, and then concludes with a restatement of the generalization, can be applied only to the particular cases specified.

(E) None of the above.

If there is still time remaining, you may review the questions in this section only. In the actual CAT GMAT, you cannot return to a question after you have confirmed your answer.

SECTION IV   DATA SUFFICIENCY   Time: 30 minutes

Directions: Each of the following problems has a question and two statements which are labeled (1) and (2). Use the data given in (1) and (2) together with other available information (such as the number of hours in a day, the definition of *clockwise*, mathematical facts, etc.) to decide whether the statements are *sufficient* to answer the question. Then fill in space

(A) if you can get the answer from (1) alone but not from (2) alone;

(B) if you can get the answer from (2) alone but not from (1) alone;

(C) if you can get the answer from (1) and (2) together, although neither statement by itself suffices;

(D) if statement (1) alone suffices *and* statement (2) alone suffices;

(E) if you cannot get the answer from statements (1) and (2) together, but need even more data.

All numbers used in this section are real numbers. A figure given for a problem is intended to provide information consistent with that in the question, but not necessarily with the additional information contained in the statements.

1. How many degrees Celsius is 100° Fahrenheit?

   (1) Degrees Celsius = 5/9 (degrees Fahrenheit) − 32

   (2) Degrees Fahrenheit = 9/5 (degrees Celsius) + 32

2. What is the area of the shaded part of the circle? *O* is the center of the circle.

   (1) The radius of the circle is 4.
   (2) *x* is 60.

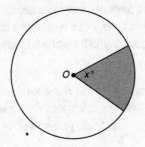

3. What was Mr. Kliman's income in 1970?

   (1) His total income for 1968, 1969, and 1970 was $41,000.
   (2) He made 20% more in 1969 than he did in 1968.

4. If *l* and *l'* are straight lines, find *y*.

   (1) *x* = 100
   (2) *z* = 80

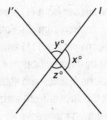

5. Fifty students have signed up for at least one of the courses German I and English I. How many of the 50 students are taking German I but not English I?

   (1) 16 students are taking German I and English I.
   (2) The number of students taking English I but not German I is the same as the number taking German I but not English I.

6. Is *ABCD* a square?

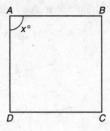

(1) $AD = AB$

(2) $x = 90$

7. The *XYZ* Corporation has 7,000 employees. What is the average yearly wage of an employee of the *XYZ* Corporation?

(1)   4,000 of the employees are executives.

(2)   The total amount the company pays in wages each year is $77,000,000.

8. Is $x > y$?

(1) $(x + y)^2 > 0$

(2) x is positive

9. What is the area of the shaded region if both circles have radius 4 and *O* and *O'* are the centers of the circles?

(1)   The area enclosed by both circles is 29π.

(2)   The line connecting *O* and *O'* is perpendicular to the line connecting *B* and *C* (*B* and *C* are the points where the two circles intersect).

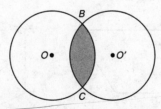

10. How long will it take to travel from *A* to *B*? It takes 4 hours to travel from *A* to *B* and back to *A*.

(1)   It takes 25% more time to travel from *A* to *B* than it does to travel from *B* to *A*.

(2)   *C* is midway between *A* and *B*, and it takes 2 hours to travel from *A* to *C* and back to *A*.

11. l, l', and k are straight lines. Are l and l' parallel?

   (1) $x = y$

   (2) $y = z$

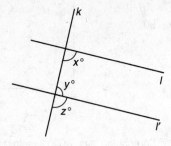

12. What is $x + y + z$?

   (1) $x + y = 3$

   (2) $x + z = 2$

13. How much cardboard will it take to make a rectangular box with a lid whose base is 7 inches long?

   (1) The width of the box will be 5 inches.

   (2) The height of the box will be 4 inches.

14. If a, b, and c are digits, is $a + b + c$ a multiple of 8? A digit is one of the integers 0, 1, 2, 3, 4, 5, 6, 7, 8, 9.

   (1) The three-digit number abc is a multiple of 8.

   (2) $a \times b \times c$ is a multiple of 8.

15. Which of the two figures, *ABCD* or *EFGH*, has the largest area?

   (1) The perimeter of *ABCD* is longer than the perimeter of *EFGH*.

   (2) *AC* is longer than *EG*.

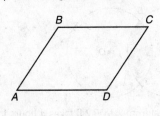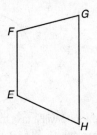

16. Is a number divisible by 9?

   (1) The number is divisible by 3.

   (2) The number is divisible by 27.

17. *PQRS* is a rectangle. The coordinates of the point *P* are (2,3). What is the area of *PQRS*?

   (1) The coordinates of the point *S* are (2,5).
   (2) The coordinates of the point *Q* are (6,3).

18. *ABCD* is a rectangle. Which region, *ABEF* or *CDFE*, has a larger area?

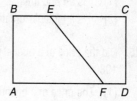

   (1) *BE* is longer than *FD*.
   (2) *BE* is longer than *CD*.

19. Is the integer *k* odd or even?

   (1) k^2 is odd.
   (2) $2k$ is even.

20. Is *x* positive?

   (1) $x^2 + 3x - 4 = 0$
   (2) $x > -2$

21. *ABCD* is a square. *BCO* is a semicircle. What is the area of *ABOCD*?

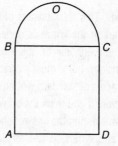

   (1) The length of *AC* is $4\sqrt{2}$.
   (2) The radius of the semicircle *BOC* is 2.

22. Do the points *P* and *Q* lie on the same circle with center (0,0)?

   (1) The coordinates of point *P* are (2,3).
   (2) The coordinates of point *Q* are (4,1).

          • *P*

             • *Q*

      •
    (0,0)

23. Did ABC Company make a profit in 1980?

    (1) ABC Company made a profit in 1979.

    (2) ABC Company made a profit in 1981.

24. Is 2^n divisible by 8?

    (1) n is an odd integer.

    (2) n is an integer greater than 5.

25. Did the price of a bushel of soybeans increase during every week of 1980?

    (1) The price of a bushel of soybeans was $2 on January 1, 1980.

    (2) The price of a bushel of soybeans was $4 on January 1, 1981.

If there is still time remaining, you may review the questions in this section only. In the actual CAT GMAT, you cannot return to a question after you have confirmed your answer.

SECTION V   SENTENCE CORRECTION   Time: 30 minutes

Directions: This test consists of a number of sentences, in each of which some part or the whole is underlined. Each sentence is followed by five alternative versions of the underlined portion. Select the alternative you consider both most correct and most effective according to the requirements of standard written English. Answer A is the same as the original version; if you think the original version is best, select answer A.

In considering the answer choices, be attentive to matters of grammar, diction, and syntax, as well as clarity, precision, and fluency. Do not select an answer that alters the meaning of the original sentence.

1. <u>If we cooperate together by dividing up the work</u>, we shall be able to finish it quickly.

    (A) If we cooperate together by dividing up the work

    (B) If we cooperate by dividing up the work

    (C) If we cooperate together by dividing the work

    (D) If we cooperate dividing up the work together

    (E) If we cooperate by dividing the work

2. <u>I think he approves my choice despite the fact I differ with him,</u>
<u>granted the generation gap between us.</u>

(A) I think he approves my choice despite the fact I differ with him,
granted the generation gap between us.

(B) Granted the generation gap between us, I think he approves my
choice despite the fact I differ with him.

(C) Despite the fact I differ with him, I think he approves my
choice, granted the generation gap between us.

(D) Despite the fact I differ with him, I think, granted the generation
gap between us, he approves my choice.

(E) Granted the generation gap between us, despite the fact that I
differ with him, I think he approves my choice.

3. The vacationers <u>enjoyed swimming in the pool, bathing in the</u>
<u>ocean, and, particularly, to snorkel</u> near the reef.

(A) enjoyed swimming in the pool, bathing in the ocean, and,
particularly, to snorkel

(B) enjoyed swimming in the pool, to bathe in the ocean, and,
particularly, to snorkel

(C) enjoyed swimming in the pool, to bathe in the ocean, and,
particularly snorkeling

(D) enjoyed swimming in the pool, bathing in the ocean, and,
particularly, snorkeling

(E) enjoyed to swim in the pool, to bathe in the ocean, and,
particularly, to snorkel

4. <u>Crossing the street, a car almost struck us.</u>

(A) Crossing the street, a car almost struck us.

(B) A car almost struck us, crossing the street.

(C) As we crossed the street, a car almost struck us.

(D) A car, crossing the street, almost struck us.

(E) Having crossed the street, a car almost struck us.

5. <u>The theme of this novel is how money doesn't make you happy.</u>

(A) The theme of this novel is how money doesn't make you happy.

(B) The theme of this novel is that money doesn't make you happy.

(C) In this novel, its theme is how money doesn't make you happy.

(D) In this novel, that money doesn't make you happy is the theme.

(E) In this novel, you are not made happy by money is the theme.

6. If some Americans <u>look at where they are going, it can be seen that our goal</u> is money.

    (A) look at where they are going, it can be seen that our goal

    (B) look back at where they are going, they see that their goal

    (C) look ahead to where they are going, it can be seen that their goal

    (D) look at where they are going, they can see our goal

    (E) look ahead to where they are going, they can see their goal

7. <u>Mary, a girl with little talent for cooking, enjoys preparing</u> pizza.

    (A) Mary, a girl with little talent for cooking, enjoys preparing

    (B) Mary is a girl who has little talent for cooking who enjoys to prepare

    (C) Mary is a girl with little talent for cooking and who enjoys preparing

    (D) Mary, who has little talent for cooking, enjoys to prepare

    (E) With little talent for cooking, Mary is a girl who enjoys to prepare

8. <u>My grandmother is the most remarkable person of all the persons I have ever met.</u>

    (A) My grandmother is the most remarkable person of all the persons I have ever met.

    (B) Of all the persons I have ever met, my grandmother is the most remarkable person.

    (C) Of all the persons I have ever met, the most remarkable person is my grandmother.

    (D) Of all the persons I have ever met, the most remarkable is my grandmother.

    (E) My grandmother, of all the persons I have ever met, is the most remarkable.

9. <u>Start the motor, and then you should remove the blocks.</u>

    (A) Start the motor, and then you should remove the blocks.

    (B) Start the motor and then remove the blocks.

    (C) Start the motor, then removing the blocks.

    (D) Start the motor, and then the blocks should be removed.

    (E) Starting the motor, the blocks should then be removed.

10. <u>He is a genius, although he is eccentric and wants recognition.</u>

   (A) He is a genius, although he is eccentric and wants recognition.
   (B) Although he is eccentric, he is a genius and wants recognition.
   (C) Although he is eccentric, he is a genius although he wants recognition.
   (D) His is a genius although he is eccentric and although he wants recognition.
   (E) Although he is eccentric and wants recognition, he is a genius.

11. <u>Every creditor feels that their claim is the most important thing</u> in the world.

   (A) Every creditor feels that their claim is the most important thing
   (B) Every creditor feels that his claim is the most important thing
   (C) Each and every creditor feels that their claim is the most important thing
   (D) Every creditor feels that their claims are the most important things
   (E) Every creditor feels that his claim is the more important thing

12. <u>The smaller firms sold either on a price or quality-of-workmanship basis.</u>

   (A) The smaller firms sold either on a price or quality-of-workmanship basis.
   (B) The smaller firms either sold on a price or quality-of-workmanship basis.
   (C) The smaller firms sold on either a price or a quality-of-workmanship basis.
   (D) The smaller firms sold on either a price or on a quality-of-workmanship basis.
   (E) Either the smaller firms sold on a price or on a quality-of-workmanship basis.

13. The matter was <u>referred back to committee since the solution to the problem was different from the one proposed earlier which was not practicable.</u>

   (A) referred back to committee since the solution to the problem was different from the one proposed earlier which was not practicable.

    (B) referred to committee since the solution to the problem was different from the one proposed earlier which was not practicable.

    (C) referred back to committee since the solution to the problem was different than the one proposed earlier which was not practical.

    (D) referred to committee since the solution to the problem was different than the one proposed earlier which was not practicable.

    (E) referred back to committee since the solution to the problem was different from the one proposed earlier which was not practical.

14. <u>Irregardless of the consequences, the police officer was forbidden from making any pinches.</u>

    (A) Irregardless of the consequences, the police officer was forbidden from making any pinches.

    (B) Irregardless of the consequences, the police officer was forbidden from making any arrests.

    (C) Regardless of the consequences, the police officer was forbidden from making any arrests.

    (D) Irregardless of the consequences, the police officer was forbidden to make any pinches.

    (E) Regardless of the consequences, the police officer was forbidden to make any arrests.

15. <u>The book having been read carefully and extensive notes having been taken, Tom</u> felt confident about the test.

    (A) The book having been read carefully and extensive notes having been taken, Tom

    (B) Tom, who read the book carefully and having taken extensive notes,

    (C) Reading the book carefully and taking extensive notes, Tom

    (D) Having read the book carefully and extensive notes having been taken, Tom

    (E) Because he had read the book carefully and had taken extensive notes, Tom

16. He has <u>not only violated the law, but also he has escaped punishment.</u>

    (A) not only violated the law, but also he has escaped punishment.

(B) violated not only the law, but also he has escaped punishment.

(C) violated not only the law, but he has escaped punishment also.

(D) not only violated the law, but also escaped punishment.

(E) not only violated the law, but has escaped punishment.

17. Ideally, <u>the fan should be placed in a different room than</u> the one you want to cool.

    (A) the fan should be placed in a different room than

    (B) the fan had ought to be placed in a different room from

    (C) the fan should be placed in a different room from

    (D) the fan had ought to be placed in a different room than

    (E) you should place the fan in a different room than

18. After viewing both movies, <u>John agreed that the first one was the best of the two.</u>

    (A) John agreed that the first one was the best of the two.

    (B) John agreed that the first was the best of the two.

    (C) John agreed that the first one was the better of the two.

    (D) John agreed that of the two the better one was the first.

    (E) John agreed that the best of the two was the first.

19. Poor product quality angers Bob, <u>who wonders if it is part of a strategy by manufacturers.</u>

    (A) who wonders if it is part of a strategy by manufacturers.

    (B) who wonders if manufacturers are part of the strategy.

    (C) that wonders if it is part of a strategy by manufacturers.

    (D) wondering if this is part of a strategy by manufacturers.

    (E) who wonders if they are part of a strategy by manufacturers.

20. He noted <u>the dog's soft hair, strong legs, and keen sense of smell.</u>

    (A) the dog's soft hair, strong legs, and keen sense of smell.

    (B) the dog's soft hair, strong legs, and that his sense of smell was keen.

    (C) the dog's soft hair, and that his legs were strong and sense of smell was keen.

    (D) the dog's soft hair, and that his legs were strong and smell was keen.

    (E) the dog's soft hair, keen smell and that his legs were strong.

21. Because of production cutbacks caused by termination of government contracts, the management announces that the services of some personnel will be dispensed with effective immediately.

   (A) Because of production cutbacks caused by termination of government contracts, the management announces that the services of some personnel will be dispensed with effective immediately.

   (B) Because of decreased production caused by loss of government contracts, the management announces the immediate firing of some personnel.

   (C) Because of loss of government contracts causing lower production, the management will have to dispense with some personnel immediately.

   (D) Because of reduced production caused by the end of government contracts, some personnel will be dismissed immediately.

   (E) The services of some personnel will be dispensed with immediately because of production cutbacks and the end of government contracts.

22. Having bowed our heads, the minister led us in prayer.

   (A) Having bowed our heads, the minister led

   (B) After we bowed our heads, the minister led

   (C) After we bowed our heads, the minister leads

   (D) After we had bowed our heads, the minister led

   (E) Having bowed our heads, the minister leads

23. She seldom ever wants to try and face the true facts.

   (A) seldom ever wants to try and face the true facts.

   (B) seldom ever wants to try and face the facts.

   (C) seldom ever wants to try to face the facts.

   (D) seldom wants to try and face the facts.

   (E) seldom wants to try to face the facts.

24. The new legislation also provides $5 billion to finance solar energy projects and for conservation measures.

   (A) also provides $5 billion to finance solar energy projects and for conservation measures.

(B)   provides also $5 billion to finance solar energy projects and for conservation measures.

(C)   also provides $5 billion in order to finance solar energy projects and for conservation measures.

(D)   also provides $5 billion to finance solar energy projects and to carry out conservation measures.

(E)   provides $5 billion for financing solar energy projects and to carry out conservation measures.

25.   The president's talk <u>was directed toward whomever was present.</u>

(A)   was directed toward whomever was present.

(B)   was directed toward whoever was present.

(C)   was directed at who was present.

(D)   was directed at whomever was present.

(E)   was directed towards whomever was present.

If there is still time remaining, you may review the questions in this section only. In the actual CAT GMAT, you cannot return to a question after you have confirmed your answer.

SECTION VI   PROBLEM SOLVING   Time: 30 minutes

Directions: Solve each of the following problems; then indicate the correct answer on the answer sheet. [On the actual test you will be permitted to use scratch paper for your calculations.]

NOTE: A figure that appears with a problem is drawn as accurately as possible so as to provide information that may help in answering the question. Numbers in this test are real numbers.

1.   If the side of a square increases by 40%, then the area of the square increases by

(A)   16%   (D)   116%

(B)   40%   (E)   140%

(C)   96%

2. If 28 cans of soda cost $21.00, then 7 cans of soda should cost

(A) $5.25   (D) $7.00
(B) $5.50   (E) $10.50
(C) $6.40

3. Plane *P* takes off at 2 A.M. and flies at a constant speed of *x* mph. Plane *Q* takes off at 3:30 A.M. and flies the same route as *P* but travels at a constant speed of *y* mph. Assuming that *y* is greater than *x*, how many hours after 3:30 A.M. will plane *Q* overtake plane *P*?

(A) $\dfrac{3}{2}x$ hrs.   (D) $\dfrac{3}{2(y-x)}$ hrs.

(B) $\dfrac{3}{2}$ hrs.   (E) $\dfrac{3x}{2(y-x)}$ hrs.

(C) $\dfrac{3}{2y}$ hrs.

4. A worker is paid $20 for each day he works, and he is paid proportionately for any fraction of a day he works. If during one week he works $\frac{1}{8}$, $\frac{2}{3}$, $\frac{3}{4}$, $\frac{1}{3}$, and 1 full day, what are his total earnings for the week?

(A) $40.75   (D) $57.50
(B) $52.50   (E) $58.25
(C) $54

Use the following table for questions 5–6.

DISTRIBUTION OF TEST SCORES IN A CLASS

Number of Students	*Number of Correct Answers*
10	36 to 40
16	32 to 35
12	28 to 31
14	26 to 27
8	0 to 25

5. What percent of the class answered 32 or more questions correctly?

(A) $16\frac{2}{3}$ (D) $43\frac{1}{3}$
(B) 20   (E) 52
(C) $26\frac{2}{3}$

6. The number of students who answered 28 to 31 questions correctly is x times the number who answered 25 or fewer correctly, where x is

(A) $\frac{2}{3}$

(B) 1

(C) $\frac{3}{2}$

(D) $\frac{7}{4}$

(E) 2

7. If the product of 3 consecutive integers is 210, then the sum of the two smaller integers is

(A) 5

(B) 11

(C) 12

(D) 13

(E) 18

8. Cereal costs $\frac{1}{3}$ as much as bacon. Bacon costs $\frac{5}{4}$ as much as eggs. Eggs cost what fraction of the cost of cereal?

(A) $\frac{5}{12}$

(B) $\frac{4}{5}$

(C) $\frac{5}{4}$

(D) $\frac{5}{3}$

(E) $\frac{12}{5}$

9. A truck gets 15 miles per gallon of gas when it is unloaded. When the truck is loaded, it travels only 80% as far on a gallon of gas as when unloaded. How many gallons will the loaded truck use to travel 80 miles?

(A) $5\frac{1}{3}$

(B) 6

(C) $6\frac{1}{3}$

(D) $6\frac{2}{3}$

(E) $6\frac{3}{4}$

10. If x and y are negative numbers, which of the following statements is (are) always true?

  I. $x - y$ is negative

  II. $-x$ is positive

  III. $(-x)(-y)$ is positive

(A) I only

(B) II only

(C) I and II only

(D) II and III only

(E) I and III only

11. Both circles have radius 4 and the area enclosed by both circles is 28π. What is the area of the shaded region?

(A) 0
(B) 2π
(C) 4π
(D) 4π²
(E) 16π

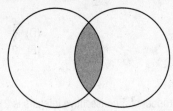

12. For each dollar spent by the sales department, the research department spends 20¢. For every $4 spent by the research department, the packing department spends $1.50. The triple ratio of the money spent by the sales department to the money spent by the research department to the money spent by the packing department can be expressed as

(A) 40 : 8 : 3   (D) 4 : 1 : 5
(B) 20 : 4 : 1   (E) 2 : 1 : 5
(C) 8 : 4 : 1

13. *ABCD* has area equal to 28. *BC* is parallel to *AD*. *BA* is perpendicular to *AD*. If *BC* is 6 and *AD* is 8, then what is *CD*?

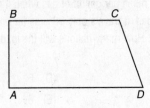

(A) $2\sqrt{2}$ (D) $2\sqrt{5}$
(B) $2\sqrt{3}$ (E) 6
(C) 4

14. A manufacturer prints books at a cost of $*x* each for the first thousand copies printed. The second thousand copies printed cost $.9*x* each. If it costs $3,264 to print 1,400 copies of a book, then *x* is

(A) 1.63   (D) 2.40
(B) 2.10   (E) 2.59
(C) 2.33

15. If X is an odd integer and Y is an even integer, which of the following statements is (are) always true?

   I. $X + Y$ is odd.

   II. XY is odd.

   III. $2X + Y$ is even.

(A) I only   (D) II and III only

(B) III only   (E) I, II, and III

(C) I and III only

16. Find the area of the region inside the circle and outside the square *ABCD*. *A*, *B*, *C*, and *D* are all points on the circle, and the radius of the circle is 4.

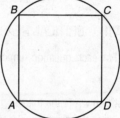

(A) $16\pi - 36$

(B) $16(\pi - 2)$

(C) $16(\pi - 1)$

(D) $16\pi - 4$

(E) 16π

17. **X* is defined as the largest integer which is less than *X*. What is the value of $(^{*}3) + (^{*}4) + (^{*}4.5)$?

(A) 9   (D) 11.5

(B) 10   (E) 12

(C) 11

18. Joan started work 2 years ago. Her starting salary was one-half of Mike's salary at that time. Each year since then Joan has received a raise of 5% in her salary and Mike has received a raise of 10% in his salary. What percentage (to the nearest percent) of Mike's current salary is Joan's current salary?

(A) 45   (D) 50

(B) 46   (E) 220

(C) 48

19. Which of the following integers has the most divisors?

(A) 88   (D) 99

(B) 91   (E) 101

(C) 95

20. The amount of fat in an ounce of food A plus the amount of protein in an ounce of food A is 100 grams. The amount of protein in an ounce of food A minus twice the amount of fat in an ounce of food A is 10 grams. How many grams of protein are there in an ounce of food A?

(A) 30   (D) 55
(B) 45   (E) 70
(C) 50

If there is still time remaining, you may review the questions in this section only. In the actual CAT GMAT, you cannot return to a question after you have confirmed your answer.

SECTION VII   CRITICAL REASONING   Time: 30 minutes

Directions: For each question, choose the best answer among the listed alternatives.

1. A politician wrote the following: "I realize there are some short-comings to the questionnaire method. However, since I send a copy of the questionnaire to every home in the district, I believe the results are quite representative...I think the numbers received are so large that it is quite accurate even though the survey is not done scientifically."

The writer of the above statement makes which of the following assumptions:

(A) Most people who received the questionnaire have replied.
(B) Most people in the district live in homes.
(C) The questionnaire method of data collection is unscientific.
(D) The large number of replies means that a high proportion of those sampled have replied.
(E) A large, absolute number of replies is synonymous with accuracy.

2. In 1970, Transylvania earned $1 million in tourist revenue. By 1990, tourist revenue doubled, and in 2000 it reached the sum of $4 million.

Each of the following, if true, may explain the trend in tourist revenue EXCEPT:

(A) The number of tourists has increased from 1970 to 2000.

(B) Average expenditure per tourist has increased.

(C) Average stay per tourist has increased.

(D) The number of total hotel rooms has increased.

(E) The average price of tourist services has increased.

3. Donors are almost never offended by being asked for too much (in fact, they are usually flattered). And if you ask for too much, your donor can always suggest a smaller amount. On the other hand, donors are frequently offended by being asked for too little. A common reaction is "So that's all they think I'm worth."

The above statement assumes that:

(A) Donors are usually never asked enough.

(B) A good fund-raiser will value the worth of the donor.

(C) It is worth the gamble to ask for large donations.

(D) Fund-raisers often think that donors are incapable of giving much.

(E) Donors are seldom offended by fund-raisers.

4. One major obligation of the social psychologist is to provide his own discipline, the other social sciences, and interested laymen with conceptual tools that will increase the range and the reliability of their understanding of social phenomena. Beyond that, responsible government officials are today turning more frequently to the social scientist for insights into the nature and solution of the problems with which they are confronted.

The above argument assumes that:

(A) Social psychologists must have a strong background in other sciences as well as their own.

(B) A study of social psychology should be a part of the curriculum of government officials.

(C) The social scientist has an obligation to provide the means by which social phenomena may be understood by others.

(D) Social phenomena are little understood by those outside the field of social psychology.

(E) A good social psychologist is obligated principally by the need to solve interdisciplinary problems.

5. New problems require new solutions. And new problems arise with new populations and new technologies. The solutions of these problems require new institutions as well as new political, economic, and social mechanisms. Yet institutions and political and economic arrangements grow slowly and die slowly. Because old institutions die slowly, new institutions should be given every chance of success.

   The writer of the above makes which of the following assumptions:

   (A) New institutions are needed because old institutions are inefficient.
   (B) New institutions are created in order to solve existing problems.
   (C) As old institutions are phased out, new ones take their place.
   (D) If there were no growth, old institutions would die more slowly.
   (E) Sociotechnological change requires new forms of institutional arrangements.

6. About 40 percent of American husbands think it is a good idea for wives with school-age children to work outside the home. Only one out of ten German household heads approves of mothers working if school-age children live at home. Every second American wife and every third German wife with school-age children has a job outside her home.

   If the above is correct, which of the following must be true?

   (A) More German than American wives work outside the home.
   (B) Employment opportunities for American wives are greater than for German wives.
   (C) German husbands have more conservative attitudes than American husbands.
   (D) German husbands would seem to be less satisfied about working wives who have school-age children than American husbands.
   (E) German women have fewer children than American women.

7. Building codes required all public buildings constructed after 1980 to have reinforced-steel bomb shelters installed.

   From which of the following can the statement above be inferred?

(A) Public buildings had to install reinforced-steel bomb shelters after 1980.

(B) No bomb shelters other than reinforced-steel shelters were installed in public buildings after 1980, but all public buildings constructed after 1980 were required to have bomb shelters.

(C) Some public buildings constructed before 1980 had installed bomb shelters.

(D) Bomb shelters were not required in public buildings before 1980, but some were installed voluntarily.

(E) Before 1980, public buildings had bomb shelters, but not necessarily made of reinforced-steel.

8. In 1950, the average child visited the dentist once a year; by 1970, the number of visits had increased to two. Today, the average child visits the dentist three times a year.

Each of the following, if true, could explain this trend EXCEPT:

(A) Dentist fees have declined over the period.

(B) Better home care of teeth has reduced the number of cavities.

(C) Dental care has become less painful.

(D) Parents are more aware of the importance of dental care.

(E) Tax benefits for deducting dental expenses have increased.

9. Attention is most often focused on net exports (exports less imports) because that figure measures the net effect of a nation's trade in goods and services with the rest of the world. In 1968, net exports were 5.8 percent of GNP (Gross National Product), and in 1975 they were 6.8 percent.

If the information above is accurate, which of the following must be true?

(A) If GNP was constant from 1968 to 1975, net exports were greater in 1975 than in 1968.

(B) Exports were greater than imports in 1975, but not in 1968.

(C) Exports increased from 1968 to 1975.

(D) In 1975, the increase in exports was nearly double that in 1968.

(E) In 1968, net exports were greater than in 1975.

10. Once a company has established an extensive sales network in a foreign market and therefore has achieved substantial sales, it

seems that these markets should be treated in a very similar fashion to those in one's own country. It is therefore those countries where only initial sales and representation have been developed where marketing methods will have to differ from domestic activities.

The above statement assumes that:

(A) Sales networks can be the same in both foreign and domestic markets.

(B) Extensive sales networks are preferable to less developed ones.

(C) Some countries develop economically faster than others.

(D) Larger markets abroad are more adaptable to domestic marketing methods.

(E) A study of marketing should consider the adaptability of advertising campaigns in different countries.

11. The principal monetary policy objective is to reduce substantially the import surplus of the coming years while resuming economic growth. Realization of this goal entails a marked structural change of the economy, which can be brought about by freezing the standard of living (per capita private consumption plus public services) and restricting investments that do not further exports.

The writer of the above policy assumes that:

(A) Economic growth will result in a structural change of the economy.

(B) Only if people consume less can the economy grow.

(C) The import surplus can be reduced if investment is restricted.

(D) Only a structural change in the economy can substantially increase imports.

(E) People will have to be persuaded to give up consumption for the national good.

12. The most commonly cited explanation for nationalization of foreign companies is a change in government. Nationalization tends to cover a wide range of industries and is not selective by country of ownership.

The above statement assumes that:

(A) Defense-related, government-related, and natural resource industries are most likely to be nationalized.

(B) The process of nationalization is not limited to any particular industry or country.

(C) Nationalization of businesses is so widespread as to cause concern.

(D) Nationalization will not occur in countries with democratic governments.

(E) Sharing ownership with local nationals will forestall takeovers by foreign governments.

13. Equality of opportunity has long been prominent as a goal in many countries. In Europe and America there has also been advocacy of more equality of income—the results after taxes of what a person gets for his efforts and the yield of his property. Many western politicians believe this concept of equality should be implemented in developing countries in order to speed economic development.

    Which of the following, if true, could weaken the argument above?

    (A) In a poor society, total income is so low that if it were distributed equally, no one could save enough to provide resources for investment.

    (B) Very large incomes may cause social dissension.

    (C) The marginal dollars in the hands of people with large incomes provide less utility than those with lower incomes.

    (D) High achievement in many societies is due to equality of incomes.

    (E) Equality of opportunity is not necessarily synonymous with equality of income.

14. The balance of trade (i.e., exports minus imports) for most countries is calculated on a yearly basis, divided into quarters. A favorable balance is indicated by export revenue greater than import costs. The terms of trade, i.e., the ratio of export to import prices, is also calculated on a yearly basis. A ratio of 100 means that aggregate export earnings just equal aggregate import costs. Favorable terms are indicated by a ratio of more than 100. Euphoria's balance of trade worsened between 1980 and 1981, and its terms of trade deteriorated.

    If the above conditions are accurate, which of the following must be true?

- (A) Euphoria paid more for aggregate imports in 1981 than in 1980.
- (B) Between 1980 and 1981, Euphoria imported more than it exported, and paid more for its exports than it paid for its imports.
- (C) Between 1980 and 1981, Euphoria exported more than it imported and earned more from its exports than it paid for its imports.
- (D) Between 1980 and 1981, Euphoria exported more than it imported, but paid more for its imports than it earned from its exports.
- (E) Euphoria earned more from aggregate exports in 1981 than in 1980.

15. A recent communique noted that China's foreign minister told officials in Italy that Beijing intends to maintain and extend its open-door policy to the West. The minister also said that China would continue with its program of political and economic changes despite a recent campaign against Western ideas and foreign aid.

The writer of the communique above makes which of the following assumptions?

- (A) China's foreign minister asserts that internal change is a matter for only the Chinese to decide.
- (B) Internal political and economic changes will not be tolerated.
- (C) China's external relations with the West will continue despite turmoil at home.
- (D) Internal changes in China will not follow Western models although foreign trade between them may continue.
- (E) China's foreign minister does not realize that an open-door policy and rejection of Western ideas are mutually exclusive.

16. In 1985, there were 20 deaths from automobile accidents per 1,000 miles traveled. A total of 20,000 miles were traveled via automobiles in 1985. In the same year, 800 people died in airplane crashes and 400 people were killed in train disasters. A statistician concluded from these data alone that it was more dangerous to travel by plane, train, and automobile, in that order.

Which of the following refutes the statistician's conclusion?

- (A) There is no common denominator by which to compare the number of deaths resulting from each mode of travel.
- (B) One year is insufficient to reach such a conclusion.

(C) More people travel by car than any other mode of transport; therefore, the probability of a car accident is greater.
(D) The number of plane flights and train trips is not stated.
(E) The probability of being killed in a train disaster and as a result of a car crash is the same.

17. From a letter to the commercial editor of a newspaper: Your article of January 9 drew attention to the large deficit in Playland's balance of payments that has worsened over the past three years. Yet, you favor the recent trade treaty signed between Playland and Workland. That treaty results in a lowering of our import duties that will flood us with Workland's goods. This will only exacerbate our balance of trade. How can you be in favor of the treaty?

Which of the following considerations would weaken the letter writer's argument?

(A) Import diversion versus import creation
(B) Prices paid by importers versus prices paid by consumers
(C) Economic goals versus political goals
(D) Duties levied increase government revenue
(E) Free trade versus protectionism

18. In 1930, there were, on the average, 10 deaths at birth (infant mortality) per 10,000 population. By 1940 there were 8.5, and by 1950, 7.0. Today there are 5.5 deaths at birth per 10,000 population, and it is anticipated that the downward trend will continue.

Each of the following, if true, would help to account for this trend EXCEPT:

(A) Medical care is more widespread and available.
(B) More effective birth control methods have been implemented.
(C) Sanitary conditions have improved.
(D) The number of pediatricians per 10,000 population has increased.
(E) Midwifery has declined in favor of medical doctors.

19. Product shipments of household appliances are expected to rise to $17 billion next year, an average annual increase of 8.0 percent over the past five years. The real growth rate, after allowing for probable price increases, is expected to be about 4.3 percent each year, resulting in shipments this year of $14 billion in 1987 dollars.

Each of the following, if true, could help to account for this trend EXCEPT:

(A) Increased consumer spending for durable products.

(B) Household formations have increased.

(C) Consumer disposable income has increased.

(D) The consumer price of electricity has decreased.

(E) Individual tax advantages have decreased.

20. Each year's increase or decrease in the trade deficit (merchandise imports greater than exports) is calculated in relation to the previous year's. In 1976, imports of private vehicles were 10 percent higher than in 1975, while imports of vehicles including commercial vans was 15 percent higher than in 1975. That 15 percent increase was one and a half times the increase recorded in 1975.

If the information above is accurate, which of the following must be true?

(A) In 1976, the increase, if any, of commercial vehicle imports was smaller than the increase in imports of private vehicles.

(B) In 1976, the increase, if any, of commercial vehicle imports was greater than the increase in imports of private vehicles.

(C) In 1975, more commercial vehicles were imported than private vehicles.

(D) In 1975, more private vehicles were imported than commercial vehicles.

(E) The average number of private vehicles imported in 1975 declined.

ANSWERS

Section I   Reading Comprehension

1. (C)	8. (E)	15. (A)	22. (D)
2. (C)	9. (B)	16. (E)	23. (C)
3. (D)	10. (B)	17. (A)	24. (E)
4. (C)	11. (A)	18. (C)	25. (E)
5. (C)	12. (D)	19. (D)	
6. (B)	13. (C)	20. (D)	
7. (A)	14. (D)	21. (E)	

Section II   Problem Solving

1. (B)	6. (D)	11. (A)	16. (B)
2. (B)	7. (E)	12. (E)	17. (E)
3. (D)	8. (C)	13. (C)	18. (D)
4. (E)	9. (D)	14. (B)	19. (E)
5. (A)	10. (C)	15. (B)	20. (C)

Section III   Critical Reasoning

1. (C)	6. (C)	11. (D)	16. (B)
2. (E)	7. (A)	12. (D)	17. (A)
3. (B)	8. (D)	13. (A)	18. (D)
4. (C)	9. (A)	14. (B)	19. (E)
5. (C)	10. (E)	15. (C)	20. (B)

Section IV   Data Sufficiency

1. (D)	8. (E)	15. (E)	22. (C)
2. (C)	9. (A)	16. (B)	23. (E)
3. (E)	10. (A)	17. (C)	24. (B)
4. (D)	11. (C)	18. (A)	25. (E)
5. (C)	12. (E)	19. (A)	
6. (E)	13. (C)	20. (C)	
7. (B)	14. (E)	21. (D)	

Section V   Sentence Correction

1. (E)	8. (D)	15. (E)	22. (D)
2. (E)	9. (B)	16. (D)	23. (E)
3. (D)	10. (E)	17. (C)	24. (D)
4. (C)	11. (B)	18. (C)	25. (B)
5. (B)	12. (C)	19. (A)	
6. (E)	13. (B)	20. (A)	
7. (A)	14. (E)	21. (D)	

Section VI   Problem Solving

1. (C)	6. (C)	11. (C)	16. (B)
2. (A)	7. (B)	12. (A)	17. (A)
3. (E)	8. (E)	13. (D)	18. (B)
4. (D)	9. (D)	14. (D)	19. (A)
5. (D)	10. (D)	15. (C)	20. (E)

Section VII   Critical Reasoning

1. **(E)**	6. **(D)**	11. **(E)**	16. **(A)**
2. **(D)**	7. **(B)**	12. **(B)**	17. **(A)**
3. **(C)**	8. **(B)**	13. **(A)**	18. **(B)**
4. **(C)**	9. **(A)**	14. **(B)**	19. **(E)**
5. **(E)**	10. **(D)**	15. **(D)**	20. **(A)**

ANALYSIS

Section I   Reading Comprehension

1. **(C)** See paragraph 2, line 1.
2. **(C)** See paragraph 1, sentence 2: "His maturer theories of society…"
3. **(D)** See paragraph 1: "…he ended life as a major social theorist… sympathetic with violent revolution…"
4. **(C)** See paragraph 3: "…Russia…is no longer a proletarian movement…but a camouflaged imperialistic effort…"
5. **(C)** See paragraph 3. Of course, it is accepted by those in (D) and (E), but also by those in (C).
6. **(B)** This can be deduced from the last paragraph.
7. **(A)** See paragraph 2.
8. **(E)** All these are mentioned in paragraph 1.
9. **(B)** See paragraph 1: "…fiscal policies should be designed to encourage economic growth."
10. **(B)** See paragraph 1: they did not.
11. **(A)** See paragraph 2: the Committee of the Whole.
12. **(D)** See paragraph 3, line 1.
13. **(C)** See paragraph 4: "In the first decade of the twentieth century, an 'executive budget' came into successful use…"
14. **(D)** See paragraph 4: it was rejected.
15. **(A)** See paragraph 5, line 1: the responsibility was given by the Budget and Accounting Act of 1921.
16. **(E)** See paragraph 5: the Director of the Bureau of the Budget serves for an indefinite term.
17. **(A)** See paragraph 1.
18. **(C)** See paragraph 1: they came at different times.
19. **(D)** See paragraph 1.
20. **(D)** Paragraphs 1 and 3 especially mention the various points of migration which the Indians reached.

21. **(E)** See paragraph 3.
22. **(D)** See paragraph 2: "...the New Mexico Indians were very success-
    ful big game hunters."
23. **(C)** See the last line of paragraph 3.
24. **(E)** All these are given in paragraph 2.
25. **(E)** Certainly, alternatives (A) and (C) do not correspond to the con-
    tents of the passage, while (B) and (D) are too general. The pas-
    sage is mainly about the migration of Indians, their cultures, and
    their acclimation to new surroundings. These subjects are in the
    domain of the anthropologist.

Section II   Problem Solving

1. **(B)** Let T be the total amount needed for the building and let L be the
   total number of people the college will ask for donations. Then
   there are $.4L$ people left to give donations and they must donate a
   total of $.25T$. So, if A denotes the amount donated per person by
   the remaining people, then $(.4L) \times A = .25T$. This equation can be

   solved for A to yield $A = \dfrac{(.25)}{(.4L)} = \left(\dfrac{5}{8} \right)\left(\dfrac{T}{L} \right)$. Since 75% of the total

   was raised by an average donation of \$60 each from 60% of the
   people, we know that $\$60 \times .6L = .75T$. So $\$36L = .75T$, which

   gives $\dfrac{T}{L} = \dfrac{\$36}{.75} = \$48$.

   Therefore $A = \left(\dfrac{5}{8} \right)\$48 = \$30$.

2. **(B)** Since $x = 3$, $2x + y = 6 + y$; so $6 + y = 10$ and $y = 4$. Therefore,
   $x - y = 3 - 4 = -1$.

3. **(D)** Since 15 minutes is $\dfrac{1}{4}$ of an hour, each worker can pack $4 \times \dfrac{1}{6}$ or

   $\dfrac{2}{3}$ of a case an hour. The factory has 40 workers, so they should

   pack $40 \times \dfrac{2}{3}$ or $\dfrac{80}{3}$ cases each hour. Therefore, in $1\dfrac{2}{3}$ or $\dfrac{5}{3}$ hours

   the factory should pack $\left(\dfrac{5}{3} \times \dfrac{80}{3} \right)$, which equals $\dfrac{400}{9}$ or $44\dfrac{4}{9}$
   cases.

4. **(E)** Simply use the properties of inequalities to solve the given inequality. Subtract $2x$ from each side to get $5x - 5 < 18$. Next add 5 to each side to obtain $5x < 23$. Finally divide each side by 5 to get $x < \dfrac{23}{5}$.

5. **(A)** Since the truck driver averaged 50 miles per hour for the first three hours, he traveled 3×50 or 150 miles during the first three hours. Since he needs to travel $180 - 150$ miles in the final hour, he should drive at 30 mph.

6. **(D)** The area of a triangle is ½ the base times the altitude. The altitude is $2B$, so the area is $(\frac{1}{2})(B)(2B)$ or B^2.

7. **(E)** If we denote the two numbers by x and y, then $xy = 10$ and $x + y = 7$. Then x is $7 - y$ and $(7 - y)y = 7y - y^2 = 10$ or $y^2 - 7y + 10 = 0$. But $y^2 - 7y + 10 = (y - 5)(y - 2)$; so the two numbers are 5 and 2. The correct answer can be selected quickly by inspection of the choices.

8. **(C)** Since the first 100 bags cost $\$x$ each, the total cost of the first 100 bags is $\$100x$. Since the remaining 50 bags are discounted 10%, each bag costs 90% of $\$x$ or $\$(.90)x$ and the 50 bags cost $\$45x$. Thus, the total cost is $\$145x$.

9. **(D)** According to the Pythagorean theorem, the length squared equals $8^2 + 15^2$, which is 289. So the length of the side opposite the right angle is 17.

10. **(C)** The first 600 copies cost a total of $600x¢$. There are $1{,}500 - 600$ or 900 copies after the first 600, each of which costs $\left(x - \dfrac{y}{10}\right)¢$; so the 900 copies cost $900\left(x - \dfrac{y}{10}\right)¢$, which equals $(900x - 90y)¢$. Therefore, the total cost is $(1500x - 90y)¢$.

11. **(A)** The sum of the angles of a parallelogram (which is 4-sided) must be $(4 - 2)\,180° = 360°$. Since the sum of the values in III is 410, III cannot be correct. The sum of the numbers in II is 360, but in a parallelogram opposite angles must be equal, so x must equal z and y must equal w. Since 60 does not equal 70, II cannot be correct. The sum of the values in I is 360 and opposite angles will be equal, so I is correct.

12. **(E)** John weighs twice as much as Marcia, so John cannot weigh the least. Marcia's weight is less than Bob's weight, so Bob's weight is not the least. Dave's weight is ½ of Lee's weight, so Lee can't weigh the least. The only possible answers are Marcia or Dave. Let J, M, B, D, and L stand for the weights of John, Marcia, Bob, Dave, and Lee, respectively. Then $D = .5L = .5(1.9)J$. So $D = .95J$. Since $J = 2M$, we know $M = .5J$. Therefore Marcia weighs the least.

13. **(C)** Since the sum of the integers is 35, the average is $35/5 = 7$. So the "middle" integer should be near 7. Since $5 + 6 + 7 + 8 + 9 = 35$, the five integers are 5, 6, 7, 8, and 9. 6 and 8 are not primes because they are divisible by 2; 9 is not prime since it is divisible by 3. Only 5 and 7 are primes, so two of the five integers are primes.

14. **(B)** Since DA is perpendicular to AC, ABD is a right triangle. So the square of DB is equal to the square of AD plus the square of AB. We know AB is 10. AD is a radius of circle 1 and, since ACB is a straight line and both circles have the same radii, ACB is equal to $AC + CB$. So $10 =$ twice the radius. Therefore the radius is 5. Since AD is 5, we have $DB = \sqrt{100 + 25} = \sqrt{5} \times \sqrt{25} = 5\sqrt{5}$.

15. **(B)** First find the market value of the house. If M is the market value, then 60% of M is $72,000. So $.6M = \$72,000$, which means $M = \$72,000/.6 = \$120,000$. The tax rate is $3 for every $1,000 or .003. Therefore the taxes are $.003 \times \$120,000 = \$360$.

16. **(B)** First evaluate *5. Using the given rule, *5 is $(5 \times 5) - 2 = 25 - 2 = 23$. So *(*5) is *23, which is $(23 \times 23) - 2 = 529 - 2 = 527$.

17. **(E)** Since $y/x = 1/3$, cross multiply to obtain $x = 3y$. Substitute $x = 3y$ into $x + 2y = 10$ to get $3y + 2y = 5y = 10$. Therefore $y = 2$, so $x = 6$. You can check that $2/6 = 1/3$ and $6 + 2(2) = 10$, so you know your answer is correct.

18. **(D)** The area of a parallelogram is the altitude times the base. Since the bottom is part of the line $y = -1$ and the top is part of the line $y = 2$, an altitude is the distance between these two lines. This distance is $|2 - (-1)| = 3$. Since a base is the segment from $(1, -1)$ to $(4, -1)$, the base is $|4 - 1| = 3$. Therefore the area is $3 \times 3 = 9$.

19. **(E)** The perimeter of a rectangle is 2(length) + 2(width). Since we know the length is y, we need to find the width. The area of a rectangle is (length) × (width). So the fact that the area is 1,000

square yards gives the equation y(width) = 1,000. Solving for the width, we get width = 1,000/y. Therefore the perimeter is $2y + 2(1,000/y) = 2y + 2,000/y$.

20. **(C)** Since the figure is a cube, *ADEH* is a square whose sides have length 10. Therefore *AE*, which is a diagonal of the square, has length $\sqrt{10^2 + 10^2} = \sqrt{200}$. Since *FE* is perpendicular to *AE*, the triangle *AEF* is a right triangle. So *AF* squared is equal to the sum of the square of *AE* and the square of *FE*. Therefore *AF* = $\sqrt{200 + 10^2} = \sqrt{200 + 100} = \sqrt{300} = \sqrt{3} \times \sqrt{100} = 10\sqrt{3}$.

Section III   Critical Reasoning

1. **(C)** It is true that the condition cited by Myra as evidence might be only temporary (A) and also that Myra uses a generalization based on only one source (B), but Lewis does not react to either of these. Lewis's reply also ignores deaths caused on roads other than freeways (E). Further, the fact that no statistics are given (D) has no bearing on Myra's conclusion. So none of these is an appropriate answer. Choice (C) is the correct answer. Myra cites the fact that the number of freeway accidents in North Carolina has decreased with the new speed limit as evidence that this new policy and freeway accidents are causally related. However, Myra fails to establish specifically that the number of freeway accidents was higher under the previous speed limit. The response from Lewis centers on this omission.

2. **(E)** In order to achieve your freedom, you must first ascertain whether your guards are honest or liars. (Remember: one can be honest, while the other can be a liar.) This is only possible by asking question 1 to both guards. Two answers in the affirmative will indicate they are both honest, while two answers in the negative will indicate they are both liars.

   If you receive a yes and a no, then whoever answered "no" must be honest and the other one (who answered "yes") must be a liar. As soon as you have ascertained the honesty or otherwise of either guard, you can ask with certainty whether a particular door leads to freedom.

   (E) combines these questions and is therefore the appropriate answer.

3. **(B)** Answer alternative (A) can be shown false from the information given—namely, that the Nuggets and the Suns have the same num-

ber of points and that the Suns have more points than the Bullets. Choices (C), (D), and (E) might be correct, but it is not possible to confirm these facts from the information given in the paragraph. Details on the number of points the Lakers have in relation to the other teams is not provided. (B) can be demonstrated to be true, since the Bullets have fewer points than the Suns, who have the same number of points as the Nuggets; the Nuggets, therefore, have more points than the Bullets. The Pistons have more points than the Nuggets and, therefore, more than the Bullets.

The information in the passage can best be summarized in the following diagram.

$$B \overset{L}{\swarrow} < S = N < P$$

4. **(C)** The 3:15 from New York will be 15 miles out of New York (and 45 miles away from New Jersey) when it has completed one quarter of its journey and this will be at 3:30 P.M. At 3:30 P.M., the 3 P.M. from New Jersey will only have traveled 30 miles and the two trains will, therefore, not have passed each other. The trains must pass each other after this time. So conclusion (A) can be made and is not the appropriate answer. Conclusion (B) can also be made. The 3:30 P.M. from New York will reach New Jersey at 4:30 P.M., which is before 5 P.M., the time that the train due in at New York at 6 P.M. has to leave. Conclusion (D) is evident from the fact that all trains travel 60 miles per hour; therefore (D) is not appropriate.

   Conclusion (C) cannot be made. As it leaves New York at 4 P.M., the outgoing train would meet the train just arriving, i.e., the 3 P.M. from New Jersey. When it reaches its destination, one hour later at 5 P.M., the 5 P.M. will just be departing from New Jersey. Between 3 and 5 P.M., 120 trains will have left New Jersey and passed the New York train.

5. **(C)** It can be argued that New York, Ohio, Pennsylvania, and California have large populations and extensive industry and thus a wide tax base from which to finance higher education. Most other states (there are some exceptions) do not have such an extensive tax base. The argument in the statement is a fallacy of analogy, incorrectly making an analogy between the four states mentioned and

most other states. Fewer high school graduates in the other states (B) and (D) could imply reduced costs and thus could possibly strengthen the argument. The fact that free education is not guaranteed (A) does not preclude its being offered and is not relevant to the argument. Alternative (E), a statement of opinion, is also not relevant; the quality of education is not mentioned in the statement.

6. **(C)** A. Brown, in choice (A), is eligible for an A grade under condition I, but that condition states that a student could receive an A (not that he must), and anyway, A. Brown may have failed the third examination. So choice (A) is possible and therefore not appropriate. Not enough information is given about B. White to determine his grade, but the data given does not preclude the giving of a B. This makes choice (B) inappropriate. D. Black qualifies for an A on condition IV and E. Gray gets a B by virtue of failing one paper in accordance with condition III, making choices (D) and (E) inappropriate. (C) is not permissible, even though C. Green came in the top decile, because he failed an examination. Therefore, he cannot receive a grade higher than a B.

7. **(A)** The statements given in choices (B) and (C) are relevant to and consistent with the stated policy. (B) is an example of fully written down equipment still being held by the company and is perfectly consistent with the stated accounting policy. (C) is also consistent with the policy as, in accordance with the last sentence on leasehold improvements, the additional costs of leasehold improvements should be written off over the number of years left on the lease. The statements given in choices (D) and (E) are not within the ambit of the policy notes. Inventories and negotiable securities are usually current assets and subject to other accounting policies, and amortization of assets other than fixed assets would be similarly dealt with elsewhere. Therefore, (D) and (E) are neither relevant to nor consistent with the policy stated in the paragraph. The statement in (A) is relevant to but not fully consistent with the accounting policy. In not separating the cost of land from that of land and buildings and depreciating it at a rate of 2%, Marton Ltd. has not acted in accordance with its own policy, which is to provide depreciation on all fixed assets except land. (A) is the correct answer.

8. **(D)** The ad emphasizes that Gallenger's new rackets are stronger and will add power to your strokes. (B) and (E) are, therefore, inferred. It is intended that the reader of the ad should relate to the judgment of former Wimbledon champions, and, therefore, should wish to follow their example; for this reason (C) can be inferred. The claim made in choice (A) is included in the ad. Choices (A), (B), (C), and (E) are all therefore inappropriate. However, the ad does not claim or infer the statement made in (D). In fact, the paragraph states that the five individuals have changed to Gallenger's new rackets, and this implies that they used something else previously. (D) is the appropriate answer.

9. **(A)** The argument is that married women who work have a higher chance of getting divorced than unemployed married women. However, the statistics do not prove this contention. The census bureau's report of divorce rates is only for married women who earn above $75,000. What about those who earn less? If, as in alternative (A), only 15 percent of married women earn more than $75,000, then what about the other 85 percent? If, among the remaining 85 percent, the divorce rate is equal to or less than that of unemployed married women, then the conclusion is false. Alternatives (B) and (C) buttress the argument. Alternative (D) states evidence that cannot weaken the statement because it does not refer to the divorce rate. Alternative (E) could weaken the statement *if* the divorce rate for employed women was known.

10 **(E)** If the shipyard is not converted into the proposed complex, it might be sold for another use, which could be more detrimental to the opposition's interests than the current plan. Alternatives (A) and (B) reveal that there are buyers for the proposed complex, but hardly rebut the opposition's argument against the project. The closure of shellfish (C) buttresses the opposition (more population). The number of existing moorings (D) also supports the opposition, i.e., there are sufficient moorings. Alternative (E) implies that another use for the shipyard may be worse than the proposed project.

11. **(D)** The head of the committee provides the answer when he supplies the reasons for not including books by Mrs. Blyton on the prescribed list. One of the reasons quoted is that in the view of the committee, the books were inferior in quality. So D is the appropriate answer.

The four remaining answers may have an element of truth in them, but they cannot be inferred from a simple reading of the text.

12. **(D)** The provision applies to annual financial statements which finish after July 15, 1988, and therefore the statements in I which finish on December 31, 1987, are not affected. The paragraph points out that in the first year of applying these provisions, the interim periods are not required to comply with the new rules. Therefore, the statements to July 30, 1988, are not affected. I, therefore, does not apply.

The statements in II are interim. Although they represent the half-yearly accounts in the year ending June 30, 1988, a fiscal year ending after the effective date, they do not have to comply with the new provisions since the six months to December 31, 1988, is an interim period in the initial year of application. (If they are presented with the June 31, 1989, accounts, the interim figures would have to be restated). II, therefore, also does not apply.

No answer choice that lists I or II is correct; and (A), (B), and (C) are therefore incorrect.

III is a case of a fiscal year ending after July 15, 1988, and even though it is a period of less than 12 months and it is the first year of application, the new provisions apply. (D) is, therefore, the appropriate answer. (Choice (E) is inappropriate since there is a correct answer—(D).)

13. **(A)** Choice (A) sums up the conclusion of the passage and is thus the appropriate answer. It combines the intention of the car manufacturers—to produce more cars—with the chosen method, dividing labor into component tasks. Choice (B) may have been a further outcome of implementing this policy, but the passage does not comment on this; therefore, (B) is not appropriate. Choice (C) mentions another direction in which the car manufacturers may have moved, i.e., opening, larger plants, etc., and this process may have been assisted by what is discussed in the passage, but again this cannot be concluded from the passge. So (C) is also inappropriate.

Choices (D) and (E) are both concomitant with the division of labor process—(D), a disadvantage, and (E), an advantage—but neither of them can be inferred from the passage and are therefore inappropriate.

14. **(B)** The statement in choice (A) cannot be inferred or concluded. We may conclude that slow growth may reduce inflation since the United States is pursuing such a policy as part of a concern to curb inflation, but we may not infer or conclude that slow growth can prevent inflation. According to the passage, investment in industry in Japan has been shown to lead to low, not high, inflation; so choice (C) is not appropriate. The statement in choice (D) is partially correct since increased productivity has lowered the rate of inflation in Japan. However, this has been coupled with lowering of production costs. Statement (D) is insufficient by itself, and so is not the correct choice. The statement in (E) is a correct interpretation of U.S. economic policy, but it is not a proven statement, and it cannot be concluded based on the paragraph provided. The text does not state that the United States must cure inflation before improving industry; it merely states that this is current policy and understanding. Choice (B) is the correct choice. Since modernization lowers costs of production, this increases competitiveness and business activity. This has been demonstrated by Japan's high productivity, export record, and low inflation. Slow growth in the United States has had the opposite effect on industry, causing a decrease in efficiency and production. Therefore, (B) is the only conclusion that can be drawn.

15. **(C)** Statement (A) cannot be deduced from the text. It is an untrue statement: a contraceptive is something that can prevent conception, and the drug discussed here does not prevent conception. Therefore, (A) is an incorrect choice. Statement (B) is also an untrue statement. The drug is reported to block egg implantation, not egg production. There is nothing in the paragraph concerning the drug's effectiveness, side effects, benefits, or dangers as compared to other abortion techniques, so there is no basis from which the reader can deduce or infer that the new drug will replace conventional abortion techniques. So (D) is not appropriate. Although the drug has been manufactured and tested in France, there is no indication that its use will be limited to that country alone, so statement (E) is not valid. The statement in (C) is the only limited statement that can be deduced from the text—that the drug RU486 can be used to induce abortion, thus terminating pregnancy.

16. **(B)** Improvement in quality and professionalism can only be ensured if the most suitable candidates are chosen. Since positive discrimination does not guarantee this, statement (C) is not valid. Similarly, statement (D) only ensures that the most suitably qualified candidate from a minority group will fill the position and he or she might be less well suited than a candidate from a non-minority group. Therefore, (D) is an incorrect choice. Positive discrimination cannot be shown to be capable of eradicating prejudice, as claimed in (E); this is a totally separate issue and is not covered within the realm of the text. Statement (A) is probably a correct statement of fact, but it is not the basis of Jane's argument. Jane's argument is that, for better or worse, positive discrimination is a tool to be used to enable minority groups to play a more significant role in society. Because applicants from minority groups will receive more favorable consideration with a policy of positive discrimination, it can be assumed that they will receive extra opportunities. These opportunities are Jane's immediate and long-term objectives. Statement (B), which states all the above in one sentence, is, therefore, the best summary of Jane's position and the correct answer.

17. **(A)** Suggestion (B) would immediately put more people in the job market, and, if they found work, there would be more people contributing to pension funds, thus increasing the amount on hand to pay pensions. Suggestion (C) is also a possible solution to the problem, since again more money would be available for paying those of pensionable age. Thus, both (B) and (C) would improve the situation and are therefore incorrect choices. Suggestions (D) and (E) would reduce the amount of money being paid out. Therefore, they would also help improve the situation and so are incorrect. Choice (A), on the other hand, is a policy that would increase the number of claimants and decrease the number of people providing contributions. This suggestion would not improve the situation; therefore (A) is the appropriate answer.

18. **(D)** In order to shift the blame for the reduction in the annual rate of growth of sales output away from Joe's new regime, we must find another reason for the lack of sales. (D) provides us with this alternative, thus weakening the conclusion in the paragraph. (D), therefore, is the appropriate answer. Although a cost is incurred in pro-

viding depreciation on the new plan and machinery, as in (A), this does not affect the conclusion drawn. (B) is simply a statement of policy, or rather lack of policy—that is, that there is no strict relationship between sales price and cost of production. (C) is a possible defense of Joe's policy, but it does not weaken the conclusion that implementation of his ideas has been to blame for the reduction in the annual rate of growth in sales output. Finally, the fact that Joe's policy of firing workers has enabled a competitor to recruit the company's ex-employees, as in (E), has no bearing on whether or not implementation of Joe's plans has resulted in the decrease in the growth of sales.

19. **(E)** Sentence (A) is a sublime idea, but it cannot be proven to be the intention of the manufacturer. Similarly, sentence (C) is true, but again, cannot be proven to be the prime motive of the manufacturer. Sentence (B) is a tactical move, not a motive, or aim. Sentence (D) is untrue, and so cannot be the prime aim of the manufacturer. Sentence (E) is the only statement that can be obtained from the paragraph, and thus is the appropriate answer.

20. **(B)** The statement by Lewis in the extract simply states that if X is greater than Y and Y is greater than Z, then X is greater than Z, i.e. the condition of being greater is more acute. Choice (B), which states this condition, is the appropriate answer. Choice (A) does not describe the argument in the extract; there is a similarity in the terms used, but the extract does not say that murder is as bad as blackmail and the latter is as bad as theft, therefore murder is as bad as theft. Therefore (A) is inappropriate. Choice (C) is inapplicable, as the extract does not state a purpose that can be applied to other situations. Similarly, (D) is not appropriate, as there is no generalization followed by specific cases. Because there is one appropriate answer, (E) is not correct.

Section IV   Data Sufficiency

1. **(D)** Statement (1) alone is sufficient. Just use 100 for degrees Fahrenheit in the formula. Statement (2) alone is also sufficient, since the formula in statement (2) can be solved to give the formula of statement (1) which we know is sufficient.

2. **(C)** (1) tells us the area of the circle is $\pi 4^2 = 16\pi$. Since there are 360° in the whole circle, (2) tells us that the shaded area is $^{60}/_{360}$ or $^1/_6$ of

the area of the circle. Thus, using both (1) and (2), we can answer the question, but since we need both the radius of the circle and the value of x, neither of them alone is sufficient. Therefore, the answer is (C).

3. **(E)** Using (1) we can find the income for 1970 if we know the income for 1968 and 1969, but (1) gives no more information about the income for 1968 and 1969. If we also use (2) we can get the income in 1969 if we know the income for 1968, but we still can't determine the income for 1968. Therefore, both together are not sufficient.

4. **(D)** Since a straight line forms an angle of 180° and l' is a straight line, we know $x + y = 180$. If we use (1) we get $y = 80$, so (1) alone is sufficient. When two straight lines intersect, the vertical angles are equal. So $y = z$; thus if we use (2) we get $y = 80$. Therefore, (2) alone is sufficient. Thus, each statement alone is sufficient.

5. **(C)** In the figure, x denotes the number taking German I but not English I, and y the number taking English I but not German I. From (1) we know that $x + 16 + y = 50$; from (2), $x = y$. Neither statement alone can be solved for x, but both together are sufficient (and yield $x = 17$).

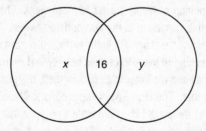

6. **(E)** (1) alone is not sufficient because it only says two sides are equal; in a square all four sides are equal. Even if we use (2) we don't know if *ABCD* is a square since *all* angles have to be right angles in a square. Therefore, both statements together are insufficient.

7. **(B)** The average yearly wage per employee is the total amount of wages divided by the number of employees. So (2) alone is sufficient since it gives the total amount of wages and we are given the number of employees. (1) alone is not sufficient, since (1) by itself does not tell us the total wages. Therefore, the answer is (B).

8. **(E)** Since the square of any nonzero number is positive, (1) says

$x + y \neq 0$ or $x \neq -y$. So (1) alone is not sufficient. If we also assume (2), we know only that x is positive and unequal to $-y$, not whether x is greater than or less than y. Thus (1) and (2) together are insufficient.

9. **(A)** Since the circles both have radius 4, the figure $OBO'C$ is a rhombus (each side is a radius) and the diagonals BC and OO' (of a rhombus) are perpendicular. So (2) does not give any new information, and is thus not sufficient alone. (1) alone is sufficient. The area of each circle is 16π since the radius of each circle is 4. If there were no shaded area, the area enclosed by both circles would be $16\pi + 16\pi = 32\pi$. Since the area enclosed by both circles is 29π, the shaded area is $32\pi - 29\pi$ or 3π. So (1) alone is sufficient but (2) alone is insufficient.

10. **(A)** Let x be the time it takes to travel from A to B and let y be the time it takes to travel from B to A. We know $x + y = 4$. (1) says x is 125% of y or $x = \frac{5}{4}y$. So using (1) we have $x + \frac{5}{4}x = 4$ which we can solve for x. Thus, (1) alone is sufficient. (2) alone is not sufficient since we need information about the relation of x to y to solve the problem and (2) says nothing about the relation between x and y. Therefore, (1) alone is sufficient but (2) alone is insufficient.

11. **(C)** (1) alone is insufficient. If x and y were right angles, (1) would imply that l and l' are parallel, but if x and y are not right angles, (1) would imply that l and l' are not parallel. (2) alone is not sufficient since it gives information only about l' and says nothing about the relation of l and l'. (1) and (2) together give $x = z$ which means that l and l' are parallel. Therefore, (1) and (2) together are sufficient but neither alone is sufficient.

12. **(E)** If we use (1), we have $x + y + z = 3 + z$, but we have no information about z, so (1) alone is insufficient. If we use (2) alone, we have $x + y + z = y + 2$, but since we have no information about y, (2) alone is insufficient. If we use both (1) and (2), we obtain $x + y + z = y + 2 = 3 + z$. We can also add (1) and (2) to obtain $2x + y + z = 5$, but we can't find the value of $x + y + z$ without more information. So the answer is (E).

13. **(C)** We need to know the surface area of the box. Since each side is a rectangle, we know the surface area will be $2LW + 2LH + 2HW$ where H is the height of the box, L is the length, and W is the width. We are given that $L = 7$, so to answer the question we need H and W. Since (1) gives only the value of W and (2) gives only

the value of H, neither alone is sufficient. But both (1) and (2) together are sufficient.

14. **(E)** The three digit number abc is $(100 \times a) + (10 \times b) + c$. If abc is a multiple of 8, then there is an integer k such that $k8 = (100 \times a) + (10 \times b) + c$. Divide this equation by 8 and you have

$$k = \left(\frac{100}{8} \times a \right) + \left(\frac{10}{8} \times b \right) + \frac{c}{8}$$

$$= \left(12a \times \frac{4a}{8} \right) + \left(b \times \frac{2b}{8} \right) + \frac{c}{8}$$

$$= 12a + b + \left(\frac{4a}{8} + \frac{2b}{8} + \frac{c}{8} \right)$$

$$= 12a + b + \left(\frac{4a + 2b + c}{8} \right)$$

So (1) alone is not enough since choosing $a = 1 = b$ and $c = 2$ will make abc (112) a multiple of 8 but $a + b + c = 4$, which is not a multiple of 8. However, choosing $a = 8 = b = c$ will make abc (888) a multiple of 8 and $a + b + c = 24$, which is also a multiple of 8. So (1) alone is not sufficient. (1) and (2) together are not sufficient, since the assignment $a = 8 = b = c$ will satisfy both (1) and (2) and $a + b + c = 24$ but the assignment $a = 2$, $b = 4$, and $c = 8$ will satisfy both (1) and (2) and $a + b + c = 14$.

15. **(E)** (1) alone is not sufficient. A four-sided figure can have both larger perimeter and smaller area than another four-sided figure, or it could have larger perimeter and larger area. (2) alone is also insufficient since the length of one diagonal does not determine the area of a four-sided figure. (1) and (2) together are also insufficient, as shown by the figure.

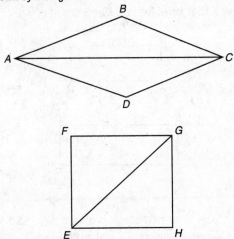

(1) and (2) are both satisfied and the area of *EFGH* is larger than *ABCD*. But (1) and (2) could still be satisfied and the area of *ABCD* be larger than the area of *EFGH*; so the answer is (E).

16. **(B)** Statement (1) alone is not sufficient, since 12 is divisible by 3 but 12 is not divisible by 9. Statement (2) alone is sufficient, since if a number is divisible by 27 then, because 27 = 9 x 3, the number must be divisible by 9.

17. **(C)** Statement (1) is not sufficient. (1) will let you figure out the length of the side *SP;* however, you need to know the length of *SR* or *PQ* to find the area. Statement (2) alone is not sufficient. (2) will allow you to find the length of *PQ*, but you also need to know the length of *SP* or *RQ*.

    Statements (1) and (2) together are sufficient.

18. **(A)** Both regions *ABEF* and *CDFE* are trapezoids, so their area is given by the formula a ($\frac{1}{2}[b_1 + b_2]$) where a is an altitude and b_1 and b_2 are the sides perpendicular to the altitude. Since *ABCD* is a rectangle, *AB = CD*, which means the altitudes are the same length for

each region. So it is sufficient to know whether $BE + AF$ is larger than $EC + FD$.

Statement (1) alone is sufficient, since, if BE is larger than FD, then $BC - BE$, which is EC, must be smaller than $AD - FD = AF$. ($AD = BC$ since $ABCD$ is a rectangle.) So $BE + AF$ is larger than $EC + FD$.

Statement (2) alone is not sufficient, since either region could be larger if BE is larger than CD (See figures).

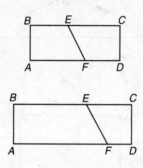

19. **(A)** The square of an even integer is always even. So if k^2 is odd, k can't be even. Therefore, k is odd and (1) alone is sufficient.

Statement (2) alone is not sufficient, since $2k$ is even for every integer k.

20. **(C)** Statement (1) alone is not sufficient. (1) implies x is equal to either -4 or 1.

Statement (2) alone is not sufficient, since there are positive numbers greater than -2 and negative numbers greater than -2.

Statements (1) and (2) together are sufficient, since the only possible value is 1.

21. **(D)** The area of the region is the area of the square plus the area of the semicircle. So you must be able to determine the length of a side of the square and the length of the radius of the semicircle. Since the radius is ½ of BC, it is sufficient to determine either the radius or the length of a side of the square. Statement (1) alone is sufficient, since the diagonal of a square is $\sqrt{2}$ times the length of a side. Statement (2) alone is sufficient, since the length of a side of the square is twice the radius.

22. **(C)** Using statements (1) and (2), you can determine the distance from P to $(0,0)$ and the distance from Q to $(0,0)$. The distances are

equal if and only if P and Q are on the same circle with center (0,0). Neither statement alone is sufficient, since you need to know both distances.

23. **(E)** Both statements together give no information about the year 1980.

24. **(B)** Since 2^n is n "copies" of 2 multiplied together, 2^n is divisible by 8 if and only if n is greater than or equal to 3. (This is because $8 = 2 \times 2 \times 2 = 2^3$). Therefore, (2) alone is sufficient.

    Statement (1) alone is not sufficient, because there are odd numbers less than 3 (for example, 1) and odd numbers greater than 3.

25. **(E)** The fact that the price is higher at the end of the year than it was at the beginning of the year does not imply that the price rose every week during the year. The price could have gone up and down many times during the year.

Section V   Sentence Correction

1. **(E)** Both *together* and *up* are unnecessary since their meaning is included in the words *cooperate* and *divide*.

2. **(E)** The important idea, *he approves my choice*, should be held to the end of the sentence. It should not be separated from *I think*, as it is the object of the verb *think*.

3. **(D)** Parallel structure requires the use of the gerund (verbal noun) as the object of the verb *enjoyed*: *swimming, bathing, snorkeling*. *Enjoy* should not be followed by an infinitive construction.

4. **(C)** The other choices all have misplaced modifiers.

5. **(B)** The clause *that money doesn't make you happy* is the predicate nominative of the verb *is*. *How* is inappropriate.

6. **(E)** The shift in pronouns from *they* to *our* is incorrect. The active verb *can see* is preferable to the passive verb *can be seen*. Also, one looks *ahead to* where one is going.

7. **(A)** No error.

8. **(D)** Suspense is created by holding *grandmother* to the end of the sentence. The word *person* does not have to be repeated.

9. **(B)** The two verbs should be parallel: *start* and *remove*.

10. **(E)** The key idea is that *he is a genius*. To create a suspenseful or periodic sentence, the writer should place *he is a genius* at the end of the sentence.

11. **(B)** The pronoun should agree in number with the noun to which it refers (*creditor/his*). *Most important* is correct here.

12. **(C)** The correlatives *either…or* should be placed as near as possible to the words with which they belong: *a price* and *a quality-of-workmanship basis.*

13. **(B)** *Referred back* is redundant. The prefix *re* means "back."

14. **(E)** *Irregardless* is not a word in current English usage. *Forbidden* requires an infinitive construction (forbidden *to make*). The word *pinch* is slang and should be avoided in writing.

15. **(E)** Active expressions are preferable to passive ones. The two subordinate reasons, reading and note-taking, should be preceded by *because.*

16. **(D)** The correlatives *not only…but also* should be placed near to the words with which they belong: *violated* and *escaped.*

17. **(C)** The correct idiom is *different from. Had ought* is not correct verb form.

18. **(C)** In sentences comparing two items, *-er* words are used. When comparing more than two items use *-est* words. Thus the correct form here is *better*. Choice D is more awkward in construction.

19. **(A)** No error. *Poor product quality* is singular, so the pronoun must also be singular—*it*. Choice B eliminates the pronoun and changes the meaning. Choice E uses a plural pronoun. Choice C uses an incorrect pronoun, *that*, in place of *who*. Choice D is awkward.

20. **(A)** No error. The phrases are all parallel: soft *hair*, strong *legs*, and keen *sense* of smell.

21. **(D)** The wordy main clause can be cut from fifteen words to six without any loss of meaning.

22. **(D)** *Having bowed our heads* is a dangling modifier. The act of bowing heads preceded the leading prayer, so the past perfect tense must be used.

23. **(E)** *Ever* and *true* are unnecessary. The infinitive *to try* is followed by *to*, not *and*.

24. **(D)** The sentence elements should be parallel: *to finance* and *to carry* are both infinitive constructions.

25. **(B)** The entire clause *whoever was present* is the object of the preposition *toward; whoever* is the subject of *was*. Therefore, *whomever*, which is in the objective case, is incorrect.

Section VI   Problem Solving

1. **(C)** If s is the original side of the square, then s^2 is the area of the original square. The side of the increased square is 140% of s or $(1.4)s$. Therefore, the area of the increased square is $(1.4s)^2$ or $1.96s^2$, which is 196% of the original area. Thus, the area has increased by 96%.

2. **(A)** If P is the price of 7 cans, then $\frac{7}{28} = \frac{P}{21}$, so $P = \frac{1}{4}$ of $21, which is $5.25.

3. **(E)** Plane P will travel $\frac{3}{2}$ of an hour before Q takes off, so it will be $\frac{3x}{2}$ miles away at 3:30 A.M. Let t denote the number of hours after 3:30 A.M. it takes Q to overtake P. By then P has flown $tx + \frac{3x}{2}$ miles and Q has flown ty miles. We want the value of t, where $ty = tx + \frac{3x}{2}$, or $t(y - x) = \frac{3x}{2}$. Therefore, $t = \frac{3x}{2(y - x)}$.

4. **(D)** Note that $\left(\frac{2}{3} + \frac{1}{3}\right)$ equals 1 full day, and that $\left(\frac{1}{8} + \frac{3}{4}\right)$ is $\frac{1}{8}$ less than 1 full day, so he works $2\frac{7}{8}$ days altogether.

$$\left(2\frac{7}{8}\right)(20) = \left(\frac{23}{8}\right)(20) = \frac{460}{8} = \$57.50.$$

5. **(D)** There were 26 (16 + 10) students who answered 32 or more questions correctly. The total number of students is 60, and $\frac{26}{60} = .43\frac{1}{3}$. Therefore, $43\frac{1}{3}$ % of the class answered 32 or more questions correctly.

6. **(C)** 12 students had scores of 28 to 31, and 8 had scores of 25 or less; so
$8x = 12$ and $x = \dfrac{12}{8} = \dfrac{3}{2}$.

7. **(B)** The product of 3 consecutive integers is of the form $(x - 1)(x)(x + 1)$ and a good approximation to this is x^3. Since $6^3 = 216$, a good guess for x is 6. 6 is correct since $5 \times 6 \times 7 = 210$. Therefore, the sum of the two smaller integers is $5 + 6$ or 11.

8. **(E)** Let C, B, and E denote the cost of cereal, bacon, and eggs respectively. Then $C = \dfrac{1B}{3}$ and $B = \dfrac{5E}{4}$, or $E = \dfrac{4B}{5}$. Therefore,
$E = \dfrac{4B}{5}$ and $B = 3C$; so we conclude that $E = \left(\dfrac{4}{5}\right) 3C = \dfrac{12C}{5}$.

9. **(D)** Since 80% of 15 is 12, the loaded truck travels 12 miles on a gallon of gas. Therefore, it will use $\dfrac{80}{12}$ or $6 \dfrac{8}{12}$ or $6 \dfrac{2}{3}$ gallons of gas to travel 80 miles.

10. **(D)** Statement I is false since if $x = -5$ and $y = -6$, then $x - y = 1$, which is not negative.
Statement II is true. Minus a negative number is always a positive number.
Statement III is true since $(-x)$ and $(-y)$ are both positive, and the product of two positive numbers is a positive number.

11. **(C)** Think of the area enclosed by both circles as three distinct sections. Then we want to know the value of b. Since each circle has radius 4, the area of each circle is $\pi(4 \times 4) = 16\pi$. So $a + b = 16\pi$ and $b + c = 16\pi$ or $a + 2b + c = 32\pi$. The area enclosed by both circles is $a + b + c$, which must be equal to 28π. Now subtract $a + b + c = 28\pi$ from $a + 2b + c = 32\pi$ to obtain $b = 4\pi$.

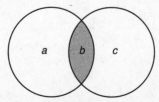

12. **(A)** Let S, R, and P be the respective amounts spent by the sales, research, and packing departments. Then S:R is 1:.2 and R:P is

4:1.5. In order to combine these into a triple ratio for S:R:P, we need to have the same number for R in both the ratios S:R and R:P. If we multiply each term of the ratio S:R by 20, we obtain 20:4. Therefore we can express the triple ratio as 20:4:1.5. However, this is not one of the given answers. If you multiply every term of a triple ratio by the same nonzero number, the triple ratio remains unchanged. So multiply each term by 2, and the triple ratio becomes 40:8:3, which is (A).

13. **(D)** Let E be the point on AD such that CE is perpendicular to AD. Then CDE is a right triangle, and CD can be computed if we know CE and DE. Since EC and AB are perpendicular to the same line, $ABCE$ is a rectangle. So AE is equal to BC, which is 6. Therefore $ED = AD - AE = 8 - 6 = 2$. Since $ABCD$ is a trapezoid, its area is the average of AD and BC multiplied by an altitude. So $28 = (1/2)(6 + 8)$(altitude) means the altitude is $28/7 = 4$. Since CE is perpendicular to AD, CE is an altitude and so CE must equal 4. Finally, using the Pythagorean relation, we have $CD = \sqrt{4^2 + 2^2} = \sqrt{20} = \sqrt{4} \times \sqrt{5} = 2\sqrt{5}$.

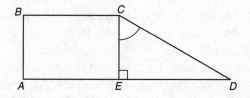

14. **(D)** The cost of 1,400 copies is the cost of the first 1,000 plus the cost of the next 400 copies. Each of the first 1,000 copies cost $x, so the first 1,000 copies cost $1,000x. The next 400 each cost $.9x, so the next 400 copies will cost $(400)(.9x) = $360x. So the total cost of the 1,400 copies should be $1,000x + $360x = $1,360x, which must equal $3,264. Therefore, $x = 3,264/1.360 = 2.40$.

15. **(C)** An odd integer can be written as $2j - 1$ for some positive integer j, and an even integer can be written as $2k$ for some positive integer k. So let $x = 2j - 1$ and $y = 2k$. Then $x + y = 2j - 1 + 2k = 2(j + k) - 1$, which is odd. So I is true. Since $xy = (2j - 1)2k = 4jk - 2k = 2(2jk - k)$, xy is even and II is false. Finally, $2x + y$ is $2(2j - 1) + 2k = 4j - 2 + 2k = 2(2j - 1 + k)$, which is even. Therefore, III is true.

16. **(B)** The area of the region is the area of the circle minus the area of the square. Since the radius of the circle is 4, the area of the circle is $\pi(4 \times 4) = 16\pi$. Since *ABCD* is a square, *ABD* is a right triangle with *AB* equal to *AD*. Since *ABD* is a right triangle, *BD* is a diameter of the circle, so *BD* equals 8. Therefore, $s^2 + s^2 = 8^2$ where *s* is the length of a side of the square. So $2s^2 = 64$ or $s^2 = 32$. Since s^2 is the area of the square, 32 is the area of the square. So the area of the region is $16\pi - 32 = 16(\pi - 2)$.

17. **(A)** Since *X is the largest integer which is less than *X*, *3 is 2 (NOT 3). In the same way *4 is 3 and *4.5 is 4. So (*3) + (*4) + (*4.5) equals $2 + 3 + 4 = 9$.

18. **(B)** Let *JS* and *JC* be Joan's starting and current salaries respectively. Let *MS* and *MC* be Mike's salary when Joan started and his current salary. We know $JS = .5MS$, and we want to find an equation relating *JC* and *MC*. Since Joan received a 5% raise each year, after 1 year her salary was $1.05JS$ and after 2 years her salary is $(1.05)(1.05)JS$. In the same way, we can see that Mike's current salary (*MC*) is $(1.10)(1.10)MS$. So $MC = (1.1)^2MS$. So $JC = (1.05)(1.05)JS = 1.1025JS = .5(1.1025)MS = (.55125)(1/(1.1)^2)MC = (.55125/1.21)MC$. Since we want the answer to the nearest percent, we must divide to three decimal places. So $.55125/1.21 = .455 = 46\%$ to the nearest percent.

19. **(A)** Since every integer has 1 and itself as divisors, we shall neglect these. Write each integer as a product of primes to determine its divisors. So $88 = 2 \times 44 = 2 \times 2 \times 22 = 2 \times 2 \times 2 \times 11$. Therefore, the divisors of 88 are 2, 4, 8, 11, 22, and 44, for a total of 6. Since $91 = 7 \times 13$ and $95 = 5 \times 19$, they both have a total of 2 divisors. $99 = 3 \times 33 = 3 \times 3 \times 11$, so the divisors of 99 are 3, 9, 11, and 33, for a total of 4. 101 is a prime, so it has no divisors. (To see that 101 is a prime, you only have to see if primes less than $\sqrt{101}$, which is less than 11, divide 101.) Therefore, 88 has the most divisors.

20. **(E)** Let *f* and *p* be the amounts of fat and protein in an ounce of food A. Then we know that $f + p = 100$ and $p - 2f = 10$. So *f* is $100 - p$, and the second equation becomes $p - 2(100 - p) = p - 200 + 2p = 3p - 200 = 10$. So $3p = 210$ or $p = 70$.

Section VII Critical Reasoning

1. **(E)** The politician assumes that a large, absolute number of replies means that the survey results are representative of the population (total homes in the district), even though a proportionately small number of replies may have resulted. Alternatives (A), (B), and (D) cannot be assumed from the statement. Alternative (C) is incorrect.

2. **(D)** The number of hotel rooms may be a function of the number of tourists and not vice versa. If average income per tourist did not increase over the time period, an increase in the number of tourists' (doubling every decade) total revenue would double (A). If the number of tourists did not double every decade, but average revenue per tourist doubled (B), total revenue would double. If the average stay per tourist increased, total revenue would increase (assuming that average revenue did not decrease) (C). If the average cost for, say, services, would have doubled during any ten year period, even assuming the same number of tourists and average revenue, total revenue would double. In short, any combination of increases in (A), (B), (C), and (E) could explain the doubling of tourist revenue in any ten year period.

3. **(C)** The assumption is that potential donors will be flattered by requests for large donations and frequently offended by requests for smaller amounts. Therefore, it is worth the gamble to start high—at worst if the potential donor may decrease his gift. Alternatives (A), (B), and (D) are not assumptions made in the statement. Alternative (E) is partially correct: Donors are seldom offended if they are asked *too much* by fund raisers.

4. **(C)** The statement refers to the social psychologist's obligation to provide a wide range of people—those in his own discipline, other social scientists, laymen, and government officials—with the tools to understand social phenomena. Alternative (E) might be a correct assumption if it were not linked to interdisciplinary problems. Alternatives (A), (B), and (D) are incorrect assumptions.

5. **(E)** New technologies and populations represent problems related to sociotechnological change, requiring new mechanisms. The other alternatives are incorrect assumptions.

6. **(D)** is true. Forty percent of American husbands approve, while 50 percent of American wives work. Ten percent of German husbands

approve, while 33 percent of German wives work. Therefore, the gap between German husbands' attitudes towards work and what their wives actually do is much greater than for American husbands and wives.

7. **(B)** Both statements may be inferred; if all public buildings constructed after 1980 were required to have reinforced-steel bomb shelters, then by definition, no bomb shelters other than reinforced-steel ones were installed after 1980. Alternative (A) is incorrect because it refers to *all* public buildings, i.e. those built before 1980. The statement mentions only those constructed *after* 1980.

8. **(B)** (A), (C), (D), and (E) should all encourage more visits to dentists. A decrease in the incidence of cavities should result in a decline of visits to dentists.

9. **(A)** The net export figure is measured in absolute terms, while the export and import figures are given as percents of GNP. Therefore, we may compare the trend in percentage terms and relate it to net exports (given in absolute terms) only as a proportion of GNP. If GNP remained constant over the period, we may compare only the percentage terms. Net exports/constant GNP was 5.8 percent in 1968 and 6.8 percent in 1975. Since GNP was constant over the two time periods, net exports were greater in 1975 than in 1968.

10. **(D)** The assumption is that domestic marketing techniques may be transferable to only those markets that have substantial sales volume. The words "marketing methods" in the last sentence refer to the word "treated" in the first sentence.

11. **(E)** If the principal monetary policy is to be attained—reducing the import surplus while resuming economic growth—per-capita consumption will have to be frozen. Thus, consumers will have to be persuaded to give up consumption to further national economic goals. The assumption is that people will be willing to put a halt to growth in their standard of living.

12. **(B)** Even though nationalization is thought to be caused by changes in government, it is not "selective" by country and covers a wide range of industries.

13. **(A)** If the idea is to speed economic development, then there is place for an argument for inequality of income. In lower income countries, investment by local entrepreneurs is possible only because

of income inequality (the wealthy have excess income which they invest).

14. **(B)** If Euphoria imported more than it exported over the period, its balance of payments worsened. If its terms of trade deteriorated, then it must have paid more for its imports than its exports, that is, earned less from its exports than it paid for its imports.

15. **(D)** While (A) may be inferred, (D) better summarizes the minister's assertion. In this case, "open-door policy" may signify increased trade since ideas and foreign aid are ruled out. There is no proof for (E), while (B) and (C) may not be inferred from the communique.

16. **(A)** Note that the casualty figure for automobile deaths is given as the ratio of number of deaths to miles traveled. In order to make a comparison with other modes of transport, the same denominator (miles traveled) would have to be used.

17. **(A)** If the treaty results in increased Workland exports to Playland at the expense of local producers (import creation), Playland's balance of payments will show a larger deficit. If however, increased Workland exports to Playland merely replace imports from other countries (import diversion), the trade balance will not change. Alternative (C) is a second best consideration, i.e. that political objectives supersede economic goals. The remaining alternatives have no bearing on Playland's balance of trade.

18. **(B)** There is no association between birth control and infant mortality. Birth control can prevent pregnancies but not death after birth.

19. **(E)** If tax advantages (deductions, etc.) decrease, less disposable income is available for spending. All other alternatives explain why total shipments of appliances have increased.

20. **(A)** First, the increase in imports of both types of vehicles was one and a half times greater in 1976 than in 1975. That means that there was a 10 percent increase in the import of both types of vehicles in 1975. Likewise, if the increase for 1976 of private vehicles was 10 percent, then the increase in 1975 was 6.7 percent. Therefore, the difference in import increases for both types of vehicles between 1975 and 1976 is 5 percent and for private vehicles, 3.3 percent. The relative increase in both types of vehicles was 5 percent, including the relative increase in private vehicles of 3.3 percent. Therefore, the residual, relative increase in commercial vehicles was 5 percent – 3.3 percent, or 1.7 percent, less than the increase in private ones. The correct answer is (A).

	Both Types	*Private*
1975	10%	6.7%
1976	15%	10.0%
Increase	5%	3.3%

EVALUATING YOUR SCORE

Tabulate your score for each section of Sample Test 1 according to the directions on pages 6–7 and record the results in the Self-Scoring Table below. Then find your rating for each score on the Self-Scoring Scale and record it in the appropriate blank.

SELF-SCORING TABLE

Section	Score	Rating
1		
2		
3		
4		
5		
6		
7		

SELF-SCORING SCALE—RATING

Section	Poor	Fair	Good	Excellent
1	0 – 11 +	12 – 16 +	17 – 21 +	22 – 25
2	0 – 8 +	9 – 12 +	13 – 17 +	18 – 20
3	0 – 8 +	9 – 12 +	13 – 17 +	18 – 20
4	0 – 11 +	12 – 16 +	17 – 21 +	22 – 25
5	0 – 11 +	12 – 16 +	17 – 21 +	22 – 25
6	0 – 8 +	9 – 12 +	13 – 17 +	18 – 20
7	0 – 8 +	9 – 12 +	13 – 17 +	18 – 20

Study the Review sections again, covering material in Sample Test 1 for which you had a rating of FAIR or POOR. Then go on to Sample Test 2.

Answer Sheet—Sample Test 2

Section I Problem Solving	Section II Reading Comprehension	Section III Data Sufficiency	Section IV Sentence Correction
1. Ⓐ Ⓑ Ⓒ Ⓓ Ⓔ	1. Ⓐ Ⓑ Ⓒ Ⓓ Ⓔ	1. Ⓐ Ⓑ Ⓒ Ⓓ Ⓔ	1. Ⓐ Ⓑ Ⓒ Ⓓ Ⓔ
2. Ⓐ Ⓑ Ⓒ Ⓓ Ⓔ	2. Ⓐ Ⓑ Ⓒ Ⓓ Ⓔ	2. Ⓐ Ⓑ Ⓒ Ⓓ Ⓔ	2. Ⓐ Ⓑ Ⓒ Ⓓ Ⓔ
3. Ⓐ Ⓑ Ⓒ Ⓓ Ⓔ	3. Ⓐ Ⓑ Ⓒ Ⓓ Ⓔ	3. Ⓐ Ⓑ Ⓒ Ⓓ Ⓔ	3. Ⓐ Ⓑ Ⓒ Ⓓ Ⓔ
4. Ⓐ Ⓑ Ⓒ Ⓓ Ⓔ	4. Ⓐ Ⓑ Ⓒ Ⓓ Ⓔ	4. Ⓐ Ⓑ Ⓒ Ⓓ Ⓔ	4. Ⓐ Ⓑ Ⓒ Ⓓ Ⓔ
5. Ⓐ Ⓑ Ⓒ Ⓓ Ⓔ	5. Ⓐ Ⓑ Ⓒ Ⓓ Ⓔ	5. Ⓐ Ⓑ Ⓒ Ⓓ Ⓔ	5. Ⓐ Ⓑ Ⓒ Ⓓ Ⓔ
6. Ⓐ Ⓑ Ⓒ Ⓓ Ⓔ	6. Ⓐ Ⓑ Ⓒ Ⓓ Ⓔ	6. Ⓐ Ⓑ Ⓒ Ⓓ Ⓔ	6. Ⓐ Ⓑ Ⓒ Ⓓ Ⓔ
7. Ⓐ Ⓑ Ⓒ Ⓓ Ⓔ	7. Ⓐ Ⓑ Ⓒ Ⓓ Ⓔ	7. Ⓐ Ⓑ Ⓒ Ⓓ Ⓔ	7. Ⓐ Ⓑ Ⓒ Ⓓ Ⓔ
8. Ⓐ Ⓑ Ⓒ Ⓓ Ⓔ	8. Ⓐ Ⓑ Ⓒ Ⓓ Ⓔ	8. Ⓐ Ⓑ Ⓒ Ⓓ Ⓔ	8. Ⓐ Ⓑ Ⓒ Ⓓ Ⓔ
9. Ⓐ Ⓑ Ⓒ Ⓓ Ⓔ	9. Ⓐ Ⓑ Ⓒ Ⓓ Ⓔ	9. Ⓐ Ⓑ Ⓒ Ⓓ Ⓔ	9. Ⓐ Ⓑ Ⓒ Ⓓ Ⓔ
10. Ⓐ Ⓑ Ⓒ Ⓓ Ⓔ	10. Ⓐ Ⓑ Ⓒ Ⓓ Ⓔ	10. Ⓐ Ⓑ Ⓒ Ⓓ Ⓔ	10. Ⓐ Ⓑ Ⓒ Ⓓ Ⓔ
11. Ⓐ Ⓑ Ⓒ Ⓓ Ⓔ	11. Ⓐ Ⓑ Ⓒ Ⓓ Ⓔ	11. Ⓐ Ⓑ Ⓒ Ⓓ Ⓔ	11. Ⓐ Ⓑ Ⓒ Ⓓ Ⓔ
12. Ⓐ Ⓑ Ⓒ Ⓓ Ⓔ	12. Ⓐ Ⓑ Ⓒ Ⓓ Ⓔ	12. Ⓐ Ⓑ Ⓒ Ⓓ Ⓔ	12. Ⓐ Ⓑ Ⓒ Ⓓ Ⓔ
13. Ⓐ Ⓑ Ⓒ Ⓓ Ⓔ	13. Ⓐ Ⓑ Ⓒ Ⓓ Ⓔ	13. Ⓐ Ⓑ Ⓒ Ⓓ Ⓔ	13. Ⓐ Ⓑ Ⓒ Ⓓ Ⓔ
14. Ⓐ Ⓑ Ⓒ Ⓓ Ⓔ	14. Ⓐ Ⓑ Ⓒ Ⓓ Ⓔ	14. Ⓐ Ⓑ Ⓒ Ⓓ Ⓔ	14. Ⓐ Ⓑ Ⓒ Ⓓ Ⓔ
15. Ⓐ Ⓑ Ⓒ Ⓓ Ⓔ	15. Ⓐ Ⓑ Ⓒ Ⓓ Ⓔ	15. Ⓐ Ⓑ Ⓒ Ⓓ Ⓔ	15. Ⓐ Ⓑ Ⓒ Ⓓ Ⓔ
16. Ⓐ Ⓑ Ⓒ Ⓓ Ⓔ	16. Ⓐ Ⓑ Ⓒ Ⓓ Ⓔ	16. Ⓐ Ⓑ Ⓒ Ⓓ Ⓔ	16. Ⓐ Ⓑ Ⓒ Ⓓ Ⓔ
17. Ⓐ Ⓑ Ⓒ Ⓓ Ⓔ	17. Ⓐ Ⓑ Ⓒ Ⓓ Ⓔ	17. Ⓐ Ⓑ Ⓒ Ⓓ Ⓔ	17. Ⓐ Ⓑ Ⓒ Ⓓ Ⓔ
18. Ⓐ Ⓑ Ⓒ Ⓓ Ⓔ	18. Ⓐ Ⓑ Ⓒ Ⓓ Ⓔ	18. Ⓐ Ⓑ Ⓒ Ⓓ Ⓔ	18. Ⓐ Ⓑ Ⓒ Ⓓ Ⓔ
19. Ⓐ Ⓑ Ⓒ Ⓓ Ⓔ	19. Ⓐ Ⓑ Ⓒ Ⓓ Ⓔ	19. Ⓐ Ⓑ Ⓒ Ⓓ Ⓔ	19. Ⓐ Ⓑ Ⓒ Ⓓ Ⓔ
20. Ⓐ Ⓑ Ⓒ Ⓓ Ⓔ	20. Ⓐ Ⓑ Ⓒ Ⓓ Ⓔ	20. Ⓐ Ⓑ Ⓒ Ⓓ Ⓔ	20. Ⓐ Ⓑ Ⓒ Ⓓ Ⓔ
	21. Ⓐ Ⓑ Ⓒ Ⓓ Ⓔ	21. Ⓐ Ⓑ Ⓒ Ⓓ Ⓔ	21. Ⓐ Ⓑ Ⓒ Ⓓ Ⓔ
	22. Ⓐ Ⓑ Ⓒ Ⓓ Ⓔ	22. Ⓐ Ⓑ Ⓒ Ⓓ Ⓔ	22. Ⓐ Ⓑ Ⓒ Ⓓ Ⓔ
	23. Ⓐ Ⓑ Ⓒ Ⓓ Ⓔ	23. Ⓐ Ⓑ Ⓒ Ⓓ Ⓔ	23. Ⓐ Ⓑ Ⓒ Ⓓ Ⓔ
	24. Ⓐ Ⓑ Ⓒ Ⓓ Ⓔ	24. Ⓐ Ⓑ Ⓒ Ⓓ Ⓔ	24. Ⓐ Ⓑ Ⓒ Ⓓ Ⓔ
	25. Ⓐ Ⓑ Ⓒ Ⓓ Ⓔ	25. Ⓐ Ⓑ Ⓒ Ⓓ Ⓔ	25. Ⓐ Ⓑ Ⓒ Ⓓ Ⓔ

Section V Critical Reasoning	Section VI Sentence Correction	Section VII Problem Solving
1. Ⓐ Ⓑ Ⓒ Ⓓ Ⓔ	1. Ⓐ Ⓑ Ⓒ Ⓓ Ⓔ	1. Ⓐ Ⓑ Ⓒ Ⓓ Ⓔ
2. Ⓐ Ⓑ Ⓒ Ⓓ Ⓔ	2. Ⓐ Ⓑ Ⓒ Ⓓ Ⓔ	2. Ⓐ Ⓑ Ⓒ Ⓓ Ⓔ
3. Ⓐ Ⓑ Ⓒ Ⓓ Ⓔ	3. Ⓐ Ⓑ Ⓒ Ⓓ Ⓔ	3. Ⓐ Ⓑ Ⓒ Ⓓ Ⓔ
4. Ⓐ Ⓑ Ⓒ Ⓓ Ⓔ	4. Ⓐ Ⓑ Ⓒ Ⓓ Ⓔ	4. Ⓐ Ⓑ Ⓒ Ⓓ Ⓔ
5. Ⓐ Ⓑ Ⓒ Ⓓ Ⓔ	5. Ⓐ Ⓑ Ⓒ Ⓓ Ⓔ	5. Ⓐ Ⓑ Ⓒ Ⓓ Ⓔ
6. Ⓐ Ⓑ Ⓒ Ⓓ Ⓔ	6. Ⓐ Ⓑ Ⓒ Ⓓ Ⓔ	6. Ⓐ Ⓑ Ⓒ Ⓓ Ⓔ
7. Ⓐ Ⓑ Ⓒ Ⓓ Ⓔ	7. Ⓐ Ⓑ Ⓒ Ⓓ Ⓔ	7. Ⓐ Ⓑ Ⓒ Ⓓ Ⓔ
8. Ⓐ Ⓑ Ⓒ Ⓓ Ⓔ	8. Ⓐ Ⓑ Ⓒ Ⓓ Ⓔ	8. Ⓐ Ⓑ Ⓒ Ⓓ Ⓔ
9. Ⓐ Ⓑ Ⓒ Ⓓ Ⓔ	9. Ⓐ Ⓑ Ⓒ Ⓓ Ⓔ	9. Ⓐ Ⓑ Ⓒ Ⓓ Ⓔ
10. Ⓐ Ⓑ Ⓒ Ⓓ Ⓔ	10. Ⓐ Ⓑ Ⓒ Ⓓ Ⓔ	10. Ⓐ Ⓑ Ⓒ Ⓓ Ⓔ
11. Ⓐ Ⓑ Ⓒ Ⓓ Ⓔ	11. Ⓐ Ⓑ Ⓒ Ⓓ Ⓔ	11. Ⓐ Ⓑ Ⓒ Ⓓ Ⓔ
12. Ⓐ Ⓑ Ⓒ Ⓓ Ⓔ	12. Ⓐ Ⓑ Ⓒ Ⓓ Ⓔ	12. Ⓐ Ⓑ Ⓒ Ⓓ Ⓔ
13. Ⓐ Ⓑ Ⓒ Ⓓ Ⓔ	13. Ⓐ Ⓑ Ⓒ Ⓓ Ⓔ	13. Ⓐ Ⓑ Ⓒ Ⓓ Ⓔ
14. Ⓐ Ⓑ Ⓒ Ⓓ Ⓔ	14. Ⓐ Ⓑ Ⓒ Ⓓ Ⓔ	14. Ⓐ Ⓑ Ⓒ Ⓓ Ⓔ
15. Ⓐ Ⓑ Ⓒ Ⓓ Ⓔ	15. Ⓐ Ⓑ Ⓒ Ⓓ Ⓔ	15. Ⓐ Ⓑ Ⓒ Ⓓ Ⓔ
16. Ⓐ Ⓑ Ⓒ Ⓓ Ⓔ	16. Ⓐ Ⓑ Ⓒ Ⓓ Ⓔ	16. Ⓐ Ⓑ Ⓒ Ⓓ Ⓔ
17. Ⓐ Ⓑ Ⓒ Ⓓ Ⓔ	17. Ⓐ Ⓑ Ⓒ Ⓓ Ⓔ	17. Ⓐ Ⓑ Ⓒ Ⓓ Ⓔ
18. Ⓐ Ⓑ Ⓒ Ⓓ Ⓔ	18. Ⓐ Ⓑ Ⓒ Ⓓ Ⓔ	18. Ⓐ Ⓑ Ⓒ Ⓓ Ⓔ
19. Ⓐ Ⓑ Ⓒ Ⓓ Ⓔ	19. Ⓐ Ⓑ Ⓒ Ⓓ Ⓔ	19. Ⓐ Ⓑ Ⓒ Ⓓ Ⓔ
20. Ⓐ Ⓑ Ⓒ Ⓓ Ⓔ	20. Ⓐ Ⓑ Ⓒ Ⓓ Ⓔ	20. Ⓐ Ⓑ Ⓒ Ⓓ Ⓔ
	21. Ⓐ Ⓑ Ⓒ Ⓓ Ⓔ	
	22. Ⓐ Ⓑ Ⓒ Ⓓ Ⓔ	
	23. Ⓐ Ⓑ Ⓒ Ⓓ Ⓔ	
	24. Ⓐ Ⓑ Ⓒ Ⓓ Ⓔ	
	25. Ⓐ Ⓑ Ⓒ Ⓓ Ⓔ	

SAMPLE TEST 2

SECTION I   PROBLEM SOLVING   Time: 30 minutes

Directions: Solve each of the following problems, then indicate the correct answer on the answer sheet. [On the actual test you will be permitted to use scratch paper for your calculations.]

NOTE: A figure that appears with a problem is drawn as accurately as possible so as to provide information that may help in answering the questions. Numbers in this test are real numbers.

1. What is the next number in the geometric progression 4, 12, 36?

    (A) 44   (D) 108
    (B) 60   (E) 144
    (C) 72

2. An angle of x degrees has the property that its complement is equal to ⅙ of its supplement where x is

    (A) 30   (D) 63
    (B) 45   (E) 72
    (C) 60

3. If $y = \dfrac{3}{(x^2)} + x$ and $x = 3$, then y is

    (A) $\dfrac{2}{3}$ (D) $\dfrac{18}{3}$

    (B) $\dfrac{10}{3}$ (E) $\dfrac{36}{6}$

    (C) $\dfrac{12}{3}$

4. Which of the following numbers is the least common multiple of the numbers 2, 3, 4, and 5?

    (A) 12   (D) 40
    (B) 24   (E) 60
    (C) 30

5. In a certain town 40% of the people have brown hair, 25% have brown eyes, and 10% have both brown hair and brown eyes. What percentage of the people in the town have neither brown hair nor brown eyes?

    (A) 35   (D) 50
    (B) 40   (E) 55
    (C) 45

6. If the altitude of a triangle increases by 5% and the base of the triangle increases by 7%, by what percent will the area of the triangle increase?

    (A) 3.33%   (D) 12%
    (B) 5%   (E) 12.35%
    (C) 6%

7. A shipping firm charges 2¢ a pound for the first 20 pounds of package weight and 1.5¢ for each pound or fraction of a pound over 20 pounds of package weight. How much will it charge to ship a package which weighs 23½ pounds?

    (A) 6¢   (D) 46¢
    (B) 8¢   (E) 47¢
    (C) 45¢

8. If paper costs 1¢ a sheet, and a buyer gets a 2% discount on all the paper he buys after the first 1,000 sheets, how much will it cost to buy 5,000 sheets of paper?

    (A) $49.20   (D) $4,920.00
    (B) $50.00   (E) $5,000.00
    (C) $3,920.00

9. Tom's salary is 150% of John's salary. John's salary is 80% of Steve's salary. What is the ratio of Steve's salary to Tom's salary?

    (A) 1 to 2   (D) 6 to 5
    (B) 2 to 3   (E) 5 to 4
    (C) 5 to 6

10. A charity solicited *P* persons over the phone who agreed to an average pledge of $*R* each. *Q* of these people who had pledged an average of $*S* each never sent in the pledged amount. Which of the following expressions represents the percentage of pledged money that the charity received?

(A) $100 \times \dfrac{PR}{QS}$

(D) $100 - \dfrac{100QS}{PR}$

(B) $100 \times \dfrac{QS}{PR}$

(E) $100\ PR - \dfrac{100QS}{PR}$

(C) $100\ PR - 100\ QS$

11. If it takes 50 workers 4 hours to dig a sewer, how long should it take 30 workers to dig the same sewer?

(A) 2 hrs., 24 min.
(B) 5 hrs., 12 min.
(C) 6 hrs., 12 min.
(D) 6 hrs., 20 min.
(E) 6 hrs., 40 min.

12. Three pounds of 05 grass seed contain 5 percent herbicide. A different type of grass seed, 20, which contains 20 percent herbicide, will be mixed with the three pounds of 05 grass seed. How much grass seed of type 20 should be added so that the resulting mixture contains 15 percent herbicide?

(A) 3 pounds
(B) 3.75 pounds
(C) 4.5 pounds
(D) 6 pounds
(E) 9 pounds

13. A car is traveling on a straight highway. At 10 o'clock, it passes a truck traveling in the same direction. The truck continues on the highway traveling at 50 mph while the car travels at 65 mph. How far apart are the car and the truck at 2 o'clock?

(A) 15 miles
(B) 30 miles
(C) 60 miles
(D) 200 miles
(E) 260 miles

Use the following graph for question 14.

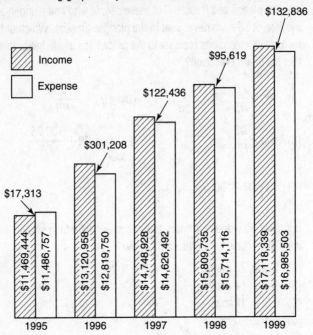

14. Which of the following statements can be inferred from the graph?

  I.   The company made a profit in all the years shown on the graph.

  II. The company's profit increased in every year between 1997 and 1999.

  III. The company's expenses increased in each year shown on the graph.

  (A) I only
  (B) II only
  (C) III only

  (D) I and III only
  (E) I, II, and III

15. If $x - 2$ is less than y then

  (A) x and y are positive
  (B) y is less than $x + 2$
  (C) y is greater than x

  (D) $y + 2$ is greater than x
  (E) none of the preceding

16. Wheat costs $2.00 a bushel and corn costs $2.62 a bushel. If the price of wheat rises 10% a month and the price of corn is unchanged, how many months will it take before a bushel of corn costs less than a bushel of wheat?

(A) 2   (D) 5
(B) 3   (E) 6
(C) 4

17. If $\frac{1}{2} + \frac{1}{4} = \frac{x}{15}$, then x is

(A) 10   (D) 13.75
(B) 11.25   (E) 14
(C) 12

18. If $x + y + z + w = 15$, then at least k of the numbers x, y, z, w must be positive where k is

(A) 0   (D) 3
(B) 1   (E) 4
(C) 2

19. If the length of a rectangle is increased by 11% and the width remains the same, then the area of the rectangle is increased by

(A) 11%   (D) 111%
(B) 21%   (E) 121%
(C) 110%

20. Which of the following figures has the largest area?

  I. A circle of radius $\sqrt{2}$.
  II. An equilateral triangle whose sides each have length 4.
  III. A triangle whose sides have lengths 3, 4, and 5.

(A) I   (D) I and II
(B) II   (E) II and III
(C) III

If there is still time remaining, you may review the questions in this section only. In the actual CAT GMAT, you cannot return to a question after you have confirmed your answer.

SECTION II   READING COMPREHENSION   Time: 30 minutes

Directions: This part contains four reading passages. You are to read each one carefully. When answering the questions, you *will* be allowed to refer to the passages. The questions are based on what is *stated* or *implied* in each passage. You have thirty minutes to complete this section.

Passage 1:

A newly issued report reveals in facts and figures what should have been known in principle, that quite a lot of business companies are going to go under during the coming decade, as tariff walls are progressively dismantled. Labor and capital valued at $12 billion are
(5) to be made idle through the impact of duty-free imports. As a result, 35,000 workers will be displaced. Some will move to other jobs and other departments within the same firm. Around 15,000 will have to leave the firm now employing them and work elsewhere.

The report is measuring exclusively the influence of free trade with
(10) Europe. The authors do not take into account the expected expansion of production over the coming years. On the other hand, they are not sure that even the export predictions they make will be achieved. For this presupposes that a suitable business climate lets the pressure to increase productivity materialize.

(15) The government is to blame for not making the position absolutely clear. It should be saying that in ten years' time tariffs on all industrial goods imported from Europe will be eliminated. There will be no adjustment assistance for manufacturers who cannot adapt to this situation.

(20) The second obstacle to adjustment is not stressed in the same way in the report; it is the attitude of the service sector. Not only are service industries unaware that the Common Market treaty concerns them too, they are artificially insulated from the physical pressures of international competition. The manufacturing sector has been forced
(25) to apply its nose to the grindstone for some time now, by the increasingly stringent import-liberalization program.

The ancillary services on which the factories depend show a growing indifference to their work obligations. They seem unaware that overmanned ships, underutilized container equipment in the
(30) ports, and repeated work stoppages slow the country's attempts to

narrow the trade gap. The remedy is to cut the fees charged by these services so as to reduce their earnings—in exactly the same way that earnings in industrial undertakings are reduced by the tariff reduction program embodied in the treaty with the European Community.

(35)   There is no point in dismissing 15,000 industrial workers from their present jobs during the coming ten years if all the gain in productivity is wasted by costly harbor, transport, financial, administrative and other services. The free trade treaty is their concern as well. Surplus staff should be removed, if need be, from all workplaces, not just from
(40) the factories. Efficiency is everybody's business.

1. The attitude of the report, as described in the passage, may best be expressed as

   (A) harshly condemnatory, because industry is not more responsive to the business climate.
   (B) optimistic that government will induce industry to make needed changes.
   (C) critical of labor unions.
   (D) pessimistic that anything can be done to reduce the trade gap.
   (E) objective in assessing the influence of free trade on employment.

2. What is the meaning of *free trade* in line 9?

   (A) unlimited sale of goods in Europe
   (B) trade on a barter basis
   (C) the elimination of tariffs
   (D) sale of price-discounted goods to European countries
   (E) trade with only Western Europe

3. It can be inferred that the term *adjustment assistance* in line 18 refers mainly to

   (A) unemployment compensation.
   (B) some sort of financial assistance to manufacturers hurt by free trade.
   (C) help in relocating plants to Europe.
   (D) aid in reducing work stoppages.
   (E) subsidy payments to increase exports.

4. The author's central recommendation seems to be that

   (A) unemployment should be avoided at all costs.
   (B) redundant labor should be removed in all sectors.
   (C) government should control the service sector.
   (D) tariffs should not be lowered.
   (E) workers should be retrained.

5. Which of the following titles best describes the content of the passage?

   (A) *The Prospects of Free Trade*
   (B) *Government Intervention in World Trade*
   (C) *Trade with the Common Market*
   (D) *What Lies Ahead?*
   (E) *Unemployment and Adjustment Assistance*

6. Which of the following will occur because of duty-free imports?

   I. Twelve billion dollars of capital will be idled.
   II. Thirty-five thousand workers will be unemployed.
   III. Fifteen thousand firms will face bankruptcy.

   (A) I only   (D) II and III only
   (B) II only   (E) I, II, and III
   (C) I and II only

7. According to the passage, the government is responsible for

   (A) increasing tariffs.   (D) adjustment assistance.
   (B) subsidizing exports.   (E) overmanned ships.
   (C) not explaining its position.

8. Tariffs will be reduced on

   (A) all manufactured goods.
   (B) manufactured and agricultural goods.
   (C) all goods.
   (D) industrial goods.
   (E) industrial and consumer goods.

9. Which industries will be affected by tariff reductions?

    I. Services

   II. Manufacturing

  III. Extracting

(A) I only

(B) II only

(C) I and II only

(D) II and III only

(E) I, II, and III

Passage 2:

      The fundamental objectives of sociology are the same as those of science generally—discovery and explanation. To *discover* the essential data of social behavior and the connections among the data is the first objective of sociology. To *explain* the data and the connec-
(5) tions is the second and larger objective. Science makes its advances in terms of both of these objectives. Sometimes it is the discovery of a new element or set of elements that marks a major breakthrough in the history of a scientific discipline. Closely related to such discovery is the discovery of relationships of data that had never been noted
(10) before. All of this is, as we know, of immense importance in science. But the drama of discovery, in this sense, can sometimes lead us to overlook the greater importance of explanation of what is revealed by the data. Sometimes decades, even centuries, pass before known connections and relationships are actually explained. Discovery and
(15) explanation are the two great interpenetrating, interacting realms of science.

      From observation or discovery we move to *explanation*. The explanation sought by the scientist is, of course, not at all like the explanation sought by the theologian or metaphysician. The scientist
(20) is not interested—not, that is, in his role of scientist—in ultimate, transcendental, or divine causes of what he sets himself to explain. He is interested in explanations that are as empirical as the data themselves. If it is the high incidence of crime in a certain part of a large city that requires explanation, the scientist is obliged to offer his explana-
(25) tion in terms of factors which are empirically real as the phenomenon of crime itself. He does not explain the problem, for example, in terms of references to the will of God, demons, or original sin. A satisfactory explanation is not only one that is empirical, however, but one that can

be stated in the terms of a *causal proposition*. Description is an
(30) indispensable point of beginning, but description is not explanation.
It is well to stress this point, for there are all too many scientists, or
would-be scientists, who are primarily concerned with data gathering,
data counting, and data describing, and who seem to forget that such
operations, however useful, are but the first step. Until we have
(35) accounted for the problem at hand, explained it causally by referring
the data to some principle or generalization already established, or
to some new principle or generalization, we have not explained
anything.

10. According to the passage, scientists are not interested in
theological explanations because

(A) scientists tend to be atheists.
(B) theology cannot explain change.
(C) theological explanations are not empirical.
(D) theology cannot explain social behavior.
(E) scientists are concerned primarily with data gathering.

11. The major objective of the passage is to

(A) show that explanation is more important than discovery.
(B) prove that sociology is a science.
(C) explain the major objectives of sociology.
(D) discuss scientific method.
(E) describe social behavior.

12. Which of the following statements best agrees with the author's
position?

(A) Science is the formulation of unverified hypotheses.
(B) Explanation is inferred from data.
(C) Causation is a basis for explanation.
(D) Generalization is a prerequisite for explanation.
(E) Empiricism is the science of discovery.

13. Judging from the contents of the passage, the final step in a study of social behavior would be to

    (A) discover the problem.
    (B) establish principles.
    (C) offer an explanation of the data by determining causation.
    (D) collect data.
    (E) establish generalizations.

14. According to the passage, which of the following activities contribute to the advance of science?

    I. Finding data relationships
    II. Expanding the limits of the empirical
    III. Establishing ultimate causes of phenomena

    (A) I only   (D) I and III only
    (B) II only   (E) I, II, and III
    (C) I and II only

15. The author's main point in the first paragraph may best be described by which of the following statements?

    (A) Science and sociology are interdisciplinary.
    (B) The first objective of sociology is discovery.
    (C) Discovery without explanation is meaningless.
    (D) Both discovery and explanation are fundamental to building a science.
    (E) It takes a long time before relationships of data are discovered.

16. According to the author, which of the following explanations would a scientist accept?

    I. Snow falls because angels are having a pillow fight.
    II. Suicide is caused by weak character.
    III. Babies weigh 20% more than the average weight of newborns if their mothers take a 2-hour nap every day during the last 3 months of pregnancy.

    (A) I only   (D) II and III only
    (B) II only   (E) I, II, and III
    (C) III only

17. The major objective of the second paragraph is

(A) to show that electrons are empirical data.

(B) to show that science changes as time passes.

(C) to demonstrate the difference between chemistry and sociology.

(D) to explain how science expands the frontiers of the observable world.

(E) to explain what the term *explanation* means.

Passage 3:

A polytheist always has favorites among the gods, determined by his own temperament, age, and condition, as well as his own interest, temporary or permanent. If it is true that everybody loves a lover, then Venus will be a popular deity with all. But from lovers she will elicit

(5) special devotion. In ancient Rome, when a young couple went out together to see a procession or other show, they would of course pay great respect to Venus, when her image appeared on the screen. Instead of saying, "Isn't love wonderful?" they would say, "Great art thou, O Venus." In a polytheistic society you could tell a good deal

(10) about a person's frame of mind by the gods he favored, so that to tell a girl you were trying to woo that you thought Venus overrated was hardly the way to win her heart.

The gods must always be symbolized in one form or another. To give them a human form is one way of doing this, technically

(15) called *anthropomorphism* (from the Greek *anthropos*, a man, and *morphé* form). People of certain temperaments and within certain types of culture seem to be more inclined to it than are others. It is, however, more noticeable in others than in oneself, and those who affect to despise it are sometimes conspicuous for their addiction to

(20) it. A German once said an Englishman's idea of God is an Englishman twelve feet tall. Such disparagement of anthropomorphism occurred in the ancient world, too. The Celts, for instance, despised Greek practice in this matter, preferring to use animals and other such symbols. The Egyptians favored more abstract and stylized symbols,

(25) among which a well-known example is the solar disk, a symbol of Rà, the sun-god.

What is really characteristic of all polytheism, however, is not the worship of idols or humanity or forests or stars; it is, rather, the worship of innumerable *powers* that confront and affect us. The
(30) powers are held to be valuable in themselves; that is why they are to be worshipped. But the values conflict. The gods do not cooperate, so you have to play them off against each other. Suppose you want rain. You know of two gods, the dry-god who sends drought and the wet-god who sends rain. You do not suppose that you can just pray to the
(35) wet-god to get busy, and simply ignore the dry-god. If you do so, the latter may be offended, so that no matter how hard the wet-god tries to oblige you, the dry-god will do his best to wither everything. Because both gods are powerful you must take both into consideration, begging the wet-god to be generous and beseeching the dry-god to
(40) stay his hand.

18. It can be inferred from the passage that polytheism means a belief in

   (A) Greek gods.
   (B) more than one god.
   (C) a god-centered world.
   (D) powerful deities.
   (E) infinite numbers of gods.

19. The author's statement in lines 9–10 that "you could tell a good deal about a person's frame of mind by the gods he favored" means that

   (A) those who believed in gods were superstitious.
   (B) worship was either anthropocentric or theocentric.
   (C) gods were chosen to represent a given way of life.
   (D) the way a person thinks depends on the power of deities.
   (E) in certain cultures, the gods served as representations of what people thought of themselves.

20. It may be inferred from the passage that the author would most likely agree that ancient cultures

    I. symbolized their deities only in human form.
    II. symbolized the gods in many forms.
    III. were mainly self-worshippers.

    (A) I only   (D) I and III only
    (B) II only   (E) I, II, and III
    (C) I and II only

21. The main point the author makes about anthropomorphism in lines 15–20 is that

    (A) certain cultures are inclined to anthropomorphism.
    (B) those who demean anthropomorphism may themselves practice it.
    (C) the disparagement of anthropomorphism is common to both ancient and modern cultures.
    (D) the Germans tend to be more theocentric than the English.
    (E) anthropomorphism is a practice common to all cultures.

22. It may be inferred from the last paragraph that polytheism entails

    (A) a commonality of interests among the deities.
    (B) predictable consequences.
    (C) incoherence and conflict among the "powers."
    (D) an orderly universe.
    (E) worshipping one god at a time.

23. Which people worshipped animals?

    (A) Romans   (D) Celts
    (B) Greeks   (E) Pagans
    (C) Egyptians

24. Anthropomorphism may be said to be symbolizing

 (A) a deity in one's own image.
 (B) a human form.
 (C) any form.
 (D) both human and spiritual forms.
 (E) an abstract form.

25. A polytheist

   I. has favorite gods.
  II. simultaneously worships more than one god.
 III. lives in Greece.

 (A) I only
 (B) II only
 (C) I and II only

 (D) II and III only
 (E) I, II, and III

If there is still time remaining, you may review the questions in this section only. In the actual CAT GMAT, you cannot return to a question after you have confirmed your answer.

SECTION III   DATA SUFFICIENCY   Time: 30 minutes

Directions: Each of the following problems has a question and two statements which are labeled (1) and (2). Use the data given in (1) and (2) together with other available information (such as the number of hours in a day, the definition of *clockwise,* mathematical facts, etc.) to decide whether the statements are *sufficient* to answer the question. Then fill in space

 (A) if you can get the answer from (1) alone but not from (2) alone;
 (B) if you can get the answer from (2) alone but not from (1) alone;
 (C) if you can get the answer from (1) and (2) together, although neither statement by itself suffices;
 (D) if statement (1) alone suffices *and* statement (2) alone suffices
 (E) if you cannot get the answer from statements (1) and (2) together, but need even more data.

All numbers used in this section are real numbers. A figure given for a problem is intended to provide information consistent with that in the question, but not necessarily with the additional information contained in the statements.

1. *ABC* is a triangle inscribed in circle *AOCB*. Is *AC* a diameter of the circle *AOCB*?

    (1)   Angle *ABC* is a right angle.
    (2)   The length of *AB* is $\frac{3}{4}$ the length of *BC*.

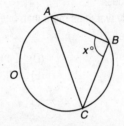

2. A cylindrical tank has a radius of 10 feet and its height is 20 feet. How many gallons of a liquid can be stored in the tank?

    (1)   A gallon of the liquid occupies .13 cubic feet of space.
    (2)   The diameter of the tank is 20 feet.

3. How many books are on the bookshelf?

    (1)   The average weight of each book is 1.2 pounds.
    (2)   The books and the bookshelf together weigh 34 pounds.

4. Is the triangle *ABC* congruent to the triangle *DEF*? *x* is equal to *y*.

    (1)   *AB* is equal to *DE*.
    (2)   *BC* is equal to *EF*.

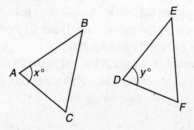

5. Decide whether the square root of the integer x is an integer.

   (1)   The last digit of x is 2.
   (2) x is divisible by 3.

6. Mr. Carpenter wants to build a room in the shape of a rectangle. The area of the floor will be 32 square feet. What is the length of the floor?

   (1)   The length of the floor will be twice the width of the floor.
   (2)   The width of the floor will be 4 feet less than the length of the floor.

7. Do the rectangle *ABCD* and the square *EFGH* have the same area?

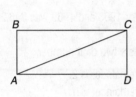 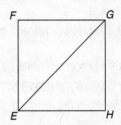

   (1) $AC = EG$, $AB = \frac{1}{2} EH$
   (2)   The area of triangle *ABC* is not equal to the area of triangle *EFG*.

8. How much does Susan weigh?

   (1)   Susan and Joan together weigh 250 pounds.
   (2)   Joan weighs twice as much as Susan.

9. Two different holes, hole *A* and hole *B*, are put in the bottom of a full water tank. If the water drains out through the holes, how long before the tank is empty?

   (1)   If only hole *A* is put in the bottom, the tank will be empty in 24 minutes.
   (2)   If only hole *B* is put in the bottom, the tank will be empty in 42 minutes.

10. Find $x + y$

(1) $x - y = 6$
(2) $-2x + 2y = -12$

11. C is a circle with center D and radius 2. E is a circle with center F and radius R. Are there any points which are on both E and C?

(1) The distance from D to F is $1 + R$.
(2) $R = 3$.

12. Mr. Parker made \$20,000 in 1967. What is Mr. Parker's average yearly income for the three years 1967 to 1969?

(1) He made 10% more in each year than he did in the previous year.
(2) His total combined income for 1968 and 1969 was \$46,200.

13. Is the integer n divisible by 9? n is a two digit number.

(1) When n is divided by 3 the remainder is 2.
(2) When n is divided by 7 the remainder is 1.

14. John and Paul are standing together on a sunny day. John's shadow is 10 feet long. Paul's shadow is 9 feet long. How tall is Paul?

(1) John is 6 feet tall.
(2) John is standing 2 feet away from Paul.

15. Is x greater than y?

(1) x^2 is greater than y^2
(2) $x + 3$ is greater than $y + 2$

16. A dozen eggs cost 90¢ in January 1980. Did a dozen eggs cost more than 90¢ in January 1981?

(1) In January 1980, the average worker had to work 5 minutes to pay for a dozen eggs.
(2) In January 1981, the average worker had to work 4 minutes to pay for a dozen eggs.

17. At 7 o'clock how many people are on line to buy tickets at a theater box office?

    (1) People are getting on the line at the rate of 2 people per minute at 7 o'clock.
    (2) People are buying tickets and leaving the line at the rate of 4 people every 2 minutes at 7 o'clock.

18. What is the value of $\frac{x}{y}$? $x > 0$.

    (1) $x = \frac{1}{4}y$
    (2) $y = 400\%$ of x

19. What is the area of the circular sector AOB? A and B are points on the circle which has O as its center.

    (1) Angle $AOB = 72°$
    (2) $OB = 4$

    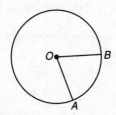

20. How many of the numbers x, y, and z are positive? x, y, and z are all less than 30.

    (1) $x + y + z = 61$
    (2) $x + y = 35$

21. How far is it from town A to town B? Town C is 15 miles west of town A.

    (1) It is 10 miles from town B to town C.
    (2) There is a river between town A and town B.

22. Is $2 < x < 4$?

    (1) $x^2 - 5x + 6 < 0$
    (2) $5x^2 - 25x > 0$

23. What percentage of families in the state have annual incomes over $25,000 and own a sailboat?

    (1) 28% of all the families in the state have an annual income over $25,000.
    (2) 40% of the families in the state with an annual income over $25,000 own a sailboat.

24. What is the two-digit number whose first digit is *a* and whose second digit is *b*? The number is greater than 9.

    (1) The number is a multiple of 51.
    (2) The sum of the digits *a* and *b* is 6.

25. What is the radius of the circle with center O?

    (1) The area of the circle is 25π.
    (2) The area of the circle divided by the diameter of the circle is equal to π times ½ of the radius of the circle.

If there is still time remaining, you may review the questions in this section only. In the actual CAT GMAT, you cannot return to a question after you have confirmed your answer.

SECTION IV   SENTENCE CORRECTION   Time: 30 minutes

Directions: This test consists of a number of sentences, in each of which some part or the whole is underlined. Each sentence is followed by five alternative versions of the underlined portion. Select the alternative you consider both most correct and most effective according to the requirements of standard written English. Answer A is the same as the original version; if you think the original version is best, select answer A.

In considering the answer choices, be attentive to matters of grammar, diction, and syntax, as well as clarity, precision, and fluency. Do not select an answer that alters the meaning of the original sentence.

1. In her candid autobiography, the author discusses her early years, her desire <u>to become an actress, and how she made</u> her debut on the stage.

   (A) to become an actress, and how she made
   (B) that she become an actress, and how she made
   (C) to become an actress, and
   (D) that she become an actress, and
   (E) that she become an actress and that she make

2. Government authorities predicted correctly that tremendous savings in the consumption of gasoline would be achieved if <u>speeding was to be limited to</u> 55 miles per hour.

   (A) speeding was to be limited to
   (B) motorists limited their speed to
   (C) speeding did not exceed
   (D) a motorist was to limit his speed to
   (E) speeding by motorists was to be limited to

3. The desktop computer has revolutionized office procedures more than <u>any machine</u> of modern times.

   (A) any machine
   (B) has any machine
   (C) any other machine
   (D) has any other machine
   (E) any other machine has

4. Bullied by his wife and intimidated by policemen and parking lot attendants alike, <u>daydreaming about being a surgeon, a crack pistol shot, and so on, enable Walter Mitty to cope with the real world.</u>

   (A) daydreaming about being a surgeon, a crack pistol shot, and so on, enable Walter Mitty to cope with the real world.
   (B) daydreaming about being a surgeon, a crack pistol shot, and so on, enables Walter Mitty to cope with the real world.
   (C) Walter Mitty reacts to the real world by his daydreams of being a surgeon, a crack pistol shot, and so on.

(D) Walter Mitty escapes from the real world his daydreams of being a surgeon, a crack pistol shot, and so on.

(E) Walter Mitty is able to cope with the real world by daydreaming of being a surgeon, a crack pistol, and so on.

5. The possibility of expropriation was believed to be unlikely in the near future due to the lack of mining technology and capital available in this small South American country.

(A) due to the lack of mining technology and

(B) because of the lack of mining technology and

(C) because there was no mining technology and

(D) because of the lack of mining technology and there was no

(E) due to the lack of mining technology, and there was no

6. The owner of a Super-11 Food Store on Glen Avenue told police he was robbed of $7,500 in store receipts by a gunman wearing a ski mask as he was about to make a night deposit.

(A) The owner of a Super-11 food store on Glen Avenue told police he was robbed of $7,500 in store receipts by a gunman wearing a ski mask as he was about to make a night deposit.

(B) Police said that the owner of a Super-11 Food Store on Glen Avenue was robbed of $7,500 in store receipts by a gunman wearing a ski mask as he was about to make a night deposit.

(C) As he was about to make a night deposit, a gunman wearing a ski mask robbed him of $7,500 in store receipts, the owner of a Super-11 Food Store on Glen Avenue told police.

(D) The owner of a Super-11 Food Store on Glen Avenue told police that, as he was about to make a night deposit, he was robbed of $7,500 in store receipts by a gunman wearing a ski mask.

(E) As the owner of a Super-11 Food Store on Glen Avenue was about to make a night deposit, he told police that he was robbed of $7,500 in store receipts by a man wearing a ski mask.

7. The doctrine applies in Canada, where there <u>is a federal law and a provincial law that are each valid and</u> consistent.

   (A) is a federal law and a provincial law that are each valid and
   (B) are a federal law and a provincial law that are each valid and
   (C) are a federal law and a provincial law both of which are each valid and
   (D) is a federal law and a provincial law both of which are each valid and
   (E) are a federal law and a provincial law that are each valid or

8. Former Postal Service employees who believe they <u>may be affected</u> by this settlement should contact their last place of USPS employment, the department advised.

   (A) may be affected
   (B) may be effected
   (C) will have been affected
   (D) will be effected
   (E) will have been effected

9. Blake is among the very few individuals <u>who critics regard as genuinely significant in the history of both</u> art and literature.

   (A) who critics regard as genuinely significant in the history of both
   (B) whom critics regard as genuinely significant in the history of both
   (C) whom critics regard as genuinely significant both in the history of
   (D) who critics regard as genuinely significant both in the history of
   (E) who is regarded by critics as genuinely significant in the history of both

10. Many scientists are alarmed over the interest in such pseudo-scientific topics as ESP, flying saucers, and the occult, fearing that <u>this interest may herald a new dark age of gullibility, ignorance, and thinking in superstitious ways</u>.

    (A) this interest may herald a new dark age of gullibility, ignorance, and thinking in superstitious ways
    (B) it may herald a new dark age of gullibility, ignorance, and thinking in superstitious ways

(C) it may herald a new dark age of gullibility, ignorance, and superstition

(D) this interest may herald a new dark age of gullibility, ignorance, and superstition

(E) they may herald a new dark age of gullibility, ignorance, and superstition

11. <u>Having broken with Freud, Jung's later writings nevertheless bore signs of the continued</u> influence of Freudian doctrine and theories.

(A) Having broken with Freud, Jung's later writings nevertheless bore signs of the continued

(B) Since breaking with Freud, Jung's later writings nevertheless bore signs of the continued

(C) Although he had broken with Freud, in his later writings Jung nevertheless showed signs of the continued

(D) Having broken with Freud, Jung's later writings nevertheless bore signs of the continual

(E) Having broken with Freud, later writings by Jung nevertheless bore signs of the continued

12. That Giotto's paintings are significant in the history of the early Renaissance is undeniable, but Giotto <u>cannot scarcely be considered</u> the equal of such masters as Leonardo and Raphael.

(A) cannot scarcely be considered

(B) can scarcely be considered

(C) cannot hardly be considered

(D) cannot scarcely be considered to be

(E) isn't hardly to be considered

13. Although the theory of continental drift <u>was not widely accepted until the mid-twentieth century, the basic concept had been</u> described as early as 1620.

(A) was not widely accepted until the mid-twentieth century, the basic concept had been

(B) was not widely accepted until the mid-twentieth century, the basic concept was

(C) was not widely accepted until the mid-twentieth century, the basic concept has been

(D)   had not been widely accepted until the mid-twentieth century,
      the basic concept has been

(E)   had not been widely accepted until the mid-twentieth century,
      the basic concept was

14. The reason I am supporting Senator Blandings is <u>because her
extensive background in foreign affairs has made her uniquely
qualified for</u> a seat on this important subcommittee.

(A)   because her extensive background in foreign affairs has made
      her uniquely qualified for

(B)   that her extensive background in foreign affairs have made
      her uniquely qualified for

(C)   that her extensive background in foreign affairs has made her
      uniquely qualified for

(D)   that her extensive background in foreign affairs has made her
      uniquely qualified to

(E)   because her extensive background in foreign affairs have
      made her uniquely qualified for

15. Even without any promotion of passenger service by Amtrak, there
<u>has been sufficient numbers of passengers leaving and arriving at
this station to warrant not only continuing the two daily stops here
but also maintaining</u> the agent and station.

(A)   has been sufficient numbers of passengers leaving and
      arriving at this station to warrant not only continuing the two
      daily stops here but also maintaining

(B)   have been sufficient numbers of passengers leaving and
      arriving at this station to warrant not only continuing the two
      daily stops here but also maintaining

(C)   have been sufficient numbers of passengers leaving and
      arriving at this station not only to warrant continuing the two
      daily stops here but also maintaining

(D)   has been sufficient numbers of passengers leaving and
      arriving at this station to not only warrant continuing the two
      daily stops here but also maintaining

(E)   have been sufficient numbers of passengers leaving and
      arriving at this station to warrant not only continuing the two
      daily stops here but also to maintain

16. Fear of future nationalistic feelings and a conviction that natural resource endowments should be exploited for the welfare of the residents of the country, <u>rather than for private profit, are</u> shared by all managers of extractive industries there.

    (A) rather than for private profit, are
    (B) rather than for private profit, is
    (C) irregardless of private profit, are
    (D) as opposed to private profit, is
    (E) and not necessarily for private profit, is

17. The lieutenant reminded his men that <u>the only information to be given to the enemy if captured was each individual's name, rank, and serial number</u>.

    (A) the only information to be given to the enemy if captured was each individual's name, rank, and serial number
    (B) the only information to be given to the enemy if they were captured was each individual's name, rank, and serial number
    (C) the only information to be given to the enemy if captured were each individual's name, rank, and serial number
    (D) , if captured, the only information to be given to the enemy was each individual's name, rank, and what his serial number was
    (E) , if they were captured, the only information to be given to the enemy was each individual's name, rank, and serial number

18. Writing a beautiful sonnet is as much an achievement as <u>to finish</u> a 400-page novel.

    (A) to finish   (D) if you finished
    (B) it is to finish   (E) to have finished
    (C) finishing

19. Anyone interested in Web site design can find a job in contemporary industry <u>if you learn</u> the basic coding languages, such as HTML and Java.

    (A) if you learn
    (B) if you will learn
    (C) if he would learn
    (D) by the study of
    (E) by studying

20. During the gasoline shortage of the 1970s caused by the actions of the OPEC nations, <u>the number of accidents on our highways decreased markedly.</u>

   (A) the number of accidents on our highways decreased markedly

   (B) the amount of accidents on our highways decreased markedly

   (C) there were less accidents on our highways

   (D) there were a fewer amount of accidents on our highways

   (E) they found there were many fewer accidents on our highways

21. <u>Being that only twenty-four states</u> have ratified the proposed amendment, we can assume that it will not be adopted.

   (A) Being that only twenty-four states

   (B) Since twenty-four states only

   (C) Being as only twenty-four states

   (D) Seeing as how only twenty-four states

   (E) Inasmuch as only twenty-four states

22. I have studied the works of George Bernard Shaw not only for their plots but <u>also because they are very witty</u>.

   (A) also because they are very witty

   (B) because they are also very witty

   (C) for their wit also

   (D) because they are very witty also

   (E) also for their wit

23. <u>The noise at the airport was deafening, which made conversation</u> difficult if not impossible.

   (A) The noise at the airport was deafening, which made conversation

   (B) The noise at the airport was deafening, and it made conversation

   (C) The deafening noise at the airport made conversation

   (D) The airport noise was deafening, which made conversation

   (E) The noise at the airport was deafening, conversation being

24. The majority of New Yorkers <u>have not been aware that one out of five English-speaking adults in the city lacks</u> critical reading and writing skills.

   (A) have not been aware that one out of five English-speaking adults in the city lacks

(B) have not been aware that one out of five English-speaking
adults in the city lack

(C) has not been aware that one out of five English-speaking
adults in the city lack

(D) has not been aware that one out of five English-speaking
adults in the city lacks

(E) have not been aware that there are one out of five English-
speaking adults in the city lacking

25. Inflation in the United States has not <u>and, we hope, never will
reach</u> a rate of 20 percent a year.

(A) and, we hope, never will reach

(B) reached and, we hope, never will

(C) and hopefully never will reach

(D) reached and, we hope, never will reach

(E) reached and hopefully never will

*If there is still time remaining, you may review the questions in this section only.
In the actual CAT GMAT, you cannot return to a question after you have
confirmed your answer.*

SECTION V   CRITICAL REASONING   Time: 30 minutes

Directions: For each question, choose the best answer among the listed
alternatives.

1. The Black Death that reached Sicily in October 1347 from the ports
of the Crimea traveled the same route as many slaves. Reflecting
the rates of transportation of rats and fleas as well as of humans,
the disease itself demonstrated the commercial integration of Western Europe. It arrived in England—having devastated France—in
the summer of 1348, reached Sweden and Poland towards the end
of 1349, and in the course of three years had infected the whole of
the West with the exceptions of Bohemia and Hungary.

Which of the following statements best summarizes the above?

(A) The spread of the Black Death was caused by the commercial
integration of Western Europe.

(B) The spread of the Black Death was caused by increasing rates
of transportation.

(C) The spread of the Black Death was caused by the transportation of slaves.

(D) The spread of the Black Death was caused by the transportation of rats and fleas.

(E) The spread of the Black Death was caused by increasing contacts with the parts of the Crimea.

2. In almost all developing countries, the initial thrust of their respective trade policies was to foster domestic industries whose production would replace imports. This was a natural and logical strategy, given that import-substituting production could count on an existing known domestic demand, promised some mitigation of national economic dependence, and could be protected easily from external competition through high tariffs, quotas, or subsidies of various kinds.

Which of the following, if true, would weaken the strategy above?

(A) Domestic demand may be unknown.

(B) Quotas are more regressive than tariffs.

(C) Subsidies and import constraints keep domestic prices high and impose a burden on consumers.

(D) Fast economic growth fosters inequality of income.

(E) A protectionist policy may be beneficial to the developing country, but disliked by economically advanced countries.

3. The 15th century was a period in which there was more reading and traveling than at any earlier period of the Middles Ages. The result was an increase of informed opinion, talk and discussion, and greater questioning over a wide range of topics, and the exchanges stimulated by travel helped to modify the opinions of many different individuals. Despite the continuance of intolerance, persecution, and extremism, belief was growing in the agreement attainable through argument, in the power of books, and in peaceful persuasion.

Which of the following statements best summarizes the above?

(A) The 15th century is best characterized by intolerance, persecution, and extremism.

(B) The 15th century is best characterized as an age of doubting.

    (C) In the 15th century, books were only available to those who traveled.

    (D) The experience of books and travel brought new classes of people new confidence and new doubts.

    (E) The 15th century was an age of peaceable persuasion.

4. The quantitative supply of labor (as well as its qualitative composition) depends on the following variables: the size of the population, its age-sex composition, marital structure, and participation rates in the labor force in accordance with these factors.

    Each of the following, if true, could affect the supply of labor EXCEPT:

    (A) Birth and death rates.

    (B) Immigration and emigration.

    (C) Educational level of the population.

    (D) Number of employment agencies.

    (E) Marital status of females.

5. In order to discourage present suburban growth patterns, which because of their low densities are uneconomic to service and wasteful of land and resources, land use policy studies should include research into innovative forms of high density, low-rise housing.

    The above statement is a response to all of the following problems EXCEPT:

    (A) The tendency to exclude light industry from residential areas means that people have to go outside their communities to seek work.

    (B) The traditional practice of using land as a commodity rather than a resource has meant that the location of new communities is often solely governed by a developer's economic convenience.

    (C) There is a lack of coordination between the planning and structure of communities and their relation to transportation networks.

    (D) Present patterns of urban growth have squandered agricultural and rural lands.

    (E) In houses designed for the standard family, there is a lack of inter- and intraunit privacy.

6. Over the last 20 years the rate of increase in total production in Workland has been second to none in the world. However, the growth is more modest when calculated per capita of total population. Over the last ten years progress has been much slower.

   If the information above is accurate, which of the following must be true?

   (A) Workland has a very large population.
   (B) Productivity per capita has not grown as fast during the past ten years.
   (C) Total production has increased faster than population growth.
   (D) The birth rate has declined.
   (E) The per capita production rate has not declined.

7. The earliest known proto-Eskimos are those of the Cape Denbigh Flint complex of northwestern Alaska, including adjacent Baffin Island. Denbigh people and their descendants were well equipped to survive in the Arctic. Their adaptive success is obvious in the speed with which they spread eastward across arctic Canada to northeast Greenland, which they reached by 2000 B.C.

   Which of the following, if true, would refute the above?

   (A) The Cape Denbigh Flint complex dates back to 3000 B.C.
   (B) The Vikings populated Greenland between 800 and 1100 A.D.
   (C) Denbigh artifacts of early settlements in northeast Greenland date back further than Denbigh artifacts found on Baffin Island.
   (D) Denbigh origin lies in the Paleolithic and the Mesolithic period—say about 4000 B.C. of Siberia.
   (E) The Denbigh people are known almost solely from their flint tools.

8. Harry Dyner was the Minister of Petroleum in a small oil-producing country. His country's oil exports were approximately 2 percent of total world oil sales. The Minister of Finance was anxious to maximize petroleum production and export to earn foreign exchange. Dyner, however, believed that increased sales would only drive down the world price of petroleum and lower his country's foreign exchange revenue.

Which of the following would best exemplify an error in Dyner's reasoning?

(A) Price of crude v. price of refined petroleum.

(B) Production goals v. financial goals.

(C) The supply produced by a single country v. aggregate supply on the market.

(D) Seasonal v. long-term supply.

(E) Long-term v. short-term demand.

9. There is no clear line between health and illness; it is easy to forget what it feels like to be really well and to get gradually used to often having a headache, feeling irritable, or tired. There is an unrecognized proportion of the population that has been tipped over the brink into ill health by ubiquitous contaminants.

Which of the following statements best describes the purpose of the above?

(A) The public must be encouraged to have regular medical examinations.

(B) The public must be warned to be aware of various physical and chemical hazards.

(C) The public must be warned to treat seriously such symptoms as headaches, irritability, and tiredness.

(D) The medical professional is not always capable of diagnosing illness.

(E) No one can really be sure if he is healthy or ill.

10. Administrators and executives are members of the most stable occupation.

The stability mentioned in the above statement could be dependent on each of the following factors EXCEPT:

(A) Training and skills.

(B) Nature of the occupation.

(C) Status.

(D) Relatively high income.

(E) Rate of turnover.

11. By far the chief export in the 15th century was textiles. Among these, woolens and worsteds predominated; linens were far less important and silks played an insignificant part. Outside this group, the only important item in the first half of the century was corn, though the exports of fish, lead, and tin were by no means negligible.

Given the above information which of the following statements is correct?

(A) Corn, though not as important an export as textiles was still an important component of the export trade.

(B) Corn was nearly as important an export as linen.

(C) Silk was a valuable export in the 15th century.

(D) Fishing was a bigger industry than wool production in the 15th century.

(E) Nontextile items were one of the chief elements in the list of products exported in the 15th century.

12. Self-employment is found more often among men and women in the 25- to 44-year-old group than among their older or younger counterparts. Some 31 percent of the men and only 19 percent of the women who operate unincorporated businesses on a full-time basis completed four or more years of college. And while self-employed men are generally better educated than their wage-and-salary counterparts, the same cannot be said of self-employed women.

If the information above is accurate, which of the following must be true?

(A) Self-employed women are generally younger than self-employed men.

(B) Self-employed men have more education than self-employed women.

(C) Women wage earners have more education than men wage earners.

(D) Salaried men are younger than self-employed men.

(E) Self-employed men and women have more education than wage-earning men and women.

13. Between 1940 and 1945 gasoline consumption in the U.S. dropped about 35 percent because of wartime rationing. In the same period, lung cancer in U.S. white males declined by approximately the same percentage. Between 1914 and 1950 lung cancer mortality increased nineteenfold and the rate of gasoline consumption increased at the same rate.

    Which of the following facts, if true, would weaken the above argument?

    (A) For each of the years between 1939 and 1949, lung cancer among urban blacks in the United States remained at the same level.
    (B) The amount of lead in gasoline increased between 1916 and 1944.
    (C) After 1950 gasoline consumption jumped.
    (D) During World War II, people suffering from cancer were forbidden to drive.
    (E) Women first began driving in large numbers between 1941 and 1951.

14. From 1920 to 1950, the amount of food production per worker and per hour increased twofold. From 1950 to 1980, food production per worker and per hour increased 1.3 times.

    Each of the following, if true, could help to account for this trend EXCEPT:

    (A) The number of farm workers increased.
    (B) The use of mechanical technology in food production decreased.
    (C) The use of chemical fertilizers decreased.
    (D) The number of hours worked per unit of output decreased.
    (E) More workers were needed to produce the same unit of output.

15. "Some men are certainly tall, others are certainly not tall; but of intermediate men, we should say, 'tall'? Yes, I *think* so or no, I shouldn't be inclined to call him tall."

    Which of the following most accurately reflects the intention of the writer of the above?

    (A) Men intermediately tall partake of "tallness" to a moderate degree.

(B) To call men tall who are not strikingly so must be to use the concept with undue imprecision.

(C) Every empirical concept has a degree of vagueness.

(D) There is really no need to be as indecisive as the writer of the above.

(E) Calling someone tall or short depends upon one's whim.

16. There are many reasons that individuals want to run their own businesses. Some foresee more personal satisfaction if they are successful in launching their own business, while others are interested mainly in the prospect of larger financial rewards. Since the late 1970s and early 1980s, tax regulations and other changes have encouraged increasing numbers of venture capitalists and entrepreneurs to start new enterprises. Since 1980, some one-half million new ventures have been started. Not all have succeeded, of course.

The above statement makes which of the following assumptions?

(A) Success in starting a new business depends in large part on sound financial planning.

(B) Social incentives motivate investors just as much as financial rewards.

(C) Financial incentives are associated with new business starts.

(D) Most new business ventures succeed initially but fail later on.

(E) Venture capitalists are motivated by nonmonetary gains.

17. A highly cohesive work group is a prerequisite for high team performance. Sociologists posit that the association between group cohesion and success is owing to the support individual team members give to one another and their acceptance of the group's goals and activities.

Each of the following, if true, either provides support for or cannot weaken the sociologists' assumption about the relationship between cohesion and success EXCEPT:

(A) A group of German researchers found that successful work teams were headed by dominant leaders.

(B) Industrial psychologists in England found that work groups who tended to participate in after hours social activities were more productive.

(C) University researchers found that there was a significant correlation between team productivity and the extent to which team members understood and complied with the group's objectives.

(D) American researchers found that successful team members tended to rate their fellow members more favorably.

(E) The winning team in a computerized business game rated their peers generally low on "stick by the rules," "extrovert," "friendly," and "positive" and high on "egocentric," "individualistic," and "discord."

18. The development of the American consumer might have been influenced by the tradition of the frontier, which made self-reliance necessary, as well as by the experience of immigration. The European consumer, on the other hand, might have been fashioned by the not-yet-forgotten experience of distinct classes and class rigidity, as well as by the former absence of geographical and occupational mobility.

The thesis above assumes that:

(A) European consumers are more experienced buyers than their counterparts in America.

(B) American consumers have not reached the sophistication of Europeans.

(C) Social class has a greater influence on consumer behavior in Europe than in America.

(D) A study of consumerism must take into consideration social class structure, tradition, acculturation, and mobility.

(E) Consumer behavior is not an exact science as evidenced by the lack of a definitive framework for understanding the differences between buyers in different countries.

19. Before the middle of the 14th century, there were no universities north of Italy, except in France and England. By the end of the 15th century, there were 23 universities in this region, from Louvain and Mainz to Rostock, Cracow, and Bratislava and the number of universities in Europe as a whole had more than doubled.

Given the above information, which of the following statements is correct?

(A) Until the age of university expansion in the 15th century, there were perhaps 11 universities in the whole of Europe.

(B) South of Italy there were 23 universities in the 14th century.

(C) In the 13th century, France and England were the only countries in Europe with universities.

(D) After the great age of university expansion in the 14th and 15th centuries, France and England were not the only northern European countries to have such centers of learning.

(E) Italy was the cradle of university expansion.

20. Between 1979 and 1983, the number of unincorporated business self-employed women increased five times faster than the number of self-employed men and more than three times faster than women wage-and-salary workers. Part-time self-employment among women increased more than full-time self-employment.

Each of the following, if true, could help to account for this trend EXCEPT:

(A) Owning a business affords flexibility to combine work and family responsibilities.

(B) The proportion of women studying business administration courses has grown considerably.

(C) There are more self-employed women than men.

(D) Unincorporated service industries have grown by 300 percent over the period; the ratio of women to men in this industry is three to one.

(E) The financial reward of having a second wage earner in the household has taken on increased significance.

If there is still time remaining, you may review the questions in this section only. In the actual CAT GMAT, you cannot return to a question after you have confirmed your answer.

SECTION VI   SENTENCE CORRECTION   Time: 30 minutes

Directions: This test consists of a number of sentences, in each of which some part or the whole is underlined. Each sentence is followed by five alternative versions of the underlined portion. Select the alternative you consider both most correct and most effective according to the requirements of standard written English. Answer A is the same as the original version; if you think the original version is best, select answer A.

In considering the answer choices, be attentive to matters of grammar, diction, and syntax, as well as clarity, precision, and fluency. Do not select an answer that alters the meaning of the original sentence.

1. Since neither of the agencies had submitted the necessary documentation, <u>each were required to reapply for the grant the following year</u>.

   (A) each were required to reapply for the grant the following year
   (B) each were required, the following year, to reapply for the grant
   (C) each was required to reapply for the grant the following year
   (D) both were required to reapply, the following year, for the grant
   (E) it was required to reapply for the grant the following year

2. Stationary missile launching sites are frequently criticized by military experts on the ground that, in comparison to mobile units, <u>they are the most</u> vulnerable to preemptive attack.

   (A) they are the most
   (B) such sites are the most
   (C) they are rather
   (D) stationary sites are most
   (E) they are more

3. The qualities needed in a president are scarcely tested in today's political campaigns, which call instead for showmanship, good looks, and <u>being able to seem eloquent</u> while saying nothing.

   (A) being able to seem eloquent
   (B) the ability to seem eloquent
   (C) having eloquence
   (D) a certain eloquence
   (E) that he seem eloquent

4. <u>Anyone who would speak</u> with authority on the poets of the Renaissance must have a broad acquaintance with the writers of classical antiquity.

   (A) Anyone who would speak
   (B) If one would speak
   (C) He which would speak
   (D) Anyone desirous for speaking
   (E) Those who have a wish to speak

5. <u>Having chosen to demand an immediate vote on the issue,</u>
   because of his belief that a sizable majority was within easy reach.

   (A) Having chosen to demand an immediate vote on the issue
   (B) An immediate vote on the issue having been demanded
   (C) He had chosen to demand an immediate vote on the issue
   (D) His demand had been for an immediate vote to be held on the
       issue
   (E) He had chosen that a vote on the issue should be held
       immediately

6. In its final report, the commission proposed, among other measures,
   <u>that the legal drinking age be raised</u> from eighteen to twenty-one.

   (A) that the legal drinking age be raised
   (B) a rise of the legal drinking age
   (C) that the legal drinking age should be raised
   (D) raising the age of drinking legally
   (E) to raise legally the drinking age

7. Since neither <u>her nor the Dean were willing</u> to veto the curriculum
   changes, they went into effect as of September 1.

   (A) her nor the Dean were willing
   (B) she nor the Dean was willing
   (C) her nor the Dean wished
   (D) she or the Dean was willing
   (E) she nor the Dean were willing

8. <u>A broad range of opinions was represented between</u> the various
   members of the steering committee.

   (A) A broad range of opinions was represented between
   (B) A broad range of opinions were represented between
   (C) A broad range of opinions had been held by
   (D) A broad range of opinions was represented among
   (E) Varying opinions were represented by

9. Undaunted by the political repercussions of his decision, <u>the new
   gasoline rationing plan was announced by the Governor</u> at the
   state office building last Friday.

   (A) the new gasoline rationing plan was announced by the Governor

(B) the Governor's new gasoline rationing plan was announced

(C) the Governor made the announcement concerning the new gasoline rationing plan

(D) the new gasoline rationing plan of the Governor was announced

(E) the Governor announced the new gasoline rationing plan

10. Mario <u>had already swum five laps when I</u> jumped into the pool.

(A) had already swum five laps when I

(B) already swam five laps when I

(C) already swam five laps when I had

(D) had already swum five laps when I had

(E) had already swam five laps when I

11. Despite their avowed opposition to the strike, no one <u>from among the dozens of nonunion workers were willing</u> to cross the picket line.

(A) from among the dozens of nonunion workers were willing

(B) of the dozens of nonunion workers were willing

(C) was willing from among the dozens of nonunion workers

(D) from among the dozens of nonunion workers was willing

(E) from the dozens of nonunion workers were willing

12. According to one recent survey, gasoline economy, low price, <u>and safety have replaced</u> style and comfort as leading factors in the choice of a new car.

(A) and safety have replaced

(B) and safe driving have replaced

(C) and safety has replaced

(D) as well as safety has replaced

(E) along with safety have replaced

13. The poetry of George Herbert is regarded by many critics as <u>equal in quality, though less influential, than the work</u> of his more famous contemporary John Donne.

(A) equal in quality, though less influential, than the work

(B) equal in quality to, though less influential than, the work

(C) qualitatively equal, though less influential than, that

(D) equal in quality, though less influential, than the work

(E) of equal quality, though of less influence, than that

14. If it is the present administration <u>whom we should blame</u> for the economic crisis, the first step toward a solution is to reject the incumbent at the polls this November.

    (A) whom we should blame
    (B) whom is to blame
    (C) who we should blame
    (D) who should be blamed
    (E) who one should blame

15. The assembly speaker has called for a shorter fall session of the legislature <u>in hopes that less amendments of a</u> purely symbolic nature will be proposed by the state's lawmakers.

    (A) in hopes that less amendments of a
    (B) hoping that fewer amendments that have a
    (C) in hopes that fewer amendments of a
    (D) in order that less amendments of a
    (E) in hope that fewer amendments of

16. <u>One of the costliest engineering projects ever undertaken, both public and private funds have been needed to support the space shuttle program.</u>

    (A) One of the costliest engineering projects ever undertaken, both public and private funds have been needed to support the space shuttle program.
    (B) One of the costliest engineering projects ever undertaken, support for the space shuttle program has come from both public and private funds.
    (C) The space shuttle program has been supported by both public and private funds, one of the costliest engineering projects ever undertaken.
    (D) From both public and private funds support has come for one of the costliest engineering projects ever undertaken; namely, the space shuttle program.
    (E) Both public and private funds have been needed to support the space shuttle program, one of the costliest engineering projects ever undertaken.

17. Parker's testimony made it clear that <u>he appointed Ryan before he had become aware</u> of Ryan's alleged underworld connections.

(A) he appointed Ryan before he had become aware

(B) he appointed Ryan before his awareness

(C) he had appointed Ryan prior to his having become aware

(D) his appointment of Ryan preceded awareness

(E) he had appointed Ryan before becoming aware

18. <u>Despite its being smaller in size than are</u> conventional automobile engines, the new Alcock Engine can still deliver the horsepower needed for most short-distance city driving.

(A) Despite its being smaller in size than are

(B) In spite of its being smaller than

(C) Although smaller than

(D) Despite its size relative to

(E) Though not comparable in size to

19. Seventy-four applications were received, <u>of whom the better were selected</u> for detailed review.

(A) of whom the better were selected

(B) from which were selected the better

(C) the best of which were selected

(D) from whom were selected the best

(E) from which they selected the best

20. <u>If the British government had had no fear of</u> the increasing hostility of the Indian populace, Gandhi's nonviolent tactics would have availed little.

(A) If the British government had had no fear of

(B) If the British government did not fear

(C) Had the British government no fear

(D) If the British government did not have fear of

(E) Would the British government not have feared

21. The official imposition of "Lysenkoism" on Soviet biologists, with its chilling effects on scientists in countless related fields, <u>illustrate vividly the danger of government interference with science</u>.

(A) illustrate vividly the dangers of government interference with science

    (B) illustrate the dangers of government interference with science vividly

    (C) illustrates vividly the dangers of government interference with science

    (D) vividly illustrate the dangers of government interference with science

    (E) vividly illustrates how dangerous can be government interference with science

22. Health care costs have been forced upward less by increases in the salaries of nurses, technicians, and other personnel <u>than by increases in the amounts</u> spent on diagnostic machinery and electronic equipment.

    (A) than by increases in the amounts

    (B) than the amounts

    (C) but by increases in the amounts

    (D) and more by increases in the amounts

    (E) than by funds

23. The press secretary announced that <u>neither himself nor the President would be</u> available for questions until they had had more time to examine the report.

    (A) neither himself nor the President would be

    (B) neither he or the President was

    (C) neither he nor the President would be

    (D) he and the President will not be

    (E) he nor the President would be

24. In routine cases, the Civilian Review Board receives all complaints about police misconduct, weighs the evidence and the seriousness of the charges, and <u>then it decides whether a formal inquiry is needed</u>.

    (A) then it decides whether a formal inquiry is needed

    (B) then decides if a formal inquiry would be needed

    (C) then it decides whether to hold a formal inquiry

    (D) then decides whether a formal inquiry is needed

    (E) decides at that point if a formal inquiry is needed or not

25. Current scientific theory suggests that the dinosaurs were, in fact, one of the most spectacularly successful <u>groups of organisms ever developed</u> in the course of evolution.

(A) groups of organisms ever developed
(B) group of organisms that have been developed
(C) groups of organisms to ever be developed
(D) groups of organisms to be developed
(E) groups of organism developed

If there is still time remaining, you may review the questions in this section only. In the actual CAT GMAT, you cannot return to a question after you have confirmed your answer.

SECTION VII   PROBLEM SOLVING   Time: 30 minutes

Directions: Solve each of the following problems; then indicate the correct answer on your answer sheet. [On the actual test you will be permitted to use scratch paper for your calculations.]

A figure that appears with a problem is drawn as accurately as possible unless the words "figure not drawn to scale" appear next to the figure. Numbers in this test are real numbers.

1. Dictionaries weigh 6 pounds each and a set of encyclopedias weighs 75 pounds. 20 dictionaries are shipped in each box. 2 sets of encyclopedias are shipped in each box. A truck is loaded with 98 boxes of dictionaries and 50 boxes of encyclopedias. How much does the truck's load weigh?

(A) 588 pounds   (D) 19,260 pounds
(B) 7,500 pounds   (E) 22,840 pounds
(C) 11,750 pounds

2. Mary is paid $600 a month on her regular job. During July in addition to her regular job, she makes $400 from a second job. Approximately what percentage of her annual income does Mary make in July? Assume Mary has no other income except the income mentioned above.

(A) 8   (D) 13
(B) $8\frac{1}{3}$ (E) 14
(C) $12\frac{1}{2}$

3. If the area of a triangle with base S is equal to the area of a square with side S, then the altitude of the triangle is

(A) $\frac{1}{2}S$ (D) $3S$

(B) S (E) $4S$

(C) $2S$

4. A train travels at an average speed of 20 mph through urban areas, 50 mph through suburban areas, and 75 mph through rural areas. If a trip consists of traveling half an hour through urban areas, $3\frac{1}{2}$ hours through suburban areas, and 3 hours through rural areas, what is the train's average speed for the entire trip?

(A) 50 mph   (D) $58\frac{4}{7}$ mph

(B) $53\frac{2}{7}$ mph   (E) $59\frac{2}{7}$ mph

(C) $54\frac{3}{7}$ mph

5. $(x - y)(y + 3)$ is equal to

(A) $x^2 - 3y + 3$ (D) $xy - 3y + y^2 + 3x$

(B) $xy - 3y + y^2$ (E) $y^2 - 3y + 3x - xy$

(C) $xy - y^2 - 3y + 3x$

6. If $x < y$, $y < z$, and $z > w$, which of the following statements is always true?

(A) $x > w$ (D) $y > w$

(B) $x < z$ (E) $x < w$

(C) $y = w$

7. What is the ratio of $\frac{2}{3}$ to $\frac{5}{4}$?

(A) $\frac{1}{4}$ (D) $\frac{20}{6}$

(B) $\frac{10}{12}$ (E) $\frac{2}{7}$

(C) $\frac{8}{15}$

8. Of the numbers, 7, 9, 11, 13, 29, 33, how many are prime numbers?

(A) none   (D) 5

(B) 3   (E) all

(C) 4

9. A company issues 100,000 shares of stock. In 1960 each of the shares was worth $9.50. In 1970 each share was worth $13.21. How much more were the 100,000 shares worth in 1970 than in 1960?

(A) $37,000   (D) $371,000
(B) $37,010   (E) $371,100
(C) $37,100

10. A worker's daily salary varies each day. In one week he worked five days. His daily salaries were $40.62, $41.35, $42.00, $42.50, and $39.53. What was his average daily salary for the week?

(A) $40.04   (D) $41.20
(B) $40.89   (E) $206.00
(C) $41.04

11. One dozen eggs and ten pounds of apples are currently the same price. If the price of a dozen eggs rises by 10% and the price of the apples goes up by 2%, how much more will it cost to buy a dozen eggs and ten pounds of apples?

(A) 2%   (D) 12%
(B) 6%   (E) 12.2%
(C) 10%

12. How many two-digit prime numbers have a remainder of 2 when divided by 7?

(A) none   (D) three
(B) one   (E) more than three
(C) two

13. If 25 men can unload a truck in 1 hour and 30 minutes, how long should it take 15 men to unload the truck?

(A) 2 hours   (D) $2\frac{1}{2}$ hours
(B) $2\frac{1}{4}$ hours   (E) 3 hours
(C) $2\frac{1}{3}$ hours

14. A car gets 20 miles per gallon of gas when it travels at 50 miles per hour. The car gets 12% fewer miles to the gallon at 60 miles per hour. How far can the car travel at 60 miles per hour on 11 gallons of gas?

    (A) 193.6 miles   (D) 204.3 miles
    (B) 195.1 miles   (E) 220 miles
    (C) 200 miles

15. Feathers cost $500 a ton for the first 12 tons and $(500 − x) a ton for any tons over 12. What is x, if it costs $10,000 for 30 tons of feathers?

    (A) 270.00   (D) 277.78
    (B) 277.00   (E) 280.00
    (C) 277.70

16. The angles of a triangle are in the ratio 2:3:4. The largest angle in the triangle is

    (A) 30°   (D) 75°
    (B) 40°   (E) 80°
    (C) 70°

17. Find the area of the trapezoid $ABCD$. $AB = CD = 5$, $BC = 10$, $AD = 16$, and BE is an altitude of the trapezoid.

    (A) 50
    (B) 52
    (C) 64
    (D) 80
    (E) 160

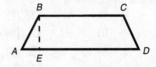

18. If x is less than 2, which of the following statements are always true?

    I. x is negative.
    II. x is positive.
    III. $2x$ is greater than or equal to x.
    IV. x^2 is greater than or equal to x.

    (A) III only   (D) I, III, and IV only
    (B) IV only   (E) none of the statements
    (C) I and III only

19. A worker is digging a ditch. He gets 2 assistants who work $\frac{2}{3}$ as fast as he does. If all 3 work on a ditch they should finish it in what fraction of the time that the worker takes working alone?

(A) $\frac{3}{7}$ (D) $\frac{4}{3}$

(B) $\frac{1}{2}$ (E) $\frac{7}{3}$

(C) $\frac{3}{4}$

20. In a survey of political preferences, 78% of those asked were in favor of at least one of the proposals: I, II, and III. 50% of those asked favored proposal I, 30% favored proposal II, and 20% favored proposal III. If 5% of those asked favored all three of the proposals, what percentage of those asked favored more than one of the three proposals?

(A) 5 (D) 17

(B) 10 (E) 22

(C) 12

If there is still time remaining, you may review the questions in this section only. In the actual CAT GMAT, you cannot return to a question after you have confirmed your answer.

ANSWERS

Section I Problem Solving

1. **(D)**	6. **(E)**	11. **(E)**	16. **(B)**
2. **(E)**	7. **(D)**	12. **(D)**	17. **(B)**
3. **(B)**	8. **(A)**	13. **(C)**	18. **(B)**
4. **(E)**	9. **(C)**	14. **(C)**	19. **(A)**
5. **(C)**	10. **(D)**	15. **(D)**	20. **(B)**

Section II Reading Comprehension

1. **(E)**	8. **(D)**	15. **(D)**	22. **(C)**
2. **(C)**	9. **(B)**	16. **(C)**	23. **(D)**
3. **(B)**	10. **(C)**	17. **(E)**	24. **(B)**
4. **(B)**	11. **(C)**	18. **(B)**	25. **(C)**
5. **(A)**	12. **(C)**	19. **(E)**	
6. **(A)**	13. **(C)**	20. **(B)**	
7. **(C)**	14. **(C)**	21. **(B)**	

Section III   Data Sufficiency

1. (A)	8. (C)	15. (E)	22. (D)
2. (A)	9. (C)	16. (E)	23. (C)
3. (E)	10. (E)	17. (E)	24. (A)
4. (E)	11. (C)	18. (D)	25. (A)
5. (A)	12. (D)	19. (C)	
6. (D)	13. (A)	20. (A)	
7. (D)	14. (A)	21. (E)	

Section IV   Sentence Correction

1. (C)	8. (A)	15. (B)	22. (E)
2. (B)	9. (B)	16. (A)	23. (C)
3. (C)	10. (D)	17. (E)	24. (D)
4. (E)	11. (C)	18. (C)	25. (D)
5. (B)	12. (B)	19. (E)	
6. (D)	13. (A)	20. (A)	
7. (B)	14. (C)	21. (E)	

Section V   Critical Reasoning

1. (A)	6. (B)	11. (A)	16. (C)
2. (C)	7. (C)	12. (B)	17. (E)
3. (D)	8. (C)	13. (A)	18. (D)
4. (D)	9. (B)	14. (D)	19. (D)
5. (E)	10. (E)	15. (C)	20. (C)

Section VI   Sentence Correction

1. (C)	8. (D)	15. (C)	22. (A)
2. (E)	9. (E)	16. (E)	23. (C)
3. (B)	10. (A)	17. (E)	24. (D)
4. (A)	11. (D)	18. (C)	25. (A)
5. (C)	12. (A)	19. (C)	
6. (A)	13. (B)	20. (A)	
7. (B)	14. (A)	21. (C)	

Section VII   Problem Solving

1. (D)	6. (B)	11. (B)	16. (E)
2. (D)	7. (C)	12. (D)	17. (B)
3. (C)	8. (C)	13. (D)	18. (E)
4. (D)	9. (D)	14. (A)	19. (A)
5. (C)	10. (D)	15. (D)	20. (D)

ANALYSIS

Section I Problem Solving

1. **(D)** Since $\dfrac{12}{4} = 3 = \dfrac{36}{12}$ the ratio of one term to the previous term is 3.

   So if x is the next term, $\dfrac{x}{36} = 3$ and $x = 3(36) = 108$.

2. **(E)** The complement of x is an angle of $90 - x$ degrees, and the supplement of x is an angle of $180 - x$ degrees. Thus, we have $90 - x = \dfrac{1}{6}\ (180 - x) = 30 - \dfrac{1}{6}x$, so $60 = \dfrac{5}{6}x$ or $x = 72$.

3. **(B)** If $x = 3$, then $x^2 = 9$, and
   $\dfrac{3}{(x^2)} = \dfrac{3}{9} = \dfrac{1}{3}$. So $\dfrac{3}{(x^2)} + x = \dfrac{1}{3} + 3 = \dfrac{10}{3}$.

4. **(E)** Since 4 is a multiple of 2, the least common multiple of 3, 4, and 5 will be the least common multiple of 2, 3, 4, 5. 3, 4, and 5 have no common factors so the least common multiple is $3 \cdot 4 \cdot 5 = 60$.

5. **(C)** Since 10% have both brown eyes and brown hair, and 25% have brown eyes, 15% of the people have brown eyes but do not have brown hair. Thus, 40% + 15% or 55% of the people have brown eyes or brown hair or both. Therefore, 100% – 55% or 45% of the people have neither brown eyes nor brown hair.

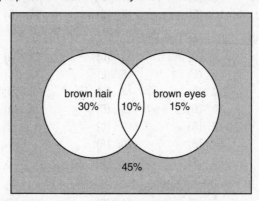

6. **(E)** Area = ½ (altitude)(base). The increased altitude is (1.05) altitude and the increased base is (1.07) base. Therefore, the increased area is ½(1.05)(1.07)(altitude)(base). So the increased area is (1.1235) area. Thus, the area has increased by 12.35%.

7. **(D)** The first 20 pounds cost $20 \cdot 2¢ = 40¢$. The package weighs $3\frac{1}{2}$ pounds more than 20 pounds, so there are 3 pounds and one fraction of a pound over 20 pounds. The weight over 20 pounds will cost $4 \cdot (1.5)¢ = 6¢$. Therefore, the total cost will be 46¢.

8. **(A)** Since $5,000 - 1,000 = 4,000$, there are 4,000 sheets which will be discounted. The 4,000 sheets cost 4,000¢ or $40.00 before the discount, so they will cost $(.98)(\$40.00)$ or $39.20 after the 2% discount. The first 1,000 sheets cost 1¢ each so they cost 1,000¢ or $10.00. Therefore, the total cost of the 5,000 sheets will be $49.20.

9. **(C)** Let T be Tom's salary, J be John's salary, and S be Steve's salary. Then the given information is $T = (1.5)J$ and $J = (.8)S$. Changing to fractions we get $T = \frac{3}{2}J$ and $J = \frac{4}{5}S$ so $S = \frac{5}{4}J$. Therefore, $\frac{S}{T} = \frac{5}{4}J / \frac{3}{2}J = \frac{5}{4} / \frac{3}{2} = \frac{5}{4} \cdot \frac{2}{3} = \frac{5}{6}$. The ratio is 5 to 6.

10. **(D)** The amount pledged is $P \times \$R$ and the amount that was not received is $Q \times \$S$. Therefore, the charity received $PR - QS$. So the percentage received is

$$\% = 100 \times \frac{(PR - QS)}{(PR)}$$

$$\% = 100 \times \left(1 - \frac{QS}{PR}\right)$$

$$\% = 100 - \frac{100QS}{PR}$$

11. **(E)** 30 workers are $\frac{3}{5}$ of 50 workers, so it should take the 30 workers $\frac{5}{3}$ as long as the 50 workers. Therefore, the 30 workers should take $= \frac{5}{3} \cdot 4 = \frac{20}{3} = 6\frac{2}{3}$ hours = 6 hours and 40 minutes.

12. **(D)** Call x the amount of type 20 grass seed that will be added. Then the total amount of grass seed will be $3 + x$ pounds. Since the resulting mixture should contain 15 percent herbicide, the total amount of herbicide will be $.15(3 + x)$. However, the total amount

of herbicide is also the herbicide from type 05 plus the herbicide from type 20. This is $.05 \times 3$ plus $.20 \times x$, which gives $.15 + .2x$. Therefore, we have the equation $.15(3 + x)$ or $.45 + .15x$, which $= .15 + .2x$. Solving for x gives $.3 = .05x$ or $x = 6$. So the correct answer is 6 pounds of type 20 must be added to the original 3 pounds.

13. **(C)** The car is traveling 15 mph faster than the truck. Since the car and truck were in the same place at 10 o'clock, 4 hours later at 2 o'clock the car will be 4 hours $\times$ 15 mph $= 60$ miles from the truck.

14. **(C)** Statement I is false since there was a loss in 1995. II is false since the profits decreased from 1997 to 1998.

15. **(D)** If $x - 2 < y$, then $x < y + 2$.

16. **(B)** The price of wheat (in dollars) will be $2(1.1)^n$ after n months. This will be greater than 2.62 when $(1.1)^n$ is greater than $2.62/2 = 1.31$. Since $1.1 \times 1.1 = 1.21$ and $1.1 \times 1.1 \times 1.1 = 1.331$, after three months the price of a bushel of corn will be less than the price of a bushel of wheat.

17. **(B)** If $\dfrac{1}{2} + \dfrac{1}{4} = \dfrac{x}{15}$, then since $\dfrac{1}{2} + \dfrac{1}{4} = \dfrac{3}{4}$ we have that $\dfrac{3}{4} = \dfrac{x}{15}$.

So $x = \dfrac{45}{4} = 11\dfrac{1}{4} = 11.25$.

18. **(B)** If three of the numbers were negative, then as long as the fourth is greater than the absolute value of the sum of the other three, the sum of all four will be positive. For example, $(-50) + (-35) + (-55) + 155 = 15$.

19. **(A)** Area $= LW$. The increased length is $1.11L$ and W is unchanged; so the increased area is $(1.11L)W = (1.11)(LW) = (1.11)A$. Therefore, the increase in area is $1.11A - A = .11A$; and the area is increased by 11%.

20. **(B)** The area of the circle is $\pi \times \sqrt{2} \times \sqrt{2} = 2\pi$. Since $3^2 + 4^2 = 5^2$, the triangle in III is a right triangle. So it has an altitude and base equal to 3 and 4. Therefore, its area is $(1/2) \times 3 \times 4 = 6$, which is less than 2π because π is greater than 3.

Let ABC be the equilateral triangle of II. Then if AD is an altitude of ABC, the right triangles ABD and ACD are congruent. So BD must equal CD, which means $BD = 4/2 = 2$. Now we can compute the length of the altitude AD by the Pythagorean relation. AD is the square root of AC squared minus CD squared. So AD is the square root of $(4^2 - 2^2 = 16 - 4 = 12)$. Hence, the area of ABC is $(1/2) \times$

$4 \times \sqrt{12} = 2 \times 2 \times \sqrt{3} = 4\sqrt{3}$. Thus II has the largest area since $4\sqrt{3}$ is larger than 2π. ($4\sqrt{3}$ is about 6.93 and 2π is only about 6.28.)

Section II   Reading Comprehension

1. **(E)** The report (on which the passage is based) is certainly not optimistic (B), but rather pessimistic in its assessment, although not specifically about the trade gap (D). Nor can the report be characterized as harshly condemnatory (A) or critical of labor unions (C). After all, as pointed out in the passage, it is labor that will suffer. The answer is (E). This is specifically supported by the first and second paragraphs.

2. **(C)** Free trade is the reduction or elimination of tariffs and duties on exports. See lines 3 and 16–17.

3. **(B)** Manufacturers that cannot increase productivity in order to lower prices will not be able to compete with duty-free imports, and will not receive adjustment assistance, i.e., subsidies or some other financial payments to buttress them in the face of foreign competition.

4. **(B)** The author's recommendation is that redundant labor should be removed. See lines 39–40.

5. **(A)** Even though the subject of trade with the Common Market (C) is discussed, the major thrust of the passage is on the consequences of free trade—in this case, with the Common Market.

6. **(A)** Only alternative I was mentioned in paragraph 1. II is incorrect because the workers will be *displaced*, not unemployed.

7. **(C)** The author blames the government for not making its position clear with regard to trade policy. See lines 15–16.

8. **(D)** The passage specifically mentions industrial goods on line 17.

9. **(B)** The manufacturing sector only will be impacted. The indifferent attitude of the service sector (paragraphs 4 and 5) is owing to the fact that it will not be affected by tariff reductions.

10. **(C)** This is stated in paragraph 2 of the passage.

11. **(C)** The major objective is to explain the objectives of sociology, which are the same as those of science. See line 1.

12. **(C)** A discussion of this point is given in paragraph 2. The other answers are either factually incorrect or incomplete.

13. **(C)** The final step or objective of science—according to the passage—is explanation (line 2), best stated as a causal proposition. See lines 27–29.

14. **(C)** I and II are mentioned in the first and second paragraphs. III is mentioned in lines 19–21 as one of the activities in which the scientist is *not* interested.

15. **(D)** Answers (B) and (E) are mentioned in the passage, but are secondary in importance to (D). Answer (C) is not correct, and answer (A) is not mentioned in the passage.

16. **(C)** The scientist would not accept I since angels are not considered empirical (see the last paragraph). He would not accept II; since the term *weak character* is not defined, it cannot be observed. The scientist would accept III since all the terms involved in the explanation are observable.

17. **(E)** All the other answers are not mentioned in the paragraph.

18. **(B)** This is mentioned in the first and the final paragraphs. In any case, the prefix *poly* means many and the suffix *theist* means one who believes in a god or gods.

19. **(E)** Answers (A), (B), and (D) cannot be inferred from the passage. Answer (C) is roughly consonant with what the author has to say, but (E) is a stronger example of the question statement.

20. **(B)** I is correct since they worshipped gods in both human and other forms. See lines 13–14.

21. **(B)** Although the author states that certain cultures are more inclined to anthropocentric worship (A), he mentions it while making the point that there are those who attribute it to others, even though practicing it themselves.

22. **(C)** The paragraph indicates that if the universe is partly controlled by the "wet-god" (it rains), then the "dry-god" lacks control. This is an example of incoherence. If you pray for rain, you must also pray to prevent the "dry-god" from exercising his powers, an example of potential conflict. Hence there is hardly a commonality of interests or order in a polytheistic system.

23. **(D)** See lines 22–24.

24. **(B)** See paragraph 2.

25. **(C)** Alternative I is found in line 1; alternative II, in lines 27–40. Alternative III is incorrect; the passage also mentions Romans.

Section III   Data Sufficiency

1. **(A)** STATEMENT (1) alone is sufficient. If angle *ABC* is a right angle, then *AOC* is a semicircle. Therefore, *AC* is a diameter.

You can keep $AB = \frac{3}{4}BC$ and change angle x, and there is always a circle through the points A, B, and C. When angle ABC is a right angle, then AC is a diameter of the circle; but when ABC is not a right angle, then AC is not a diameter of the circle.

Therefore, STATEMENT (1) alone is sufficient, but STATEMENT (2) alone is not sufficient.

2. **(A)** To find how many gallons the tank will hold, we need to calculate the volume of the tank and then divide this by the volume of one gallon of the liquid. Therefore, STATEMENT (1) alone is sufficient.

    STATEMENT (2) alone is not sufficient (note that it gives no further information about the tank). We need to know how much space a gallon of the liquid occupies.

    Therefore, STATEMENT (1) alone is sufficient, but STATEMENT (2) alone is not.

3. **(E)** STATEMENT (1) alone is not sufficient. We still need the total weight of the books; then we can divide by the average weight to obtain the number of books.

    STATEMENT (2) tells how much the books and the bookshelf together weigh, but we don't know how much the books weigh.

    So STATEMENTS (1) and (2) together are not sufficient.

4. **(E)** STATEMENT (1) alone is not sufficient, since many noncongruent triangles can have a side and an angle which are equal.

    By the same reasoning, STATEMENT (2) alone is not sufficient.

    STATEMENTS (1) and (2) together are not sufficient. For two triangles to be congruent, they must have two pairs of corresponding sides and the *included* angles equal. For example, the following two triangles satisfy STATEMENTS (1) and (2) and $x = y$ but they are not congruent.

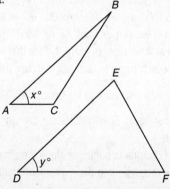

Therefore, STATEMENTS (1) and (2) together are not sufficient.

5. **(A)** The key to solving this problem is the fact that the last digit of a square of an integer is the last digit of the last digit of the integer squared. For example, the last digit of the square of 94 is 6 because the last digit of 16 (which is the square of 4) is 6. If you square each digit {0,1,2,...8,9}, you will see that the only possible last digits for a square are 0,1,4,5,6, and 9. Thus, if the last digit of x is 2, x can *not* be a square. So the square root of x is not an integer. So STATEMENT (1) alone is sufficient. Since 12 is divisible by 3 and is not a square but 36, which is a square, is divisible by 3, STATEMENT (2) alone is not sufficient.

6. **(D)** STATEMENT (1) alone is sufficient. If $L =$ the length of the floor, then STATEMENT (1) says the width is $\frac{1}{2}L$. The area of the floor is length times width or $(L)(\frac{1}{2}L)$ or $\frac{1}{2}L^2$. Since the area is equal to 32 square feet, we have $\frac{1}{2}L^2 = 32$ so $L^2 = 64$ and $L = 8$ feet.

    STATEMENT (2) alone is sufficient. Let $W =$ the width of the floor. Then STATEMENT (2) says $W = L - 4$. So the area is $L(L - 4)$ or $L^2 - 4L$ which equals 32. Therefore, L satisfies $L^2 - 4L - 32 = 0$, and since $L^2 - 4L - 32 = (L - 8)(L + 4)$, $L^2 - 4L - 32 = 0$ if and only if $L = 8$ or $L = -4$. Since $L = -4$ has no meaning for the problem, $L = 8$.

    So STATEMENT (1) alone is sufficient, and STATEMENT (2) alone is sufficient.

7. **(D)** We have to determine whether $(AB)(BC)$ which is the area of the rectangle $ABCD$ is equal to $(EH)^2$ which is the area of the square $EFGH$.

    STATEMENT (1) alone is sufficient. Since ABC is a right triangle, $BC = \sqrt{(AC)^2 - (AB)^2}$, and using STATEMENT (1) we have $BC = \sqrt{(EG)^2 - \frac{1}{4}(EH)^2}$. Using the fact that $EFGH$ is a square, we know $(EG)^2 = 2(EH)^2$, so we can express BC in terms of EH. Using STATEMENT (1) we can express AB as 1/2EH, so $(AB)(BC)$ can be expressed as a multiple of $(EH)^2$. Notice that to answer the question you don't have to actually set up the equation. If you work it out you will find that the area of $ABCD$ is $\frac{\sqrt{7}}{4}(EH)^2$, so the areas are not equal. *Don't* waste time carrying out the extra work on the test.

    STATEMENT (2) alone is sufficient since the diagonal of a rectangle divides the rectangle into two congruent triangles. Therefore, the area of *ABCD* is equal to the area of *EFGH* if and only if the area of *ABC* is equal to the area of *EFG*.

8. **(C)** STATEMENT (2) says $J = 2S$, where $J =$ Joan's weight and $S =$ Susan's weight. But since we don't know Joan's weight, STATEMENT (2) alone is not sufficient.

STATEMENT (1) says $J + S = 250$; so if we use STATEMENT (2) we have $2S + S = 250$ or $S = \dfrac{250}{3} = 83\frac{1}{3}$. But STATEMENT (1) alone is not sufficient. If we use only STATEMENT (1), we don't know how much Joan weighs. Therefore, STATEMENTS (1) and (2) together are sufficient, but neither statement alone is sufficient.

9. **(C)** In each minute, hole *A* drains ¹⁄₂₄ of the tank according to STATEMENT (1). Since we have no information about *B*, STATEMENT (1) alone is not sufficient.

In each minute, hole *B* drains ¹⁄₄₂ of the tank according to STATEMENT (2), but STATEMENT (2) gives no information about hole *A*. So STATEMENT (2) alone is not sufficient.

If we use STATEMENTS (1) and (2), then both holes together will drain $\dfrac{1}{24} + \dfrac{1}{42}$ or $\dfrac{7+4}{6 \times 28}$ or $\dfrac{11}{168}$ of the tank each minute. Therefore, it will take $\dfrac{168}{11}$ or $15\frac{3}{11}$ minutes for the tank to be empty. So STATEMENTS (1) and (2) together are sufficient, but neither statement alone is sufficient.

10. **(E)** STATEMENTS (1) and (2) are equivalent, since $x - y = 6$ if and only if $-2x + 2y = -2(x - y) = (-2)(6) = -12$. Each statement tells us only what $x - y$ is, and we have no other information. Therefore, each statement alone is insufficient. But since the two statements alone are the same, even together they are not sufficient.

11. **(C)** STATEMENT (2) alone is not sufficient, because we must know how close the circles are, and we know only the radius of each circle. STATEMENT (1) alone is not sufficient. If *R* is less than .5, then (1) implies that the circle with center *F* is completely inside the circle with center *D*, so there are no points *E* and *C*. However, if *R* is greater than .5, then the two circles must cross, because (1 + *R*) + *R* is greater than 2. (So we can form a triangle with *DF* as one side and a radius of each circle as the other sides. The third vertex of this triangle must be on both circles.)

(1) and (2) together are sufficient, because *R* is greater than .5, so

statement (1) implies that the two circles intersect. Thus, (C) is the correct choice.

12. **(D)** It is sufficient to be able to find his total income for the years 1967 through 1969 since we divide the total income by 3 to obtain the average income.

   STATEMENT (1) alone is sufficient. Since we know his income for 1967, we can find his income in 1968 and 1969 by using STATEMENT (1). Therefore, we can find the total income. STATEMENT (2) alone is sufficient. Add the combined income from 1968 and 1969 to the income from 1967 (which is given), and we have the total income. Therefore, STATEMENTS (1) and (2) are each sufficient.

13. **(A)** STATEMENT (1) alone is sufficient. If n is divisible by 9, it must be divisible by 3. Since (1) implies that n is not divisible by 3, (1) alone is sufficient.

   STATEMENT (2) alone is not sufficient. 36 is divisible by 9 and its remainder is 1 when divided by 7. However, 15 is not divisible by 9 and its remainder is 1 when divided by 7. So the correct choice is (A).

14. **(A)** STATEMENT (1) alone is sufficient. If P = Paul's height, then we can write a proportion $\dfrac{P}{6} = \dfrac{9}{10}$ since their shadows are proportional to their heights. $\left[\text{Thus, } P = \dfrac{54}{10} = 5.4 \text{ feet.} \right]$

   STATEMENT (2) alone is not sufficient. The distance they are apart does not give us any information about their heights.

   Therefore, STATEMENT (1) alone is sufficient, but STATEMENT (2) alone is not sufficient.

15. **(E)** STATEMENT (1) alone is not sufficient. Note that $4 = (-2)^2 > 1 = (-1)^2$ but $-2 < -1$.

   STATEMENT (2) alone is not sufficient. If $x + 3$ is greater than $y + 2$, then x can be less than y or greater than y. For example, ½ is greater than 0, and ½ + 3 is greater than 0 + 2. However, ½ is less than 1, while ½ + 3 is greater than 1 + 2.

   STATEMENTS (1) and (2) together are not sufficient. For example, $x = -\frac{1}{2}$ is less than $y = \frac{1}{4}$, $-\frac{1}{2} + 3$ is greater than $2 + \frac{1}{4}$, and $(-\frac{1}{2})^2 = \frac{1}{4}$ is greater than $\frac{1}{16} = (\frac{1}{4})^2$. Also, $y = \frac{1}{4}$ is less than $x = 2$, $(\frac{1}{4})^2$ is less than 2^2, and $2 + 3$ is greater than $\frac{1}{4} + 2$. So STATEMENTS (1) and (2) together are not sufficient.

16. **(E)** STATEMENTS (1) and (2) together are insufficient. You need to know whether the wages of the average worker changed. 4 minutes of work in January 1981 could be worth more or less than 90¢.

17. **(E)** Both STATEMENTS (1) and (2) tell you how the line is changing at 7 o'clock. However, you need information about the length of the line at some time in order to use information about how it changes to get the length of the line. For example, if 100 people were on line (1) and (2) could be true, but both (1) and (2) could also be true if 50 people were on line. So, (1) and (2) together are not sufficient to answer the question.

18. **(D)** STATEMENT (1) alone is sufficient. Since $x > 0$, (1) implies $y > 0$. Hence, we can divide the equations $x = \frac{1}{4}y$ by y to get the value of x/y.

STATEMENT (2) alone is sufficient since $y = 4x$ is equivalent to STATEMENT (1).

19. **(C)** STATEMENT (1) alone is not sufficient. Using (1) you can deduce that the area of the sector is $^{72}\!/_{360}$ of the area of the circle, but you can't find the area of the circle.

STATEMENT (2) alone is not sufficient. OB is a radius of the circle, so (2) gives you the area of the circle but you can't deduce what fraction of the circle the sector is. However, STATEMENT (1) gives that information, so STATEMENTS (1) and (2) together are sufficient.

20. **(A)** STATEMENT (1) alone is sufficient. Since all the numbers are less than 30, all three must be positive for their sum to be larger than 60.

STATEMENT (2) alone is insufficient. (2) implies that x and y are positive, but gives no information about z.

21. **(E)** STATEMENTS (1) and (2) together are not sufficient. You need to know what direction it is from town B to town C, besides the distance between the towns.

22. **(D)** The key to this problem is to factor the expressions. You can factor STATEMENT (1) into $(x - 3)(x - 2)$. If the expression is negative that means $x - 3$ and $x - 2$ must have *opposite* signs. This can only happen if $2 < x < 3$. Thus, (1) alone is sufficient.

STATEMENT (2) alone is sufficient since the expression factors into $5x(x - 5)$. To be positive both $5x$ and $x - 5$ must have the same sign. This will happen if $x < 0$ or if $x > 5$. This means x does *not* satisfy $2 < x < 4$. So (2) alone is sufficient.

Remember answering the question does not only mean answering yes. Deciding that a statement can not be true also answers the question.

23. **(C)** STATEMENTS (1) and (2) are sufficient. 40% of the 28% are families who both have income over $25,000 and own a sailboat. Note that STATEMENT (2) alone is not sufficient. The percentage of families who own a sailboat and have an income over $25,000 is a percentage of families in the state. In STATEMENT (2), the percentage given is a percentage of families with income over $25,000.

24. **(A)** Two digit numbers are the integers from 0 to 99. Since you are told that the number is greater than 9, the only possible choices are integers 10, 11. . . . .99.

    STATEMENT (1) alone is sufficient since there is only one multiple of 51 ($51 = 51 \times 1$) in the list of possibilities.

    STATEMENT (2) alone is not sufficient since 15 and 51 both satisfy (2) and are two digit numbers greater than 9.

25. **(A)** Since the area of a circle is equal to πr^2 and the radius is positive, STATEMENT (1) alone is sufficient.

    STATEMENT (2) is true for all circles, so it gives no information about the radius of this particular circle.

Section IV   Sentence Correction

1. **(C)** Choices (A), (B), and (E) lack parallel structure; parallel nouns should be used: *years*, *desire*, and *debut*. Choice (D) unnecessarily changes the infinitive *to become.*

2. **(B)** Choices (A), (C), and (E) imply that driving a car at any speed is speeding. Choice (D) is wrong, because the subjunctive mood is required in the *if* clause.

3. **(C)** Choices (A) and (B) contain a faulty comparison. The desktop computer *is* a modern machine, and so the word *other* must be included. In choices (D) and (E), the word *has* is unnecessary and awkward.

4. **(E)** Choices (A) and (B) suffer from dangling participles. In addition, choice (A) has an error in agreement between the singular (*daydreaming*) and the plural verb (*enable*). Choices (C) and (D) change the meaning of the sentence.

5. **(B)** *Due to* should not be used in place of the compound preposition *because of.* Choice (C) has an error in agreement between the

singular verb (*was*) and the compound subject (*technology* and *capital*). Choice (D) is wordy and awkward.

6. **(D)** Choice (D) corrects the misplaced modifiers in choices (A), (B), and (C). Choice (E) seems to say that the owner told police as he was about to make a night deposit.

7. **(B)** The compound subject requires a plural verb. Choice (C) uses incorrect language: *both of which are each* and choice (E) changes the meaning by using *or* instead of *and*.

8. **(A)** *Affected* (*influenced by* or *acted upon*) is the correct word. Choice (C) uses the wrong tense.

9. **(B)** The pronoun *who* is the object of the verb *regard;* therefore, it should be in the objective case, *whom*. Choice (C) misplaces the modifier *both*.

10. **(D)** To maintain parallel construction, the noun *superstition* should replace the gerund phrase *thinking in superstitious ways*. The reference of *it* or *they* in choices (B), (C), and (E) is not completely clear.

11. **(C)** All the choices but (C) include a dangling modifier, since Jung's *writings* had not broken with Freud.

12. **(B)** *Cannot scarcely, cannot hardly*, and *isn't hardly* are considered double negatives.

13. **(A)** The past perfect tense *had been described* is needed to make clear the order in which the events occurred.

14. **(C)** The correct expression is *the reason is that*. Choice (B) has an error in agreement: *background...have*. The idiom *is qualified for*, not *qualified to* (D).

15. **(B)** The plural subject *numbers* requires a plural verb. Choice (C) misplaces *not only:* "to warrant *not only* continuing...*but also* maintaining." Choice (E) lacks parallel construction: *not only continuing...but also to maintain*.

16. **(A)** With a compound subject (*feelings* and *conviction*), the plural verb *are* should be used. In choice (C), *irregardless* is nonstandard English.

17. **(E)** Choices (D) and (E) correct the misplaced modifier, but choice (D) has an error in parallel structure. The noun clause *what his serial number was* is not parallel with *name* and *rank*.

18. **(C)** *Finishing* is parallel to *writing*.

19. **(E)** Choices (A) and (B) suffer from the change of persons (from *any-*

one to *you*). In choice (C) *would learn* is the wrong tense. Choice (D) is wordy.

20. **(A)** The word *number* is used when the quantity can be counted. Choices (C) and (D) incorrectly use *less* and *fewer, fewer accidents* and *lesser amount* would be correct. In choice (E) *they* has no reference.

21. **(E)** *Being that* in choices (A) and (C) is incorrect. The placement of *only* in choice (B) is wrong. Choice (D), *Seeing as how…* is non-standard.

22. **(E)** Parallel structure is violated in choices (A), (B), and (D). The placement of *also* in choice (C) is poor, for it ends the sentence on an anticlimactic note.

23. **(C)** In choices (A) and (D) *which* refers to the entire sentence rather than to a specific antecedent. (B) is not as strong a sentence as (C). Choice (E) has a dangling modifier.

24. **(D)** *The majority* calls for a singular verb (*has*). In choice (C) *lacks* should be used to agree with its subject, *one*.

25. **(D)** Choices (A), (B), and (E) omit important parts of the verb. *Hopefully* in choices (C) and (E) is wrong; although many people use it this way, most grammarians do not accept it as a substitute for *we hope*. (Strictly speaking, *hopefully* should only be used to mean *in a hopeful way*, as in *The farmer searched the skies hopefully looking for signs of rain*.)

Section V   Critical Reasoning

1. **(A)** The plague was spread by the commercial integration of Western Europe, as it is said in sentence 2 of the passage. Answer choices (C), (D), and (E) are all too specific and do not summarize the entire paragraph. Choice (B) is also incorrect. The plague was not spread because ships moved faster. It spread because of greater commerce between countries of Europe; when there was little trade between countries, diseases generally remained isolated in the area in which they began.

2. **(C)** An import substitution policy is designed to develop local industry and is frequently promoted by a protectionist policy, i.e., tariffs, quotas, and other constraints that either prohibit imports or tax them highly. By restricting imports or increasing their cost, locally produced products may be priced more highly than if import competition were allowed. Therefore, consumers ulti-

mately pay the cost of higher priced (and often inferior) locally produced goods. Alternative (E) is partially correct. A protectionist policy (limiting imports) may benefit developing countries by allowing local industry to develop and may be anathema to trading partners, but this hardly weakens the argument for a policy of economic independence as given in the statement. If answer choice (A) were true, there would be nothing to protect because there could be no imports. Answer (B) is, in fact, true, but the quotas may be even more protective than tariffs. In any case, both quotas and tariffs are only the means to carry out the strategy. The inequality issue (D) cannot be deduced from the passage.

3. **(D)** The second sentence mentions the questioning that led to modified opinions ("new doubts"). The last sentence mentions a growing belief that change will be favorable ("new confidence"). Answer choices (A) and (E) only partially summarize the statement. Answer (B) is inaccurate; there was also mention of optimism. Answer (C) cannot be inferred.

4. **(D)** The birth and death rates and the immigration and emigration rates affect the size of the population, so choices (A) and (B) obviously affect the supply of labor. The educational level (C) affects the participation rate, in the labor force, and marital status (E) is said in the given paragraph to be a factor in the labor force. The only factor that could not, according to the passage, affect the supply of labor is the number of employment agencies (D). Employment agencies are involved in the distribution and direction of the labor supply, but they do not affect the quantitative supply of labor.

5. **(E)** Choices (A), (B), (C), and (D) all refer to the community and land use and are relevant to the given statement. Statement (E) relates to housing design, a topic not referred to in the given paragraph.

6. **(B)** Two factors are noted in the given passage. First, the per capita production rate has not been as high as the production increase, without regard to population size. Second, the rate of increase over the last ten years has been slower. Therefore (B) is correct. Productivity per capita has not grown as fast during the past ten years. There is no indication about the size of the Workland population given in the paragraph, and so we cannot know whether or not (A) is true. The paragraph says that growth in production is

more modest when calculated per capita of total population; we can infer that population growth has increased faster than total production, so (C) is incorrect. We can also infer that the birth rate has not declined and that per capita production has declined, so (D) and (E) are also incorrect.

7. **(C)** Alternative (C) implies a westward migration—from Greenland to Baffin Island into Alaska proper—instead of an eastward migration as stated in the passage. Answer choice (A) supports the statement chronologically. Even if answer choice (B) is true, the Eskimos or their descendants inhabited Greenland before the Vikings. Answer (E) is not associated with the movement of Eskimos or their descendants.

8. **(C)** Since Dyner's country produces only 2% of the world petroleum supply, its output can hardly affect world prices. If this is true, then answers (A), (D), and (E) cannot falsify his reasoning. Answer (B) has some connection to the argument—production goals (i.e., increased production) v. financial goals (i.e., foreign exchange savings)—but it does not signify an error in Dyner's reasoning.

9. **(B)** Choice (B) is the best answer. The statement is an admonition for people to be aware of "contaminants," a reference to physical and chemical hazards. Alternatives (A) and (C) might be implied, but neither is as good a choice as (B). Alternative (D) is not implied. Alternative (E) might be implied, but it is not the major message of the statement.

10. **(E)** The factors listed in (A), (B), (C), and (D) all affect occupational mobility. The rate of turnover (E) is another way of measuring mobility; it is not an explanatory variable, or, in other words, it is not a factor that affects stability or mobility.

11. **(A)** Textiles are mentioned as the major export, and among textiles, woolens and worsteds as the most important. Apart from textiles, corn is mentioned as the only other significant export. Therefore, (A) is correct. Linen and silks were mentioned as insignificant exports, so choices (B) and (C) are not appropriate. Since textile export was the most important export, and woolens an important component of the textile export, it can be inferred that wool production was more important to industry than fishing, which produced only insignificant export; therefore, choice (D) is incorrect. Choice (E) is clearly incorrect: the first sentence of the passage states that by far the chief export in the 15th century was textiles.

12. **(B)** 31% of men who operate unincorporated businesses (self-employed), completed four or more years of college, against 19% of women in the same category. We can then conclude that self-employed men have more education than self-employed women. The passage states that self-employed people are often in the 25-to-44-year-old group; no distinction is made between the sexes, so we cannot know whether or not self-employed women are generally younger than self-employed men, so choice (A) is not appropriate. The passage compares the education of self-employed men and wage-earning men and the education of self-employed women and wage-earning women, but it does not compare wage-earning women with wage-earning men, so we cannot know if statement (C) is true. According to the passage, salaried men are often younger or older than self-employed counterparts, so (D) is not necessarily true. The last part of the passage states that self-employed women do not have more education than their wage-earning counterparts, so (E) cannot be true.

13. **(A)** The statement implies a correlation between a decline in gasoline consumption (less pollution) and a decrease in the incidence of lung cancer among white males. If lung cancer among blacks did not decrease over the same time period, one could assume that another causal or intermediate variable—other than gasoline consumption—may explain the decrease in lung cancer among white males. Answer choice (C) does not explain associations in variables occurring between 1914 and 1950. Answer choices (D) and (E) do not explain the relationship between gasoline consumption and cancer. Choice (B) supports the argument.

14. **(D)** The statement is evidence of declining productivity. If fewer hours are needed to produce the same output, productivity should increase. In choice (A), an increase in the number of workers to achieve the same output indicates a decline in productivity. Using less technology (B) and fertilizers (C) will lower productivity. Using more workers to achieve the same output (E) is a decrease in productivity.

15. **(C)** Choice (C) reflects the intention of the writer of the passage, which stresses the facts of usage. Choice (A) implies a metaphysical (platonic) theory about the use of the word tall. Choice (B) is an opinion opposed to that of the writer. Alternative (D) is a judgment on the behavior described in the abstract. Choice (E) is a judgment based on fantasy.

16. **(C)** While personal satisfaction is a motivating factor, the statement shows that business starts increased—since 1980—along with a set of tax changes, promoting financial gains. (B) is the second best answer. However, it cannot be inferred that social motives are "just as" strong as the financial motive, given that the passage states that tax regulations motivated increasing numbers of entrepreneurs to invest. Answer choice (A) may be correct, but there is nothing in the passage to substantiate it. Choice (D) may be eliminated because of the word "most." There is no evidence in the passage to support answer choice (E).

17. **(E)** Answer choice (E) weakens the argument. Team members rated their peers low on characteristics of cohesion and high on characteristics of group discord and lack of harmony. Answer choices (B), (C), and (D) support the statement's assumption. Choice (A) neither supports nor weakens it. A dominant leader may or may not contribute to cohesion, depending on whether or not he or she unites or divides the group.

18. **(D)** There is no evidence for (A) or (B); nothing in the passage discusses buying experience or sophistication. Choice (C) cannot be inferred; the inference in the passage is that social class affects behavior, not that social class is more of an influence in Europe than in America. There is no assumption about the science of consumer behavior (E). All the factors in (D) are assumed to have influence on consumer behavior, both in Europe and in America.

19. **(D)** The passage states that university expansion—north of Italy outside France and England—took place between the mid-14th century and the end of the 15th century. There is nothing in the passage about the number of universities in the whole of Europe, so we have no way of knowing if (A) is correct. Statement (B) is not substantiated by what is in the passage—namely, that "by the end of the 15th century, there were 23 universities" in a wide region. There is nothing in the passage that states that France and England were the only countries with universities in the 13th century, so (C) is not appropriate. Similarly, nothing in the passage states or implies that Italy was the cradle of university expansion (E).

20. **(C)** Even if it were true that there are more self-employed women than men it does not explain why this number increases five times faster than men. Answer choice (A) supports the argument by

showing that it has become more convenient for women to be self-employed. Choice (B) gives a means to that end. Answer (D) provides evidence to support the claim, and (E) is an example of a motivating factor that induced more women to work.

Section VI Sentence Correction

1. **(C)** The pronoun *each* is singular, and requires the singular verb *was required.*
2. **(E)** When only two things are being compared (in this case, stationary sites and mobile units), the word *more* rather than *most* should be used.
3. **(B)** To maintain parallel structure, a phrase beginning with a noun (*ability*) is needed.
4. **(A)** The original wording is the clearest and simplest.
5. **(C)** As originally written, the sentence is a fragment, since it lacks an independent subject and verb. Choice (C) supplies them (*He had chosen*).
6. **(A)** No error.
7. **(B)** The pronoun *she* is needed, since it is part of the compound subject of the verb *was willing;* the verb must be singular to agree with the nearest subject (*Dean*).
8. **(D)** Use *among* when three or more people or things are involved.
9. **(E)** The underlined phrase must begin with *the Governor;* otherwise, the phrase which precedes it has no clear reference. Choice (C) is verbose and rather vague.
10. **(A)** No error.
11. **(D)** The pronoun *no one* is singular, and requires the singular verb *was*. Choice (C) is awkward in comparison to choice (D).
12. **(A)** The sentence is correct as originally written. Note that the compound subject ("X, Y, and Z") requires a plural verb—in this case, *have replaced.*
13. **(B)** The comparative phrases *equal...to* and *less...than* must be complete in order for the sentence to make sense.
14. **(A)** Correct as originally written. The pronoun *whom* is correct, since it is the object of the verb *should blame.*
15. **(C)** Use *fewer* for countable items (such as amendments); use *less* for noncountable substances (for example, sand, water, or time).
16. **(E)** The phrase beginning *One of the costliest* must be adjacent to the

phrase *the space shuttle program*, in order to make the reference clear.

17. **(E)** The past perfect tense *had appointed* is needed to clarify the order in which the events occurred.

18. **(C)** The other choices are verbose, vague, or both.

19. **(C)** Use the pronoun *whom* only for people, never for things. Choice (E) introduces *they*, a pronoun without a reference. *Best* is needed here.

20. **(A)** No error. In most *if* clauses, the past subjunctive form of the verb—with *had* —must be used.

21. **(C)** The singular verb *illustrates* is needed, since the subject is the singular *imposition*.

22. **(A)** Correct as originally written. Parallelism calls for repetition of the pronoun *by* (*less by…than by…*).

23. **(C)** The pronoun should be *he*, since it is part of the compound subject of the verb *would be*.

24. **(D)** The pronoun *it* is unnecessary, since the subject of the verb—*the Civilian Review Board*—has already appeared.

25. **(A)** No error.

Section VII   Problem Solving

1. **(D)** Each box of dictionaries weighs $6 \times 20 = 120$ pounds. Each box of encyclopedias weighs $2 \times 75 = 150$ pounds. So the load weighs $98 \times 120 + 50 \times 150 = 19,260$ pounds.

2. **(D)** Mary makes $600 a month on her regular job. Therefore, she receives $600 \cdot 12 = \$7,200$ a year from her regular job. Her only other income is $400. So her total yearly income is $7,600. She makes $600 + $400 = $1,000 during July, so she makes $1,000/7,600 = 5/38$ which is about .13 of her annual income during July. Therefore, Mary makes about 13% of her annual income in July.

3. **(C)** The area of the triangle is $\frac{1}{2}(\text{altitude})(\text{base}) = \frac{1}{2}(\text{altitude})S$. The area of the square is S^2. Therefore, $\frac{1}{2}S(\text{altitude}) = S^2$, so the altitude must be $2S$.

4. **(D)** The train will average 50 mph for 3½ hours, 75 mph for 3 hours and 20 mph for half an hour. So the distance of the trip is $(3\frac{1}{2})(50) + (3)(75) + (\frac{1}{2})(20) = 175 + 225 + 10 = 410$ miles. The trip takes 7 hours. Therefore, the average speed is $410/7 = 58\frac{4}{7}$ mph.

5. **(C)**
$$(x - y)(y + 3) = x(y + 3) - y(y + 3)$$
$$= xy + 3x - y^2 - 3y$$
$$= xy - y^2 - 3y + 3x$$

6. **(B)** If $x < y$ and $y < z$, then $x < z$. All the other statements may be true but are not always true.

7. **(C)** The ratio is $\dfrac{2}{3} \Big/ \dfrac{5}{4}$ which is equal to $\dfrac{2}{3} \cdot \dfrac{4}{5} = \dfrac{8}{15}$.

8. **(C)** 3 divides 9 evenly and 3 divides 33 evenly, so 9 and 33 are not primes. 7, 11, 13, and 29 have no divisors except 1 and themselves, so they are all primes. Thus, the set of numbers contains 4 prime numbers.

9. **(D)** Each share is worth $13.21 - $9.50 or $3.71 more in 1970 then it was in 1960. So 100,000 shares are worth ($3.71)(100,000) or $371,000.00 more in 1970 than they were in 1960.

10. **(D)** Add up all the daily wages for the week: $40.62 + 41.35 + 42.00 + 42.50 + 39.53 = $206.00. Divide $206.00 by 5 to get the average daily wage, $41.20.

11. **(B)** If the price of a pound of apples rises 2%, then the price of ten pounds of apples rises 2%. This is because the percentage change is the same for any amount sold. Since a dozen eggs and ten pounds of apples currently cost the same, each costs one half of the total price. Therefore, one half of the total is increased by 10% and the other half is increased by 2%, so the total price is increased by ½ (10%) + ½ (2%) = 6%.

12. **(D)** The best way to do this problem is to look at all the two-digit numbers that have a remainder of 2 when divided by 7 and see how many are prime. It is easy to look at this list, since each successive entry is 7 more than the previous entry. The list is 16, 23, 30, 37, 44, 51, 58, 65, 72, 79, 86, 93. To check whether a number is prime you only have to see if it is divisible by primes that are less than or equal to the number's square root. Since these are all two-digit numbers, their square roots are all less than 10. The only primes less than 10 are 2, 3, 5, and 7. Now, since 16, 30, 44, 58, 72, and 86 are even, they are not prime. 51 and 93 are divisible by 3 and 65 is divisible by 5 so the only possible primes are 23, 37, and 79. Since none of these is divisible by 7, they are all prime. The correct choice is (D).

13. **(D)** Each man does $\frac{1}{25}$ of the job in $1\frac{1}{2}$ hours. Thus, 15 men will do

$\frac{15}{25}$ or $\frac{3}{5}$ of the job in $1\frac{1}{2}$ hours. So 15 men will complete the job

in $\frac{5}{3} \cdot \frac{3}{2} = \frac{5}{2} = 2\frac{1}{2}$ hours. Another method gives $\frac{15}{25} = \frac{3/2}{x}$ where

x is the time 15 men will take to complete the job. Therefore,

$15x = \frac{3}{2} \cdot 25 = \frac{75}{2}$ so $x = \frac{5}{2} = 2\frac{1}{2}$.

14. **(A)** The car gets 100% – 12% or 88% of 20 miles to the gallon at 60 miles per hour. Thus, the car gets (.88)(20) or 17.6 miles to the gallon at 60 mph. Therefore, it can travel (11)(17.6) or 193.6 miles.

15. **(D)** The first 12 tons cost (12)($500) or $6,000. When you purchase 30 tons, you are buying 18 tons in addition to the first 12 tons so the additional 18 tons will cost $(500 – x)(18). Since $10,000 – $6,000 = $4,000, we get $9,000 – 18x = $4,000, and 18x = $5,000. So x = 277.78.

16. **(E)** The sum of the angles of a triangle is 180°. Let x be the number of degrees in the largest angle; then the other angles are ½x and ¾x degrees. Therefore, ½x + ¾x + x = 9/4x = 180°, so x = 80°.

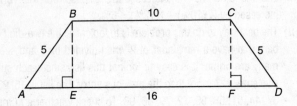

17. **(B)** If we draw $CF \perp AD$, then $\triangle ABE \cong \triangle DCF$ and $AE = FD = 3$. Then $BE = 4$. Thus the area of the trapezoid, which equals the product of the altitude and the average of the bases, equals (4)(½) (10 + 16) = 52.

18. **(E)** Since –1 (a negative number) is less than 2, and 1 (a positive number) is less than 2, neither I nor II is always true.

Since −1 is less than 2 and 2 × −1 = −2, which is less than −1, III is not true.

Finally, since ½ is less than 2 but ½ × ½ = ¼, which is less than ½, IV is also not always true. Therefore, none of the statements is always true.

19. **(A)** Since each assistant does ⅔ as much as the worker, all 3 will accomplish 1 + 2(⅔) or ⅞ as much as the worker by himself. So they will finish the job in 1 ÷ ⅞ or 3/7 as much time as it would take the worker by himself.

20. **(D)** The percent favoring at least one of the proposals is NOT the sum of 50, 30, and 20 because someone favoring 2 of the proposals will be counted twice and someone favoring all three will be counted 3 times. The correct relation is 78 = 50 + 30 + 20 − (percent favoring 2 of the proposals) − 2 (percent favoring all 3). Thus 78 = 100 − (percent favoring 2) − 2(5), which can be solved to give the percentage favoring 2 of the proposals or 100 − 10 − 78 = 12. Therefore, the percentage favoring more than one proposal is 12 + 5 = 17.

EVALUATING YOUR SCORE

Tabulate your score for each section of Sample Test 2 according to the directions on pages 6–7 and record the results in the Self-Scoring Table below. Then find your rating for each score on the Self-Scoring Scale and record it in the appropriate blank.

SELF-SCORING TABLE

Section	Score	Rating
1		
2		
3		
4		
5		
6		
7		_

SELF-SCORING SCALE—RATING

Section	Poor	Fair	Good	Excellent
1	0–8+	9–12+	13–17+	18–20
2	0–11+	12–16+	17–21+	22–25
3	0–11+	12–16+	17–21+	22–25
4	0–11+	12–16+	17–21+	22–25
5	0–8+	9–12+	13–17+	18–20
6	0–11+	12–16+	17–21+	22–25
7	0–8+	9–12+	13–17+	18–20

Study again the Review sections covering material in Sample Test 2 for which you had a rating of FAIR or POOR. Then go on to Sample Test 3.

Answer Sheet—Sample Test 3

Section I Reading Comprehension	Section II Reading Comprehension	Section III Problem Solving	Section IV Critical Reasoning
1. Ⓐ Ⓑ Ⓒ Ⓓ Ⓔ	1. Ⓐ Ⓑ Ⓒ Ⓓ Ⓔ	1. Ⓐ Ⓑ Ⓒ Ⓓ Ⓔ	1. Ⓐ Ⓑ Ⓒ Ⓓ Ⓔ
2. Ⓐ Ⓑ Ⓒ Ⓓ Ⓔ	2. Ⓐ Ⓑ Ⓒ Ⓓ Ⓔ	2. Ⓐ Ⓑ Ⓒ Ⓓ Ⓔ	2. Ⓐ Ⓑ Ⓒ Ⓓ Ⓔ
3. Ⓐ Ⓑ Ⓒ Ⓓ Ⓔ	3. Ⓐ Ⓑ Ⓒ Ⓓ Ⓔ	3. Ⓐ Ⓑ Ⓒ Ⓓ Ⓔ	3. Ⓐ Ⓑ Ⓒ Ⓓ Ⓔ
4. Ⓐ Ⓑ Ⓒ Ⓓ Ⓔ	4. Ⓐ Ⓑ Ⓒ Ⓓ Ⓔ	4. Ⓐ Ⓑ Ⓒ Ⓓ Ⓔ	4. Ⓐ Ⓑ Ⓒ Ⓓ Ⓔ
5. Ⓐ Ⓑ Ⓒ Ⓓ Ⓔ	5. Ⓐ Ⓑ Ⓒ Ⓓ Ⓔ	5. Ⓐ Ⓑ Ⓒ Ⓓ Ⓔ	5. Ⓐ Ⓑ Ⓒ Ⓓ Ⓔ
6. Ⓐ Ⓑ Ⓒ Ⓓ Ⓔ	6. Ⓐ Ⓑ Ⓒ Ⓓ Ⓔ	6. Ⓐ Ⓑ Ⓒ Ⓓ Ⓔ	6. Ⓐ Ⓑ Ⓒ Ⓓ Ⓔ
7. Ⓐ Ⓑ Ⓒ Ⓓ Ⓔ	7. Ⓐ Ⓑ Ⓒ Ⓓ Ⓔ	7. Ⓐ Ⓑ Ⓒ Ⓓ Ⓔ	7. Ⓐ Ⓑ Ⓒ Ⓓ Ⓔ
8. Ⓐ Ⓑ Ⓒ Ⓓ Ⓔ	8. Ⓐ Ⓑ Ⓒ Ⓓ Ⓔ	8. Ⓐ Ⓑ Ⓒ Ⓓ Ⓔ	8. Ⓐ Ⓑ Ⓒ Ⓓ Ⓔ
9. Ⓐ Ⓑ Ⓒ Ⓓ Ⓔ	9. Ⓐ Ⓑ Ⓒ Ⓓ Ⓔ	9. Ⓐ Ⓑ Ⓒ Ⓓ Ⓔ	9. Ⓐ Ⓑ Ⓒ Ⓓ Ⓔ
10. Ⓐ Ⓑ Ⓒ Ⓓ Ⓔ	10. Ⓐ Ⓑ Ⓒ Ⓓ Ⓔ	10. Ⓐ Ⓑ Ⓒ Ⓓ Ⓔ	10. Ⓐ Ⓑ Ⓒ Ⓓ Ⓔ
11. Ⓐ Ⓑ Ⓒ Ⓓ Ⓔ	11. Ⓐ Ⓑ Ⓒ Ⓓ Ⓔ	11. Ⓐ Ⓑ Ⓒ Ⓓ Ⓔ	11. Ⓐ Ⓑ Ⓒ Ⓓ Ⓔ
12. Ⓐ Ⓑ Ⓒ Ⓓ Ⓔ	12. Ⓐ Ⓑ Ⓒ Ⓓ Ⓔ	12. Ⓐ Ⓑ Ⓒ Ⓓ Ⓔ	12. Ⓐ Ⓑ Ⓒ Ⓓ Ⓔ
13. Ⓐ Ⓑ Ⓒ Ⓓ Ⓔ	13. Ⓐ Ⓑ Ⓒ Ⓓ Ⓔ	13. Ⓐ Ⓑ Ⓒ Ⓓ Ⓔ	13. Ⓐ Ⓑ Ⓒ Ⓓ Ⓔ
14. Ⓐ Ⓑ Ⓒ Ⓓ Ⓔ	14. Ⓐ Ⓑ Ⓒ Ⓓ Ⓔ	14. Ⓐ Ⓑ Ⓒ Ⓓ Ⓔ	14. Ⓐ Ⓑ Ⓒ Ⓓ Ⓔ
15. Ⓐ Ⓑ Ⓒ Ⓓ Ⓔ	15. Ⓐ Ⓑ Ⓒ Ⓓ Ⓔ	15. Ⓐ Ⓑ Ⓒ Ⓓ Ⓔ	15. Ⓐ Ⓑ Ⓒ Ⓓ Ⓔ
16. Ⓐ Ⓑ Ⓒ Ⓓ Ⓔ	16. Ⓐ Ⓑ Ⓒ Ⓓ Ⓔ	16. Ⓐ Ⓑ Ⓒ Ⓓ Ⓔ	16. Ⓐ Ⓑ Ⓒ Ⓓ Ⓔ
17. Ⓐ Ⓑ Ⓒ Ⓓ Ⓔ	17. Ⓐ Ⓑ Ⓒ Ⓓ Ⓔ	17. Ⓐ Ⓑ Ⓒ Ⓓ Ⓔ	17. Ⓐ Ⓑ Ⓒ Ⓓ Ⓔ
18. Ⓐ Ⓑ Ⓒ Ⓓ Ⓔ	18. Ⓐ Ⓑ Ⓒ Ⓓ Ⓔ	18. Ⓐ Ⓑ Ⓒ Ⓓ Ⓔ	18. Ⓐ Ⓑ Ⓒ Ⓓ Ⓔ
19. Ⓐ Ⓑ Ⓒ Ⓓ Ⓔ	19. Ⓐ Ⓑ Ⓒ Ⓓ Ⓔ	19. Ⓐ Ⓑ Ⓒ Ⓓ Ⓔ	19. Ⓐ Ⓑ Ⓒ Ⓓ Ⓔ
20. Ⓐ Ⓑ Ⓒ Ⓓ Ⓔ	20. Ⓐ Ⓑ Ⓒ Ⓓ Ⓔ	20. Ⓐ Ⓑ Ⓒ Ⓓ Ⓔ	20. Ⓐ Ⓑ Ⓒ Ⓓ Ⓔ
21. Ⓐ Ⓑ Ⓒ Ⓓ Ⓔ	21. Ⓐ Ⓑ Ⓒ Ⓓ Ⓔ		
22. Ⓐ Ⓑ Ⓒ Ⓓ Ⓔ	22. Ⓐ Ⓑ Ⓒ Ⓓ Ⓔ		
23. Ⓐ Ⓑ Ⓒ Ⓓ Ⓔ	23. Ⓐ Ⓑ Ⓒ Ⓓ Ⓔ		
24. Ⓐ Ⓑ Ⓒ Ⓓ Ⓔ	24. Ⓐ Ⓑ Ⓒ Ⓓ Ⓔ		
25. Ⓐ Ⓑ Ⓒ Ⓓ Ⓔ	25. Ⓐ Ⓑ Ⓒ Ⓓ Ⓔ		

Section V Data Sufficiency	Section VI Problem Solving	Section VII Sentence Correction
1. Ⓐ Ⓑ Ⓒ Ⓓ Ⓔ	1. Ⓐ Ⓑ Ⓒ Ⓓ Ⓔ	1. Ⓐ Ⓑ Ⓒ Ⓓ Ⓔ
2. Ⓐ Ⓑ Ⓒ Ⓓ Ⓔ	2. Ⓐ Ⓑ Ⓒ Ⓓ Ⓔ	2. Ⓐ Ⓑ Ⓒ Ⓓ Ⓔ
3. Ⓐ Ⓑ Ⓒ Ⓓ Ⓔ	3. Ⓐ Ⓑ Ⓒ Ⓓ Ⓔ	3. Ⓐ Ⓑ Ⓒ Ⓓ Ⓔ
4. Ⓐ Ⓑ Ⓒ Ⓓ Ⓔ	4. Ⓐ Ⓑ Ⓒ Ⓓ Ⓔ	4. Ⓐ Ⓑ Ⓒ Ⓓ Ⓔ
5. Ⓐ Ⓑ Ⓒ Ⓓ Ⓔ	5. Ⓐ Ⓑ Ⓒ Ⓓ Ⓔ	5. Ⓐ Ⓑ Ⓒ Ⓓ Ⓔ
6. Ⓐ Ⓑ Ⓒ Ⓓ Ⓔ	6. Ⓐ Ⓑ Ⓒ Ⓓ Ⓔ	6. Ⓐ Ⓑ Ⓒ Ⓓ Ⓔ
7. Ⓐ Ⓑ Ⓒ Ⓓ Ⓔ	7. Ⓐ Ⓑ Ⓒ Ⓓ Ⓔ	7. Ⓐ Ⓑ Ⓒ Ⓓ Ⓔ
8. Ⓐ Ⓑ Ⓒ Ⓓ Ⓔ	8. Ⓐ Ⓑ Ⓒ Ⓓ Ⓔ	8. Ⓐ Ⓑ Ⓒ Ⓓ Ⓔ
9. Ⓐ Ⓑ Ⓒ Ⓓ Ⓔ	9. Ⓐ Ⓑ Ⓒ Ⓓ Ⓔ	9. Ⓐ Ⓑ Ⓒ Ⓓ Ⓔ
10. Ⓐ Ⓑ Ⓒ Ⓓ Ⓔ	10. Ⓐ Ⓑ Ⓒ Ⓓ Ⓔ	10. Ⓐ Ⓑ Ⓒ Ⓓ Ⓔ
11. Ⓐ Ⓑ Ⓒ Ⓓ Ⓔ	11. Ⓐ Ⓑ Ⓒ Ⓓ Ⓔ	11. Ⓐ Ⓑ Ⓒ Ⓓ Ⓔ
12. Ⓐ Ⓑ Ⓒ Ⓓ Ⓔ	12. Ⓐ Ⓑ Ⓒ Ⓓ Ⓔ	12. Ⓐ Ⓑ Ⓒ Ⓓ Ⓔ
13. Ⓐ Ⓑ Ⓒ Ⓓ Ⓔ	13. Ⓐ Ⓑ Ⓒ Ⓓ Ⓔ	13. Ⓐ Ⓑ Ⓒ Ⓓ Ⓔ
14. Ⓐ Ⓑ Ⓒ Ⓓ Ⓔ	14. Ⓐ Ⓑ Ⓒ Ⓓ Ⓔ	14. Ⓐ Ⓑ Ⓒ Ⓓ Ⓔ
15. Ⓐ Ⓑ Ⓒ Ⓓ Ⓔ	15. Ⓐ Ⓑ Ⓒ Ⓓ Ⓔ	15. Ⓐ Ⓑ Ⓒ Ⓓ Ⓔ
16. Ⓐ Ⓑ Ⓒ Ⓓ Ⓔ	16. Ⓐ Ⓑ Ⓒ Ⓓ Ⓔ	16. Ⓐ Ⓑ Ⓒ Ⓓ Ⓔ
17. Ⓐ Ⓑ Ⓒ Ⓓ Ⓔ	17. Ⓐ Ⓑ Ⓒ Ⓓ Ⓔ	17. Ⓐ Ⓑ Ⓒ Ⓓ Ⓔ
18. Ⓐ Ⓑ Ⓒ Ⓓ Ⓔ	18. Ⓐ Ⓑ Ⓒ Ⓓ Ⓔ	18. Ⓐ Ⓑ Ⓒ Ⓓ Ⓔ
19. Ⓐ Ⓑ Ⓒ Ⓓ Ⓔ	19. Ⓐ Ⓑ Ⓒ Ⓓ Ⓔ	19. Ⓐ Ⓑ Ⓒ Ⓓ Ⓔ
20. Ⓐ Ⓑ Ⓒ Ⓓ Ⓔ	20. Ⓐ Ⓑ Ⓒ Ⓓ Ⓔ	20. Ⓐ Ⓑ Ⓒ Ⓓ Ⓔ
21. Ⓐ Ⓑ Ⓒ Ⓓ Ⓔ		21. Ⓐ Ⓑ Ⓒ Ⓓ Ⓔ
22. Ⓐ Ⓑ Ⓒ Ⓓ Ⓔ		22. Ⓐ Ⓑ Ⓒ Ⓓ Ⓔ
23. Ⓐ Ⓑ Ⓒ Ⓓ Ⓔ		23. Ⓐ Ⓑ Ⓒ Ⓓ Ⓔ
24. Ⓐ Ⓑ Ⓒ Ⓓ Ⓔ		24. Ⓐ Ⓑ Ⓒ Ⓓ Ⓔ
25. Ⓐ Ⓑ Ⓒ Ⓓ Ⓔ		25. Ⓐ Ⓑ Ⓒ Ⓓ Ⓔ

SAMPLE TEST 3

SECTION I   READING COMPREHENSION   Time: 30 minutes

Directions: This part contains three reading passages. You are to read each one carefully. When answering the questions, you *will* be allowed to refer back to the passages. The questions are based on what is *stated* or *implied* in each passage. You have thirty minutes to complete this section.

Passage 1:

The following passage was written in 1964.

The main burden of assuring that the resources of the federal government are well managed falls on relatively few of the five million men and women whom it employs. Under the department and agency heads there are 8,600 political, career, military, and foreign service

(5)   executives—the top managers and professionals—who exert major influence on the manner in which the rest are directed and utilized. Below their level there are other thousands with assignments of some managerial significance, but we believe that the line of demarcation selected is the best available for our purposes in this attainment.

(10)   There is no complete inventory of positions or people in federal service at this level. The lack may be explained by separate agency statutes and personnel systems, diffusion among so many special services, and absence of any central point (short of the President himself) with jurisdiction over all upper-level personnel of the govern-

(15)   ment.

Top presidential appointees, about 500 of them, bear the brunt of translating the philosophy and aims of the current administration into practical programs. This group includes the secretaries and assistant secretaries of cabinet departments, agency heads and their deputies,

(20)   heads and members of boards and commissions with fixed terms, and chiefs and directors of major bureaus, divisions, and services. Appointments to many of these politically sensitive positions are made on recommendation by department or agency heads, but all are presumably responsible to presidential leadership.

(25)   One qualification for office at this level is that there be no basic disagreement with presidential political philosophy, at least so far as administrative judgments and actions are concerned. Apart from the bipartisan boards and commissions, these men are normally identi-

fied with the political party of the president, or are sympathetic to it,
(30) although there are exceptions.

There are four distinguishable kinds of top presidential appointees,
including:

— Those whom the president selects at the outset to establish
immediate and effective control over the government (e.g.,
(35) Cabinet secretaries, agency heads, his own White House staff
and Executive Office Personnel).

— Those selected by department and agency heads in order to
establish control within their respective organizations (e.g.—
assistant secretaries, deputies, assistants to, and major line
(40) posts in some bureaus and divisions).

— High-level appointees who—though often requiring clearance
through political or interest group channels, or both—must
have known scientific or technical competence (e.g.—the Surgeon General, the Commissioner of Education).

(45) — Those named to residual positions traditionally filled on a
partisan patronage basis.

These appointees are primarily regarded as policy makers and
overseers of policy execution. In practice, however, they usually have
substantial responsibilities in line management, often requiring a
(50) thorough knowledge of substantive agency programs.

1. According to the passage, about how many top managerial
   professionals work for the federal government?

   (A) five million   (D) nine thousand
   (B) two million   (E) five hundred
   (C) twenty thousand

2. No complete inventory exists of positions in the three highest levels
   of government service because

   (A) no one has bothered to count them.
   (B) computers cannot handle all the data.
   (C) separate agency personnel systems are used.
   (D) the president has never requested such information.
   (E) the Classification Act prohibits such a census.

3. Top presidential appointees have as their central responsibility the

   (A) prevention of politically motivated interference with the actions of their agencies.
   (B) monitoring of government actions on behalf of the president's own political party.
   (C) translation of the aims of the administration into practical programs.
   (D) investigation of charges of corruption within the government.
   (E) maintenance of adequate controls over the rate of government spending.

4. One exception to the general rule that top presidential appointees must be in agreement with the president's political philosophy may be found in

   (A) most cabinet-level officers.
   (B) members of the White House staff.
   (C) bipartisan boards and commissions.
   (D) those offices filled on a patronage basis.
   (E) offices requiring scientific or technical expertise.

5. Applicants for presidential appointments are usually identified with or are members of

   (A) large corporations.
   (B) the foreign service.
   (C) government bureaus.
   (D) academic circles.
   (E) the president's political party.

6. Appointees that are selected directly by the president include

   (A) U.S. marshals and attorneys.
   (B) military officers.
   (C) agency heads.
   (D) assistant secretaries.
   (E) congressional committee members.

7. Appointees usually have to possess expertise in

   (A) line management.   (D) strategic planning.
   (B) military affairs.   (E) constitutional law.
   (C) foreign affairs.

8. According to the passage, presidential appointees are regarded primarily as

   (A) political spokesmen.
   (B) policy makers.
   (C) staff managers.
   (D) scientific or technical experts.
   (E) business executives.

9. Appointees selected by department and agency heads include

   (A) military leaders.   (D) diplomats.
   (B) cabinet secretaries.   (E) residual position holders.
   (C) deputy secretaries.

Passage 2:

The first and decisive step in the expansion of Europe overseas was the conquest of the Atlantic Ocean. That the nation to achieve this should be Portugal was the logical outcome of her geographical position and her history. Placed on the extreme margin of the old,
(5) classical Mediterranean world and facing the untraversed ocean, Portugal could adapt and develop the knowledge and experience of the past to meet the challenge of the unknown. Some centuries of navigating the coastal waters of Western Europe and Northern Africa had prepared Portuguese seamen to appreciate the problems which the
(10) Ocean presented and to apply and develop the methods necessary to overcome them. From the seamen of the Mediterranean, particularly those of Genoa and Venice, they had learned the organization and conduct of a mercantile marine, and from Jewish astronomers and Catalan mapmakers the rudiments of navigation. Largely excluded
(15) from a share in Mediterranean commerce at a time when her increasing and vigorous population was making heavy demands on her resources, Portugal turned southwards and westwards for opportunities of trade and commerce. At this moment of national destiny it was fortunate for her that in men of the calibre of Prince Henry, known as

(20) the Navigator, and King John II she found resolute and dedicated leaders.

The problems to be faced were new and complex. The conditions for navigation and commerce in the Mediterranean were relatively simple, compared with those in the western seas. The landlocked
(25) Mediterranean, tideless and with a climatic regime of regular and well-defined seasons, presented few obstacles to sailors who were the heirs of a great body of sea lore garnered from the experiences of many centuries. What hazards there were, in the form of sudden storms or dangerous coasts, were known and could be usually anticipated.
(30) Similarly the Mediterranean coasts, though they might be for long periods in the hands of dangerous rivals, were described in sailing directions or laid down on the portolan charts drawn by Venetian, Genoese, and Catalan cartographers. Problems of determining positions at sea, which confronted the Portuguese, did not arise. Though
(35) the Mediterranean seamen by no means restricted themselves to coastal sailing, the latitudinal extent of the Mediterranean was not great, and voyages could be conducted from point to point on compass bearings; the ships were never so far from land as to make it necessary to fix their positions in latitude by astronomical observa-
(40) tions. Having made a landfall on a bearing, they could determine their precise position from prominent landmarks, soundings or the nature of the sea bed, after reference to the sailing directions or charts.

10. Before the expansion of Europe overseas could take place

(A) vast sums of money had to be raised.

(B) an army had to be recruited.

(C) the Atlantic Ocean had to be conquered.

(D) ships had to be built.

(E) sailors had to be trained.

11. One of Portugal's leaders, known as the Navigator, was in reality

(A) Christopher Columbus.   (D) Prince Henry.

(B) King John II.   (E) Prince Paul.

(C) a Venetian.

12. Portugal was adept at exploring unknown waters because she possessed all of the following except

    (A) a navy.
    (B) past experience.
    (C) experienced navigators.
    (D) experienced mapmakers.
    (E) extensive trade routes.

13. In addition to possessing the necessary resources for exploration, Portugal was the logical country for this task because of her

    (A) wealth.
    (B) navigational experience.
    (C) geographical position.
    (D) prominence.
    (E) ability.

14. The Portuguese learned navigational methods and procedures from all of the following except

    (A) Jews.
    (B) Catalans.
    (C) Genoese.
    (D) Venetians.
    (E) Aegeans.

15. Mediterranean sailors generally kept close to shore because

    (A) they were afraid of pirates.
    (B) they feared being forced to a lee shore.
    (C) they lacked navigational ability.
    (D) they feared running into storms.
    (E) the latitudinal extent of the Mediterranean was not great.

16. Hazards such as sudden storms and dangerous coasts were

    (A) predictable risks.
    (B) unknown risks.
    (C) unknown to the area.
    (D) a major threat to exploration.
    (E) no threat to navigation.

17. Sailing close to the coast enabled sailors to

    (A) reach their destination faster.
    (B) navigate without sailing directions.
    (C) determine their positions from landmarks.
    (D) determine their longitude and latitude.
    (E) avoid dangerous shoals.

Passage 3:

I decided to begin the term's work with the short story since that form would be the easiest for [the police officers], not only because most of their reading up to then had probably been in that genre, but also because a study of the reaction of people to various situations was
(5) something they relied on in their daily work.

The officer must remain neutral and clearly try to present a picture of the facts, while the artist usually begins with a preconceived message or attitude which is then transmitted through the use of carefully selected details of action described in words intended to provoke asso-
(10) ciations and emotional reactions in the reader. Only at the end of the term did the captain point out to me that he and his men also try to evaluate the events they describe and that their description of a sequence of events must of necessity be structured and colored by their understanding of what has taken place.

(15) The policemen's reactions to events and characters in the stories were surprisingly unprejudiced.... They did not object to writers whose stories had to do with their protagonist's rebellion against society's accepted values. Nor did stories in which the strong father becomes the villain and in which our usual ideals of manhood are
(20) turned around offend them. The many hunters among my students readily granted the message in those hunting tales in which sensitivity triumphs over male aggressiveness, stories that show the boy becoming a man because he *fails* to shoot the deer, goose, or catbird. The only characters they did object to were those they thought unrealistic. As
(25) the previous class had done, this one also excelled in interpreting the ways in which characters reveal themselves, subtly manipulate and influence each other; they, too, understood how the story usually saves its insight, its revelation, for the end.

This almost instinctive grasp of the writing of fiction was revealed
(30) when the policemen volunteered to write their own short stories.... They not only took great pains with plot and character, but with style and language. The stories were surprisingly well written, revealing an understanding of what a solid short story must contain: the revelation of character, the use of background description and language to create
(35) atmosphere and mood, the need to sustain suspense and yet make each event as it occurs seem natural, the insight achieved either by the characters in the story or the reader or both. They tended to favor

surprise endings. Some stories were sheer fantasies, or derived from previous reading, films, or television shows. Most wrote stories,
(40) obviously based on their own experiences, that revealed the amazing distance they must put between their personal lives and their work, which is part of the training for being a good cop. These stories, as well as their discussions of them, showed how coolly they judged their own weaknesses as well as the humor with which they accepted some of
(45) the difficulties or injustices of existence. Despite their authors' unmistakable sense of irony and awareness of corruption, these stories demonstrated how clearly, almost naively, these policemen wanted to continue to believe in some of the so-called American virtues—that courage is worth the effort and will be admired; that hard word will be
(50) rewarded; that life is somehow good; and that, despite the weariness, boredom, and occasional ugliness and danger, despite all their dislike of most of their routine and despite their own occasional grousing and complaints, they somehow did like being cops; that life, even in a chaotic and violent world, is worth it after all.

18. Compared to the artist, the policeman is

(A) ruled by action, not words.
(B) factual and not fanciful.
(C) neutral and not prejudiced.
(D) stoic and not emotional.
(E) aggressive and not passive.

19. Policemen reacted to story events and characters

(A) like most other people.
(B) according to a policeman's stereotyped image.
(C) like dilettantes.
(D) unrealistically.
(E) without emotion.

20. To which sort of characters did policemen object?

  I. Unrealistic
 II. Emotional
III. Sordid

(A) I only   (D) II and III only

(B) II only   (E) I, II, and III

(C) I and II only

21. According to the passage, a short story should contain

    (A) elegant prose.   (D) real-life experiences.

    (B) suspense.   (E) irony.

    (C) objectivity.

22. The instructor chose the short story because

    I. it was easy for the students.

    II. students had experience with it.

    III. students would enjoy it.

    (A) I only   (D) II and III only

    (B) II only   (E) I, II, and III

    (C) I and II only

23. Like writers, policemen must

    (A) analyze situations.   (D) intervene quickly.

    (B) behave coolly.   (E) attend college.

    (C) have an artistic bent.

24. According to the passage, most policemen wrote stories about

    (A) films.   (D) their work.

    (B) previous reading.   (E) politics.

    (C) American history.

25. According to the author, policemen view their profession as

    (A) full of corruption.

    (B) worth the effort.

    (C) full of routine.

    (D) poorly paid.

    (E) dangerous but adventuresome.

If there is still time remaining, you may review the questions in this section only. In the actual CAT GMAT, you cannot return to a question after you have confirmed your answer.

SECTION II   READING COMPREHENSION   Time: 30 minutes

Directions: This part contains three reading passages. You are to read each one carefully. When answering the questions, you *will* be able to refer to the passages. The questions are based on what is *stated* or *implied* in each passage. You have thirty minutes to complete this section.

Passage 1:

In the past, American colleges and universities were created to serve a dual purpose—to advance learning and to offer a chance to become familiar with bodies of knowledge already discovered to those who wished it. To create and to impart, these were the hallmarks of
(5) American higher education prior to the most recent, tumultuous decades of the twentieth century. The successful institution of higher learning had never been one whose mission could be defined in terms of providing vocational skills or as a strategy for resolving societal problems. In a subtle way Americans believed postsecondary educa-
(10) tion to be useful, but not necessarily of immediate use. What the student obtained in college became beneficial in later life—residually, without direct application in the period after graduation.

Another purpose has now been assigned to the mission of American colleges and universities. Institutions of higher learning—public
(15) or private—commonly face the challenge of defining their programs in such a way as to contribute to the service of the community.

One need only be reminded of the change in language describing the two-year college to appreciate the new value currently being attached to the concept of a service-related university. The traditional
(20) two-year college has shed its pejorative "junior" college label and is generally called a "community" college, a clearly value-laden expression representing the latest commitment in higher education.

This novel development is often overlooked. Educators have always been familiar with those parts of the two-year college curriculum that
(25) have a "service" or vocational orientation. Knowing this, otherwise perceptive commentaries on American postsecondary education underplay the impact of the attempt of colleges and universities to relate to, if not resolve, the problems of society. Whether the subject under review is student unrest, faculty tenure, the nature of the
(30) curriculum, the onset of collective bargaining, or the growth of collegiate bureaucracies, in each instance the thrust of these discus-

sions obscures the larger meaning of the emergence of the service-university in American higher education. Even the highly regarded critique of Clark Kerr, currently head of the Carnegie Foundation, which
(35) set the parameters of academic debate around the evolution of the so-called "multiversity," failed to take account of this phenomenon.

Taken together the attrition rate (from known and unknown causes) was 48 percent, but the figure for regular students was 36 percent while for Open Admissions categories it was 56 percent. Surprisingly,
(40) the statistics indicated that the four-year colleges retained or graduated more of the Open Admissions students than the two-year colleges, a finding that did not reflect experience elsewhere. Not surprisingly, perhaps, the figures indicated a close relationship between academic success defined as retention or graduation and high school averages.
(45) Similarly, it took longer for the Open Admissions students to generate college credits and graduate than regular students, a pattern similar to national averages. The most important statistics, however, relate to the findings regarding Open Admissions students, and these indicated as a projection that perhaps as many as 70 percent would not graduate
(50) from a unit of the City University.

1. The dropout rate among regular students in Open Admissions was approximately

(A) 35%.   (D) 65%.
(B) 45%.   (E) 75%.
(C) 55%.

2. According to the passage, in the past it was *not* the purpose of American higher education to

(A) advance learning.   (D) train workers.
(B) solve societal problems.   (E) prepare future managers.
(C) impart knowledge.

3. One of the recent, important changes in higher education relates to

(A) student representation on college boards.
(B) faculty tenure requirements.
(C) curriculum updates.
(D) service-education concepts.
(E) cost constraints.

4. It was estimated that what percentage of Open Admissions students would fail to graduate from City University?

   (A) 40%   (D) 70%
   (B) 50%   (E) 80%
   (C) 60%

5. According to the passage, the two-year college may be described as

   I.   a junior college.
   II. service-oriented.
   III. a community college.

   (A) I only   (D) II and III only
   (B) II only   (E) I, II, and III
   (C) I and II only

6. The service role of colleges aims to

   (A) improve services.
   (B) gain acceptance among educators.
   (C) serve the community.
   (D) provide skills for future use.
   (E) make graduates employable.

7. The attrition rate for Open Admissions students was greater than the rate for regular students by what percent?

   (A) 10%   (D) 40%
   (B) 20%   (E) 46%
   (C) 36%

8. Clark Kerr failed to take account of

   (A) the "communiversity."   (D) the service-university.
   (B) collegiate bureaucracies. (E) Open Admissions.
   (C) faculty tenure.

9. The *average* attrition rate for regular and Open Admissions students was

   (A) 36%.   (D) 75%.
   (B) 46%.   (E) 92%.
   (C) 56%.

Passage 2:

Businessmen had been concerned about slowing economic growth that had been a major factor in the unemployment of some 30 million people in the West. As a result, businessmen pressured politicians to curb imports, increase export subsidies, or both. Automakers
(5) in the UK and USA, as well as steelmakers in Pittsburgh and Bonn wanted help in reducing unemployment. The same is true for other affected industries, such as textile, clothing and shoe manufacturers in Western countries.

Therefore, governments are tempted to take the easy way out and
(10) increase trade restrictions, even those devoted to free market economics as the Reagan administration. Evidence of this is the fact that Washington had implemented new restrictions against the importation of cars, textiles and sugar. Steel was to be next on the list of restricted imports. However, the United States is not the only country being pres-
(15) sured to impose trade restrictions. European countries have also defended domestic markets and stimulated exports through their use of subsidies.

A most urgent task for the leaders of the industrial world was to change the divisive atmosphere before more restrictive trade practices
(20) would be implemented. According to C. Fred Bergsten, words have been stronger than deeds. The condition of world trade was gloomy. World trade stood at $2 trillion on an annual basis in 1980. During the first half of 1980, C. Fred Bergsten estimated that world trade had actually declined as the world economy did not grow. However, according to
(25) his view, increased protectionism was not the cause of the trade slowdown, at least for the time being. The major cause was slow economic growth, recession and the resulting decline in the demand for imports.

Today there are additional problems that could be damaging to the economy. Even though tariffs and non-tariff barriers (such as quotas
(30) on imports) are low as the result of three months of intensive trade negotiations over the last two decades, new trade restraints have surfaced. These new restraints take the form of voluntary agreements between nations to limit the import of certain goods.

When the same industries are protected by several countries, the
(35) negotiations become more difficult. Take for example, the steel industry. Since 1977 the European Economic Community has been trying to eliminate excess steel capacity through the implementation of bilat-

eral import quotas in order to lessen the impact on steelworkers. The
United States has faced similar pressure at home and a worldwide
(40) excess supply of steel. As a result, the United States enacted a "voluntary" quota system in 1969. After a period of no restraint, the U.S.
introduced a complex trigger price mechanism in 1978.

10. According to the passage, new "trade restraints" are evidenced by

    (A) voluntary trade agreements.

    (B) political suasion.

    (C) lower than market prices.

    (D) abrogating agreements.

    (E) increased product standards.

11. Increased protectionism has been caused by

    (A) the "cold war."

    (B) United States economic policy.

    (C) increased unemployment.

    (D) a breakdown in international law.

    (E) a growth in cartels.

12. A slowdown in world trade has been caused by

    (A) protectionism.

    (B) slower population growth.

    (C) less trade with Communist countries.

    (D) economic recession.

    (E) increased oil prices.

13. The U.S. Government has increased barriers to the import of

    (A) autos, textiles, and sugar.   (D) shoes, textiles, and sugar.

    (B) autos, textiles, and steel.   (E) shoes, textiles, and steel.

    (C) autos, electronics, and steel.

14. The best possible theme for the passage would be

    (A) "Reagan Administration's Economic Policies."

    (B) "International Trade Agreements in the 1960s."

(C) "Tokyo Round of Trade Negotiations."

(D) "A Perilous Time for World Trade."

(E) "Problems and Prospects for World Exports."

15. In recent years, trade between nations has been constrained by

(A) voluntary agreements limiting imports.

(B) rhetoric expressed by labor leaders.

(C) misalignment among world currencies.

(D) the free international exchange of goods.

(E) restrictive monetary and fiscal policies.

16. While imports are restrained by barriers, exports are encouraged through

(A) bargaining.   (D) advertising.

(B) lowering prices.   (E) dealing.

(C) subsidies.

17. A means to increase steel capacity in the European Economic Community has been the use of

(A) voluntary quotas.   (D) trigger prices.

(B) bilateral quotas.   (E) restraints.

(C) voluntary and bilateral quotas.

Passage 3:

The pollution problems of the atmosphere resemble those of the water only partly. So far, the supply of air has not been deficient as was the case with water, and the dimensions of the air-shed are so vast that a number of people still hold the opinion that air need not be
(5) economized. However, scientific forecasts have shown that the time may be already approaching when clear and biologically valuable air will become problem No. 1.

Air being ubiquitous, people are particularly sensitive about any reduction in the quality of the atmosphere, the increased contents of
(10) dust and gaseous exhalations, and particularly about the presence of odors. The demand for purity of atmosphere, therefore, emanates much more from the population itself than from the specific sectors of the national economy affected by a polluted or even biologically aggressive atmosphere.

(15) The households' share in atmospheric pollution is far bigger than

that of industry which, in turn, further complicates the economic
problems of atmospheric purity. Some countries have already col-
lected positive experience with the reconstruction of whole urban
sectors on the basis of new heating appliances based on the combus-
(20) tion of solid fossil fuels; estimates of the economic consequences of
such measures have also been put forward.

In contrast to water, where the maintenance of purity would seem
primarily to be related to the costs of production and transport, a far
higher proportion of the costs of maintaining the purity of the atmo-
(25) sphere derives from environmental considerations. Industrial sources
of gaseous and dust emissions are well known and classified; their
location can be accurately identified, which makes them controllable.
With the exception, perhaps, of the elimination of sulphur dioxide,
technical means and technological processes exist which can be used
(30) for the elimination of all excessive impurities of the air from the various
emissions.

Atmospheric pollution caused by the private property of individuals
(their dwellings, automobiles, etc.) is difficult to control. Some sources
such as motor vehicles are very mobile, and they are thus capable of
(35) polluting vast territories. In this particular case, the cost of antipollution measures will have to be borne, to a considerable extent, by
individuals, whether in the form of direct costs or indirectly in the form
of taxes, dues, surcharges, etc.

The problem of noise is a typical example of an environmental
(40) problem which cannot be solved only passively, i.e., merely by
protective measures, but will require the adoption of active measures,
i.e., direct interventions at the source. The costs of a complete
protection against noise are so prohibitive as to make it unthinkable
even in the economically most developed countries.

18. According to the passage, the population at large

(A) is unconcerned about air pollution controls.
(B) is especially aware of problems concerning air quality and
     purity.
(C) regards water pollution as more serious than air pollution.
(D) has failed to recognize the economic consequences of
     pollution.
(E) is unwilling to make the sacrifices needed to ensure clean air.

19. Scientific forecasts have shown that clear and biologically valuable air

    (A) is likely to remain abundant for some time.
    (B) creates fewer economic difficulties than does water pollution.
    (C) may soon be dangerously lacking.
    (D) may be beyond the capacity of our technology to protect.
    (E) has already become difficult to obtain.

20. According to the passage, which of the following contributes *most* to atmospheric pollution?

    (A) industry
    (B) production
    (C) households
    (D) mining
    (E) waste disposal

21. The costs involved in the maintenance of pure water are determined primarily by

    I.   production costs.
    II. transport costs.
    III. research costs.

    (A) I only   (D) II and III only
    (B) III only   (E) I, II, and III
    (C) I and II only

22. According to the passage, atmospheric pollution caused by private property is

    (A) easy to control.   (D) decreasing.
    (B) impossible to control. (E) negligible.
    (C) difficult to control.

23. According to the passage, the problem of noise can be solved through

    I.   active measures.
    II. passive measures.
    III. tax levies.

    (A) I only   (D) II and III only
    (B) III only   (E) I, II, and III
    (C) I and II only

24. According to the passage, the costs of some antipollution measures will have to be borne by individuals because

    (A) individuals contribute to the creation of pollution.

    (B) governments do not have adequate resources.

    (C) industry is not willing to bear its share.

    (D) individuals are more easily taxed than producers.

    (E) individuals demand production, which causes pollution.

25. Complete protection against noise

    (A) may be forthcoming in the near future.

    (B) is impossible to achieve.

    (C) may have prohibitive costs.

    (D) is possible only in developed countries.

    (E) has been achieved in some countries.

If there is still time remaining, you may review the questions in this section only. In the actual CAT GMAT, you cannot return to a question after you have confirmed your answer.

SECTION III   PROBLEM SOLVING   Time: 30 minutes

Directions: Solve each of the following problems; then indicate the correct answer on the answer sheet. [On the actual test you will be permitted to use scratch paper for your calculations.]

NOTE: A figure that appears with a problem is drawn as accurately as possible so as to provide information that may help in answering the question. Numbers in this test are real numbers.

  1. Water has been poured into an empty rectangular tank at the rate of 5 cubic feet per minute for 6 minutes. The length of the tank is 4 feet and the width is one-half of the length. How deep is the water in the tank?

    (A) 7.5 inches   (D) 7 feet, 6 inches

    (B) 3 feet, 7.5 inches   (E) 30 feet

    (C) 3 feet, 9 inches

2. If $2x - y = 4$, then $6x - 3y$ is

(A) Cannot be determined
(B) 6
(C) 8
(D) 10
(E) 12

3. The next number in the arithmetical progression 5, 11, 17,... is

(A) 18
(B) 22
(C) 23
(D) 28
(E) 33

4. If x, y, z are chosen from the three numbers -3, $\dfrac{1}{2}$, and 2, what is the largest possible value of the expression $\left(\dfrac{x}{y}\right) z^2$?

(A) $-\dfrac{3}{8}$
(B) 16
(C) 24
(D) 36
(E) 54

5. A survey of n people found that 60 percent preferred brand A. An additional x people were surveyed who all preferred brand A. Seventy percent of all the people surveyed preferred brand A. Find x in terms of n.

(A) $\dfrac{n}{6}$
(B) $\dfrac{n}{3}$
(C) $\dfrac{n}{2}$
(D) n
(E) $3n$

6. The hexagon *ABCDEF* is regular. That means all its sides are the
    same length and all its interior angles are the same size. Each side
    of the hexagon is 2 feet. What is the area of the rectangle *BCEF*?

    (A) 4 square feet
    (B) $4\sqrt{3}$ square feet
    (C) 8 square feet
    (D) $4 + 4\sqrt{3}$ square feet
    (E) 12 square feet

7. A warehouse has 20 packers. Each packer can load $\frac{1}{8}$ of a box in 9
    minutes. How many boxes can be loaded in $1\frac{1}{2}$ hours by all 20
    packers?

    (A) $1\frac{1}{4}$ (D) 20
    (B) $10\frac{1}{4}$ (E) 25
    (C) $12\frac{1}{2}$

8. In Motor City 90% of the population own a car, 15% own a motor-
    cycle, and everybody owns one or the other or both. What is the
    percentage of motorcycle owners who own cars?

    (A) 5%   (D) 50%
    (B) 15%   (E) 90%
    (C) $33\frac{1}{3}$%

9. Jim's weight is 140% of Marcia's weight. Bob's weight is 90% of
    Lee's weight. Lee weighs twice as much as Marcia. What percent-
    age of Jim's weight is Bob's weight?

    (A) $64\frac{2}{7}$ (D) $128\frac{4}{7}$
    (B) $77\frac{7}{9}$ (E) $155\frac{5}{9}$
    (C) 90

10. Towns A and C are connected by a straight highway that is 60
    miles long. The straight-line distance between towns A and B is

50 miles, and the straight-line distance from town B to town C is 50 miles. How many miles is it from town B to the point on the highway connecting towns A and C which is closest to town B?

(A) 30   (D) 50
(B) 40   (E) 60
(C) $30\sqrt{2}$

11. A chair originally cost $50.00. The chair was offered for sale at 108% of its cost. After a week the price was discounted 10% and the chair was sold. The chair was sold for

(A) $45.00   (D) $49.50
(B) $48.60   (E) $54.00
(C) $49.00

12. A worker is paid x dollars for the first 8 hours he works each day. He is paid y dollars per hour for each hour he works in excess of 8 hours. During one week he works 8 hours on Monday, 11 hours on Tuesday, 9 hours on Wednesday, 10 hours on Thursday, and 9 hours on Friday. What is his average daily wage in dollars for the five-day week?

(A) $x + \dfrac{7}{5}y$

(B) $2x + y$

(C) $\dfrac{5x + 8y}{5}$

(D) $8x + \left(\dfrac{7}{5}\right)y$

(E) $5x + 7y$

13. A club has 8 male and 8 female members. The club is choosing a committee of 6 members. The committee must have 3 male and 3 female members. How many different committees can be chosen?

(A) 112,896   (D) 112
(B) 3,136   (E) 9
(C) 720

14. A motorcycle costs $2,500 when it is brand new. At the end of each year it is worth $\frac{4}{5}$ of what it was at the beginning of the year. What is the motorcycle worth when it is 3 years old?

(A) $1,000
(B) $1,200
(C) $1,280
(D) $1,340
(E) $1,430

15. Which of the following inequalities is the solution to the inequality $7x - 5 < 12x + 18$?

(A) $x < -\dfrac{13}{5}$

(B) $x > -\dfrac{23}{5}$

(C) $x < -\dfrac{23}{5}$

(D) $x > \dfrac{23}{5}$

(E) $x < \dfrac{23}{5}$

Use the following table for questions 16–17.

Type of vehicle	Cost of fuel for 200-mile trip
Automobile	$15
Motorcycle	$ 5
Bus	$20
Truck	$50
Airplane	$70

16. If the wages of a bus driver for a 200-mile trip are $70, and the only costs for a bus are the fuel and the driver's wages, how much should a bus company charge to charter a bus and driver for a 200-mile trip in order to obtain 120% of the cost?

(A) $24
(B) $90
(C) $94
(D) $104
(E) $108

17. If 3 buses, 4 automobiles, 2 motorcycles, and 1 truck each make a 200-mile trip, what is the average fuel cost per vehicle?

(A) $5

(B) $15

(C) $18

(D) $20

(E) $24

18. If $x + 2y = 2x + y$, then $x - y$ is equal to

(A) 0

(B) 2

(C) 4

(D) 5

(E) cannot be determined

19. Mary, John, and Karen ate lunch together. Karen's meal cost 50% more than John's meal and Mary's meal cost $\frac{5}{6}$ as much as Karen's meal. If Mary paid $2 more than John, how much was the total that the three of them paid?

(A) $28.33

(B) $30.00

(C) $35.00

(D) $37.50

(E) $40.00

20. If the angles of a triangle are in the ratio 1 : 2 : 2, then the triangle

(A) is isosceles

(B) is obtuse

(C) is a right triangle

(D) is equilateral

(E) has one angle greater than 80°

If there is still time remaining, you may review the questions in this section only. In the actual CAT GMAT, you cannot return to a question after you have confirmed your answer.

SECTION IV   CRITICAL REASONING   Time: 30 minutes

Directions: For each question, choose the best answer among the listed alternatives.

1. When Jane and Arnold Martin take a walk in the local downtown area with their four children, heads turn. With one boy easily mistaken for a Scandinavian, one child a Mexican, another Chinese, and the fourth black-skinned, it seems like an outing of the United Nations. In fact, the four kids are all adopted and each has been part of the Martin family since he or she was a few months old.

"We explained adoption to each of them as soon as they could understand," says Jane. "It's so natural to them now. In fact, they once thought every child was adopted."

"Ever since 1970, when we were married we have longed for children of our own, but despite medical tests and treatments we were unable to have any, and now, at last, we have a family. It is one of life's bitter ironies that some women would do almost anything to get rid of a fetus, while others would do almost anything to have one."

Which one of the following do you think reflects the opinion of Jane Martin?

(A) It is a sad fact that many unwanted babies are born and sometimes abandoned by their mother.

(B) The adoption of the children has fulfilled our yearnings for a family.

(C) We will tell our children they are adopted as soon as they express an interest.

(D) It is possible to go to South America and buy babies and bring them back to the States.

(E) We believe that abortion is sinful.

2. The following is an extract from a contract between company A Ltd. and an individual X, X being the sole shareholder and an employee of another company—B Ltd., wherein A agrees to purchase the 2,400 shares held by X in B Ltd. for $1,000,000 on January 15, 1988.

X agrees to sell 2,400 shares of B Ltd.'s Common Stock to A Ltd. in consideration of $1,000,000 due and payable on January 15, 1988, by check or bankers' draft.

A Ltd., B Ltd., and X represent and warrant that they have undertaken all necessary action to put B Ltd. in a financial condition so the acquisition of these shares from X conform to statutory requirements.

X agrees that he will not, without consent of B Ltd. or A Ltd., disclose any material confidential information obtained during his employment with B Ltd., except as may be required by judicial proceedings.

Which of the following statements most fairly represents the facts?

(A) B Ltd. will not purchase the shares if A Ltd. discloses material confidential information regarding B Ltd. before January 15.

(B) Following January 15, 1988, A Ltd. will have a wholly owned subsidiary—namely, B Ltd.

(C) If X were selling only 600 shares, then the proceeds should be $250,000.

(D) In the above, X can contract in the name of B Ltd. because X was the sole shareholder.

(E) B Ltd. and X have joint liability for all contracts until January 15, 1988.

3. Richard is a terrible driver. He has had at least five traffic violations in the past year.

Which of the following can be said about the above claim?

(A) This is an example of an argument that is directed against the source of the claim rather than the claim itself.

(B) The statement is fallacious because it contains an illegitimate appeal to authority.

(C) The above argument obtains it strength from a similarity of two compared situations.

(D) The argument is built upon an assumption that is not stated but rather is concealed.

(E) In the above statements, there is a shifting in the meaning of terms, causing a fallacy of ambiguity.

4. Valerie Fitzgerald, the author of *Zemindar*, was born and grew up in that part of India in which the events described in her book took place. Her family, and in particular her father, had a great interest in the period of the Indian Mutiny, engendered perhaps by the fact that her Irish grandmother survived the Siege of Agra at the age of six.

Trying to invoke the Zemindari life was easy for Valerie Fitzgerald, as she spent many childhood winters on a large estate outside Delhi, managed by her father, and later spent many holidays, on another estate, northeast of Lucknow and just at the foot of the Himalayas, in what used to be Oudh.

Valerie Fitzgerald says of the writing of Zemindar which took place over a span of nine years, "I have no recollection of just when, or more important, why I set about telling the story of the Siege. I suppose it was because I realized I had the right background—and because no one else, as far as I knew, had ever tried it."

Which of the following facts can be elicited from the foregoing paragraphs?

(A) *Zemindar* is the story of the early life of the author, Valerie Fitzgerald.

(B) Miss Fitzgerald cannot remember precisely the reason for writing the book *Zemindar.*

(C) Many of Miss Fitzgerald's winters were spent in the estates in India collecting and collating information to include in her book on the Siege of Agra.

(D) Miss Fitzgerald is the only author ever to have written a book on the Siege of Agra.

(E) Her grandmother's experience at the age of six in witnessing the Siege of Agra was the foremost influence on Miss Fitzgerald's decision to write *Zemindar.*

5. The exchange rate is the ruling official rate of exchange of dollars for other currencies. It determines the value of American goods in relation to foreign goods. If the dollar is devalued in terms of other currencies, American exports (which are paid for in dollars) become cheaper to foreigners and American imports (paid for by purchasing foreign currency) become more expensive to holders of dollars.

What conclusion can be drawn from the above?

(A) There are certain disadvantages for the United States economy attached to devaluation.

(B) The prospect of devaluation results in a speculative outflow of funds.

(C) By encouraging exports and discouraging imports, devaluation can improve the American balance of payments.

(D) The difference between imports and exports is called the Trade Gap.

(E) It is possible that inflation neutralizes the beneficial effects of devaluation.

6. You have three boxes, each containing two balls, one containing a black pair; one, a white pair; and the third, one white ball and one black ball. On each box are pictures of two balls—either two black ones, two white ones, or one white and one black. You are told that the markings on the boxes are all wrong. You are asked to ascertain the colors of the balls contained in each box.

Which of the following statements can be inferred from the above?

(A) You can take out one ball from the box marked with two black balls and, without looking at the second ball, know what each box actually contains.

(B) You can take out one ball from the box marked with two white balls and, without looking at the second ball, know what each box actually contains.

(C) You can take out one ball from the box marked with one white ball and one black ball and, without looking at the second ball, know what each box contains.

(D) You cannot know which balls are contained in which box until you take a ball out of more than one box.

(E) You cannot know which boxes contain which color balls until you take a ball out of all three boxes.

7. In the human body, platelets promote blood clotting by clumping together. Aspirin has been found to prevent clotting by making platelets less sticky. Research has now shown that heart attacks and strokes caused by blood clots could be avoided by taking one aspirin a day. Statistics show that the incidence of second heart attacks has been reduced by 21% and overall mortality rates by 15% as a result of taking aspirin.

Unfortunately, the drug has several unpleasant side effects, including nausea, gastric bleeding, and, in severe cases, shock. In children, it has been linked to Reye's syndrome, a rare, but occasionally fatal, childhood illness.

On balance, however, for men aged 40 and over, an aspirin a day may present an excellent prophylactic measure for a disease that affects 1.5 million Americans yearly and claims the lives of about 540,000.

Which of the following conclusions can most properly be drawn from the information above?

(A) All people should take an aspirin a day to prevent heart attacks.

(B) Painkillers prevent heart attacks.

(C) Smokers can safely continue smoking, provided that they take at least one aspirin a day.

(D) The majority of people suffering second subsequent cardiac arrests could have been saved by taking an aspirin a day.

(E) Aspirin can be used to reduce mortality rates in patients who have already suffered heart attacks.

8. More and more organizations in the world today are prepared to carry out criminal acts in order to achieve their ends. Often these acts involve the taking of innocent people as hostages. One of the most urgent problems on the agenda of most Western European governments is terrorism and how to deal with it. In handling the situations that arise, all agree that swift and effective action must be taken to combat the terrorist, but for some reason, when terrorism arrives on their doorstep—in the form of a hijacked airplane, for example—some governments give in all too quickly to the demands of the terrorist. It is understandable that governments must act to safeguard the welfare of their citizens and other innocent people caught up in the criminal act. However, what the governments seem to ignore is that if you give in to the terrorist once, he or she will play upon your weakness and therefore be encouraged to indulge in terrorist acts on future occasions.

Which of the following conclusions best describes the views of the writer of the above passage?

(A) There is a subtle, but certain difference between state terrorism and terrorist acts carried out by individuals or members of illegal terrorist groups.

(B) One man's terrorist is another man's freedom fighter!

(C) Governments make no distinction between terrorism carried out for financial gain and that carried out in the name of a political organization.

(D) Surrender to blackmail and you invite more blackmail!

(E) There seems to be no solution to the problem of terrorist incidents occurring in Western European countries and other democracies.

9. In the past, to run for one's country in the Olympics was the ultimate achievement of any athlete. Nowadays, an athlete's motives are more and more influenced by financial gain, and consequently we do not see our best athletes in the Olympics, which is still only for amateurs.

Which of the following will most weaken the above conclusion?

(A) The publicity and fame that can be achieved by competing in the Olympics makes athletes more "marketable" by agents and potential sponsors, while allowing the athletes to retain their amateur status.

(B) The winning of a race is not as important as participating.

(C) There is a widely held belief that our best Olympic athletes receive enough in terms of promotion and sponsorship.

(D) It has been suggested that professional athletes should be allowed to compete in the games.

(E) Athletics as an entertainment is like any other entertainment job and deserves a financial reward.

10. The function of a food technologist in a large marketing chain of food stores is to ensure that all foodstuffs which are offered for sale in the various retail outlets meet certain standard criteria for nonperishability, freshness, and fitness for human consumption.

It is the technologist's job to visit the premises of suppliers and food producers (factory or farm), inspect the facilities and report thereon. His responsibility also includes receiving new products from local and foreign suppliers and performing exhaustive quality control testing on them. Finally, he should carry out surprise spot-checks on goods held in the marketing chain's own warehouses and stores.

What conclusion can best be drawn from the preceding paragraph?

(A) A university degree in food technology is a necessary and sufficient condition for becoming a food technologist.

(B) Imported products, as well as home-produced goods, must be rigorously tested.

(C) The food technologist stands between the unhygienic producer and the unsuspecting consumer.

(D) Home-produced foodstuffs are safer to eat than goods imported from abroad because they are subject to more regular and closer inspection procedures.

(E) Random checking of the quality of goods stored on the shelves in a foodstore is the best way of ensuring that foodstuffs of an inferior quality are not purchased by the general public.

11. The daily journey from his home to his office takes John Bond on average an hour and thirty-five minutes by car. A friend has told him of a different route that is longer in mileage, but will only take an hour and a quarter on average, because it contains stretches of roads where it is possible to drive at higher speeds.

   John Bond's only consideration apart from the time factor is the cost, and he calculates that his car will consume 10% less gasoline if he takes the suggested new route. John decides to take the new route for the next two weeks as an experiment.

   If the above were the only other considerations, which one of the following may have an effect on the decision John has made?

   (A) Major road work is begun on the shorter (in distance) route, which holds up traffic for an extra ten minutes. The project will take six months, but after it, the improvements will allow the journey to be made in half an hour less than at present.

   (B) There is to be a strike at local gas stations and the amount of gasoline drivers may purchase may be rationed.

   (C) John finds a third route which is slightly longer than his old route, but shorter than the suggested route.

   (D) The old route passes the door of a work colleague, who without a ride, would have to go to work by bus.

   (E) None of the above.

12. All elephants are gray.
   And all mice are gray.
   Therefore, I conclude that all elephants are gray.

   The argument above is invalid because

   (A) the writer bases his argument on another argument that contains circular reasoning.

(B) the writer has illogically classified two disparate groups together when there is no relationship between them, except that they both have the same attribute.

(C) the writer has made a mistaken analogy between two dissimilar qualities.

(D) the writer has used a fallacy which involves the ambiguous description of animals by their color.

(E) the writer has failed to express his reasoning fully.

13. There are three main factors that control the risks of becoming dependent on drugs. These factors are the type of drug, the personality of the individual, and the circumstances in which the drug is taken. Indeed, it could be said that the majority of the adult population have taken alcohol, yet few have become dependent on it. Also, many strong drugs that have been used for medical purposes have not caused the patient to become addicted.

However, it can be demonstrated that people who have taken drugs for fun are more likely to become dependent on the drug. The dependence is not always physiological but may remain psychological, although the effects are still essentially the same. Those at greatest risk appear to be personalities that are psychopathic, immature, or otherwise unstable.

Psychological dependence is very strong with heroin, morphine, cocaine, and amphetamines. Physiological dependence is great with heroin and morphine, but less with amphetamines, barbiturates, and alcohol.

Which of the following conclusions can be drawn from the text?

(A) One cannot become addicted to certain drugs if one has a strong personality.

(B) Taking drugs for "kicks" increases the possibility of becoming dependent on drugs.

(C) Psychological dependence is greatest with heroin.

(D) Alcohol is a safe drug since very few people become dependent on it.

(E) Long-term use of certain drugs for medical purposes does not cause addiction.

14. Sally overslept. Therefore, she did not eat breakfast. She realized
     that she was late for school, so she ran as fast as she could and
     did not see a hole in the ground which was in her path. She
     tripped and broke her ankle. She was then taken to the hospital
     and while lying in bed was visited by her friend, who wanted to
     know why she had slept so late.

     Which of the following conclusions can be made from the above
     passage?

     (A) Because Sally did not eat her breakfast, she broke her ankle.
     (B) Sally's friend visited her in the hospital because she wanted
          to know why she was late for school.
     (C) Sally did not notice the hole because she overslept.
     (D) Sally broke her ankle because she went to bed late the
          previous night.
     (E) Sally's broken ankle meant she did not go to school that day.

15. The owners of a local supermarket have decided to make use of
     three now-redundant checkout counters. They believe that they
     will attract those customers who lately have been put off by the
     long checkout lines during the mid-morning and evening rush
     hours. The owners have concluded that in order to be successful,
     the increased revenue from existing and added counters will have
     to be more than the increase in maintenance costs for the added
     counters.

     The underlying goal of the owners can be summarized thus:

     (A) To improve services to all customers.
     (B) To attract people who have never been to the store.
     (C) To make use of the redundant counters.
     (D) To keep maintenance costs on the added counters as low as
          possible.
     (E) To increase monthly profits.

16. In the United States, there is increasing concern over the use of
     radiation, particularly radiation for medical uses. Mammograms,
     or breast X rays, can reveal the early stages of breast cancer, the
     leading cause of cancer death in American women.

          Public awareness of the risk of breast cancer, particularly
     among those younger than 50, was heightened during the 1970s

by the publicity given to the mastectomies of prominent women, including then-First Lady Betty Ford. The establishment in 1973 of a free nationwide screening program resulted in an unprecedented rush for mammograms.

Within three years, several hundred thousand women had been examined and 1,800 breast cancer cases detected. However, studies showed that mammograms can cause as well as identify cancer, and researchers involved in the studies concluded that the mammography program produced five cancer cases for every one it detected.

Which one of the following would most strengthen the conclusion drawn by the researchers?

(A) Tests have shown that mammography does not increase the survival rates of women younger than 50.

(B) Drug therapy to cure cancers of the breast were found to be successful.

(C) It has been decided that all women over 50 may be given a mammogram every three years.

(D) The breast has been shown as being extremely sensitive to radiation-induced cancer.

(E) The research studies showed that over 50% of women tested were smokers.

17. The cost of housing in many parts of the United States has become so excessive that many young couples, with above-average salaries, can only afford small apartments. Mortgage commitments are so huge that they cannot consider the possibility of starting a family. A new baby would probably mean either the mother or father giving up a well-paid position. The lack of or great cost of child-care facilities precludes the return of both parents to work.

Which of the following adjustments could practically be made to the situation described above which would allow young couples to improve their housing prospects?

(A) Encourage couples to remain childless.

(B) Encourage couples to have one child only.

(C) Encourage couples to postpone starting their families until a later age than previously acceptable to society.

(D) Encourage young couples to move to cheaper areas of the United States.

(E) Encourage fathers to remain at home until mothers return to work.

18. Unless new reserves are found soon, the world's supply of coal is being depleted in such a way that with demand continuing to grow at present rates, reserves will be exhausted by the year 2050.

   Which of the following, if true, will most weaken the above argument?

   (A) There has been a slowdown in the rate of increase in world demand for coal over the last 5 years from 10% to 5%.

   (B) It has been known for many years that there are vast stocks of coal under Antarctica which have yet to be economically exploited.

   (C) Oil is being used increasingly in place of coal for many industrial and domestic uses.

   (D) As coal resources are depleted, more and more marginal supplies, which are more costly to produce and less efficient in use, are being mined.

   (E) None of the above.

19. In accordance with their powers, many state authorities are introducing fluoridation of drinking water. This follows the conclusion of 10 years of research that the process ensures that children and adults receive the required intake of fluoride that will strengthen teeth. The maximum level has been set at one part per million. However, there are many who object, claiming that fluoridation removes freedom of choice.

   Which of the following will weaken the claim of the proponents of fluoridation?

   (A) Fluoridation over a certain prescribed level has been shown to lead to a general weakening of teeth.

   (B) There is no record of the long-term effects of drinking fluoridated water.

   (C) The people to be affected by fluoridation claim that they have not had sufficient opportunity to voice their views.

   (D) Fluoridation is only one part of general dental health.

   (E) Water already contains natural fluoride.

20. Mr. and Mrs. Smith and their son John want to cross the Dart River. The only way across is with Mr. Jones and his rowboat. Mr. Jones will not allow anyone to row his boat and will take only one passenger at a time. John is only a little boy so he cannot be left alone on the riverbank.

Which of the following conditions are not part of the successful passage of the Smiths across the river?

(A) Mr. Smith crosses the river first.

(B) Mr. Smith crosses the river last.

(C) Mr. and Mrs. Smith do not cross together.

(D) John crosses the river first.

(E) John crosses the river second.

If there is still time remaining, you may review the questions in this section only. In the actual CAT GMAT, you cannot return to a question after you have confirmed your answer.

SECTION V   DATA SUFFICIENCY   Time: 30 minutes

Directions: Each of the following problems has a question and two statements which are labeled (1) and (2). Use the data given in (1) and (2) together with other available information (such as the number of hours in a day, the definition of *clockwise*, mathematical facts, etc.) to decide whether the statements are *sufficient* to answer the question. Then fill in space

(A) if you can get the answer from (1) alone but not from (2) alone;

(B) If you can get the answer from (2) alone but not from (1) alone;

(C) If you can get the answer from (1) and (2) together, although neither statement by itself suffices;

(D) If statement (1) alone suffices *and* statement (2) alone suffices;

(E) if you cannot get the answer from statements (1) and (2) together, but need even more data.

All numbers used in this section are real numbers. A figure given for a problem is intended to provide information consistent with that in the question, but not necessarily with the additional information contained in the statements.

1. Is x greater than y?

(1) $3x = 2k$

(2) $k = y^2$

2. Is *ABCD* a parallelogram?

    (1) $AB = CD$
    (2) *AB* is parallel to *CD*

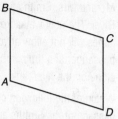

3. What was Mr. Smith's combined income for the years 1965–1970? In 1965 he made $10,000.

    (1) His average yearly income for the years 1965–1970 was $12,000.
    (2) In 1970, his income was $20,000.

4. What is the two-digit number whose first digit is *a* and whose second digit is *b*? The number is greater than 9.

    (1) $2a + 3b = 11a + 2b$
    (2) The two-digit number is a multiple of 19.

5. *k* is a positive integer. Is *k* a prime number?

    (1) No integer between 2 and $\sqrt{k}$ inclusive divides *k* evenly.
    (2) No integer between 2 and $\dfrac{k}{2}$ inclusive divides *k* evenly, and *k* is greater than 5.

6. The towns *A*, *B*, and *C* lie on a straight line. *C* is between *A* and *B*. The distance from *A* to *B* is 100 miles. How far is it from *A* to *C*?

    (1) The distance from *A* to *B* is 25% more than the distance from *C* to *B*.
    (2) The distance from *A* to *C* is $\dfrac{1}{4}$ of the distance from *C* to *B*.

7. Is *AB* perpendicular to *CD*?

    (1) $AC = BD$
    (2) $x = y$

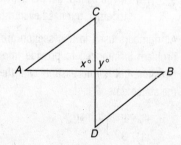

8. What is the value of $x - y$?

   (1) $x + 2y = 6$
   (2) $x = y$

9. The number of eligible voters is 100,000. How many eligible voters voted?

   (1) 63% of the eligible men voted.
   (2) 67% of the eligible women voted.

10. If $z = 50$, find the value of x.

   (1) $RS \neq ST$
   (2) $x + y = 60$

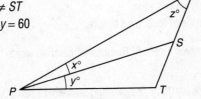

11. How much was the original cost of a car that sold for $2,300?

   (1) The car was sold for a discount of 10% from its original cost.
   (2) The salesperson received $150.

12. The hexagon $ABCDEF$ is inscribed in the circle with center O. What is the length of AB?

   (1) The radius of the circle is 4 inches.
   (2) The hexagon is a regular hexagon.

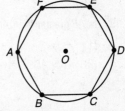

13. How many rolls of wallpaper are necessary to cover the walls of a room whose floor and ceiling are rectangles 12 feet wide and 15 feet long?

   (1) A roll of wallpaper covers 20 square feet.
   (2) There are no windows in the walls.

14. What was the percentage of defective items produced at a factory?

   (1) The total number of defective items produced was 1,234.
   (2) The ratio of defective items to nondefective items was 32 to 5,678.

15. Is *ABC* a right triangle? $AB = 5$; $AC = 4$.

(1) $BC = 3$
(2) $AC = CD$

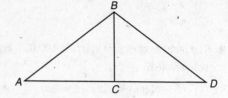

16. Did the price of energy rise last year?

(1) If the price of energy rose last year, then the price of food would rise this year.
(2) The price of food rose this year.

17. How much was a certain Rembrandt painting worth in January 1971?

(1) In January 1977 the painting was worth $2,000,000.
(2) Over the ten years 1968–1977 the painting increased in value by 10% each year.

18. A sequence of numbers $a_1, a_2, a_3, \ldots$ is given by the rule $a_n^2 = a_{n+1}$. Does 3 appear in the sequence?

(1) $a_1 = 2$
(2) $a_3 = 16$

19. Is *AB* greater than *AC*?

(1) $z > x$
(2) $AC > AD$

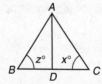

20. *x* and *y* are integers that are both less than 10. Is *x* greater than *y*?

(1) *x* is a multiple of 3.
(2) *y* is a multiple of 2.

21. Is $\dfrac{1}{x}$ greater than $\dfrac{1}{y}$?

(1) *x* is greater than 1.
(2) *x* is less than *y*.

22. *AB* intersects *CD* at point *O*.
    Is *AB* perpendicular to *CD*? *AC* = *AD*.

    (1) Angle *CAD* is bisected by *AO*.
    (2) *BC* = *AD*

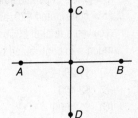

23. Plane *X* flies at *r* miles per hour from *A* to *B*. Plane *Y* flies at *S* miles per hour from *B* to *A*. Both planes take off at the same time. Which plane flies at a faster rate? Town *C* is between *A* and *B*.

    (1) *C* is closer to *A* than it is to *B*.
    (2) Plane *X* flies over *C* before plane *Y*.

24. Is $\dfrac{x}{12} > \dfrac{y}{40}$?

    (1) $10x > 3y$
    (2) $12x < 4y$

25. What is the area of the circular section *AOB*? *A* and *B* are points on the circle which has *O* as its center.

    (1) Angle *AOB* = 36°
    (2) *OB* = *OA*

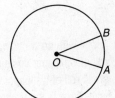

If there is still time remaining, you may review the questions in this section only. In the actual CAT GMAT, you cannot return to a question after you have confirmed your answer.

SECTION VI   PROBLEM SOLVING   Time: 30 minutes

Directions: Solve each of the following problems; then indicate the correct answer on the answer sheet. [On the actual test you will be permitted to use scratch paper for your calculations.]

NOTE: A figure that appears with a problem is drawn as accurately as possible so as to provide information that may help in answering the question. Numbers in this test are real numbers.

1. In a group of people solicited by a charity, 30% contributed $40, 45% contributed $20, and the rest contributed $2. If the charity received a total of $300 from the people who contributed $2, how much was contributed by the entire group?

(A) $1,200

(D) $12,900

(B) $2,400

(E) $25,800

(C) $12,600

2. A car currently travels 15 miles on a gallon of gas but after a tune-up the car will use only $\frac{3}{4}$ as much gas as it does now. How many miles will the car travel on a gallon of gas after the tune-up?

(A) 15

(D) $18\frac{2}{3}$

(B) $16\frac{1}{2}$

(E) 20

(C) $17\frac{1}{2}$

3. Successive discounts of 20% and 15% are equal to a single discount of

(A) 30%

(D) 35%

(B) 32%

(E) 36%

(C) 34%

4. A wall with no windows is 11 feet high and 20 feet long. A large roll of wallpaper costs $25 and will cover 60 square feet of wall. A small roll of wallpaper costs $6 and will cover 10 square feet of wall. What is the least cost for enough wallpaper to cover the wall?

(A) $75

(D) $120

(B) $99

(E) $132

(C) $100

5. Mary, John, and Karen ate lunch together. Karen's meal cost 50% more than John's meal and Mary's meal cost $\frac{5}{6}$ as much as Karen's meal. If John paid $10 for his meal, what was the total that the three of them paid for lunch?

(A) $28.33

(D) $37.50

(B) $30.00

(E) $40.00

(C) $35.00

Use the following graphs for questions 6–7.

PER CAPITA HEALTHCARE EXPENDITURES

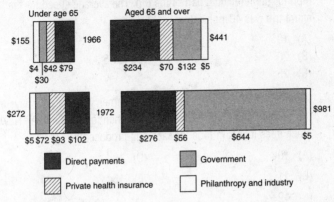

Source: Social Security Bulletin

6. Between 1966 and 1972, the per capita amount spent by the government on personal health care for those under age 65 increased by *x*% where *x* is

   (A) 100
   (B) 120
   (C) 140
   (D) 220
   (E) 240

7. Which of the following statements about expenditures for personal health care between 1966 and 1972 can be inferred from the graphs?

   I. The total amount spent for those aged 65 and over in 1972 was more than 3 times as much as the total amount spent on those under 65.

   II. Between 1966 and 1972, the amount spent per capita by those aged 65 and over increased in each of the four categories (direct payments, government, private health insurance, philanthropy/industry).

   III. The government paid more than half the amount of expenditures for those aged 65 and over in 1972.

   (A) I only
   (B) II only
   (C) III only
   (D) I and III only
   (E) II and III only

8. A car traveled 75% of the way from town A to town B at an average speed of 50 mph. The car travels at an average speed of S mph for the remaining part of the trip. The average speed for the entire trip was 40 mph. What is S?

(A) 10

(B) 20

(C) 25

(D) 30

(E) 37.5

9. A hen lays $7\frac{1}{2}$ dozen eggs during the summer. There are 93 days in the summer and it costs $10 to feed the hen for the summer. How much does it cost in food for each egg produced?

(A) 10¢

(B) $11\frac{1}{9}$¢

(C) $12\frac{3}{13}$¢

(D) $13\frac{1}{13}$¢

(E) 15¢

10. If the diameter of a circle has length d, the radius has length r, and the area equals a, then which of the following statements is (are) true?

   I. $a = \pi d^2$

   II. $d = 2r$

   III. $\dfrac{a}{d} = \pi \dfrac{r}{2}$

(A) only II

(B) I and II only

(C) I and III only

(D) II and III only

(E) I, II, and III

11. If hose A can fill up a tank in 20 minutes, and hose B can fill up the same tank in 15 minutes, how long will it take for the hoses together to fill up the tank?

(A) 5 minutes

(B) $7\frac{1}{2}$ minutes

(C) $8\frac{4}{7}$ minutes

(D) $9\frac{2}{7}$ minutes

(E) 12 minutes

12. It takes Eric 20 minutes to inspect a car. John only needs 18 minutes to inspect a car. If they both start inspecting cars at 8:00 A.M., what is the first time they will finish inspecting a car at the same time?

(A) 9:30 A.M.

(B) 9:42 A.M.

(C) 10:00 A.M.

(D) 11:00 A.M.

(E) 2:00 P.M.

13. In the figure angles *A, B, C, D, E, F, G, H* are all 90 degrees and
    AB = AH = EF = DE. Also, *BC = CD = HG* and the Cartesian coordi-
    nates of *A, C,* and *E* are (1,2), (2,5), and (5,4) respectively. What is
    the area of the figure *ABCDEFG*?

    (A) 6
    (B) 7
    (C) 8
    (D) 10
    (E) 12

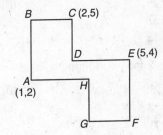

Use the following table for questions 14–15.

CAR PRODUCTION AT PLANT T FOR ONE WEEK IN 1960

	Number of cars produced	Total daily wages
MONDAY	900	$30,000
TUESDAY	1,200	$40,000
WEDNESDAY	1,500	$52,000
THURSDAY	1,400	$50,000
FRIDAY	1,000	$32,000

14. What was the average cost in wages per car produced for the week?

    (A) $25   (D) $32
    (B) $26   (E) $34
    (C) $29

15. Which of the following statements about the production of cars and
    the wages paid for the week can be inferred from the table?

    I.   One-fourth of the cars were produced on Wednesday.
    II. More employees came to the plant on Friday than on Monday.
    III. Two-fifths of the days accounted for $\frac{1}{2}$ the wages paid for the
         week.

    (A) I only   (D) I and III only
    (B) II only   (E) I, II, and III
    (C) I and II only

16. If $\dfrac{x}{y} = 4$ and y is not 0, what percentage (to the nearest percent)

of x is $2x - y$?

(A) 25   (D) 175
(B) 57   (E) 200
(C) 75

17. If $x > 2$ and $y > -1$, then

(A) $xy > -2$ (D) $-x > 2y$
(B) $-x < 2y$ (E) $x < 2y$
(C) $xy < -2$

18. What is the area of the rectangle $ABCD$, if the length of AC is 5 and the length of AD is 4?

(A) 3
(B) 6
(C) 12
(D) 15
(E) 20

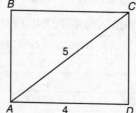

19. If electricity costs k¢ an hour, heat \$$d$ an hour, and water w¢ an hour, how much will all three cost for 12 hours?

(A) $12(k + d + w)$¢
(B) \$$(12k + 12d + 12w)$
(C) \$$(k + 100d + w)$
(D) \$$\left(12k + \dfrac{12d}{100} + 12w\right)$
(E) \$$(.12k + 12d + .12w)$

20. If $x = y = 2z$ and $x \cdot y \cdot z = 256$, then x equals

(A) 2   (D) $4\sqrt[3]{2}$
(B) $2\sqrt[3]{2}$ (E) 8
(C) 4

If there is still time remaining, you may review the questions in this section only. In the actual CAT GMAT, you cannot return to a question after you have confirmed your answer.

SECTION VII   SENTENCE CORRECTION   Time: 30 minutes

Directions: This test contains a number of sentences, in each of which some part or the whole is underlined. Each sentence is followed by five alternative versions of the underlined portion. Select the alternative you consider both most correct and most effective according to the requirements of standard written English. Answer A is the same as the original version; if you think the original version is best, select answer A.

In considering the answer choices, be attentive to matters of grammar, diction, and syntax, as well as clarity, precision, and fluency. Do not select an answer that alters the meaning of the original sentence.

1. <u>Although I calculate that he will be here</u> any minute, I cannot wait much longer for him to arrive.

   (A) Although I calculate that he will be here
   (B) Although I reckon that he will be here
   (C) Because I calculate that he will be here
   (D) Although I think that he will be here
   (E) Because I am confident that he will be here

2. <u>The fourteen-hour day not only has been reduced</u> to one of ten hours but also, in some lines of work, to one of eight or even six.

   (A) The fourteen-hour day not only has been reduced
   (B) Not only the fourteen-hour day has been reduced
   (C) Not the fourteen-hour day only has been reduced
   (D) The fourteen-hour day has not only been reduced
   (E) The fourteen-hour day has been reduced not only

3. The trend toward a decrease is further evidenced in the longer weekend <u>already</u> given to employees in many business establishments.

   (A) already   (D) ready
   (B) all ready   (E) all in all
   (C) allready

4. <u>Using it wisely,</u> leisure promotes health, efficiency, and happiness.

   (A) Using it wisely,   (D) Because it is used wisely,
   (B) If used wisely,   (E) Because of usefulness,
   (C) Having used it wisely,

5. Americans are learning that their concept of a research worker, <u>toiling alone in his laboratory and who discovers miraculous cures</u> has been highly idealized and glamorized.

   (A) toiling alone in his laboratory and who discovers miraculous cures
   (B) toiling in his laboratory by himself and discovers miraculous cures
   (C) toiling alone in his laboratory to discover miraculous cures,
   (D) who toil alone in the laboratory and discover miraculous cures
   (E) toiling in his laboratory to discover miraculous cures by himself

6. <u>We want the teacher to be him</u> who has the best rapport with the students.

   (A) We want the teacher to be him
   (B) We want the teacher to be he
   (C) We want him to be the teacher
   (D) We desire that the teacher be him
   (E) We anticipate that the teacher will be him

7. <u>If he were to win the medal</u>, I for one would be disturbed.

   (A) If he were to win the medal,
   (B) If he was to win the medal,
   (C) If he wins the medal,
   (D) If he is the winner of the medal,
   (E) In the event that he wins the medal,

8. The scouts were told <u>to take an overnight hike, pitch camp, prepare dinner, and that they should be in bed by 9 P.M.</u>

   (A) to take an overnight hike, pitch camp, prepare dinner, and that they should be in bed by 9 P.M.
   (B) to take an overnight hike, to pitch camp, to prepare dinner, and that they should be in bed by 9 P.M.
   (C) to take an overnight hike, pitch camp, prepare dinner, and be in bed by 9 P.M.
   (D) to take an overnight hike, pitching camp, preparing dinner and going to bed by 9 P.M.
   (E) to engage in an overnight hike, pitch camp, prepare dinner, and that they should be in bed by 9 P.M.

9. The dean informed us that the <u>applicant had not and never will be accepted by the college because of his high school record</u>.

    (A) applicant had not and never will be accepted by the college because of his high school record

    (B) applicant had not and never would be accepted by the college because of his high school record

    (C) applicant had not been and never will be excepted by the college because of his high school record

    (D) applicant had not been and never would be excepted by the college because of his high school record

    (E) applicant had not been and never would be accepted by the college because of his high school record

10. The <u>government's failing to keep it's pledges</u> will earn the distrust of all the other nations in the alliance.

    (A) government's failing to keep it's pledges

    (B) government failing to keep it's pledges

    (C) government's failing to keep its pledges

    (D) government failing to keep its pledges

    (E) governments failing to keep their pledges

11. Her brother along with her parents <u>insist</u> that she remain in school.

    (A) insist

    (B) insists

    (C) are insisting

    (D) were insisting

    (E) have insisted

12. Most students like to read <u>these kind of books</u> during their spare time.

    (A) these kind of books

    (B) these kind of book

    (C) this kind of book

    (D) this kinds of books

    (E) those kind of books

13. <u>She not only was competent but also friendly</u> in nature.

    (A) She not only was competent but also friendly

    (B) Not only was she competent but friendly also

    (C) She not only was competent but friendly also

    (D) She was not only competent but also friendly

    (E) She was not only competent but friendly also

14. In the normal course of events, <u>John will graduate high school and enter</u> college in two years.

    (A) John will graduate high school and enter
    (B) John will graduate from high school and enter
    (C) John will be graduated from high school and enter
    (D) John will be graduated from high school and enter into
    (E) John will have graduated high school and enter

15. With the exception of <u>Frank and I, everyone in the class finished</u> the assignment before the bell rang.

    (A) Frank and I, everyone in the class finished
    (B) Frank and me, everyone in the class finished
    (C) Frank and me, everyone in the class had finished
    (D) Frank and I, everyone in the class had finished
    (E) Frank and me everyone in the class finished

16. Many middle-class individuals find that they cannot obtain good medical attention, <u>despite they need it badly</u>.

    (A) despite they need it badly
    (B) despite they badly need it
    (C) in spite of they need it badly
    (D) however much they need it
    (E) therefore, they need it badly

17. During the winter of 1973, Americans <u>discovered the need to conserve energy and attempts were made to meet the crisis</u>.

    (A) discovered the need to conserve energy and attempts were made to meet the crisis
    (B) discovered the need to conserve energy and that the crisis had to be met
    (C) discovered the need to conserve energy and attempted to meet the crisis
    (D) needed to conserve energy and to meet the crisis
    (E) needed to conserve energy and attempts were made to meet the crisis

18. <u>When one eats in this restaurant, you often find</u> that the prices are high and that the food is poorly prepared.

   (A) When one eats in this restaurant, you often find
   (B) When you eat in this restaurant, one often finds
   (C) As you eat in this restaurant, you often find
   (D) If you eat in this restaurant, you often find
   (E) When one ate in this restaurant, he often found

19. Ever since the bombing, there has been much opposition <u>from they who maintain that it was an unauthorized war</u>.

   (A) from they who maintain that it was an unauthorized war
   (B) from they who maintain that it had been an unauthorized war
   (C) from those who maintain that it was an unauthorized war
   (D) from they maintaining that it was unauthorized
   (E) from they maintaining that it had been unauthorized

20. John was <u>imminently qualified for the position because he had studied computer programming and how to operate an IBM machine</u>.

   (A) imminently qualified for the position because he had studied computer programming and how to operate an IBM machine
   (B) imminently qualified for the position because he had studied computer programming and the operation of an IBM machine
   (C) eminently qualified for the position because he had studied computer programming and how to operate an IBM machine
   (D) eminently qualified for the position because he had studied computer programming and the operation of an IBM machine
   (E) eminently qualified because he had studied computer programming and how to operate an IBM machine

21. <u>I am not to eager to go to this play because it did not get good reviews</u>.

   (A) I am not to eager to go to this play because it did not get good reviews.
   (B) Because of its poor reviews, I am not to eager to go to this play.
   (C) Because of its poor revues, I am not to eager to go to this play.
   (D) I am not to eager to go to this play because the critics did not give it good reviews.
   (E) I am not too eager to go to this play because of its poor reviews.

22. <u>It was decided by us that the emphasis would be placed on the result that might be attained</u>.

  (A) It was decided by us that the emphasis would be placed on the result that might be attained.
  (B) We decided that the emphasis would be placed on the results that might be attained.
  (C) We decided to emphasize the results that might be attained.
  (D) We decided to emphasize the results we might attain.
  (E) It was decided that we would place emphasis on the results that might be attained.

23. <u>May I venture to say that I think this performance is the most superior</u> I have ever heard.

  (A) May I venture to say that I think this performance is the most superior
  (B) May I venture to say that this performance is the most superior
  (C) May I say that this performance is the most superior
  (D) I think this performance is superior to any
  (E) This performance is the most superior of any

24. <u>Completing the physical examination, the tonsils were found to be diseased</u>.

  (A) Completing the physical examination, the tonsils were found to be diseased.
  (B) Having completed the physical examination, the tonsils were found to be diseased.
  (C) When the physical examination was completed, the tonsils were found to be diseased.
  (D) The physical examination completed, the tonsils were found to be diseased.
  (E) The physical examination found that the tonsils were diseased.

25. Today this is a totally different world <u>than we have seen</u> in the last decade.

  (A) than we have seen   (D) than what we seen
  (B) from what we have seen   (E) than we have seen
  (C) from what we seen

If there is still time remaining, you may review the questions in this section only. In the actual CAT GMAT, you cannot return to a question after you have confirmed your answer.

ANSWERS
Section I Reading Comprehension

1. (D)	8. (B)	15. (E)	22. (C)
2. (C)	9. (C)	16. (A)	23. (A)
3. (C)	10. (C)	17. (C)	24. (D)
4. (C)	11. (D)	18. (C)	25. (B)
5. (E)	12. (E)	19. (A)	
6. (C)	13. (C)	20. (A)	
7. (A)	14. (E)	21. (B)	

Section II Reading Comprehension

1. (A)	8. (D)	15. (A)	22. (C)
2. (B)	9. (B)	16. (C)	23. (C)
3. (D)	10. (A)	17. (B)	24. (A)
4. (D)	11. (C)	18. (B)	25. (C)
5. (D)	12. (D)	19. (C)	
6. (E)	13. (A)	20. (C)	
7. (B)	14. (D)	21. (C)	

Section III Problem Solving

1. (C)	6. (B)	11. (B)	16. (E)
2. (E)	7. (E)	12. (A)	17. (C)
3. (C)	8. (C)	13. (B)	18. (A)
4. (D)	9. (D)	14. (C)	19. (B)
5. (B)	10. (B)	15. (B)	20. (A)

Section IV Critical Reasoning

1. (B)	6. (C)	11. (C)	16. (D)
2. (B)	7. (E)	12. (B)	17. (C)
3. (D)	8. (D)	13. (B)	18. (E)
4. (B)	9. (A)	14. (C)	19. (B)
5. (C)	10. (C)	15. (E)	20. (D)

Section V Data Sufficiency

1. (E)	8. (B)	15. (A)	22. (A)
2. (C)	9. (E)	16. (E)	23. (E)
3. (A)	10. (E)	17. (C)	24. (A)
4. (A)	11. (A)	18. (D)	25. (E)
5. (D)	12. (C)	19. (A)	
6. (D)	13. (E)	20. (E)	
7. (B)	14. (B)	21. (C)	

Section VI   Problem Solving

1. **(D)**	6. **(C)**	11. **(C)**	16. **(D)**
2. **(E)**	7. **(C)**	12. **(D)**	17. **(B)**
3. **(B)**	8. **(C)**	13. **(D)**	18. **(C)**
4. **(B)**	9. **(B)**	14. **(E)**	19. **(E)**
5. **(D)**	10. **(D)**	15. **(D)**	20. **(E)**

Section VII   Sentence Correction

1. **(D)**	8. **(C)**	15. **(C)**	22. **(D)**
2. **(E)**	9. **(E)**	16. **(D)**	23. **(D)**
3. **(A)**	10. **(C)**	17. **(C)**	24. **(E)**
4. **(B)**	11. **(B)**	18. **(C)**	25. **(B)**
5. **(C)**	12. **(C)**	19. **(C)**	
6. **(B)**	13. **(D)**	20. **(D)**	
7. **(A)**	14. **(B)**	21. **(E)**	

ANALYSIS

Section I   Reading Comprehension

1. **(D)** Note that the question asks "about how many," which requires an approximate figure. Of all the alternative answers, (D) comes closest to the 8,600 employees given in paragraph 1.
2. **(C)** See paragraph 2, lines 1 and 2.
3. **(C)** See paragraph 3, line 1: "Top presidential appointees,...bear the brunt of translating the philosophy and aims of the current administration into practical programs."
4. **(C)** See paragraph 4, sentence 2.
5. **(E)** See paragraph 4, last line.
6. **(C)** See paragraph 5: "Those whom the president selects..." and following.
7. **(A)** See paragraph 6: "...they usually have substantial responsibilities in line management...."
8. **(B)** Paragraph 6, line 1: "These appointees are primarily regarded as policy makers...."
9. **(C)** See paragraph 5: "Those selected by department and agency heads..." and following.
10. **(C)** See paragraph 1, line 1: "The first and decisive step in expansion of Europe overseas was the conquest of the Atlantic Ocean."

11. **(D)** See paragraph 1, lines 19–20: "…in men of the calibre of Prince Henry, known as the Navigator.…"

12. **(E)** In paragraph 1, the sentence containing the statement "Portugal could adapt and develop the knowledge and experience of the past to meet the challenge of the unknown…," meets answer (B); also in this paragraph there is mention of experienced Portuguese seamen and a mercantile marine (A), rudiments of navigation (C), and mapmakers (D). Since extensive trade routes are never mentioned, the correct answer is (E).

13. **(C)** Portugal was the logical nation for this task because of her "geographical position and her history." Wealth (A) and navigational experience (B) are resources in context with the question, while (D) and (E) are vague.

14. **(E)** See paragraph 1.

15. **(E)** See paragraph 2, lines 36–38: Seamen kept close to shore because "…the latitudinal extent of the Mediterranean was not great, and voyages could be conducted from point to point on compass bearings," not because of the other reasons given in the question.

16. **(A)** See paragraph 2, lines 28–29: "…hazards…in the form of sudden storms or dangerous coasts, were known and could be usually anticipated."

17. **(C)** See paragraph 2, lines 40–41: "Having made a landfall on a bearing, they could determine their precise position from prominent landmarks.…"

18. **(C)** The correct answer is given in paragraph 2. The policeman must be neutral and present the facts, while the "artist usually begins with a preconceived message or attitude…," i.e., prejudiced. While artists are "emotional," no mention is made that policemen are stoic (D).

19. **(A)** The writer explains that the policemen's reactions were "surprisingly unprejudiced." The rest of paragraph 3 explains that policemen reacted to story events and characters according to alternative (A).

20. **(A)** The only characters that policemen objected to were unrealistic. See paragraph 3.

21. **(B)** Only "suspense" was given in the passage (in paragraph 4).

22. **(C)** Alternatives I and II may be found in the first paragraph.

23. **(A)** Policemen must "also try to evaluate the events they describe...."
The "also" refers to artists and writers. See paragraph 2, and also
paragraph 1: "...they had to be able to take in the details of a
situation quickly...."

24. **(D)** Policemen wrote about their work. See paragraph 4.

25. **(B)** Alternative (B) sums up their feeling. Corruption and routine
were mentioned as minor annoyances. The issues of pay and
adventure were not mentioned. See paragraph 4.

Section II   Reading Comprehension

1. **(A)** The dropout rate on an average for all Open Admissions students
was 48%; for regular students, 36%; and for Open Admissions
categories, 56% (lines 37–40).

2. **(B)** See paragraph 1: "The successful institution of higher learning
had never been one whose mission could be defined in terms of
providing vocational skills or...resolving societal problems." This
is the sort of question that must be read carefully; it asks for an
answer that is *not* among the alternatives given in the passage.

3. **(D)** The idea that a university must relate to the problems of society
is given in paragraphs 2, and 4.

4. **(D)** See the last sentence.

5. **(D)** The two-year college is described in paragraph 3 as a "service-
related" and "community" college. It is no longer called a
"junior" college.

6. **(E)** The idea of the service-oriented college is to produce "productive" students and, as stated in the third paragraph, to provide
programs "to meet the demands of regional employment
markets,..." i.e., to make graduates employable.

7. **(B)** The attrition rate for Open Admissions students was 56 percent,
and that for regular students 36 percent, a difference of 20
percent. See lines 37–40.

8. **(D)** The phrase "this phenomenon" in line 36 refers to the preceding discussion of the service-university, and not just to the
"multiuniversity."

9. **(B)** The attrition rate for Open Admissions students was 56 percent
and for regular students, 36 percent. The average of 56 percent
and 36 percent is 46 percent. See lines 37–40.

10. **(A)** See the example of steel in the last paragraph.

11. **(C)** Increased barriers to trade—protectionism—have been caused by recession and unemployment.

12. **(D)** Trade probably fell as the world economy stayed flat.

13. **(A)** Washington has raised new barriers against imports in autos, textiles, and sugar.

14. **(D)** Alternatives (B) and (E) can be eliminated since the subject of the passage is not trade agreements or world exports (trade, of course, includes imports as well). Alternative (A) is not plausible, because the passage does not emphasize "domestic" but rather international economic policy. The "Tokyo Round," (C), was not mentioned in the passage. Alternative (D) certainly reflects the passage, which is pessimistic about the future of world trade.

15. **(A)** New trade restraints, often bound up in voluntary agreements to limit particular imports.

16. **(C)** Exports are promoted through subsidies.

17. **(B)** Bilateral quotas were used by the European Economic Community.

18. **(B)** See paragraph 2, sentence 1: "…people are particularly sensitive about any reduction in the quality of the atmosphere.…"

19. **(C)** This is implied in paragraph 1.

20. **(C)** See paragraph 3: "The households' share in atmospheric pollution is far bigger than that of industry.…" The key word in the question is "most."

21. **(C)** Both production *and* transportation costs are important. Although paragraph 1 states that the costs of maintaining clean water are "primarily" production costs, paragraph 4 states that this problem is "related to the costs of production and transport…"

22. **(C)** See paragraph 5, lines 32–33: "Atmospheric pollution caused by the private property of individuals…is difficult to control."

23. **(C)** See paragraph 6: both active and passive resources. No mention is made of levying taxes.

24. **(A)** See paragraph 5: "*In this particular case*, the cost of anti-pollution measures will have to be borne, to a considerable extent, by individuals.…" "In this particular case" refers to the situation also described in the paragraph where pollution is caused by the private property of individuals.

25. **(C)** See paragraph 6: While noise abatement is not impossible to achieve, the "costs of a complete protection against noise are so prohibitive...."

Section III   Problem Solving

1. **(C)** The volume of water that has been poured into the tank is 5 cubic feet per minute for 6 minutes, or 30 cubic feet. The tank is rectangular, so its volume is length × width × height, with the answer in cubic units. The width is $\frac{1}{2}$ the length, or $\frac{1}{2}$ of 4 feet, or 2 feet. The volume, which we already know is 30 cubic feet, is, therefore, 4 feet × 2 feet × the height. The height (depth of the water in the tank) is, therefore, $\frac{30}{8} = 3\frac{3}{4}$ feet = 3 feet 9 inches.

2. **(E)** $6x - 3y$ is $3(2x - y)$. Since $2x - y = 4$, $6x - 3y = 3 \cdot 4$ or 12.

3. **(C)** The progression is arithmetic and $11 - 5 = 6 = 17 - 11$, so every term is 6 more than the previous term. Therefore, the next term after 17 is $17 + 6$ or 23.

4. **(D)** Since -3 has the largest absolute value of the three given numbers, using z as -3 will make z^2 as large as possible. Since $\frac{x}{y}$ is a quotient, to make it as large as possible, use the smallest positive number for y and the largest positive number for x. So if you use $x = 2$ and $y = \frac{1}{2}$, then $\frac{x}{y}$ is as large as possible. Therefore, the largest value of the expression is $\left(\frac{2}{\left(\frac{1}{2}\right)}\right)(-3)^2 = 4(9) = 36$

5. **(B)** The total number of people surveyed was $n + x$. Since 70% of the total preferred brand A that means $.7(n + x)$ preferred brand A. However 60% of the n people and all of the x people preferred brand A. So $.6n + x$ preferred brand A. Therefore, $.7(n + x)$ must equal $.6n + x$. So we have $.7n + .7x = .6n + x$. Solving for x gives $.1n = .3x$ or $x = n/3$.

6. **(B)** A picture always helps. You are given that BC and EF are each 2 feet. Since the area of a rectangle is length times width, you must find the length (CE or BF). Look at the triangle ABF. It has two equal sides ($AB = AF$), so the perpendicular from A to the line BF will divide ABF into two congruent right triangles, AHF and AHB, each

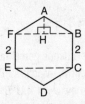

with hypotenuse 2. The angle *FAB* is 120°, since the total of all the angles of the hexagon is 720°. (You can find the sum of the angles of any convex polygon by connecting all vertices to a fixed interior point, *P*. In the case of the hexagon this will give 6 triangles.)

The total of all the triangles' angles is $6 \times 180° = 1{,}080°$. Since the angles at the fixed point, which are not part of the hexagon angles, will add up to 360°, the sum of the hexagon's angles is $1{,}080° - 360° = 720°$. So each of the two triangles is a $30° - 60° - 90°$ triangle with hypotenuse 2. So $AH = 1$ and *FH* and *HB* must equal $\sqrt{3}$. Therefore, *BF* is $2\sqrt{3}$ and the area is $2 \times 2\sqrt{3} = 4\sqrt{3}$ square feet.

7. **(E)** Since each packer loads ⅛ of a box in 9 minutes, the 20 packers will load ²⁰⁄₈ or 2½ boxes in 9 minutes. There are 90 minutes in 1½ hours; so the 20 packers will load $10 \times 2½$ or 25 boxes in 1½ hours.

8. **(C)** You want the ratio of the percentage who own both a car and a motorcycle to the percentage who own a motorcycle. You know that 15% own a motorcycle so you need to find the percentage who own both a car and a motorcycle. Let *A* stand for the percentage who own both a car and a motorcycle. Then (the percentage who own a car) + (the percentage who own a motorcycle) − *A* must equal the percentage who own one or the other or both. Since 100% own one or the other or both, we obtain 90% + 15% − *A* = 105% − *A* = 100%. So *A* = 5%. Since 15% own motorcycles, the percentage of motorcycle owners who own

cars is $\frac{5\%}{15\%} = \frac{1}{3} = 33\frac{1}{3}\%$.

9. **(D)** To do computations, change percentages to decimals. Let J, M, B, and L stand for Jim's, Marcia's, Bob's, and Lee's respective weights. Then we know $J = 1.4M$, $B = .9L$, and $L = 2M$. We need to know B as a percentage of J. Since $B = .9L$ and $L = 2M$, we have $B = .9(2M) = 1.8M$. $J = 1.4M$ is equivalent to $M = (1/(1.4))J$. So $B = 1.8M = 1.8(1/(1/4))J = (1\tfrac{2}{7})J$. Converting $1\tfrac{2}{7}$ to a percentage, we have $1\tfrac{2}{7} = 1.28\tfrac{4}{7} = 128\tfrac{4}{7}\%$, so (D) is the correct answer.

10. **(B)** The towns can be thought of as the vertices of a triangle.

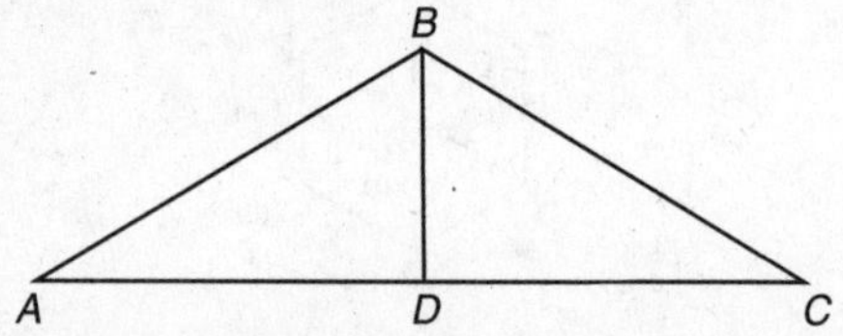

Since the distance from A to B is equal to the distance from B to C, the triangle is isosceles. The point D on AC which is closest to B is the point on AC such that BD is perpendicular to AC. (If BD were not perpendicular to AC, then there would be a point on AC closer to B than D; in the picture, E is closer to B than D is.)

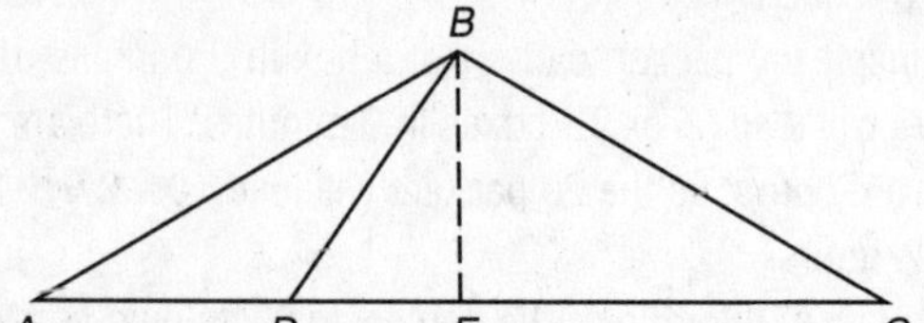

So the triangles ABD and CBD are right triangles with two corresponding sides equal. Therefore ABD is congruent to CBD. Thus $AD = DC$, and since AC is 60, AD must be 30. Since ABD is a right triangle with hypotenuse 50 and another side = 30, the remaining side (BD) must be 40.

11. **(B)** Since 108% of \$50 = (1.08)(50) = \$54, the chair was offered for sale at \$54.00. It was sold for 90% of \$54 since there was a 10% discount. Therefore, the chair was sold for (.9)(\$54) or \$48.60.

12. **(A)** Here is a table of the hours worked:

	Mon.	Tues.	Wed.	Thurs.	Fri.	Wages for week
	8	8	8	8	8	$5x$
excess over 8 hrs	0	3	1	2	1	$(0 + 3 + 1 + 2 + 1)y = 7y.$

The average daily wage equals $\dfrac{(5x + 7y)}{5}$, or $x + \dfrac{7}{5}y$.

13. **(B)** There are 8 choices for the first female, then 7 choices for the second female, and 6 choices for the third female on the committee. So there are $8 \times 7 \times 6$ different ways to pick the three females in order. However, if member A is chosen first, then member B, then member C, the same three females are chosen as when C is followed by A and B is chosen last. In fact, the same three members can be chosen in $3 \times 2 \times 1$ different orders. So to find the number of different groups of 3 females, DIVIDE $8 \times 7 \times 6$ by $3 \times 2 \times 1$ to obtain 56.

    In the same way, there are $8 \times 7 \times 6 = 336$ ways to choose the three males in order, but any group of three males can be put in order $3 \times 2 \times 1 = 6$ different ways. So there are $^{336}/_6 = 56$ different groups of three males. Therefore, there are $56 \times 56 = 3{,}136$ different committees of 3 males and 3 females.

14. **(C)** Let x_n be what the motorcycle is worth after n years. Then we know $x_0 = \$2{,}500$ and $x_{n+1} = \frac{4}{5} \times x_n$. So $x_1 = \frac{4}{5} \times 2{,}500$, which is $\$2{,}000$. x_2 is $\frac{4}{5} \times 2{,}000$, which is 1,600, and finally x_3 is $\frac{4}{5} \times 1{,}600$, which is 1,280. Therefore, the motorcycle is worth $\$1{,}280$ at the end of three years.

    OR

    $x_3 = \frac{4}{5}x_2 = \frac{4}{5}(\frac{4}{5}x_1) = (\frac{4}{5})(\frac{4}{5})(\frac{4}{5}x_0) = {}^{64}/_{125}x_0. \ (^{64}/_{125})2500 = 1280.$

15. **(B)** Simply use the properties of inequalities to solve the given inequality. Subtract $12x$ from each side to get $-5x - 5 < 18$. Next add 5 to each side to obtain $-5x < 23$. Finally, divide each side by -5 to get $x > -\dfrac{23}{5}$. Remember that if you divide each side of an inequality by a negative number the inequality is reversed. You can make a quick check of your answer by using $x = -5$ which is not $> -\dfrac{23}{5}$ and $x = -4$, which is $> -\dfrac{23}{5}$ in the original inequality. Since $x = -5$ does not satisfy the original inequality (-40 is not < -42) and $x = -4$ does satisfy the inequality (-33 is < -30), the answer is correct.

16. **(E)** Since the only costs are $20 for fuel and $70 for the driver's wages, the total cost is $90. Therefore, the company should charge 120% of $90, which is (1.2)($90) or $108.

17. **(C)** The total fuel cost will be $3 \cdot 20 + 4 \cdot 15 + 2 \cdot 5 + 1 \cdot 50$, which is $180. Since there are 10 vehicles, the average fuel cost is 180/10 or $18 per vehicle.

18. **(A)** Since $x + 2y = 2x + y$, we can subtract $x + 2y$ from each side of the equation and the result is $0 = x - y$.

19. **(B)** Let M, J, and K be the amounts paid by Mary, John, and Karen respectively. Then $K = 1.5J$, $M = \frac{5}{6}K$, and $M = J + 2$. So M, which is $\frac{5}{6}K$ must $= \left(\frac{5}{6}\right)(1.5)J = \left(\frac{5}{6}\right)\left(\frac{3}{2}\right)J = \left(\frac{5}{4}\right)J$. Therefore, we have $\left(\frac{5}{4}\right)J = J + 2$ or $\left(\frac{1}{4}\right)J = 2$, which means $J = 8$. So $K = 1/.5J$, or 12 and $M = J + 2$, or 10. So the total is $8 + 12 + 10 = \$30$.

20. **(A)** The angles are in the ratio 1:2:2, so 2 angles are equal to each other, and both are twice as large as the third angle of the triangle. Since a triangle with two equal sides must have the sides opposite equal, the triangle is isosceles. (Using the fact that the sum of the angles of a triangle is 180°, you can see that the angles of the triangle are 72°, 72° and 36°, so only (A) is true.)

Section IV   Critical Reasoning

1. **(B)** When trying to infer someone's opinion from limited information, such as that contained in the extract, one must be careful not to use conjecture or even assumption, if the latter is based on uncertainty. It is highly probable that Jane considers it sad that some babies are unwanted and abandoned, but she has not stated this, and therefore answer alternative (A) is not appropriate. Answer alternative (C) is not correct. Careful reading of the text will reveal that she states that she has already told her children that they are adopted. Answer (D) may be factually correct, but it is not an opinion, and anyway it is not relevant to the question. Jane may possibly consider abortion sinful, but she does not state this or even imply it; she says only that it is ironic that there is a difference of attitudes among women concerning having babies; alternative (E) is, therefore, not appropriate. Alternative

(B) is the appropriate answer, as can be demonstrated by Jane's declaration, "At last, we have a family!"

2. **(B)** Because A Ltd. is indeed buying 100% of the shares of the company B Ltd. (100% because X is said to be the sole share-holder), then, following payment of the sum and completion of the contract, A Ltd. will indeed have a wholly-owned subsidiary—B Ltd. Therefore, (B) is the correct answer. Answer alternative (A) is inappropriate because it is not necessarily true. Unless required by judicial proceedings, it is X that is bound not to disclose material confidential information. Nothing is said about such a requirement being imposed on A Ltd. Selling only 25% of the shares in a company, as envisaged in answer alternative (C), is very likely worth less than 25% of the value of buying 100% of the shares in a company because in the latter case the acquiring party is purchasing control of the company. Therefore, (C) is inappropriate. Alternative (D) is not correct because, although it may be true, it is not relevant to the question. (E) is inappropriate and most probably untrue, as limited companies are separate entities and, unless there are other agreements to the contrary, do not share liability with their owners.

3. **(D)** Analysis of the two sentences indicates the presence of an assumption that anyone who has had at least five traffic violations in a year is a terrible driver. This assumption is understood but is not stated. Rather, it is a hidden assumption, making (D) the appropriate answer. Alternative (A) is incorrect because there is no attack on the source of the claim. (B) is wrong because there is no appeal to authority—illegitimate or not. (C) is not the correct answer because there is no comparison of two similar situations in the statement. (E) is incorrect because there is no term with a confusing or double meaning.

4. **(B)** While Miss Fitzgerald was born and grew up in that part of India in which the book is based, it is not stated anywhere that *Zemindar* is an autobiography; therefore, (A) is incorrect. Alternative (C) is only half true. According to the text, Miss Fitzgerald's winters were spent on various estates in India, but these winters were during her childhood and not, according to what is written, during the time when she was preparing the book. (D) may be correct, but there is no way of being certain. Miss Fitzgerald only states that as far

as she knows, she is the only one to have tried it. Alternative (E) cannot be inferred from the passage. While it is clear that the experience of her grandmother sowed the seeds of interest in her father and this was no doubt handed on to Miss Fitzgerald, this is not stated as the greatest influence on the decision to write *Zemindar*. A careful reading of the third paragraph reveals that Miss Fitzgerald has "no recollection of just when, or more important, why I set about telling the story of the Siege." Therefore (B) is the correct answer.

5. **(C)** The best conclusion that can be drawn from the statement is one that sums up the facts that are given in one sentence; thus, (C) is the best answer. Although the given paragraph states that if there is devaluation of the dollar, American imports will become more expensive, this will not necessarily be a disadvantage for the U.S. economy. Hence, (A) is not appropriate. Alternative (B) is also inappropriate, because it highlights a disadvantage that may arise from the expectation of devaluation, but which is not dealt with in the paragraph. Alternatives (D) and (E) are both helpful pieces of information, but they cannot be concluded from the given text.

6. **(C)** By removing one ball from the box marked with two black balls or removing one ball from the box marked with two white balls, you cannot ascertain the color of the ball left in the box, let alone the color of the balls in the third box. Therefore, answer alternatives (A) and (B) are inappropriate. (D) and (E) are also inappropriate because it is possible, by taking out just one ball from the box marked with one white ball and one black ball, to ascertain the colors of all the balls contained in each box. The appropriate answer is (C). If you take one ball from the box wrongly marked with one white ball and one black ball, and if the ball is white, it must be one of the white pair. The mixed pair would then have to be in the box marked with two black balls and the remaining box must therefore contain the black pair.

7. **(E)** According to the passage, all people cannot take aspirin without undesirable side effects, and in some cases, the danger caused by aspirin itself outweighs its benefits. The passage, by saying "On balance, however, for men aged 40 and over, an aspirin a day may present…" also implies that not all, but only some people (men over 40) should take an aspirin a day. Alternative

answer (A) clearly cannot be concluded from the passage. Answer alternative (B) is also inappropriate. No painkiller other than aspirin is mentioned in the passage, and it cannot be inferred that all painkillers reduce the "stickiness" of platelets. (C) is incorrect. Smoking is not mentioned in the passage and since studies of the effects of smoking and aspirin have not been reported, no conclusions can be drawn. (D) is wrong because the statistics given in the passage say that 15% of second heart attack victims were saved from death by taking aspirin, and 15% does not constitute a majority. (E) is the correct choice since it simply states that mortality rates can be reduced in patients who have already suffered a heart attack (as stated in the passage), without giving any specific statistics.

8. **(D)** The writer has strong views on terrorist acts and on the policies adopted by Western European governments in handling them. The writer's main premise is that these governments are wrong when they concede to any of the demands of a hijacker or other terrorist—or any other criminal for that matter—because then they are conveying an impression of weakness and the perpetrator will feel that he or she will be able to win concessions and achieve his or her aims on subsequent occasions. Therefore, (D) is the correct answer. The statements in alternatives (A), (B), and (C) may all be statements with which the writer may concur, but they cannot be concluded with certainty from the text. Statement (E), on the other hand, is a statement with which the writer would probably not agree, but in any case, it cannot be inferred or concluded from the paragraph.

9. **(A)** It is fact that athletes can attract sponsorship and make money and that participation in the Olympics can aid this process. On the basis that it is true that athletes are more and more attracted by the profit motive, the conclusion that the best athletes do not compete in the Olympics is weakened. Therefore, A is the appropriate answer. Alternative (B) is an oft-stated maxim, but in this case, it is not relevant to the argument. The fact that people believe that amateur athletes are receiving adequate alternative remuneration does not bear on the argument for allowing genuine professional athletes into the games. So, (C) is inappropriate. Choice (D) comes close to weakening the argument,

because if professional (as well as amateur) athletes were allowed to compete, presuming the participants were selected on merit, then the best athletes would be seen. However, it has only been a suggestion, perhaps in the past, (in which case it was not adopted) or in the future (in which case its adoption is not certain). Choice (E) represents an opinion that might or might not be held by the writer, but, whether or not the author agrees, it does not weaken the argument; therefore (E) is inappropriate.

10. **(C)** The paragraph demonstrates from beginning to end that the function of the food technologist is to prevent unfit foodstuffs from being marketed by the stores and passed on to the consumer, who relies on the store's control procedures. (C), therefore, is the most appropriate answer. Answer alternative (A) is inappropriate because it cannot be inferred from the text (even if it were true). Answer (B) and possibly answer (D) are factually correct, but these conclusions cannot be drawn from the text itself. (E) is not a correct interpretation of the facts; random checking is not the best way, since below-standard goods are caught in the net only by chance.

11. **(C)** John's decision is to experiment with the new longer (in mileage) route for two weeks, and it is this decision that we have to consider. Choice (C), by offering a third alternative, gives John another possibility and, therefore, another outcome. It may affect his decision, and therefore, is the appropriate answer. Alternatives (A), (B), and (D) alter factors within the calculation affecting the decision, but taken individually and not making any other changes, will definitely not result in a different decision being made. These three are, therefore, not appropriate answers. The existence of a definite answer—in this case, (C)—means that alternative (E) is not appropriate.

12. **(B)** There is only one argument in the passage based on two separate premises upon which the writer has based his conclusion. Choice (A) is inappropriate because there is no other argument. Choice (C) is incorrect because the qualities are the same (gray). (D) is inappropriate because the description is not ambiguous, and (E) is wrong because the writer has stated an argument—albeit invalid.

13. **(B)** Although a strong personality might have some resistance to the psychological dependence factors of drug use, it cannot be stated with any certainty that a strong personality can prevent physiological dependence. In this way, (A) is not a reasonable conclusion. Psychological dependence on heroin is greater than that of drugs such as alcohol and marijuana, but it is not stated to be the "greatest" since psychological dependence is also great with cocaine and amphetamines. There is no conclusive evidence in the text to support this view, (C) is not, therefore, a reasonable conclusion.

A safe drug implies no danger of addiction, and since it cannot be shown that there is no danger of addiction to alcohol, statement (D) is also not valid.

Although short-term use of certain drugs for medical purposes rarely produces dependence, long-term use of certain drugs often causes physiological dependence; in this respect (E) is not a valid assumption.

(B) is the only conclusion that can probably be true. Statistics show that many hard-drug addicts and regular users started their habit by taking drugs for "kicks." Also the search for drugs to be used for "kicks" almost inevitably causes exposure to localities where harder and more addictive drugs are available, thus increasing the chances of attempting more addictive drugs for "kicks." The passage states that the circumstances in which the drug is taken is one factor controlling the risk of becoming dependent and also that is can be demonstrated that people who have taken drugs for fun are more likely to become dependent on the drug.

14. **(C)** Here we have a chain of events where the conclusion of one argument becomes the premise for another. Only (C) can be concluded from the facts given in the passage—that is, because Sally overslept, she ran toward school, and because she ran, she did not notice the hole. Choice (A) is inappropriate because the chain of events is not linked by the fact that Sally did not eat her breakfast. The passage does not include a consequence emanating from that fact. Choice (B) is not appropriate because there is no way to link Sally's friend to the events in the passage. Similarly, facts not included preclude (D) from being the appropriate answer. Finally, (E) cannot be inferred, as we do not know

what Sally did later that day; she may have been released from the hospital and gone to school.

15. **(E)** Services will be improved, it is hoped, for a certain segment of customers—those that shop during the rush hours—but not for all customers. This fact makes choice (A) inappropriate. To attract new customers is not stated in the passage as an objective, so (B) is inappropriate. The utilization of excess capacity, as in (C) is a useful by-product of the new system, but it is not the main goal. If maintenance costs are kept low, it will probably make the achievement of the main goal that much easier, but this is not the major objective so choice (D) is not appropriate. The principal purpose of the owners is to make more money from the change, by increasing income more than the added costs. Therefore, (E) is the appropriate answer.

16. **(D)** Choice (D) supports the conclusion of the researchers by providing information that can help account for their conclusion. (D) is, therefore, the appropriate answer. Alternative answer (A) could possibly be inferred from the data in the paragraph, but it does not strengthen the conclusion on the mammography program. The finding stated in (B) has no bearing on the conclusion in the paragraph. Choice (C) provides a decision that was probably made following the publication of the results of the program, but it has no direct relevance to the conclusion drawn. The fact that 50% of the women tested were smokers (E) would tend to invalidate much of the experimental results and any conclusions drawn, but is not directly relevant to the conclusion; therefore, (E) is not correct.

17. **(C)** Encouraging couples to remain childless would have a negative social effect and would not be practical, so answer alternative (A) is not a reasonable suggestion. The income loss involved in having one child is equal to that involved in having two or more children (assuming the loss of the income of one parent or the expense of child care), so suggestion (B) is also invalid. If couples move to cheaper areas in the country, as suggested in (D), the chances are that work would be less available or possibly that the couple would have a less positive economic future, so the change may not necessarily be financially advantageous. If fathers stayed at home rather than mothers, there would be no improvement in financial status, so suggestion (E) is invalid.

Suggestion (C) is the only sensible solution, since financial stability is likely to increase with the length of time in employment.

18. **(E)** Even if the rate of increase in demand has slowed from 10% per annum to 5% per annum over the last five years, that means that demand is still increasing at 5% per annum. If, as the passage states, demand continues to grow at the present rate—that is, by 5% per annum—the world's resources will be used up by the year 2050. Therefore, the argument is not weakened by the statement in answer alternative (A). Choice B introduces the matter of supply, but apparently the reserves in Antarctica have not been discovered recently, and this, therefore, does not affect the argument that stocks will be depleted unless new reserves are found. Choice (C) informs us that there is an alternative to coal which is being used increasingly. However, the questions of the supply of and the rate of growth of demand for oil do not affect the argument in the paragraph. Choice (D) states an economic fact of life that will have to be faced if the statements in the paragraph are true. It may lead to a search for alternative fuels and consequent decrease in demand for coal, but this is uncertain and cannot be inferred. So, neither (A), (B), (C), or (D) are appropriate. Choice (E) is, therefore, the correct answer.

19. **(B)** Choice (A) contains an important point which would have been considered in setting the maximum treatment level. So it does not weaken the argument of the authorities and is inappropriate. Choice (C) is incorrect as the passage states that the authorities are carrying out this policy in accordance with their powers. Choice (D) is a fact that would be acknowledged by both sides and weakens neither's case, while choice (E) is also a well-known fact, which like the fact in (A), would have been taken into consideration by the researchers, so it is also not appropriate. The fact that the authorities have no record of the long term good or damage of fluoridation is a significant weakness in their case, and therefore, (B) is the appropriate answer.

20. **(D)** Since John cannot be allowed to remain alone, Mr. Smith must cross the river with Mr. Jones and he must be first or last across the river in order to be with John when Mrs. Smith is crossing. Therefore, both (A) and (B) are possibilities that would lead to the Smiths' successful crossing of the river. Since John cannot

be left alone and since Mr. Jones will not allow anyone else to row his boat and neither will he take two passengers together, as (C) states, Mr. and Mrs. Smith cannot cross together. (C) is, therefore, a necessary condition and is therefore not an appropriate answer. (E) is a possible condition, since either Mr. or Mrs. Smith will be on the opposite bank waiting for John so he will not be alone. This too is not an appropriate answer. John, however, cannot be the first to cross the river or else he would be left alone on the opposite riverbank. (D) is, therefore, the appropriate answer.

Section V   Data Sufficiency

1. **(E)** Since STATEMENT (1) describes only x and STATEMENT (2) describes only y, both are needed to get an answer. Using STATEMENT (2), STATEMENT (1) becomes $3x = 2k = 2y^2$, so $x = \dfrac{2y^2}{(3)}$. However, this is not sufficient, since if $y = -1$ then $x = \frac{2}{3}$ and x is greater than y, but if $y = 1$ then again $x = \frac{2}{3}$ but now x is less than y. Therefore, STATEMENTS (1) and (2) together are not sufficient.

2. **(C)** $ABCD$ is a parallelogram if AB is parallel to CD and BC is parallel to AD. STATEMENT (2) tells you that AB is parallel to CD, but this is not sufficient since a trapezoid has only one pair of opposite sides parallel. Thus, STATEMENT (2) alone is not sufficient.

   STATEMENT (1) alone is not sufficient since a trapezoid can have the two nonparallel sides equal.

   However, using STATEMENTS (1) and (2) together we can deduce that BC is parallel to AD, since the distance from BC to AD is equal along two different parallel lines.

3. **(A)** STATEMENT (1) alone is sufficient. The average is the combined income for 1965–1970 divided by 6 (the number of years). Therefore, the combined income is 6 times the average yearly income.

   STATEMENT (2) alone is not sufficient since there is no information about his income for the years 1966–1969.

4. **(A)** Two digit numbers are the integers from 0 to 99. Since you are told that the number is greater than 9, the only possible choices are integers 10, 11,…99.

   STATEMENT (1) alone is sufficient since (1) is equivalent to $9a = b$.

In this case if a is greater than 1, then $9a$ is not a digit and if a is 0, then the number is not greater than 9. Thus there is only one possible choice, $a = 1$, which yields the number 19, that satisfies (1).

STATEMENT (2) alone is not sufficient since 19, 38, 57, 76, and 95 satisfy (2) and are two digit numbers greater than 9.

So (A) is the correct choice.

5. **(D)** k is a prime if none of the integers 2, 3, 4,... up to $k-1$ divide k evenly. STATEMENT (1) alone is sufficient since if k is not a prime then $k = (m)(n)$ where m and n must be integers less than k. But this means either m or n must be less than or equal to $\sqrt{k}$ since if m and n are both larger than $\sqrt{k}$, $(m)(n)$ is larger than $\left(\sqrt{k}\right)\left(\sqrt{k}\right)$ or k. So STATEMENT (1) implies k is a prime.

   STATEMENT (2) alone is also sufficient, since if $k = (m)(n)$ and m and n are both larger than $\dfrac{k}{2}$, then $(m)(n)$ is greater than $\dfrac{k^2}{4}$; but $\dfrac{k^2}{4}$ is greater than k when k is larger than 5. Therefore, if no integer between 2 and $\dfrac{k}{2}$ inclusive divides k evenly, then k is a prime.

6. **(D)** Since we are given the fact that 100 miles is the distance from A to B, it is sufficient to find the distance from C to B. This is so, because 100 minus the distance from C to B is the distance from A to C. STATEMENT (1) says that 125% of the distance from C to B is 100 miles. Thus, we can find the distance from C to B, which is sufficient. Since the distance from A to C plus the distance from C to B is the distance from A to B, we can use STATEMENT (2) to set up the equation 5 times the distance from A to C equals 100 miles.

   Therefore, STATEMENTS (1) and (2) are each sufficient.

7. **(B)** STATEMENT (1) alone is not sufficient. If the segment AC is moved further away from the segment BD, then the angles x and y will change. So STATEMENT (1) does not ensure that CD and AB are perpendicular.

   STATEMENT (2) alone is sufficient. Since AB is a straight line, $x + y$ equals 180. Thus, if $x = y$, x and y both equal 90 and AB is perpendicular to CD. So the correct answer is (B).

8. **(B)** STATEMENT (2) alone is sufficient, since $x = y$ implies $x - y = 0$.

   STATEMENT (1) alone is not sufficient. An infinite number of pairs satisfy STATEMENT (1), for example, $x = 2$, $y = 2$, for which $x - y = 0$, or $x = 4$, $y = 1$, for which $x - y = 3$.

9. **(E)** Since there is no information on how many of the eligible voters are men or how many are women, STATEMENTS (1) and (2) together are not sufficient.

10. **(E)** We need to find the measure of angle *PSR* or of angle *PST*. Using STATEMENT (2), we can find angle *PTR*, but STATEMENT (1) does not give any information about either of the angles needed.

11. **(A)** STATEMENT (1) is sufficient since it means 90% of the original cost is $2,300. Thus, we can solve the equation for the original cost.

    STATEMENT (2) alone is insufficient, since it gives no information about the cost.

12. **(C)** Draw the radii from *O* to each of the vertices. These lines divide the hexagon into six triangles. STATEMENT (2) says that all the triangles are congruent since each of their pairs of corresponding sides is equal. Since there are 360° in a circle, the central angle of each triangle is 60°. And, since all radii are equal, each angle of the triangle equals 60°. Therefore, the triangles are equilateral, and *AB* is equal to the radius of the circle. Thus, if we assume STATEMENT (1), we know the length of *AB*. Without STATEMENT (1), we can't find the length of *AB*.

    Also STATEMENT (1) alone is not sufficient, since *AB* need not equal the radius unless the hexagon is regular.

13. **(E)** We need to know the area of the walls. To find the area of the walls, we need the distance from the floor to the ceiling. Since neither STATEMENT (1) nor (2) gives any information about the height of the room, together they are not sufficient.

14. **(B)** STATEMENT (2) alone is sufficient. If (2) holds, then $\dfrac{32}{32 + 5,678}$ represents the ratio of defective items to total items produced. Since any fraction can be changed into a percentage by multiplying by 100, STATEMENT (2) alone is sufficient.

    STATEMENT (1) alone is not sufficient since the total number of items produced is also needed to find the percentage of defective items.

    Therefore B is the correct choice.

15. **(A)** STATEMENT (1) alone is sufficient. Since $3^2 + 4^2 = 5^2$, *ABC* is a right triangle by the Pythagorean Theorem.

    STATEMENT (2) alone is not sufficient since you can choose a point D so that $AC = CD$ for *any* triangle *ABC*.

16. **(E)** (1) and (2) are not sufficient. The price of food could rise for other reasons besides the price of energy rising.

17. **(C)** (1) alone is obviously insufficient. To use (2) you need to know what the painting was worth at some time between 1968 and 1977. So (2) alone is insufficient, but by using (1) and (2) together you can figure out the worth of the painting in January 1971.

18. **(D)** (1) alone is sufficient since the rule enables you to compute all successive values once you know a_1. Also the rule and (1) tell you that the numbers in a sequence will always increase. Thus, since $a_2 = 4$, 3 will never appear. In the same way, by using (2) and the rule for the sequence you can determine that $a_2 = 4$ and a_1 is 2 or –2, so the reasoning used above shows that 3 will never appear.

19. **(A)** (1) alone is sufficient. If $z > x$ then the side opposite angle *ABC* is larger than the side opposite angle *ACB*. (2) alone is insufficient since *D* can be anywhere between *B* and *C*, so you can't decide whether *AD* is larger or smaller than *AB*.

20. **(E)** If $x = 9$ and $y = 8$, then (1) and (2) would be true and $x > y$. However, if $x = 6$ and $y = 8$, (1) and (2) would still be true although $x < y$.

21. **(C)** STATEMENT (2) alone is not sufficient. –1 is less than 2 and $\frac{1}{-1}$ is less than $\frac{1}{2}$ but 1 is less than 2 and $\frac{1}{1}$ is greater than $\frac{1}{2}$.

    STATEMENT (1) alone is insufficient since there is no information about *y*.

    STATEMENTS (1) and (2) together imply that *x* and *y* are both greater than 1 and for two positive numbers *x* and *y*, if *x* is less than *y* then $\frac{1}{x}$ is greater than $\frac{1}{y}$.

22. **(A)** STATEMENT (1) alone is sufficient. Since angle *CAD* is bisected by *AO*, the triangles *AOD* and *AOC* are congruent by side-angle-side ($AO = AO$). Therefore, angle AOD = angle *AOC*. Since the sum of the angles is 180° (*CD* is a straight line) the two angles are right angles and *AB* is $\perp$ *CD*.

STATEMENT (2) alone is insufficient. We can choose B so that $BC = AD$ whether or not $AB \perp CD$.

23. **(E)** Since C is closer to A, if plane X is flying faster than plane Y, it will certainly fly over C before plane Y. However, if plane X flies slower than plane Y, and C is very close to A, plane X would still fly over C before plane Y does. Thus, STATEMENTS (1) and (2) together are not sufficient.

24. **(A)** To compare two fractions, the fractions must have the same denominator. The least common denominator for both fractions is 120. Using this fact, $\dfrac{x}{12} = \dfrac{10x}{120}$ and $\dfrac{y}{40} = \dfrac{3y}{120}$. So the relation between the fractions is the same as the relation between $10x$ and $3y$. Therefore, STATEMENT (1) alone is sufficient. STATEMENT (2) alone is not sufficient. Using $y = 13$ and $x = 4$, STATEMENT (2) is true and $\dfrac{x}{12}$ is greater than $\dfrac{y}{40}$. However, using $y = 10$ and $x = 2$, STATEMENT (2) is still true, but now $\dfrac{x}{12}$ is less than $\dfrac{y}{40}$.

25. **(E)** Since the area of a circle is πr^2, the area of the circular section of AOB is the fraction $x/360$ times πr^2, where angle $AOB = x°$. (There are 360° in the entire circle.) Using STATEMENT (1), we know $x = 36$ so $(36/360)\pi r^2 = 1/10 \pi r^2$. However STATEMENT (1) gives no information about the value of r, so STATEMENT (1) alone is insufficient.

STATEMENT (2) gives no information about the value of r, so STATEMENTS (1) and (2) together are insufficient.

Section VI Problem Solving

1. **(D)** $\dfrac{300}{2} = 15$, so there were 150 people who contributed $2. Since this group was 100% − 30% − 45% = 25% of the total group, there were $\dfrac{150}{.25} = 600$ people in the total group. So the amount contributed by those who gave $40 was .30 × 600 × $40 = $7,200. The amount contributed by those who gave $20 was .45 × 600 × $20 = $5,400. Therefore the total was $7,200 + $5,400 + $300 = $12,900.

2. **(E)** After the tune-up, the car will travel 15 miles on $\frac{3}{4}$ of a gallon of gas. So it will travel $\frac{15}{3/4}$ or $\frac{4}{3} \times 15$ or 20 miles on one gallon of gas.

3. **(B)** The price after a discount of 20% is 80% of P, the original price. After another 15% discount, the price is 85% of 80% of P or $(.85)(.80)P$, which equals $.68P$. Therefore, after the successive discounts, the price is 68% of what it was originally, which is the same as a single discount of 32%.

4. **(B)** The area of the wall is 11 feet $\times$ 20 feet = 220 square feet. Since a large roll of wallpaper gives more square feet per dollar, you should try to use large rolls. $\frac{220}{60} = 3$ with a remainder of 40. So if you buy 3 large rolls, which cost $3 \times \$25 = \$75$, you will have enough to cover the entire wall, except for 40 square feet. You can cover 40 square feet by either buying 1 large roll or 4 small rolls. A large roll costs $25 but 4 small rolls cost only $24. So the minimum cost is $75 + $24 = $99.

5. **(D)** If John paid $10, then Karen paid 150% of $10, or $15. So Mary paid $\frac{5}{6} \times \$15 = \$12.50$. The total is $10 + $15 + $12.50 = $37.50

6. **(C)** In 1966, the government spent $30 per capita on people under 65; by 1972 the per capita amount for those under 65 was $72. Therefore, the increase was $42. Since $\frac{42}{30} = 1.4 = 140\%$, the correct answer is (C).

7. **(C)** STATEMENT I cannot be inferred since the graph gives only per capita amounts. The total amount will also depend on the number of people in each group.
STATEMENT II is false since private health insurance decreased from $70 to $56 per capita.
STATEMENT III is true since $644 is more than ½ of $981.
Therefore, only statement III can be inferred from the graphs.

8. **(C)** This problem can be worked out by some complicated algebra if you let D be the distance between the towns and T be the

total time of the trip. However, it is much easier to work it out if you simply choose a convenient number for the distance. So let the distance between town A and town B be 1000 miles. Then 75% of the distance is 750 miles, so the car traveled for $\frac{750}{50} =$ 15 hours at 50 mph. If the car averaged 40 mph for the entire trip, then the entire trip took $\frac{1000}{40} = 25$ hours. So the car must have taken $25 - 15 = 10$ hours for the part of the trip it traveled at S mph. It traveled $1000 - 750 = 250$ miles at S mph, so S is $\frac{250}{10} = 25$. A common mistake is to solve the equation $.75(50) + .25S = 40$ for S. This approach would be correct if the car traveled 75% of the TIME at 50 mph and 25% of the TIME at S mph. However, you are given that the car traveled 75% of the DISTANCE at 50 mph and since the speed changes the time it takes to travel, 75% of the distance will not be 75% of the time.

9. **(B)** $7\frac{1}{2}$ dozen is $\frac{15}{2} \times 12 = 90$, so during the summer the hen lays 90 eggs. The food for the summer costs $10, so the cost in food per egg is $\frac{\$10}{90} = \frac{\$1}{9} = 11\frac{1}{9}$ ¢.

10. **(D)** STATEMENT I is not true since the diameter is not equal to the radius and the area of the circle is πr^2.

STATEMENT II is true since the length of a diameter is twice the length of a radius.

STATEMENT III is true since $a = \pi r^2 = \pi r(d/2) = \pi(r/2)d$. Therefore, $a/d = \pi(r/2)$.

Therefore, only STATEMENTS II and III are true.

11. **(C)** Since hose A takes 20 minutes to fill the tank, it fills up $\frac{1}{20}$ of the tank each minute. Since hose B fills up the tank in 15 minutes, it fills up $\frac{1}{15}$ of the tank each minute. Therefore, hose A and hose B together will fill up $\frac{1}{20} + \frac{1}{15}$ or $\frac{3+4}{60}$ or $\frac{7}{60}$ of the tank each minute. Thus, it will take $\frac{60}{7}$ or $8\frac{4}{7}$ minutes to fill the tank.

12. **(D)** Since Eric will finish k cars after $k \times 20$ minutes and John will finish j cars after $j \times 18$ minutes, they both will finish inspecting cars at the same time when $k \times 20 = j \times 18$. Since k and j must be integers (they represent the number of cars finished) this question is asking you to find a common multiple of 20 and 18. The question asks for the first time they will finish a car simultaneously, so you must find the least common multiple. The following 3 steps will find the Least Common Multiple

   (A) $20 = 4 \times 5 = 2 \times 2 \times 5$
   $18 = 2 \times 3 \times 3$

   (B) Delete 2 from one of the products

   (C) So the L.C.M. is $2 \times 2 \times 5 \times 3 \times 3 = 180$

   So Eric and John will finish inspecting a car at the same time 180 minutes after they start, or at 11:00 A.M.

13. **(D)** Since the angle B is 90 degrees, the coordinates of B are (1,5) so $AB = 3$ and $BC = 1$. To find the area, break the figure into three smaller figures by extending the line CD until it meets AH at point J and extending line GH until it meets DE at point K. Then the area sought is the sum of the areas of $ABCJ$, $JDKH$, and $KEFG$. All three figures are rectangles because all their angles are 90 degrees. The area of $ABCJ$ is 3×1 since AB is 3 and BC is 1. The area of $JDKH$ is $JD \times JH$. Since the coordinates of D, J, and K are (2,4), (2,2), and (4,4) respectively, the area of $JDKH$ is $2 \times 2 = 4$. Finally, since $EF = AB = 3$ and $KE = 1$, the area of $KEFG$ is $3 \times 1 = 3$. Therefore, the area of the figure is $3 + 4 + 3 = 10$.

14. **(E)** There were 6,000 cars produced and the total wages paid for the week was ($30,000 + $40,000 + $52,000 + $50,000 + $32,000) or $204,000. Therefore, the average cost in wages per car $= \dfrac{\$204,000}{6,000} = \$34$.

15. **(D)** STATEMENT I is true since the total number of cars produced was 6,000 and ¼ of 6,000 is 1,500.

   STATEMENT II cannot be inferred since there are no data about the number of employees. If some employees are paid more than others, there may be fewer employees present who receive higher wages.

STATEMENT III is true since $102,000 was paid on Wednesday and Thursday and $102,000 is ½ of the weekly total of $204,000. Therefore, only STATEMENTS I and III can be inferred from the graph.

16. **(D)** Since $\dfrac{x}{y} = 4$, we know $x = 4y$. So $2x - y = 2\,(4y) - y = 7y$.

Therefore $\dfrac{(2x - y)}{x}$ is $\dfrac{7y}{4y} = \dfrac{7}{4}$, or 175%.

17. **(B)** Since $x > 2$, then $-x < -2$; but $y > -1$ implies $2y > -2$. Therefore, $-x < -2 < 2y$ so $-x < 2y$. None of the other statements is always true. (A) is false if x is 5 and $y = -\frac{1}{2}$; (C) is false if $x = 3$ and $y = -\frac{1}{2}$; (D) is false if $x = 3$ and $y = 3$, and (E) is false if $x = 3$ and $y = -\frac{1}{2}$.

18. **(C)** Since *ABCD* is a rectangle, all its angles are right angles. The area of a rectangle is length times width; the length of *AD* is 4. Using the Pythagorean theorem we have $4^2 + (\text{width})^2 = 5^2$, so the (width)^2 is $25 - 16 = 9$. Therefore, the width is 3, and the area is $4 \times 3 = 12$.

19. **(E)** The electricity costs 12*k*¢ for 12 hours, the heat costs $12*d* for 12 hours, and the water costs 12*w*¢ for 12 hours. So the total is 12*k*¢ + $12*d* + 12*w*¢ or $.12*k* + $12*d* + $.12*w* which is $(.12*k* + 12*d* + .12*w*).

20. **(E)** Since $x = 2z$ and $y = 2z$, $x \cdot y \cdot z = (2z)(2z)(z) = 4z^3$; but $x \cdot y \cdot z = 256$ so $4z^3 = 256$. Therefore, $z^3 = 64$ and z is 4; so $x = 8$.

Section VII   Sentence Correction

1. **(D)** Do not use *calculate* or *reckon* when you mean *think*.

2. **(E)** Since the words *but also* precede the phrase, *to one of eight or even six*, the words *not only* should precede the phrase, *to one of ten hours*. This error in parallel structure is corrected in choice E.

3. **(A)** *Already* is an adverb; *all ready* is an adjectival construction. *Allready* is a misspelling. Choices D and E do not convey the thought of the sentence.

4. **(B)** One way of correcting a dangling participle is to change the participial phrase to a clause. Choices B and D substitute clauses for the phrase. However, choice D changes the meaning of the sentence.

5. **(C)** In the underlined phrase, we find two modifiers of worker— *toiling* and *who discovers....* The first is an adjective and the second a clause. This results in an error in parallel structure. Choice C corrects this by eliminating one of the modifiers of *worker*. Choice E does the same thing but creates a change in the thought of the sentence. Choice D corrects the error in parallel structure but introduces an error in agreement between subject and verb—*who* (singular) and *toil* (plural).

6. **(B)** "He" is the subject of the sentence which takes who as the relative pronoun.

7. **(A)** No error.

8. **(C)** This choice does not violate parallel structure.

9. **(E)** The omission of an important word (*been*) is corrected in choice E. *Excepted* (which means to *exclude*) is the wrong word to use in this sentence.

10. **(C)** Choice C corrects errors in the possessive form of *government* (needed before a verbal noun) and *it*.

11. **(B)** This corrects the error in agreement: *Her brother...insists.*

12. **(C)** This is also an error in agreement: *Kind* is singular and requires a singular modifier (*this*).

13. **(D)** This choice eliminates the error in parallel structure.

14. **(B)** The correct idiom is *graduate from*. The active case is preferred to the passive used in choice C. Choice D adds an unnecessary word, *into*.

15. **(C)** This corrects the two errors in this sentence—the error in case (*me* for *I*) and the error in tense (*had finished* for *finished*).

16. **(D)** *Despite* should be used as a preposition, not as a word joining clauses.

17. **(C)** This corrects the lack of parallel structure.

18. **(C)** This was an unnecessary shift of pronoun. Do not shift from *you* to *one*. Choice D changes the meaning unnecessarily.

19. **(C)** The demonstrative pronoun *those* is needed here—*from those* (persons).

20. **(D)** Choice D corrects the error in diction and the error in parallel structure.

21. **(E)** Choice E corrects the misuse of the word *too*.

22. **(D)** Active verbs are preferred to passive verbs.

23. **(D)** The phrase *May I venture to say that* is unnecesary, as is *most* before *superior*.

24. **(E)** This answer eliminates the misplaced modifier, *completing*, and the passive verb, *were found*.

25. **(B)** The correct idiom is *different from*.

EVALUATING YOUR SCORE

Tabulate your score for each section of Sample Test 3 according to the directions on pages 6–7 and record the results in the Self-Scoring Table below. Then find your rating for each score on the Self-Scoring Scale and record it in the appropriate blank.

SELF-SCORING TABLE

Section	Score	Rating
1		
2		
3		
4		
5		
6		
7		

SELF-SCORING SCALE—RATING

Section	Poor	Fair	Good	Excellent
1	0–11+	12–16+	17–21+	22–25
2	0–11+	12–16+	17–21+	22–25
3	0–8+	9–12+	13–17+	18–20
4	0–8+	9–12+	13–17+	18–20
5	0–11+	12–16+	17–21+	22–25
6	0–8+	9–12+	13–17+	18–20
7	0–11+	12–16+	17–21+	22–25

Study again the Review sections covering material in Sample Test 3 for which you had a rating of FAIR or POOR.

NOTES

NOTES

NOTES

NOTES

Be prepared for a business education with Barron's Books

BARRON'S

How to Prepare for the GMAT—Graduate Management Admission Test w/optional CD-ROM
13th Edition
Eugene D. Jaffe, M.B.A., Ph.D. and Stephen Hilbert, Ph.D.
Updated with information reflecting the Graduate Management Admission Test as it is given today—which is as a computer-adaptive exam—this manual presents a diagnostic test with answers and analysis plus five full-length model exams with all questions answered and explained. Subject review sections are focused to help test-takers correct their weaknesses in essay writing, reading comprehension, sentence correction, critical reasoning, and math. The CD-ROM simulates an actual computer-adaptive test and scores the test-taker's results automatically.
Book only: ISBN 0-7641-2352-1, paperback, $16.95, Canada $24.50
Book w/CD-ROM: ISBN 0-7641-7459-2, paperback, $29.95, Canada $43.50

Essays that Will Get You into Business School
2nd Edition
Dan Kaufman, Chris Dowhan and Adrienne Dowhan

From the Reviews:
Praise for the previous Edition of Essays that Will Get You into College:

"This book should help any student write a better essay and may motivate some to create super efforts. It does tend to make the problem of writing an essay to be far simpler than one might have imagined. But, the quality of its advice should reassure book store operators to keep this good one on sale."

—*College Spotlight, May-June 2002*

This edition, updated with many new sample essays, will help college students who are seeking admission to graduate schools of business administration. Essay-writing advice is followed by approximately 75 essays written by applicants who were accepted by leading business schools. Updated with much new material, the newly revised titles in this series present between 50 and 75 model essays designed to inspire students who must prepare original essays of their own as part of today's entrance process into colleges and graduate schools. Students will also find extensive advice on the do's and don'ts for writing a successful essay plus instruction on the process of organizing ideas, writing a rough draft, then rewriting a final finished essay for presentation. Essays cover many categories, including sports, work experiences, ethnicity, cross-cultural experiences, and much more.
ISBN 0-7641-2035-2, paperback, $11.95, Canada $17.50

Guide to Graduate Business Schools
13th Edition
Eugene Miller
Updated with current information, fees, and figures, this book describes more than 600 business schools in the United States and Canada. Information presented includes admission requirements, academic programs offered, tuition and related fees, career placement services, new trends, and more. The author also advises on self-assessment and the way to choose the school that most closely fits the individual student's needs.
ISBN 0-7641-2295-9, paperback, $16.95, Canada $24.50

BARRON'S
Business Review